GW00384136

The Mad Bad Line

The Mad Bad Line

THE FAMILY OF LORD ALFRED DOUGLAS

by

BRIAN ROBERTS

'You had yourself often told me how many of your race there had been who had stained their hands in their own blood; your uncle certainly, your grandfather, possibly; and many others in the mad, bad line from which you are come.'
—Oscar Wilde to Lord Alfred Douglas in *De Profundis*

HAMISH HAMILTON
London

First published in Great Britain 1981
by Hamish Hamilton Ltd
Garden House 57-59 Long Acre London WC2E 9JZ

British Library Cataloguing in Publication Data

Roberts, Brian
  The mad bad line.
  I. Title
  929'.2'09411   DA758.3.Q5/
ISBN 0-241-10637-0

Photoset by Rowland Phototypesetting Ltd
Bury St Edmunds, Suffolk
Printed in Great Britain by
St Edmundsbury Press Ltd, Bury St Edmunds, Suffolk

For Alan Hartford

Contents

Illustrations

Between pages 148 and 149

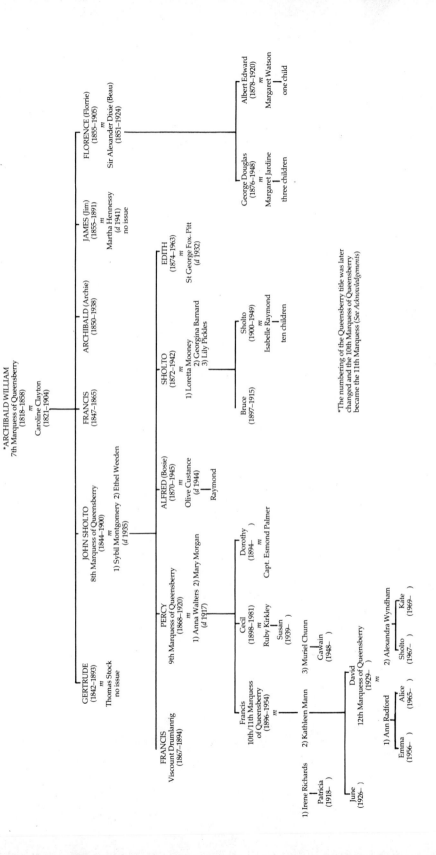

*ARCHIBALD WILLIAM
7th Marquess of Queensberry
(1818–1858)
m
Caroline Clayton
(1821–1904)

GERTRUDE
(1842–1893)
m
Thomas Stock
no issue

JOHN SHOLTO
8th Marquess of Queensberry
(1844–1900)
m
1) Sybil Montgomery 2) Ethel Weeden
(d 1935)

FRANCIS
(1847–1865)

ARCHIBALD (Archie)
(1850–1938)

JAMES (Jim)
(1855–1891)
m
Martha Hennessy
(d 1941)
no issue

FLORENCE (Florrie)
(1855–1905)
m
Sir Alexander Dixie (Beau)
(1851–1924)

George Douglas
(1876–1948)
m
Margaret Jardine
three children

Albert Edward
(1878–1920)
m
Margaret Watson
one child

FRANCIS
Viscount Drumlanrig
(1867–1894)

PERCY
9th Marquess of Queensberry
(1868–1920)
m
1) Anna Walters 2) Mary Morgan
(d 1917)

ALFRED (Bosie)
(1870–1945)
m
Olive Custance
(d 1944)

Raymond

SHOLTO
(1872–1942)
m
1) Loretta Mooney 2) Georgina Barnard 3) Lily Pickles

EDITH
(1874–1963)
m
St George Fox-Pitt
(d 1932)

Bruce
(1897–1915)

Sholto
(1900–1949)
m
Isabelle Raymond
ten children

Francis
10th/11th Marquess
of Queensberry
(1896–1954)
m

Cecil
(1898–1981)
m
Ruby Kirkley

Susan
(1939–)

Dorothy
(1894–)
m
Capt. Esmond Palmer

2) Kathleen Mann

3) Muriel Chunn

Gawain
(1948–)

David
12th Marquess of Queensberry
(1929–)
m

1) Irene Richards

Patricia
(1918–)

June
(1926–)

1) Ann Radford

Emma
(1956–)

Alice
(1965–)

2) Alexandra Wyndham

Sholto
(1967–)

Kate
(1969–)

*The numbering of the Queensberry title was later
changed and the 10th Marquess of Queensberry
became the 11th Marquess (See Acknowledgements)

Part One

Chapter One

'The Bold and Gallant Drum'

Archibald William Douglas, seventh Marquess of Queensberry, was found shot through the chest in the grounds of his Scottish estate, Kinmount, at four o'clock in the afternoon of 6 August 1858. Beside his body lay a double-barrelled gun from which a single shot had been fired. The bullet had entered his chest at an angle and travelled through his heart to his back. His two cousins, who made the discovery, reported that he had been dead for half an hour.

Early accounts of the tragedy all agreed that the Marquess had been killed by an accidental explosion of his gun. This seemed the only logical conclusion. The Marquess was, after all, a mere forty years of age, the father of a large and devoted family of four sons and two daughters, popular with his neighbours, well-loved by his tenants and, as he never tired of demonstrating, in the best of health. His behaviour on the day of his death had appeared perfectly normal; he had shown no signs of nervousness, strain or depression. Indeed he had returned from London the day before, after attending the races at Goodwood, in remarkably good form. His wife and younger children were away at the time, visiting relations at Moffat, but his eldest daughter, Gertrude, was at home. She had not the slightest doubt about her father's high spirits. Outgoing and hearty as ever, he seemed delighted to be back in Scotland.

On the morning of his death he had announced that he was going to spend the afternoon shooting rabbits. He had tried to persuade Gertrude to join him but was hardly surprised when she refused. Gertrude, a quiet, somewhat serious-minded girl, then approaching her sixteenth birthday, was no sportswoman. When she pleaded that she was due to meet her mother and the rest of the family at the nearby Ecclefechan railway station after lunch, her father had accepted the excuse happily enough. He had left the house alone at two o'clock that afternoon with his gun tucked under his arm.

An hour or so later some men working in the grounds saw him shoot a crow and then move on to an adjoining field. That was the last time he was seen alive. Several gun shots were heard shortly afterwards, but they ended abruptly at half-past three. From then on there was silence.

Just before four o'clock, the Marquess's two cousins, Mr Johnstone

Douglas and his brother, arrived looking for him. They were directed to the spot from which the shots had come. Their search did not last long.

'The two gentlemen,' it was reported, 'proceeded a little further down the grounds, and were overwhelmed with horror on discovering the body of his Lordship prostrate on the earth and covered with blood. Life was found to be extinct, and the limbs were beginning to stiffen.'

Solemnly the Marquess's body was carried back to Kinmount House. Four labourers, having scrambled into black clothes, shouldered the roughly made litter and crossed the fields at a slow measured pace. They were followed by a ragged procession of weeping servants. It was a sombre, feudal rite which the Marquess's younger daughter, Florence— or Florrie as she was known—was to remember for the rest of her life.

Florrie was only three years old at the time. Earlier that afternoon she had arrived home with her mother and then she and her twin brother, James, had been taken for a drive by their nurse. On returning to the house, the children were puzzled by the crowd blocking the doorway. They were pushed into the hall by their nurse who, having whispered to one of the servants, suddenly gave a scream. Once inside the twins were even more bewildered. Their mother, tense and dazed, was standing at the door; one of their older brothers lay face down on a sofa sobbing; another brother stood beside him, white faced and trembling; and their elder sister cowered in the background 'weeping bitterly.' Then came a shuffling of feet and four men entered the hall carrying 'something covered up in a cloak' and crossed to the library. Their mother followed and silently closed the library door. Only then were the twins told what had happened.

'It's papa,' whispered their brother Archie. 'Papa's dead. The gun killed him like it kills a rabbit.'

[2]

But there was more to Lord Queensberry's death than that. Not everyone was prepared to accept that he had been killed like a rabbit; not everyone saw him as a devoted father, a generous landlord and a back-slapping sportsman. Those who knew him well were baffled by the accident. The published accounts left too many questions unanswered; there were too many inconsistencies and too few witnesses for the tragedy not to cause speculation. Hardly was the Marquess in his grave before the gossip started. Indeed the local newspaper, the *Dumfries Standard*, could not wait for him to be buried before launching in. Its obituary, published the day before his funeral, was far from complimentary.

'Sudden and sad has been the latter end of the seventh Marquess of Queensberry,' it observed. 'Born in high rank, the inheritor of a house, which, though not one of the wealthiest, occupies a distinguished place on the roll of the Scottish peerage . . . he has perished in a moment. Five days ago he was in the flush of health, in the pride of manhood's prime, now nothing remains but a heap of senseless ashes. . . . Faults he had not a few. That passion for the turf, and kindred pursuits still more questionable, absorbed much of his time and energies, brought clouds about his otherwise radiant path. . . . What might he not have become had he avoided the vortex in which he was so involved? . . . We entertained high expectations of the deceased nobleman and it was because we did so and were disappointed that we speak thus.'

This obituary, gleefully republished in the London *Times,* was followed by others, equally carping. By and large the Marquess was dismissed as a good-natured but reckless, feckless and self-indulgent aristocrat who had frittered away his heritage. The best that could be said of him was that he was 'one of the most universal of sportsmen, as far as his small means permitted, that the three kingdoms possessed. Nothing came amiss to him—hunting, shooting, the gloves, horse-racing, deer-stalking, fishing. . . .' Even so, claimed *The Field*, his sportsmanship had long since begun to degenerate. 'Of late years,' it grumbled, 'the Marquess has only appeared on the turf as a spectator, but he occasionally betted heavily on the principal events, from which he rarely absented himself.' That was something on which they were all agreed: the seventh Marquess of Queensberry was an inveterate and not very successful gambler.

But it was the way in which he died that mystified most people. Could such an experienced sportsman have killed himself by accident? It seemed most unlikely. Admittedly he was said to be 'one of the most careless men that ever handled a gun,' but was he so careless that he could have shot himself? As far as was known he had never so much as scratched himself accidentally. He might have been impetuous but he was not foolish. He was too old a hand in the field to endanger his own life. What is more, his body had been found in open country; there was no suggestion that he had tripped, fallen into a ditch, or become entangled in a bush. If, as was claimed, the gun had exploded unexpectedly, would the shot have pierced his heart with such deadly accuracy? Surely not.

'It is surmised,' noted a journalist, 'that one barrel exploded while the Marquess was loading the other. Our sporting friends, however, will not require to be told that, under such circumstances, any but a left handed man would be shot through the right breast, and not the left. Was then the Marquess a left handed man? It is indeed just possible that the deceased might have held the gun away from him in such a position that the left handed barrel should have pointed towards his left breast. But if this was so, in what condition would the other barrel have been found? It is hardly likely that the final tap of the ramrod on the last wadding should have caused the explosion of the other barrel; but at all events, even the ramrod would have been displaced or blown away. Was it so? In the third place, was the nipple of the loaded barrel capped or not? If so it is obviously impossible that the accident could have happened as described.'

None of these tantalising questions were answered. There was no public inquest, no official findings were published; the press was left to draw its own conclusions. This the press was only too ready to do. Sporting journals had a field day; fanciful theories followed wild assumptions. Only one suggestion came within the bounds of probability. The Marquess, it was argued, could have been sitting on a stone and, feeling drowsy, he might have allowed his gun to slip between his thighs until it pointed at his chest. In such a position, he could have started up on seeing a rabbit, caught the trigger with his foot, and caused the gun to fire. So taken with this theory was Mr William Bishop that he immediately published a pamphlet on the rules of handling a gun. He wished, he said sternly, to prevent accidents similar to that which had killed his 'esteemed and deeply lamented friend the Marquess of Queensberry.' The more cynical remained unconvinced.

It was the *Evening Herald* that had the last word. 'In sporting circles,' it announced, 'a belief is expressed that the death was not accidental; [the Marquess] had lately sustained severe losses.' Suicide was thought more feasible; particularly when the suicide involved a member of the emotional, head-strong and totally unpredictable Douglas family.

[3]

The Gaelic for Douglas is *dub glas,* meaning 'dark water.' But apparently the name Douglas was loosely applied to an early Scottish chieftain known as 'the dark grey man.' And that, according to legend, is how the clan Douglas came into being. Actually the origins of the family are unknown. They can, it is said, be traced back to the eighth century but it was four or five centuries later that they came into prominence. By that time they were well established as powerful land owners both in England and Scotland, but mostly in Scotland. As the Douglas estates lay on the border, they were acknowledged as guardians of the north against the encroachments of the English, particularly of the Percies with their estates to the south. This is how the Douglas family gained their formidable reputation as opponents of the English crown.

For centuries the Douglas chieftains swashbuckled their way through history, terrorising, fighting and dying in the service of God, Scotland and their patron saint, St Bryde. From warrior overlords they rose to become earls, marquesses, and eventually dukes. Few of them enjoyed a serene old age. Some were killed in battle, others died in captivity, still others committed suicide or were murdered by their own relations, a few were killed in duels, and at least one was said to be the victim of sorcery. Their careers were as colourful as their nick-names. There was a Hardy Douglas, a Black Douglas, a Red Douglas, a Grim Douglas, a Gross Douglas, a Great Douglas, a Dull Douglas, a Tyneman Douglas and even a Bell-the-Cat Douglas—a catchword he adopted when plotting to murder the favourite of James III.

The Queensberry title came into the family in the seventeenth century. Sir William Douglas of Drumlanrig, a loyal supporter of the Stuarts, was elevated to the Scottish peerage as Viscount Drumlanrig by James IV of Scotland—in return, they say, for entertaining the King in 1617—and then, in 1633, he was created first Earl of Queensberrie (sic). From that time on the eldest son of the family was usually styled Drumlanrig, either as Earl or Viscount. This was an inheritance which many of them had good reason to regard as a curse. For, by and large, the Queensberry heirs were notably lacking in good luck.

An exception was the heir of the second Earl of Queensberry. His father had gamely upheld family tradition by supporting the Stuart King, Charles I, in the Civil War and was made to pay dearly for his loyalty by Cromwell; but he, as third Earl, was richly recompensed when the monarchy was restored. Not only was the third Earl made a Privy Councillor, Justice-General and Lord High Treasurer of Scotland, as well as Governor of Edinburgh Castle, but he was showered with additional titles. In 1682 he was created Lord Douglas of Kinmount, Middlebie and Dornock; Viscount Nith, Torthowald and Ross; Earl of Drumlanrig and Sanquhar and, at the same time, first Marquess of Queensberry.

Then, in the following year, the family tree came into full flower when he was created first Duke of Queensberry. One would have imagined that a dukedom, with a handsome clutch of lesser titles, would have satisfied the most ambitious family; but it was not enough for the Queensberrys. Proud Scots though they were, they always hankered after an English peerage. This yearning was to develop into an obsession. The prize—which was repeatedly snatched from them—was first won by the second Duke of Queensberry when Queen Anne (the Queensberrys had turned their coat during 'The Glorious Revolution' of 1688) made him Duke of Dover, as a reward for his services to the 1707 Act of Union between England and Scotland. But the esteemed English title did not remain in the family long. Lost through untimely deaths, it was not revived—or replaced rather—until early in the nineteenth century when the most reprehensible of all the Dukes of Queensberry—that notorious and colourful lecher 'Old Q'—was created Baron Douglas of Amesbury. But alas, with Old Q dying unmarried, if not celibate, the prize once more slipped from the family's grasp.

Old Q's death brought a reshuffling of the Queensberry titles as well.

The dukedom, in terms of its patent, went to the Duke of Buccleuch who from then on was known as the Duke of Buccleuch and Queensberry. The original Queensberry peerage, however, passed to Old Q's distant relation Sir Charles Douglas of Kelhead—a descendant of the first Earl of Queensberry—who became the fifth Marquess of Queensberry.

Apparently, the fifth Marquess of Queensberry's only noteworthy achievement was in securing once again that elusive English title. On 7 June 1833 he was created Baron Solway of Kinmount with 'remainder to the heirs-male of his body.' But try as he might, he could not produce the required heir male. The Queensberry curse remained constant. When he died in 1837, he left eight daughters. The Queensberry title went to his younger brother John, who became the sixth Marquess.

This sixth Marquess married his cousin Sarah, daughter of John Sholto Douglas, a pious Protestant lady, in 1817, and they had two children—a son and a daughter. The daughter, Georgina, was born in 1819. The son was Archibald William who, as seventh Marquess of Queensberry, was found dead beside his gun at Kinmount.

[4]

Archibald William rarely thought of himself as seventh Marquess of Queensberry. The title came to him too late for him to feel at home with it. His father died in December 1856 and he was to die less than two years later. Most of his life was spent as Viscount Drumlanrig and it was by that ill-omened title he was best known. One of his more romantic descendants claimed that he was called 'the Bold and Gallant Drum.' This could possible be true. Bold he unquestionably was and, with women, he could certainly be gallant. To his more intimate friends, though, he was known simply as 'Drum.'

Born in Edinburgh on 18 April 1818, Drumlanrig had from childhood displayed all the aggressive traits of his family. Very little of his mother's Protestant piety rubbed off on him and as a schoolboy at Eton he was known better as a bruiser of noses than as a browser in books. He dearly loved a fight. He would take on anyone: his school mates, his seniors, even the local roughs. 'A rare pugilist was spoilt,' claimed Nat Langham, the well-known prize fighter, 'when Lord Drumlanrig was born to a peerage.'

After leaving Eton, Drumlanrig entered the Life Guards as a cornet. His military career was short and undistinguished. Most of his army years seem to have been spent in clubbing together with his fellow officers to arrange prize-fights or in organising hunts. Although he was never an elegant horseman, Drumlanrig was considered 'one of the hardest riders across country' of his day. Why he left the army is not known. It might have been boredom—he was easily bored; it might have been his racing debts; it could even have been the result of his marriage, some three years earlier, to the attractive Caroline Clayton. Perhaps it was a combination of all three.

Drumlanrig's marriage certainly had a profound influence on his life. Caroline Clayton was an exceptional young woman. A wide-eyed, ring-letted young beauty, vivacious, quick-witted and fiercely independent, she had all the sparkling qualities that appealed to Drumlanrig. Her family, if not as noble, was every bit as spirited as his. Sir William Clayton, her father, was a distinguished soldier who had served with Wellington in the Peninsular wars, been wounded at Quatrebras, and fought at Waterloo; her Irish Catholic mother, the heiress Alice O'Donnel of county Mayo—where Caroline was born—came from a military family which claimed descent from the original kings of Ulster.

At the time of Drumlanrig's meeting with Caroline, Sir William Clayton was MP for Marlow. His Buckinghamshire home, Harleyford House, was a popular centre for visiting politicians, sportsmen and exiled royalty. One of the more regular visitors was Prince Louis Napoleon, the dreamy-eyed Bonaparte Pretender, whose frequent boating trips on the Thames with young Caroline had caused considerable local speculation. It had also raised the Clayton family's hopes. Her mother would have welcomed a match with a Catholic Prince and it may well have been imperial ambition that made Sir William object to the wayward Drumlanrig as a suitor for his younger daughter. At any rate he refused consent to the couple's marriage.

Sir William should have known his daughter better. At nineteen Caroline was every bit as impetuous, self-willed and defiant as her lover. She was quick to agree to Drumlanrig's suggestion that they elope. Bundling into a post-chaise, the couple raced to the Scottish border where they hired two horses and galloped to Gretna Green, to be married across the anvil on 28 May 1840. Sir William was presented with a *fait accompli*. His reaction is not recorded, but the marriage seems to have convinced him of Caroline's determination. Within a matter of days the couple were back in London and hastily remarried at St Mary's Church, Marylebone, with Sir William's consent if not his blessing. Their brief honeymoon was spent in Buckinghamshire.

Caroline never forgot her elopement. It was one of the few truly romantic episodes of her life. Even in old age she delighted in being described as the 'Gretna Green Marchioness.' The love match was, for her, proof of her husband's early devotion. In time the memory of it became the one ray of light in the clouded sky of her marriage. Drumlanrig, though, had little need of such memories. Never one for senti-ment, he rarely gave a thought to the past. On the few occasions that he was reminded of his Gretna Green marriage he tended to treat it as a joke, something that had been fun at the time but was better forgotten. This difference in their attitudes was touchingly illustrated many years later.

One of their coachmen, deciding to elope with a housemaid, borrowed Drumlanrig's favourite stallion to ride to Gretna Green. On the return journey, the horse went lame. When Drumlanrig heard about it he was furious. The newly-weds were summoned, lectured on their stupidity, and sacked. They had hardly left the room when an agitated Caroline rushed in to plead for them.

'Oh Archie,' she cried, 'would you have minded how many horses were lamed when you eloped with me?' Evidently the thought had not occurred to Drunlanrig. 'He was restored to good humour,' runs the story, 'and allowed the culprits to remain under the Queensberry domain.' That this is said to have happened at a late stage in Drumlanrig's marriage, makes it all the more remarkable. By that time Drumlanrig was not easily swayed by sentiment.

The early years of the marriage appear to have been happy enough. Drumlanrig was still in the army and Caroline was content as a soldier's wife. They had been reconciled with their families, and their first child—a daughter, Gertrude Georgina—was born on 21 August 1842. To all intents and purposes the couple seemed set for a conventionally aristocratic life.

But behind this serene facade things were very different. For one thing, Drumlanrig was not cut out for a military career. Painfully bored, he looked to his various sporting activities for excitement. He became a regular race-goer and began to bet heavily. His gambling was both reckless and disastrous; no judge of horseflesh he relied too much on stable gossip and his own prejudices. All too often, they say, he displayed 'a fatal propensity to select one horse in a big race for whom he had conceived an often baseless antipathy, and laid such a sum against him as it would have surely crippled him to pay, if, indeed, he was able to pay at all.' The results were predictable.

His first severe loss was on the 1843 Derby. Like many others Drumlanrig was convinced the race was to be rigged; the favourite was to be nobbled leaving the field open to a much fancied rival. But the conspiracy was defeated, the favourite came in, and losses on the race were enormous. Drumlanrig was among the worst sufferers. Only by borrowing £10,000 from his sister Georgina, who risked her life's savings to bail him out, was he able to settle his debts. As security he agreed to pay Georgina five per cent annually on the loan and to insure his life in her favour. The debt hung over him for years.

Whether Caroline knew about his losses is not certain. But for Drumlanrig, an impoverished junior army officer, it was a matter of great anxiety. Not that it cured his gambling. It started a chain of debts; debts that ruined his prospects as the Queensberry heir, destroyed his confidence as a husband and father, and plagued him for the rest of his life. To escape his responsibilities he threw himself ever more frantically into frivolous pastimes.

And his responsibilities continued to mount. On 20 July 1844 his first son, John Sholto, was born. That same year he left the army. He was now twenty-six, the father of two children, living on a small family allowance, neither trained nor eager to find employment and already in debt.

Not until three years later did Drumlanrig show signs of pulling himself together. Or rather, of finding himself a position in which he was able to pull himself together. In 1847, Mr Hope Johnstone, the sitting MP for Dumfriesshire, retired and Drumlanrig was elected in his place unopposed. He entered Parliament as a follower of Sir Robert Peel, the dissident Tory Prime Minister. His politics were described as those of a 'moderate liberal.' He received no pay as an MP but his election was not without its perks. Within the next couple of years he was made Colonel of the Dumfries Militia and Lord Lieutenant of Dumfries. Nor was he a political light-weight. If nothing else, Drumlanrig's election proved that his weaknesses were more a matter of temperament than a lack of intelligence. In the election of 1852 he was again returned unopposed and joined Lord Aberdeen's coalition of Whigs and Peelites. Under Aberdeen his talents were recognised by his appointment as a Privy Councillor and Comptroller of Her Majesty's Household. He seemed at last to have found his feet.

Unfortunately he lacked staying power. Politics interested but never absorbed him. Bored by the day-to-day routine of Parliament, he was more often in the back parlours of prize-fighter's taverns than in the House of Commons. The prospect of a political debate could never match the promise of a sparring bout. 'Nothing pleased him more,' declared a sporting crony, 'than to put on the gloves with some aspiring novice who was about to try conclusions in a four-and-twenty foot ring with some lad from the black country.' These bouts were often staged at the quaintly named Rum-pum-Pus Club, run by his old admirer Nat Langham. The club was founded to encourage aristocratic fight enthusiasts and Drumlanrig was one of its star performers. His moment of glory came when he was asked to take on the up-and-coming prize-fighter Jem Mace. Dressed in his nobleman's ruffled shirt and tight trousers, he stood up to the bare-chested Mace for all of two rounds before throwing in the towel. Then, to show there were no hard feelings, he rewarded Mace with a couple of guineas. Drumlanrig liked, above all things, to be thought of as a good loser.

His graciousness was no less evident on the race-course. He never missed a big race and his gambling debts became legendary. Those who tried to estimate his losses had to admit defeat. They could only stand amazed at the risks he took. One of his 'narrowest shaves' was on the Two

Thousand Guineas of 1855, when the favourite, St Hubert, was pipped at the post. 'The betting,' said a spectator, 'was prodigiously heavy and the excitement commensurate. . . . In the end, Lord of the Isles won, all out, by a neck, and Lord Drumlanrig, who stood an impossible sum against St Hubert, looked on without moving a muscle. No narrow escape, and no constant repetition of them, could shake his steady nerves.'

That was the impression he gave as a gambler. To his racing chums he was a man of tremendous resolution. In looks, one of them claimed, he 'bore undeniable tokens of the iron courage and recklessness which were his most marked characteristics . . . he was absolutely without an idea of what fear meant.' Yet there is reason to believe that this impression was deceptive, that his seemingly nerveless front was nothing more than a pose. Behind the mask lay a mass of doubts and uncertainties.

Drumlanrig was a good-looking man; sturdy, ruddy-faced, hearty and affable. When relaxed among friends he could be a delightful companion. Only when faced with a challenge, particularly a sporting challenge, did his easy-going manner falter.

For him sport was always competitive: he had either to win or to prove himself. Even the most casual day's hunt became a test, demanding all his concentration. At the start of a chase he was taciturn, edgy and, at times, downright surly. On these occasions he was best left alone. Once in the saddle, however, his pent up nerves would find release; he would gallop ahead of the field in a frenzy, yelling at the top of his voice and causing confusion among the other riders. 'He was far too wild,' one of them grumbled. 'In fact, sport when he was out was always rather critical; as at times he and his huntsmen were at different sides of the field blowing their horns against each other.'

Nor did the frenzied rider find it easy to unwind. To help him his attendants carried a pipe for him to puff during the intervals; but, it was pointed out, 'they never gave him a very good one as he was sure to bite a piece off it.' The tense, excitable Marquess gave a very different impression as a huntsman than he did as the supposedly nonchalant gambler. Caught off guard in the field, Drumlanrig displayed all the symptoms of an ill-controlled neurotic.

Sport, alas, was not his only distraction. The *Dumfries Standard* hinted at 'kindred pursuits still more questionable'; others were more specific. He was a notorious womaniser. 'Fox-hunting, steeple-chasing, pugilism, the fair sex and—last, but not least—the Turf,' sighed a despairing friend, 'claimed him for their own, and prevented him from bestowing that time and attention upon politics, without which no man, however gifted, can hold his own in the House of Commons.'

Details of Drumlanrig's sex life are vague. His affairs were evidently many and varied and although he did not flaunt his mistresses, people talked. No doubt Caroline knew about them. His children, on the other hand, seem never to have doubted his fidelity. They grew up believing their father was a paragon whose gambling was nothing more than an aristocratic indulgence which, in any case, most of them shared. His eldest son, John Sholto, might have suspected otherwise but if he did he never let on. So closely kept was this family secret that one of Drumlanrig's descendants could claim, in all innocence, that his respected ancestor led an 'uneventful and blameless life.' It says much for Caroline's loyalty that such a legend was handed down.

For loyal Caroline was. At the beginning of her husband's political career she was constantly at his side. Known in court circles as 'the beautiful Lady Drumlanrig,' she played her part as hostess to perfection. It was as much Caroline's tact as her husband's abilities that won Drumlanrig the high regard of Queen Victoria while he was Comptroller of the Royal Household. For all that, Caroline did not enjoy her role. She was not cut out to be a hostess; the social round bored her. Essentially serious-minded, she became more so as she grew older. She was far happier when she could escape to her father's home, Harleyford House, where she could be alone with her children and recapture her own childhood. As she and Drumlanrig drifted apart, as they inevitably did, Harleyford became more and more her refuge.

Her second son, Francis William Bouverie, was born there on 8 February 1847 and a third son, Archibald Edward, was born on 17 June 1850. Three years later she gave birth to yet another son who died within a matter of hours, and the last of her six children—the twins, Florence Caroline and James Edward Sholto—were born at the Drumlanrigs' London house in Wilton Crescent on 25 May 1855. It was a good-sized, conventional Victorian family. Unfortunately it did not reflect Victorian virtues. Drumlanrig's fecklessness ruined whatever hopes Caroline might have had for a stable domestic life. By the time the twins were born the relationship between husband and wife had become hopelessly strained. Nor was the rift helped when, in July 1856, Drumlanrig abruptly resigned his Court appointment and quit politics.

[5]

As it happened, it was neither Drumlanrig's gambling nor his philandering that prompted his resignation. It was another, very different, hereditary weakness—the longing for an English peerage. This was as fatal to his career as any of his vices.

When, in January 1855, the Aberdeen coalition fell, as a result of mismanagement during the Crimean War, it was replaced by the more energetic administration of Lord Palmerston. Drumlanrig, although nominally a Peelite, agreed to serve under Palmerston but his loyalty had

a price. He requested that the English Barony of Solway, formerly held
by his uncle—the fifth Marquess of Queensberry—be 'revived in his
person.' Unfortunately his estimate of his worth was not shared by the
new Prime Minister. After protracted negotiations Palmerston refused
the request and, in a fit of petulance, Drumlanrig resigned.

His wild, but characteristic, gesture left him without position or
prospects. For not only did he resign his post as Comptroller of the Royal
Household and his seat in Parliament but he withdrew as Lord Lieutenant of Dumfries. His local supporters were shocked. 'Had prudence and
patriotism been his counsellors . . .' complained the *Dumfries Standard*,
'[he] might easily have climbed higher up the ladder and become an
influential servant of the State.' But prudence was never Drumlanrig's
strong point. When, a few months later, his father died and he succeeded
as seventh Marquess of Queensberry he had only his title to console him.

His change of status made no difference to his way of life. If anything,
he could now devote more of his time to sport. The only real drawback
was his age. He was now approaching forty, at a time when forty was
considered middle-aged. His days as an active sportsman were limited.
Aware of this, he put himself to the test. During the last year or so of
Drumlanrig's life there was more than a hint of desperation in his attempts to assert his virility.

In the sporting field his behaviour became more erratic; his energy was
inexhaustible, his manner more intense. He developed a passion for
otter-hunting. With a pack of otter-hounds he would hunt the Arran
waters 'swimming along beside them nearly all day.' Next to riding,
swimming now became his favourite sport. On his last visit to London he
made a great show of swimming the Thames below Greenwich for no
other reason than to impress his friends with his fitness. And, of course,
his gambling continued.

Experience had taught him nothing. He refused all advice, relied entirely on his own judgement, stuck firmly to his prejudices. His inability
to pick a winner was matched only by his confidence in spotting a loser.
Nothing could have been more foolish. Yet he continued to gamble until
—or so his friends believed—he faced ruin.

The story of his last, most disastrous, bet was published twenty-seven
years after his death. It had long been talked about but it did not appear in
the *Sporting Times* until 13 June 1885, when he was featured as a 'Turf
Celebrity.' According to this article, Drumlanrig (as the writer insisted in
calling the newly created Marquess) arrived in London for the 1858
Goodwood Cup a few weeks before the race. At that time betting was
slight but the favourite appeared to be Saunterer, a horse owned by James
Merry.

'Lord Drumlanrig,' explained the article, 'dropped in one night at
Owen Swift's public house—a haunt which he often frequented. There,

as ill-luck would have it, he chanced to come in contact with Norman Buchanan, the favourite commissioner, the compatriot, and often the boon companion of Mr James Merry . . . and when in a swaggering, half-inhebriated manner Buchanan offered to take twenty monkeys to one—£10,000 to £500—that Mr Merry's Saunterer won, he was instantly shot by Lord Drumlanrig. The latter had taken up the erroneous impression that Saunterer would not stay half the distance for the Goodwood Cup, and no entreaties, no warnings, no objurations emanating from his friends could shake him from his firm resolve to stand £10,000—which he did not possess—against the horse. It was in vain that Mathew Dawson, who then trained for Mr Merry, assured Lord Drumlanrig that Saunterer was bound to win. Into the details of that melancholy race, beyond saying that Saunterer won in a canter, we decline to enter.'

There can be no doubt that the bet was laid and lost. This is what gave rise to the rumours after the Marquess's death. Whether, as the article goes on to imply, it was the sole cause of his supposed suicide is another matter.

To suggest that he did not have £10,000 to settle his debt is absurd. He was by no means the richest peer in Scotland but he was not poor. He had recently inherited the Kinmount estate from which the rent roll alone is said to have been worth £20,000 annually. Besides this he also owned Torthowald Castle and other family properties. His fortune at the time of his death was estimated at something like £780,000. Admittedly this money was largely tied up, but as a substantial landowner he would have had little difficulty in raising a loan. If driven to it he could even have sold part of his property (as his son did) to meet his debts. He would not have been happy about selling his land, but it would have been less drastic than suicide.

All the same, suicide seems highly likely. His contemporaries certainly believed he killed himself and, if further proof were needed, the *Sporting Times* article provided it. Or, at least, it appeared to do so. The writer claimed to have seen a letter which the Marquess wrote to his current mistress shortly before his death. This letter was supposed to have 'told its own tale' and was 'subsequently shown to many of his and her friends.' Unfortunately—or conveniently—the lady herself had since died and the letter could neither be produced nor quoted. Whatever the truth, the facts of the article were never challenged.

But there is more to the suicide theory than gossip. There is the personality of the Marquess himself. Had he been an emotionally stable man, the arguments against suicide might appear reasonable. But he was hardly that. His death could easily have resulted from pressures less obvious than his gambling debts. There was his failure to obtain an English peerage, the sudden end of his political career, the dread of middle-age and the deterioration in his relationship with his wife. All these things could have contributed to his loss of self-esteem. His disastrous bet, and the subsequent ridicule, might have been the final blow. Members of his family are known to have killed themselves for less.

It is the history of his family that lends weight to the theory that the seventh Marquess of Queensberry committed suicide. Not only his ancestors but his children suffered from bouts of manic-depression. So severe were these attacks that they often threw the sufferers completely off-balance. 'I will kill myself . . . I can't live and it's so utterly easy to die,' wrote one of his grandchildren. This was merely a threat but it was a threat which was repeated again and again. The thought of suicide sprang all too easily to the minds of the Marquess's descendants at times of crisis. Not all of them stopped at threats.

Chapter Two

Drumlanrig's Legacy

Kinmount, the Queensberry estate, was four miles north of the little town of Annan, on the high road to Dumfries. The property, formerly known as Kelhead and then Kilnmount, had originally been granted to the Norman family of de Careol or Carlyle—thought to be the ancestors of the historian Thomas Carlyle, who was born in the nearby village of Ecclefechan—in the thirteenth century and had remained in their possession for some four hundred years. In 1633, however, it was acquired by the first Earl of Queensberry. Eventually it became part of the inheritance of Sir Charles Douglas, the fifth Marquess of Queensberry.

An imposing mansion, surrounded by tree-studded lawns and facing a huge lake, was built on the estate in the early 1700s but, being 'fitted with a good deal of timber,' was destroyed by fire later that century. Several lives were lost in the fire and when, in 1815, the fifth Marquess decided to rebuild the house, orders were given that no wood was to be used. The result was the huge grey stone building, elegantly proportioned but severe in outline, that came be known as Kinmount House. At the time it was considered a 'poor substitute' for the earlier, infinitely more picturesque mansion but with the years it weathered, matured, and took on beauty of its own. Set against a background of Scotch firs and magnificent copper beeches, its massive portico, decorative balustrading, graceful terraces and handsome conservatories showed to full advantage. Inside it was no less impressive. The spacious, pillared hall, with galleries running round the first and second floors, was lit by a high glass cupola; huge double doors led into the main rooms of the lower floor—library, reception-rooms, morning-room and dining-room—whose tall windows looked out on the park-like grounds. From the upper storey of the central tower it was possible to gaze across the countryside to the silver thread of the Solway glinting in the distance. The family was justly proud of its Scottish seat.

That pride was not shared by the recently widowed Lady Queensberry. Accustomed to the gentler charms of Harleyford—a mellow, red-bricked, eighteenth century house, whose lawns sloped to the banks of the Thames—she found Kinmount bleak, impersonal and haunted by sad memories. She spent very little time there after her husband's death.

Accompanied by her younger children, she moved about England, renting houses or staying with relations and spending long periods on the Continent, wandering from one fashionable resort to another. Her youngest daughter later boasted that by the time she was ten she had visited every major city in Europe. When Lady Queensberry did return to Scotland she preferred to live at Glen Stuart, a smaller family house hidden in the woods on the Kinmount estate.

The children, particularly the twins, adored Glen Stuart. During these restless years it became an anchor for them, the place nearest to being a home. They felt free and secure there and loved nothing more than exploring the woods, tracking squirrels, climbing trees, bird nesting and collecting flowers. The great love of nature they acquired remained with them all their lives; they never really felt happy in a town. Little Florrie tried to express her feelings about Glen Stuart in a childish poem.

> *Glen Stuart, where dear Jim and others play*
> *Joining with me in many frolics gay*
> *It is our 'home Sweet Home' as truly dear*
> *As the more stately Kinmount rising near*
>
> *Dear Kinmount, yes I love your lordly pile*
> *But better still I love my wood-girt isle*
> *Glen Stuart, where we wander and we play*
> *Making amidst its scenes sweet holiday.*

Dear Jim was, of course, her twin James and the 'others' would, for a while at least, have included her brother Archie. Her older brothers, John and Francis, were at school in England and her sister, Gertrude, lived a life of her own, often staying with her Clayton grandparents or with friends in London. It was Florrie, Jim and Archie who remained with their mother and who were most influenced by her incessant journeyings. Of the three, Archie was probably the favourite. He was eight years old when his father died, 'a gentle, kindly, quiet lad, very different in temperament to the twins or his elder two brothers,' and, being more sensitive than the others, he was more deeply affected by the tragedy. Over the next few years, young as he was, Archie became his mother's confidant. They drew very close and remained so until he too was sent to a preparatory school in England.

The twins were left to their indulgent nurse, 'Nan'—whom they idolised—and to their own devices. Never happier than in Scotland, always searching for excitement, they enjoyed their freedom to the full. Like most twins they were inseparable. 'We two are twins, my dear brother and I,' Florrie wrote proudly in another of her poems, 'and our hearts are cemented in one.' They had the same tastes, they had the same friends, they played the same games, they even wore the same clothes. To her, he was 'Dearest'; to him, she was 'Darling.' Together they would organise the local children into games of cricket, rounders and football. Together they planned raiding parties on the neighbouring gardens and raced their ponies across the Scottish moors or, on their European holidays, climbed the Bavarian mountains. All these decidedly masculine activities left their mark on Florrie; they turned her into (although she came to hate the term) a tomboy.

Hers was far and away the dominant personality. Where Jim was inclined to be moody, fractious and sulky, Florrie was forthright, out-spoken and daring. There was nothing that Jim could do that she could not equal. There was no horse, however wild, that she could not ride; there was no mountain torrent, however fierce, that she would not swim; there was no precipice, however steep, that she would not climb. She was completely without fear. She thought of herself as a boy, she spoke of herself as a boy, throughout her life she rode astride her saddle like a man. 'Come kiss your boy,' she once commanded her mother. 'He'll try to be a good chap till he dies.'

But it was not all rounders and raiding parties for the twins. Their childhood might have been unrestricted but it was not carefree; they were still subject to their mother's whims and this meant constant upheavals; tearful partings from their friends and, occasionally, painful partings from each other. The first and probably most traumatic of these disruptions occurred three years after their father's death. It had far reaching effects.

[2]

Next to Glen Stuart, the family's favourite resting place was Harleyford. Few months went by without a visit to Lady Queensberry's parents and these visits sometimes lasted for weeks on end. After the isolation of Scotland, Harleyford provided sufficient diversions and excitements to please them all. The children had free run of the extensive grounds and there were the additional attractions of the Thames and the tiny island on the river owned by the Clayton family as well as the special treats ar-ranged by their doting grandfather. Their mother, on the other hand, was happy enough to relax in the company of her family and her many old friends. Life was rarely dull at Harleyford.

Old Sir William Clayton was no longer an MP—having lost his seat after a fierce contest in 1842—but his house was still a popular meeting place for politicians of all parties. Week-end gatherings at Harleyford could be highly entertaining. For not only was Sir William a man of many friends and diverse tastes, but his views on most subjects were far from conventional. This was particularly true of his religious opinions. Married to a devout Catholic, he had insisted on his children being brought up as Protestants—his elder daughter's husband became an Anglican Bishop—but he, to the embarrassment of his more conservative guests, made no secret of his own scepticism. It made for lively after-dinner talk. One of Florrie's most vivid childhood memories was of her grandfather championing George Jacob Holyoake, the well-known secularist, against the criticism of the cynical, but conformist, Benjamin Disraeli.

'When I was a little girl,' she later told Holyoake, 'I heard your praises sung at a large dinner party at Harleyford by my grandfather . . . who was a great admirer of yours. I was six, and was seated on Disraeli's knee for desert, eating almonds and raisins, and listening very attentively to the discussion of your merits and demerits. I sympathised with my grandfather's estimate of you, and, when Mr Disraeli did not, I put up a tiny hand to his cheek and, pulling his face round, said: "Mr Disraeli, Florrie likes Mr Holyoake too." '

It was a pretty gesture but it would hardly have pleased her mother. Lady Queensberry disapproved strongly of her father's dinner-table arguments, especially with the children present. She had her own views on religion and since the death of her husband those views had become more pronounced. ''She absolutely and steadfastly,' it is said, 'believed in the doctrines of Christianity—in heaven, in hell, in devils and in angels; and it is quite certain her beliefs were shared by her children, to whom she taught them assiduously.' Emotional, lonely and obviously discontent, Lady Queensberry had turned more and more to her mother's faith and by the time the twins were six years old she had decided to become a Catholic. Whether her father knew of this decision is uncertain—it is a secret she seems to have shared only with her son Archie—but once her mind was made up nothing could dissuade her.

Sometime in 1861, Lady Queensberry and the eleven-year old Archie were received into the Catholic Church at Brompton Oratory in London.

When the news of her conversion leaked out, it was not her family but her husband's family that was outraged. Her mother-in-law, the staunchly Presbyterian Dowager Marchioness of Queensberry, was particularly incensed. She immediately took steps to stop the rot. Guardians had been appointed to supervise the education of the younger children and these guardians were now called in to rescue the twins and Archie. On her return to Scotland, Lady Queensberry was summarily informed that her children were to be removed from her care.

Her reaction was very much what might have been expected. She took flight. Hurriedly packing a trunk, she bundled the twins and their nurse into a carriage and drove to Ecclefechan railway station. Then, travelling by train to Folkestone, she snatched Archie from his preparatory school. They caught the next channel steamer to France.

[3]

Hardly had Lady Queensberry arrived in Boulogne than the alarms sounded. 'Police,' it was later reported, 'were after her everywhere—they went to America, even to Australia—at last, through information given by a lady, she was discovered in France.' Who the informer was is not known, but there can be no doubt about Lady Queensberry's reaction. Once she learned that her hiding place had been discovered, she panicked. Helped by a Catholic friend, Mrs Eleanor Leslie, she made a desperate appeal to her old admirer, the Emperor Napoleon III—formerly Prince Louis Napoleon—for protection. According to Florrie the Emperor immediately supplied guards to keep 'watch and ward' over the children. These guards remained with them throughout their stay in France.

Florrie, who idolised Napoleon III, might have been exaggerating. It is doubtful whether a private family feud would have warranted a permanent guard, but there can be no doubt that the Emperor did intervene. It was, says Eleanor Leslie, largely due to official French protection that 'Lady Queensberry was allowed to keep her children in peace, and bring them up as she pleased.'

Many years later Florrie wrote about her childhood in a book called *The Story of Ijain: or, the Evolution of a Mind.* Ijain was her pet name and, although the book is written in the third person, it is an obvious piece of autobiography. The only reason for attempting to disguise the characters and places—the family name is given as Dugald, the Queensberry title as Torthowald, Harleyford as Marleyford and so on—was to save her mother unnecessary embarrassment. But few knowledgeable readers could have been fooled. The book is illustrated with photographs of Florrie and Jim ('Rorie') as children, family letters are reproduced, the story is faithful to verifiable events, and footnotes are provided to substantiate the more obscure passages. Florrie's incurable weakness for romanticism is very much in evidence, but *Ijain* is no more fictionalised than her other autobiographical writings. In any event, it contains the only detailed account of the family's years in 'exile.'

They eventually settled, she says, in a 'large old-fashioned, roomy house in one of the squares or places of the ancient town of Nantes.' If Napoleonic soldiers kept a permanent guard on the house, they were singularly unobtrusive. Certainly their presence made no difference to the friendships that Lady Queensberry formed with her royalist neighbours. The district surrounding Nantes was at that time crowded with French legitimists who, contemptuous of the new Napoleon, welcomed the Queensberry family as fellow exiles. They were convinced that the newly arrived 'Scottish Marquise'—a Douglas and a Catholic—was every bit as loyal to the deposed Stuarts as they were to the Bourbons, and Lady Queensberry did nothing to disillusion them. It all helped to make for a friendly, pleasant existence. Florrie was to remember her visits to the châteaux of these die-hard, often eccentric, French aristocrats with amused affection.

A particular friend was the Vicomtesse de Kersabiec (de Rersabiec in *Ijain*) who lived near the coast a few miles from Nantes. Somewhat younger than her neighbours, Madame de Kersabiec was popular with the entire Queensberry family. Her house became a second home for the children. Archie and Madame de Kersabiec's eldest son struck up a great friendship, were always together, and both being 'religiously inclined' were taught for a while by the Kersabiec's chaplain. For the twins the visits to the coast were sheer delight. Their days were spent on the beach, clambering over rocks, hunting crabs and netting shrimps or sometimes, as a special treat, they were allowed to go out with the local fishermen on sardine runs. Even the excitements of the Glen Stuart woods seemed tame in comparison.

But bright as most days were, they were not entirely cloudless for Florrie. Niggling doubts tended to spoil her fun. If she is to be believed, she was troubled even at this early age by the cruelty of hunting living creatures. Always, she says, she felt 'sorry for the sardines, as they lay gasping on the decks of the smacks, and she did not like to see the shrimps lying in packed heaps in the baskets, or the crabs with their claws tied together.' This could, though, have been hindsight. Many years were to pass before she openly rebelled against what she called 'the suffering or loss of liberty to sentient life.'

Other members of the family soon made their way to France. The first to arrive was Florrie's sister, the twenty-year-old Gertrude, who not only joined the family but was received into the Catholic Church. How much she was influenced in this by her mother's example it is difficult to say. Shy and somewhat reserved, Gertrude nonetheless had a strongly independent streak and it is doubtful whether she would meekly have followed in her mother's footsteps. She was quite capable of making her own decisions and any decisions she made would have been the result of firmly held convictions. There was nothing frivolous about Gertrude. She appears, in fact, to have been contemplating the step for some time but it was not until she arrived in France, in March 1863, that she was received into the Church. Madame de Kersabiec stood as her sponsor, or godmother, and Gertrude threw herself into her new religion with all the pent-up passion of a Victorian virgin. She punctiliously observed every fast day and feast day and made a point of attending the earliest Mass of the day; she immersed herself in good works and assisted local charities; she haunted the neighbouring convents, revered saintly relics and made pilgrimages to nearby shrines. The rattle of rosary beads were music to her ears. It was not for nothing that in *Ijain*, Gertrude is called Bryde—St Bryde was the patron saint of the Douglas family.

Gertrude was followed by Francis, Lady Queensberry's second son. Having recently left Eton, Francis was now studying for an army commission and it was decided that he should continue his studies in France. A tutor was engaged to coach him. There was little chance, however, of Francis following his mother and sister on the path to Rome. When the possibility was hinted at he was quick to dismiss it. He adamantly refused, he said, to 'be chopped and changed about.' Religion of any sort held few attractions for him. 'Single harness is bad enough,' he once grunted, 'but double harness is a worse yoke. There is a chance of bolting in the first, but very little in the other.'

This was very much the attitude of his elder brother, John Sholto, now the eighth Marquess of Queensberry, who also paid a brief visit to France. Like Francis, Queensberry—as the family now called him—had also completed his formal schooling. He was now a midshipman in the Royal Navy. His stay at Nantes was confined to a short leave from his ship, but he was there long enough to establish himself as a 'great favourite' with the local royalists.

It was probably at Gertrude's prompting that Lady Queensberry decided to have the twins baptised as Catholics. They were too young to decide for themselves and, unlike Archie, they were not in the least 'religiously inclined.' Sundays, for them, were a penance: days of dull prayers and clothes which fitted 'like straight jackets.' Left to themselves they would have been happier on the beach than in church. But, to the delight of their mother and sister and to their own discomfort—they hated having water sprinkled over them—they were duly baptised. The ceremony was brief but its consequences were costly.

'That baptism,' complained Florrie, 'was not likely to be forgotten by the children, for it brought to them, the first great sorrow of their lives, in the loss of Nan.' Nan, of course, was their beloved nurse. She had been with the family for as long as the twins could remember and was, in many ways, closer to them than their mother. It had been Nan who had comforted them when their father died, Nan who had broken the news of their mother's conversion. Throughout the recent upheavals she had remained loyal, even though she strongly disapproved of Lady Queensberry's new religion. As an upright member of the Free Kirk, she considered all 'Papists as creations of the devil' and had accompanied the family to France 'in fear and trembling.' Her uneasiness had not been helped by Gertrude's excessive piety, but it was the twin's baptism that finally broke her spirit. To have her 'wee bairns' thrust into the arms of the Scarlet Woman proved more than she could take. Tearfully she handed in her notice and fled 'the land of darkness.' The twins were heartbroken.

New arrangements were made for the children's schooling. Another tutor was engaged for Archie and Jim; Florrie who showed ' a disinclination to assimiliate her new religion' was bundled off to a convent school for young ladies. This was the second blow for the twins. Having lost their nurse they now were, for the first time, parted from each other. This produced even greater heartache than their separation from Nan. There were painful scenes: tears, tantrums, foot-stamping and sulks, but it made no difference. Florrie had to go, and go she did.

But not for long. Wilful, stubborn and rebellious, she refused to settle down at school and when her brother Francis visited her a week later she cried bitterly and pleaded with him to take her away. So obvious was her distress that Francis, appalled and angry, went straight back to Nantes and demanded that she be brought home. His mother, never at her strongest when defied by the children, agreed. A few days later the triumphant twins were reunited.

This was not the end of Florrie's educational conflicts; not by any manner of means. There were, in the future, to be other convents, more partings and more unhappiness. But Florrie remained unteachable and unrepentant. Time and again she was sent home by angry nuns who pronounced her 'a little heathen', quite beyond their control. It bothered her not at all. The older she got the more defiant she became and the less she needed family intervention. Determined to get her own way, she was quite capable of driving the most saintly teachers to distraction.

For the time being, though, she was placed in the care of a governess. This unfortunate Irish Catholic lady was a Miss O'Ryan, who was brought out from England for her thankless task. And thankless it undoubtedly was. Florrie did not actively dislike Miss O'Ryan, but could never resist teasing her. To the twins she was known as Tomtit, and they went out of their way to torment her. Their outrageous behaviour, embarrassing questions and hair-raising practical jokes—mostly devised by Florrie—often frightened the poor woman out of her wits.

Lady Queensberry's exile lasted about two years. It came to an end when a compromise was reached with the children's guardians. Florrie claims that this compromise was forced upon the guardians when they discovered that it was impossible to penetrate the ever-watchful Napoleonic guard, but the fact that the old Dowager Marchioness of Queensberry was becoming increasingly frail (she died shortly afterwards) might well have strengthened her mother's hand. However it was brought about, the agreement allowed Lady Queensberry sole charge of the children's education 'until such time as, by Scotch law, they could make their own choice.'

With this, and an assurance that she would be free from 'further molestation,' Lady Queensberry closed the house in Nantes. In the spring of 1864, she returned to England with the twins. Gertrude and Archie had preceded her, Francis was touring Europe before sitting his army examination and Queensberry, having recently left the navy, was preparing to matriculate at Cambridge.

[4]

Of all the children, John Sholto, the eighth Marquess of Queensberry, was most like his father. He had his father's trim, athletic build—five foot seven, broad shouldered and slim hipped—his father's black wiry hair, ruddy complexion, prominent nose and darting eyes. He was like him too in other ways. He shared his father's love of horses, love of fighting, love of swimming, love of gambling and love of women. He had more than his father's share of obstinacy, conceit and uncertain temper. Like the young Drumlanrig, John Sholto was impetuous, reckless, combative and temperamental. He could, when it suited him, be charming but, when crossed, he became truculent and abusive. He was very much a Queensberry, very much his father's son.

It was not entirely a matter of heredity. Father and son had always been close. As a child John Sholto had little formal schooling; he spent more time in the hunting field with his father than in the schoolroom with his tutor. He could shoot better than he could spell and learned to ride before he learned to read. At the age of twelve he was sent to a naval training school at Portsmouth, where he was frequently visited by his father. The bond between them was broken only by his father's death two years later. Indeed, John Sholto was the only member of the family for whom the unfortunate seventh Marquess appears to have shown some concern during the last crisis in his life. Before returning to Scotland, after that fateful Goodwood race, he hurried to Portsmouth to see his eldest son. It is doubtful whether the boy appreciated the significance of that visit but its purpose may have been to take a last, though unspoken, goodbye.

John Sholto was naturally shocked and distressed by his father's death. In his case, however, the blow was tempered by his sudden change in status. Mingled with his sadness was the knowledge that he had not only lost his father but had, in effect, replaced him. Overnight he became the Marquess of Queensberry, the owner of a large estate and the nominal head of his family. Never notable for self-restraint he could now assert himself with authority. It was an awesome transformation in the life of a fourteen-year-old boy and one which left its mark. As time was to show, his instant elevation to the Scottish peerage did nothing to balance his already lop-sided personality. 'Thinking over all I knew of him,' one of his more perceptive female acquaintances remarked, 'I came to the conclusion that he had become his own master too soon. A little more discipline in early years was all that was wanting.' That was simplifying things a little, but it was a point worth making.

The only discipline he knew came from his naval training. But it was a discipline softened by privilege. From his preparatory school he was transferred to the training ship *Britannia* and became a midshipman, but he remained the Marquess of Queensberry. To his friends he was known as 'Q', a lordly but popular all-rounder, whose place in Scotland was open house for those he chose to entertain. He was never short of companions on his leaves. Periodically Kinmount would be invaded by a horde of rowdy midshipmen who were given free run of the house, the grounds and the stables. Even the presence of Lady Queensberry—before her exile in France—was not allowed to spoil the hospitality of her domineering son. Servants were kept on the run, rooms were ransacked, cricket pitches were marked out on the lawns, extra horses were hired for hunts and, for a week or ten days, Kinmount and its surrounds echoed with the shouts of Queensberry's 'brother middies.'

'They managed to make everything extremely lively and pleasant,' enthused young Florrie, '[we] often participated in some of the young officers' rollicking pastimes, one of these being paper chases on horse-back, a very lively game indeed.'

The twins enjoyed it all enormously. And so, for quite different reasons, did their elder sister. Gertrude, then an attractive girl of eighteen, was very popular with her brother's fellow officers and her friendship with one of them developed into a distinct sentimental attachment. They were never officially engaged but it was taken for granted that they would be married as soon as the young officer completed his first spell of foreign service. As it happened, he was posted abroad shortly after the family fled to France and did not return until some three years later. By that time Gertrude had become a Catholic and as her lover was 'a Huguenot, fervid and pronounced' the idea of marriage became impossible. Gertrude resolutely refused to marry if her children could not be brought up as Catholics and the equally determined young man would not consent 'to see any child of his in the grip of Rome.' With a display of tortured rectitude on both sides—Gertrude sobbing but speechless, the young man vowing never to marry anyone else—they decided to part.

Apparently the young man kept his vow. Forty years later, Florrie reported that he was still a naval officer, still dedicated to the service and still unmarried. Gertrude sought a more immediate solution. A week or so after the parting, her friends were startled by a short paragraph in the gossip column of a society newspaper. 'Lady Gertrude Douglas,' it announced, 'who not long since joined the Church of Rome, has been received into a Roman Catholic religious order.' Few could have doubted Gertrude's sincerity. From the time she was received into the Church, she seemed destined to become a nun.

Queensberry's career was unaffected by the family upheavals. He no longer spent his leaves at Kinmount, but he remained just as popular with his hearty companions. His one visit to Nantes was a huge success. Shortly afterwards he was made a lieutenant and posted with his ship, H.M.S. *Forte*, to West Africa. He was away for little over a year. Not much is known about his naval career but the one story to survive probably speaks for the rest. On arriving at Madeira, on the way to West Africa, the *Forte* docked for refuelling. Queensberry and four of his fellow officers went ashore and, defying orders, decided to have some fun by galloping through the town. So rowdy were they that they were immediately set upon by the local Portuguese—'fifteen policemen and sixty or seventy inhabitants'—against whom they put up such a fight that the island guard was turned out to restore peace. After three hours in gaol the five officers were secretly released after dark—on payment of a fine by the commanding officer of the *Forte*—and returned to their ship expecting the worst. But Queensberry's title evidently stood him in good stead. Instead of being disciplined, he and his companions were warmly congratulated. The only regret expressed by the *Forte*'s commander was that the officers had not 'marked' their opponents a little more.

On his return to England, at the beginning of 1864, Queensberry resigned his commission and applied for admission to Cambridge. Goodness knows what prompted this decision. He might, as was later claimed, have wanted to prepare himself 'to take charge of his considerable estates' or, like his father, he might simply have become bored with service life. In either case, he abruptly ended his naval career at the age of nineteen and, as far as is known, never showed the slightest interest in the sea or ships again.

He was admitted to Magdalene College, Cambridge, at the beginning of the 1864 University year and matriculated at the end of the Michaelmas term. That was as far as his academic ambitions went. No scholar himself, he remained contemptuous of formal education throughout his life. He had never, he liked to boast, 'known a degree to be worth twopence to anybody.'

Far more to his taste were the opportunities that Cambridge offered his insatiable appetite for sport. If his short stay at the University did little to broaden his mind, it undoubtedly helped to refine his athletic interests. Mixing exclusively with a group of hearty, but not unintelligent, undergraduates he learned to take sport more seriously and to give thought to the unscientific way in which most games were played. He became a skilful cricketer and a finely tuned long distance runner. In all his activities he was influenced by his friendship with John Graham Chambers.

A year older than Queensberry, Chambers was one of those God-like creatures who stride to University, from the playing-fields of an English public-school, in a blaze of glory. A champion walker, outstanding oarsman and superb swimmer, Chambers was a recognised expert on most sports and the idol of the Cambridge games-playing set. He had been admitted to Trinity College from Eton two years before Queensberry arrived at Cambridge, had twice rowed against Oxford in the University Boat race, had won the Colquhoun sculls in 1863 and was president of the University Boat Club. He was, claimed one of his many admirers, 'one of the best pedestrians and oarsmen Cambridge ever turned out.' For all that, Chambers was a modest, almost self-effacing, youngster for whom the betterment of sport was a selfless crusade. He sought not adulation but dedication, not applause but achievement. In Queensberry he found a surprisingly eager disciple.

Not by nature a hero-worshipper, Queensberry nevertheless revered successful sportsmen. He not only revered them but would go to great lengths to win their approval. As a child an approving nod from his father had always offset his lack of ability; as an adult he continued to seek approving nods from his sporting heroes. If he could not equal a champion's skills, he would bask in a champion's respect. This, in his opinion, was the essence of good sportsmanship. It was only when he was over-looked or ignored—in any field—that he became resentful, jealous and surly. Chambers gave him the respect he craved and Queensberry was happy to accept his guidance. They became great friends. The friendship lasted long after they had left Cambridge and brought Queensberry his only unsullied claim to fame.

Fame, though, was not uppermost in his mind on leaving Cambridge. Having matriculated at University he began to prepare for his role as land-owner and head of his reunited family. In July of the following year he would be twenty-one and his coming-of-age was to be celebrated at Kinmount by a huge gathering of the Douglas clan.

Chapter Three

The Shadow of the Matterhorn

Curiously enough the one sport in which Queensberry showed little interest was mountaineering. This is surprising because, in the late 1850s and early 1860s, no sport was more fashionable. These were the years known as the 'Golden Age' of mountaineering. It was an age inspired by the publication in 1856 of *Wanderings Amongst the High Alps* by Alfred Wills (the man who forty years later was to preside over the trial of Oscar Wilde at the Old Bailey).

In his book Wills described his ascent of the Wetterhorn, two years earlier. It made exciting and, for many, inspiring reading. Not only was the narrative fascinating in detail but it sounded a note of high endeavour which proved irresistible to adventurous young Victorians. 'I am not ashamed to own,' wrote Wills on reaching the top of the mountain, 'that I experienced . . . a profound and almost irrepressible emotion. We felt as in the more immediate presence of Him who had reared this tremendous pinnacle.' To a generation familiar with Ruskin's poetic appreciation of mountains and Alpine scenery, this suggestion of mystical experience combined with rugged, often perilous, effort served as a clarion call. Over the next few years hordes of steely-eyed young men—and a handful of incongruously dressed young women—made their way to Switzerland in the hopes of scoring a 'first' on one of its virgin peaks. When Wills's book was published, the summits of most mountains in the Alps were virtually unknown to man; a decade later there were few that had not been climbed.

It was a very selective sport. The cost of travel, equipment and experienced local guides put mountaineering beyond the reach of all but the relatively rich. But for those who could afford it there was no lack of encouragement. This was particularly true of England where hardly a sporting paper or magazine did not feature a mountaineering column, mountaineering notes or a thrilling rock climbing serial. Added impetus was given to the sport in 1857 with the formation of the London Alpine Club—the world's first mountaineering association, of which Wills became a president—which quickly became the foremost authority on Alpine matters. Not until five years later was its Austrian equivalent formed and this was followed by Swiss, German, French and Italian clubs. But for many years mountain climbing remained primarily, and peculiarly, a very British occupation.

If Queensberry did not respond to this national enthusiasm, his brother Francis certainly did. Of all the family, Francis was far and away the most accomplished. As much an athlete as Queensberry—he was a particularly powerful swimmer—his love of sport was balanced by more scholarly interests. He was far more sensitive, more considerate, more open-minded and decidedly more intelligent than his older brother. Francis was the only one of the Queensberry boys to be sent to a well-known public school (Eton) and—with the possible exception of Archie—the only one to show any real aptitude for serious study. His passion for mountaineering seems, in fact, to have resulted more from his reading than from the fashionable craze. But passion it was. The desire to conquer untrodden heights became an obsession with him. Francis was never happier than when clinging to a sheer rock face.

By the time he was eighteen Francis was a seasoned climber. He had learned the rudiments of mountaineering during the period he spent in the Alps while studying for his army examinations in France and, after completing his studies, he had again visited Switzerland on his tour of Europe. On neither occasion does he appear to have performed any outstanding climbs—his greatest achievement on his European tour was in swimming the Hellespont—but his skills, his knowledge and his confidence improved enormously. He had got to know the Swiss guides, learned how to handle climbing equipment, made valuable friends and, as a final accolade, was admitted to the London Alpine Club. All he lacked was reputation. This was something he was prepared to remedy. Given the right opportunity, the right mountain, Francis was all set to make a spectacular ascent.

His chance came shortly after his eighteenth birthday. On his return from Europe, at the beginning of 1865, Francis sat his examination for a direct army commission. He passed first in order of merit and was offered the choice of a commission in the Guards or the Black Watch. He chose the Black Watch. But before joining his regiment he determined to test himself in the Alps. After visiting Florrie—who was suffering one of her periodic incarcerations in a convent school—Francis left for Switzerland, promising to be back in time for Queensberry's coming-of-age celebrations, on 20 July, at Kinmount. He seemed, said Florrie, 'livelier, more carefree and full of fun than I had ever known him.'

His high spirits were also evident in Switzerland. These sunny summer days, coming on top of his successful army examinations, were probably the happiest and certainly the most promising of his life. They started triumphantly. Within a matter of weeks he had chalked up some impressive 'firsts' by struggling to the top of the Thrifthorn, Unter Gabelhorn and Wellenkuppe, but these did not count as major peaks. His next attempt was more ambitious.

He decided to tackle the formidable Ober Gabelhorn, a mountain that had defeated veteran climbers and frightened off others. Accompanied by two well-known guides, Peter Taugwalder and Joseph Viennin, Francis made the climb on 8 July and succeeded in reaching the summit. It was his most noteworthy climb to date and one of which he could be proud. But as a lasting achievement, it proved disappointing. To his untold dismay, another British climber, A. W. Moore—one of the greatest of Victorian mountaineers—had tarnished Francis's victory by beating him to the top the day before. Francis's ascent of the Ober Gabelhorn, although creditable, could only rank as a worthy 'second.' The glory he craved, his claim to mountaineering immortality, still eluded him.

But he refused to be beaten. His holiday was running short; in less than two weeks he was due back in Scotland, but there was still time for that spectacular climb. With the Ober Gabelhorn conquered there was only one virgin peak in the Monte Rosa group that offered the necessary challenge. This was the mighty and mysterious Mount Cervin or, as it was better known to Englishmen, the Matterhorn. Whether Francis had considered climbing the Matterhorn before is not known, but once his mind was made up there was no stopping him. Temperate in many ways, he could be as impetuous as any member of his family when courage was called for.

And courage was certainly called for now. Although not the highest peak in the Alps, the Matterhorn was one of the most forbidding. Rising to a height of 14,691 feet on the Swiss–Italian border, its sharp-edged summit appeared from the Swiss side, awesome and inaccessible. Most attempts to reach the summit had been made on the terraced walls of the Italian side but they had all failed. Local legend had it that the upper reaches of the mountain were inhabited by demons and even hard headed mountaineers were known to refer to those levels as the Devil's territory. No man had ever climbed high enough to dispel the legend. In 1862 no less than seven attacks had been made on the Matterhorn; the highest any party reached was 13,970 feet. Demons or no demons, the prospect facing the eighteen-year-old Francis was daunting.

He took heart from his guides. At Zermatt, the little Swiss town at the foot of the Matterhorn, he consulted Peter Taugwalder who told him that an ascent from the Swiss side might well be possible. This was all the encouragement Francis needed. The climb, as he knew, could not be made without expert guidance and it was probably at Taugwalder's suggestion that he set off across the Théodule Pass—accompanied by one of Taugwalder's sons, 'young' Peter Taugwalder—to enlist the help of Jean-Antoine Carrel, the Italian guide who knew the Matterhorn better than any man alive. He arrived at Breuil, on the Italian side of the mountain, at midday on 11 July where, as misfortune would have it, he met Edward Whymper, another young British climber. Whymper was also set upon conquering the Matterhorn. They decided to join forces.

[2]

Edward Whymper was one of the best-known, and least liked, climbers of his day. In mountaineering literature his name is seldom introduced without a string of derogatory adjectives. He has been described as stubborn, opinionated, aloof, selfish, quarrelsome and friendless. At the same time he is generally acknowledged as a courageous mountaineer of considerable ability. He was twenty-five when Francis met him and had been acquainted with the Alps for a number of years. Next to Jean-Antoine Carrel, few men were more knowledgeable about the Matterhorn than Edward Whymper.

The son of a London wood-engraver, Whymper had taken up mountaineering almost by accident. Like his father he had started life as a wood-engraver and soon became recognised as a master craftsman. In 1860 the publisher W. Longman had commissioned him to make a series of sketches for the Alpine Club's first publication *Peaks, Passes and Glaciers*. This had started him on his climbing career. Eager to make a name for himself, Whymper had quickly discarded his original ambition of becoming an Artic explorer and turned to mountaineering. At first his sights were fixed on the Weisshorn or the Matterhorn—then two of the highest unclimbed peaks—but after the Weisshorn was mastered in 1861, by Professor John Tyndall, Whymper concentrated almost exclusively on the Matterhorn.

Over the next few years he made several attacks on the mountain. In August 1861, shortly after abandoning the Weisshorn, he climbed to a height of 12,650 feet with an unnamed guide but was infuriatingly outstripped by Jean-Antoine Carrel and one of his brothers. (On this climb Carrel carved his name and mark on a rock at the highest point—13,230 feet—then reached by man.) The following year Whymper returned for five more attempts: two made with Carrel, two with guides and one which he undertook alone—falling nearly 180 feet 'in seven or eight bounds' while descending. In 1863, on a seventh, equally unsuccessful climb, he was again joined by Carrel.

The alliance between Wymper and Carrel was largely one of convenience. Neither man liked the other. Whymper was jealous of Carrel's superior knowledge—'the cock of the valley,' he called him—and Carrel, an Italian patriot, resented the Englishman's invasion of his territory. But their rivalry was not openly declared until 1865 when, after a year's absence, Whymper again returned to confront the Matterhorn.

His first climb this year was made without Carrel. It ended, as usual, in failure. So difficult was the ascent that, on returning, two of his guides wanted to cry off. '*Anything* but Matterhorn, dear Sir,' one of them pleaded, '*anything* but Matterhorn.' His third and most valued guide, Michel Croz, also had to leave in order to meet a new client at Chamonix. Whymper had no alternative but to turn to Carrel for assistance. Somewhat reluctantly Carrel agreed and, after paying off the two apprehensive guides, Whymper set about planning his second attempt—this time by a new route. Unfortunately, while he was still preparing, a well-equipped party organised by the Italian Alpine Club arrived at Breuil and made it clear that they intended to beat him to the top. Carrel, who had been half expecting the Italian party, then promptly ended his contract with Whymper and announced that he would join his fellow countrymen. Whymper was furious. Carrel's defection, he declared, left him 'bamboozled and humbugged.' After years of unsuccessful attempts on the mountain, he was now alone and apparently helpless. His guides had already left, he was without companions, and the Italians were about to claim his long coveted prize.

Even so he refused to despair. There was still a vestige of hope. The weather was bad, the mountain was shrouded in mist, and the Italian party—for all its impressive equipment—was large and cumbersome. Given a bit of luck, it might still be possible for him to defeat them by crossing the Théodule and making an attempt from the Swiss side.

His luck materialised in the form of Francis Douglas and young Taugwalder. Not only did Francis agree to join him but he brought the 'good news' that 'old' Peter Taugwalder thought an ascent from the Swiss side possible. This, and Francis's growing reputation, was all the encouragement Whymper needed. 'Lord Francis Douglas . . .' he declared, 'was nimble as a deer and was becoming an expert mountaineer. Just before our meeting he had ascended the Ober Gabelhorn . . . and this gave me a high opinion of his powers; for I had examined that mountain all round, a few weeks before, and had declined its ascent on account of its apparent difficulty.'

Together with a porter, they crossed the Théodule the following morning, carrying Whymper's stores. 'All four were heavily laden . . .' he says. 'Of rope alone there was about 600 feet. There were three kinds. First, 200 feet of the Manilla rope; second, 150 feet of a stouter and probably stronger rope than the first; and third, more than 200 feet of a lighter and weaker rope than the first, of a kind that I had used formerly (stout sash-line).' This rope—which Whymper had good reason to remember in detail—was dumped in a little chapel on the slopes of the mountain before the party hurried on to Zermatt where they signed on 'old' Peter Taugwalder. Francis and Whymper then went to book into the Monte Rosa Hotel.

Here they had another stroke of luck. Sitting on a wall in front of the hotel they found Michel Croz, Whymper's favourite guide. Croz told them that the client he had expected to meet at Chamonix had been taken ill and that, being free, he had now been hired by the Reverend Charles Hudson who was also about to climb the Matterhorn from the Swiss side. That evening Francis and Whymper met Hudson in the dining-room of the hotel and discussed an all-British expedition. It promised well. At thirty-seven, Charles Hudson was already a veteran mountaineer. Handsome, tough, and one of the founders of the London Alpine Club—more than a quarter of whose members were clergymen—Hudson was the personification of muscular Christianity. Whymper was delighted at winning his support and finding him so modest. 'Although he had done the greatest mountaineering feats . . .' he noted approvingly, 'he was the last man to speak of his own doings.' There was little chance of Charles Hudson overshadowing Edward Whymper. It seemed, in any case, a sensible arrangement. They all agreed that 'it was undesirable that two independent parties should be on the mountain at the same time with the same object.'

There was only one snag. Hudson had taken great pains in preparing for his climb. He had arrived with specially designed equipment—'a kind of ladder' he had invented for scaling precipices—and had persuaded the Anglican chaplain at Zermatt, Joseph M'Cormick, and a Mr Birbeck to join him. Also in his party was a nineteen-year-old student, Douglas Hadow, who had just left Harrow and was spending his first season in the Alps. Lack of time would not allow them to use Hudson's equipment (if they were to beat the Italians) and his two older companions readily bowed out, but Hudson insisted that young Hadow be included. This worried Whymper. 'Before admitting his friend, Mr Hadow,' he claimed, 'I took the precaution to inquire what he had done in the Alps, and, as well as I can remember, Mr Hudson's reply was, "Mr Hadow had done Mont Blanc in less time than most men." He then mentioned several other excursions that were unknown to me, and added, in answer to a further question, "I consider he is a sufficiently good man to go with us." Mr Hadow was admitted without any further question.'

Either Whymper or Hudson was lying. Young Douglas Hadow's experience was minimal; certainly he was not qualified to undertake such a potentially dangerous climb as the ascent of the Matterhorn. If Whymper did query Hadow's inclusion then Hudson was foolish to answer as he is said to have done; if no questions were asked then Whymper behaved irresponsibly. In either case, taking Hadow with them was a grave mistake.

It is also not certain who was in charge. Hudson was older and every bit as experienced as Whymper yet, from the outset, Whymper appears to have taken the lead. What was to happen on the mountain? No clear decision was reached, no division of duties suggested. The risks involved in such a vague arrangement should have been obvious.

But it did not seem to bother them. It was agreed that Michel Croz and 'old' Peter Taugwalder should act as guides and that two of Taugwalder's sons, Peter and Joseph, would accompany them as porters. This meant— with Whymper, Francis, Hudson and Hadow—the party would consist of eight men. That was as far as their planning went. They had more exciting things to discuss. Uppermost in all their minds was the thought of reaching the summit of the Matterhorn before the Italians.

[3]

The climb started at 5:30 on the morning of 13 July 1865. It was a crisp summer's day, the mist had cleared and the sparkling, snow-covered mountain stood out sharply against a cloudless sky. They marched in pairs at a steady pace (each foreigner with a local man) picked up Whymper's supplies at the mountain chapel, and by midday had reached a horizontal platform on the eastern face which seemed an ideal camping spot. Here a halt was called and a tent erected.

Whymper was astonished at their relatively easy progress. So far the ropes had not been needed and they had encountered no difficulties. Places which looked, from below, 'entirely impracticable were so easy that we could *run about*,' he exclaimed. To save time the following morning, Croz and young Peter Taugwalder were sent ahead to reconnoitre. They returned at three o'clock that afternoon and reported that there should be no difficulty in reaching the summit the following day, 'We passed the remaining hours of daylight,' recorded the ecstatic Whymper, 'some basking in the sunshine, some sketching or collecting.'

Shortly before dawn the following morning, they assembled to prepare for the day's climb. The tent was briskly dismantled and—despite Whymper's protest that they were tempting Providence—one of the poles was retained to serve as a flagpole at the summit. They no longer needed two porters and it was agreed that Joseph Taugwalder should return to Zermatt with their surplus supplies while his brother, Peter, continued with the rest of the party. By daylight they were all set for the last stage of the ascent.

Once again the going was easy. They followed the route pioneered by Croz and young Taugwalder the day before and Whymper was surprised to see the entire slope of the eastern face rising above them 'like a huge natural staircase.' Why others had found it so perilous seemed a mystery. Not until they were obliged to turn to the north side did it become necessary to use ropes. Before doing so they changed the order of ascent, with Croz leading and Whymper following. 'Now,' muttered Croz, as he started to climb, 'now for something altogether different.'

But if it was different it was far from impossible. Whymper considered it no worse than any hazard a 'fair mountaineer' might be expected to tackle. At times it was difficult to get a firm hold, in places the exposed rocks were covered with patches of ice and occasionally Whymper had to reach for Croz's hand to pull himself up. But this was all part of climbing. Francis and Hudson refused even to be helped, Hadow, on the other hand, found it extremely tough going. The youngster, says Whymper, 'was not accustomed to this kind of work, and required continual assistance.' Cautiously, spider-like, they edged their way over the rocks until, to their amazement, they stumbled upon the blissful sight of a snow-covered slope stretching to the top. Whymper was exultant.

'The last doubt vanished!' he trumpeted. 'The Matterhorn was ours!'

But was it? What about those audacious Italians and their superior equipment? Where were they? Had they, by chance, found an easier way up the southern slope and already staked their claim? These were questions that had plagued the Britishers every step of the way. Whenever they had had the chance to stop and talk, they had talked about little else. Now the moment of truth was about to arrive.

Whymper could hardly wait for the others to join him before breaking loose—it was later claimed he cut himself free—and racing to the top. Croz panted beside him and they reached the summit together. There was not a mark, not a footstep to be seen. 'At 1:40 p.m.' noted the suddenly sobered Whymper, 'the world was at our feet, and the Matterhorn was conquered.' It was an awesome thought.

Even so he could still not believe his luck. The summit of the Matterhorn is not a solitary peak but a horizontal ridge and it was not until Whymper had examined this ridge from end to end and found no footsteps that he was satisfied. Then, peering over the Italian end, he at last saw what he had been looking for. There, hundreds of feet below, no more than tiny dots in the snow, were the Italians. This was Whymper's real moment of triumph. He could not restrain himself. Letting out a loud whoop, he waved his hat in the air and signalled to Croz.

'Croz! Croz! come here', he yelled. The guide joined him and the two men, cheering like schoolboys, tried to attract their rivals' attention. At first there was no response and Whymper, determined to make his presence known, became desperate. He started hurling rocks over the cliff and told Croz to do the same. They worked themselves into a frenzy. 'We drove our sticks in,' says Whymper, 'and prized away at the crags, and soon a torrent of stones poured down. . . . There was no mistake about it this time. The Italians turned and fled.'

It was a foolish thing to have done. No mountaineer in his right senses deliberately lets loose a rain of stones. It was also unnecessary. The

Italians had already seen and recognised them. They did not flee, as Whymper claims, but turned away resignedly. Later even Whymper was to admit that Carrel, with all his experience, deserved to share in the victory.

By this time Francis, Hudson and the rest had reached the summit. The entire party gathered at the north end of the ridge. Standing solemnly in a circle they watched Croz plant the tent pole in a mound of snow. Only then did it dawn upon them that they had not brought a flag. However, Croz was equal to the occasion. Tearing off his blue peasant's blouse, he fixed it to the pole. 'It made a poor flag,' admits Whymper, 'and there was no wind to float it out, yet it was seen all around.'

They remained on the summit for an hour.

Climbing down a mountain can be just as treacherous as climbing up, if not more so. This was something that Whymper and Hudson realised only too well. They planned the order of descent with care. The sure-footed Croz was placed in the lead and he was followed by young Hadow who, it was thought, might need his help; Hudson 'almost equal to a guide' was positioned behind Hadow and then came Francis and the elder Taugwalder. Whymper and young Taugwalder were to bring up the rear. It was a sensible arrangement but, with an inexperienced climber in their midst, it was inadequate. No instructions were given for possible emergencies, no warnings were sounded about likely dangers, everything was more or less left to luck. Whymper did suggest to Hudson that they should attach a rope to the rocks at 'the difficult part' but, as he somewhat off-handedly admitted, 'it was not definitely settled.' In fact, very little had been definitely settled.

There was a last-minute hitch before the descent began. Someone suddenly remembered that it was customary to leave the names of the first climbing party in a bottle at the summit of a mountain. Whymper was asked to do this and he and young Taugwalder stayed behind as the others moved off.

By the time they caught up again, the rest of the party were heaving themselves over the edge of what Whymper called 'the difficult part.' This, of course, was the rocky shoulder leading to the east face which had proved slightly tricky on the ascent. Still cock-a-hoop with his success, Whymper was not unduly worried to find that Hudson had not acted on his suggestion by roping the party to the rocks; nor did he and young Taugwalder bother to rope themselves to the others. Everyone, he claimed airily, seemed to be taking 'great care.'

Care was needed. As they inched their way down the head-spinning heights it became more and more difficult to find a foothold. Only one man moved at a time; not until he was firmly planted did the next follow. Even so it was not long before Croz had to reach up and help the fumbling

Hadow by placing his feet in position, step by step. This, although not unusual, was hardly reassuring. Francis, in fact, became distinctly uneasy. After they had been going a little while he asked Whymper to tie on behind the older Taugwalder. He was afraid, he said, that if one of the others slipped 'Taugwalder would not be able to hold his ground.'

He was wrong. Within minutes of his speaking the slip occurred. Hadow missed his footing, crashed into Croz and the two of them tumbled over the cliff. Hudson was jerked off his feet and the rope between Francis and Taugwalder tightened. Taugwalder stood firm. The rope held for a second and then, to everyone's horror, snapped. Francis was sent reeling headlong after the others.

It all happened in a flash. 'For a few seconds,' claims the stunned Whymper, 'we saw our unfortunate companions sliding downwards on their backs, and spreading out their hands, endeavouring to save themselves. They passed from our sight uninjured, disappeared one by one, and fell from precipice to precipice. . . .'

The three survivors were unable to move for half an hour. Paralysed by the shock, they remained rooted where they stood. The Taugwalders were on the verge of hysterics, shaking alarmingly and crying 'like infants.' Whymper, wedged between them, was overcome by disgust. 'The father's fear,' he snorted, 'was natural—he trembled for his son; the young man's fear was cowardly—he thought of self alone.' At last old Taugwalder pulled himself together, changed his position and tied himself to a rock. Only then was his terrified son persuaded to descend. As soon as they were together, Whymper asked to see the rope that was broken. To his horror he found it was the feeble sash cord—the oldest and weakest of the three grades. 'It was not brought and should not have been employed,' he explained angrily, 'for the purpose for which it was used.' But it was too late for recriminations. He or Hudson should have discovered the mistake earlier.

They spent the night on the mountain and arrived at Zermatt the following morning. A search party was sent out immediately. It returned six hours later to report that the bodies had been seen 'lying motionless in the snow.' To his credit, Whymper refused to listen to the suggestion that, because the following day was a Sunday, any further search should be postponed for twenty-four hours. Exhausted as he was—he had not slept that day—he set off an hour or two after midnight on the off-chance of finding one or other of his friends alive. With him went the Anglican chaplain, Joseph M'Cormick, two other Englishmen and five local guides.

They reached the plateau on which the bodies had been sighted at half-past eight that morning. The last stretch of snow was crossed in silence. They were apprehensive of what they might find. 'When we looked up,' wrote M'Cormick in a letter to *The Times*, 'at the 4,000 feet above us, and observed how they must have bumped from rock to rock

. . . we knew they could not be alive, and we feared that they would be so awfully mangled that we should not be able to recognise them. Our worst fears were realised.'

There were three bodies—or, rather, battered remains—and they were identifiable only by their clothing. Croz was found first and near him lay Hadow. Hudson was some fifty yards away. Of Francis there was no sign. A search was made and eventually his gloves, his belt and one of his boots were found. But that was all.

'His body,' M'Cormick reported sadly, 'must either have remained on some of the rocks above or been buried deeply in the snow.'

[4]

'I have not been able to find a trace of darling Francy's body,' Queensberry wrote to his family from Zermatt a week later. 'When I got here, I found they had already searched and were going to search for it again . . . I am convinced it is useless to search further, and that his dear body is resting beyond the power of mortal man to reach him.'

The telegram announcing the tragedy had reached Kinmount a few days earlier. Preparations for Queensberry's coming-of-age celebrations were in full swing and the house was crowded with people. His mother, with Archie and the twins in tow, had just arrived from the Isle of Wight. Beds were being aired, vases were being filled with flowers, larders and pantries were being stocked. The rooms were loud with the chatter of friends and relatives and the corridors were full of scurrying servants.

The news from Switzerland put a sudden end to all this pleasurable activity. Kinmount was closed immediately; those guests who had already arrived silently packed and left; those who were expected were put off; Lady Queensberry and the children moved to Glen Stuart and a wire was sent to Gertrude's convent asking permission for her to join her mother and family.

Queensberry found relief in action. Throwing a few things into a suitcase, he caught the next train south and then hurried on to Switzerland. It was an agonising journey. He was too dazed to think clearly. Overnight his coming-of-age party had been turned into a wake, leaving him confused by grief and the need to play his part as head of the family. He arrived at Zermatt wild-eyed and distraught.

Determined to assert himself, he waved aside all advice and set about organising his own search party. 'The brother of Lord Francis Douglas (the Marquis of Queensberry) is here,' reported a French journalist, 'for the purpose of discovering his remains; he has offered a large sum to anyone who can find the body.' But it was not as simple as that. The peasants of Zermatt were cautious; they were highly suspicious of strangers, even titled strangers, offering to pay for their services. With the exception of the professional guides, most of them regarded mountaineering as an eccentric and dangerous pastime for foreigners with more money than sense. They saw no urgency in Queensberry's appeal. Why should they rush to search for a man who was undoubtedly dead? Queensberry waited impatiently at the Monte Rosa hotel but no volunteers turned up. At last he could bear the suspense no longer and decided to start out on his own.

It was, as he later admitted, a senseless decision. Night had already fallen, he had no experience of mountaineering and only the vaguest idea of which direction to take. Earlier he had been assured that a new search party was being formed and that he would be allowed to join it. But this made no difference. He wanted action and he wanted it at once. 'I was alone in my room,' he explained, 'I felt I could not wait until the next day, but must go and look for him at once. I was half mad with misery, or I don't suppose I should have tried to do such a thing, and how I managed to get as far as I did, all alone and without a guide, beats me entirely, as it has others.'

Certainly it was an extraordinary feat. Floundering through the snow in the moonlight he climbed the slopes of the mountain until he reached 'the base' of the Matterhorn. It took him several hours; it was already beginning to get light before he started on the next stage. His confidence was no longer what it had been. He had no equipment, no warm clothes, and was wearing only a pair of thick walking boots. From time to time he was forced to dodge as stones and rocks came bounding down from above. But he refused to turn back. 'I can't tell you all I went through . . .' he wrote to his family. 'I struggled on; I don't know how I got forward. . . . At length I reached a spot far up, which they tell me is called the Hut. Here I found myself stranded. Though I made several attempts, I could get no higher, and, what is more, I could not get down again. I heard avalanches falling, and I realised the impossibility of the task I had set myself. . . . It was fearfully cold, and I was half perished, but I tried to keep myself warm as best I could.'

Luckily he had left a note in his room at the hotel, explaining what he was trying to do. It was found early next morning and two guides set out immediately. They found him, half dead with cold, some hours later. His safe arrival back at Zermatt was a source of wonder. That he should have attempted such a climb was considered the height of foolishness; few had expected him to return alive. '[He] would probably have been killed,' clucked a disapproving newspaper reporter, 'had not the guides been sent in quest of him.'

But this rash adventure, frightening and futile as it appeared, was of great significance to Queensberry. He never forgot his night on the Matterhorn. Alone on the mountain he had had time to think and his thoughts had taken a strange turn. 'Those thoughts,' he was to say at the time, 'brought me a lot of comfort in my misery.' But they did more than that. The ideas that came to him that night, vague and confused as they were, had a decisive influence on his life. They resulted in what many of his more conventional friends regarded as his 'eccentric views on religion.'

Numb with cold, still steeped in misery, he watched the sun rise and flood the mountain 'in changing crimson hues' until, suddenly, the entire mountainside seemed to be 'bathed in glorious light.' Miraculously the Matterhorn came alive. Never before had he been more impressed by the dawning of the day, never had he been so moved by the beauty of the earth's renewal. He saw it not as a mystical transformation but as an awe-inspiring natural phenomenon. He was not concerned with possible causes but with breathtaking reality. It opened up new realms of thought. He thought about Francis. He thought about the Matterhorn. He thought about life and death. He found himself wondering what had happened to his brother on the mountain. What, he asked himself, happened to the men when they die? Where was Francis now?

'I thought and thought where he was,' he confessed later, 'and called him, and wondered if I should ever see him again. . . . And then I had some wonderful thoughts. They came to me like a flash of lightning. It was about the relation of the body and soul of man.'

He found it difficult to explain his revelation. Not given to abstract thinking, he was mystified by his lightning experience. Only later did he attempt to clarify his thoughts and even then—expressed in blank verse —they remained poetically obscure. They centred on the Matterhorn. He saw the mountain as a symbol of enduring life. Or, as he put it: 'A monument of the eternal hand; a monument which, towering to the skies, bears witness to the everlasting laws of endless life proceeding from decay.' The mountain had claimed Francis, but it had not destroyed him. Life, thought the young Queensberry, could never be destroyed. That which appeared to die merely returned to the elements to be renewed—as the mountain had been renewed by the coming of the day. All living things, including man, were part of an eternal cycle. 'For,' he wrote, 'naught which death destroys in Nature's scheme but bursts afresh in other forms of life; and thus all life remains eternal still, for death is life, and life eternity.'

These surprising, emotionally inspired thoughts, brought Queensberry the comfort he was seeking. They also helped to form the basis of his philosophy. Unaware of their pantheistic implications, he considered them original and profound. They seemed to dispose of supernatural explanations of the universe, yet offer hope of immortality. They called for reverence, but did not demand subservience. They explained man's nature without limiting his freedom. In time he was to elaborate these thoughts and shape them to match his own prejudices, but he never doubted their truth. They were to guide him along some curious and unexpected paths.

In Zermatt, though, he had little time for philosophising. As soon as he had recovered from his ordeal he wrote home despairing of finding Francis's body. This did not mean that he had given up looking. A search party was being organised and he intended to stay until the search was over. But he held out little hope.

'I shall come home soon,' he told the ten-year-old Florrie. 'You must be good to poor mother; she will feel this terribly. She loved him so dearly.'

[5]

Lady Queensberry needed the support of her family. She was completely crushed by the tragedy. She moved about Glen Stuart ashen-faced and speechless. She clung to the hope that Francis might still be alive. She took what courage she could from the fact that his body had not been found. She waited impatiently for news from Switzerland.

If a story that appeared in the newspapers can be believed, her suffering was intensified by a premonition she had had on the day Francis died. She had not then left for Kinmount and was working in the garden of a house she had rented on the Isle of Wight. 'All at once,' said the report, 'she experienced a sudden revulsion of the heart; she thought she felt that her son was in danger, and she uttered a fervent prayer to his Angel Guardian. For three days the impression remained in her mind that Lord Francis was dying by famine.' The newspaper did not say how it had got hold of this dubious story. It seems to have been given out by Lady Queensberry's servants. For, not content with premonitions, the story went on to tell of 'a domestic' who, that same day, 'had a vision in which she saw the young man covered with wounds, and in the last stage of inanition.'

Whatever its origins, the report was typical of many others. The newspapers were full of ugly rumours. Most of them concerned Francis and few spared his family's feelings. Reporting the tragedy, for instance, the *Journal de Genève*—obviously relying on garbled accounts—had no hesitation in stating that the fall was caused 'when Lord Douglas suddenly slipped, and, giving a violent shock to the cord threw down . . . all the band.' This was tactlessly repeated by *The Times* and other English newspapers.

There was worse to come. The most disturbing rumour was started at Zermatt. The townspeople, it was said, firmly believed that the elder Taugwalder had deliberately cut the rope to save himself from being dragged down with the others. This was seized upon in England and led to a public outcry. Mountaineering was loudly condemned as treacherous and dangerous. Even Queen Victoria joined in by enquiring whether the sport could not be prohibited by law.

So malicious was the rumour-mongering that Alfred Wills, as President of the Alpine Club, appealed to Whymper to give a full account of the accident. Whymper's reply was published in *The Times*. He gave details of the climb and was highly critical of the Taugwalders' behaviour after the fall, but brushed aside the accusation of treachery. The rope, he insisted, had snapped. Even so the rumours persisted. Several years later Whymper still found it necessary to deny that Taugwalder had cut the rope. 'In regard to this infamous charge,' he thundered, 'I say that he *could* not do so at the moment of the slip, and that the end of the rope in my possession shows that he did not do so beforehand.' To prove his point he published photographs of the frayed rope end.

Seasoned climbers tended to accept Whymper's explanation. There seemed, on the face of it, no reason to doubt him. After all, why should he lie to defend Taugwalder? How did it benefit him? He was in no way responsible for the guide's behaviour. The Taugwalders, father and son, had been employed by Francis, not Whymper. Would Whymper deliberately court criticism when he could escape all blame by pointing to Taugwalder's treachery? It made no sense. Nor, for that matter, did the accusations make sense. From the very outset it was doubted whether Taugwalder, or any guide, could have acted quickly enough to have cut the rope, let alone fake the frayed ends. To men who climbed mountains, an accident seemed far more likely than a conspiracy.

Not that this exonerated Whymper. Far from it. If treachery could be ruled out, neglect could not. Few were prepared to defend Whymper on this score. As the instigator of the expedition, it was argued, he should have taken more care. Preparations for the climb had been far too slapdash. There had been little or no organisation. Whymper could, and should, have shown more foresight. Under no circumstances should the inexperienced Hadow have been allowed to join the party. More attention should have been given to the selection of the rope. The sash cord should have been kept strictly in reserve. Whymper should have been present when the descent began. There were endless points of detail which should have been considered.

It was even suggested that Whymper had ruined a length of the stouter rope by cutting himself free when he joyously raced Croz to the summit. This, it was claimed, accounted for Taugwalder having to tie himself to Francis with the fatally weak sash cord. Negligence seemed to have been compounded by foolishness. To make matters worse, three days after the tragedy the Italian party succeeded in reaching the summit of the Matterhorn from the far more dangerous southern slopes. Even the jaundiced Whymper had to acknowledge this as 'the most desperate piece of mountain scrambling upon record.' Yet the desperate scramble had been accomplished without a casualty. It all went to show what efficient organisation could do.

That Whymper was accused—and continued to be accused—of incompetence is hardly surprising. Few climbs have caused as much controversy as the first ascent of the Matterhorn.

[6]

It was a controversy from which the Queensberry family remained aloof. Whether they accepted Whymper's arguments or not was never made clear. They kept their opinions to themselves. They were in no mood for public wrangling. Their thoughts were entirely upon their loss.

When Queensberry finally returned from Zermatt he brought with him a sleeve which might or might not have been torn from Francis's coat. This was all that had been found. Parties of volunteers scoured the footholds of the Matterhorn but whatever hopes they had of finding Francis's body were smothered with each fresh fall of snow. In the end they gave up. Reluctantly they were forced to agree with Whymper that the body had been 'arrested on the rocks above.' There seemed no other explanation.

For Francis's family it was no explanation at all. They preferred not to think of it. Desperately they tried to cloak their suffering in palliatives of their own making. Lady Queensberry and Gertrude (home from her convent and released from her vows) consoled themselves with religion. Queensberry brooded on his recent 'revelation.' Little Florrie poured her heart out in anguished poetry, but it was no use. The ache, the sense of emptiness, could not be softened. It was the lack of finality which made their grief so unbearable. Had Francis's body been found, wept over, and buried they might in time have accepted his death. As it was, they were plagued by nagging doubts, by a feeling of incompleteness. They never ceased to hope that one day the body would be discovered intact, preserved by the snow, and buried with dignity. The Matterhorn—'that huge, majestic tomb'—held a morbid fascination for them. Zermatt became a place of pilgrimage. Mountains and death by climbing featured prominently in the books they wrote. Francis was never far from their thoughts. His death, far more than their father's, cast a shadow over all their lives. Not for nothing did Florrie, in *Ijain* forty years later, change the name of the Matterhorn to the 'Spectrehorn.'

It was Lady Queensberry, though, who was most directly affected by the tragedy. Her personality seemed to change overnight. She remained as restless, as unpredictable and as impetuous as she had ever been, but her emotions were more subdued. The last vestiges of her youthful high-spirits vanished and she became pensive, withdrawn and self-critical. Her excitability gave way to fretfulness, her vivacity to earnestness. So marked was the change in her outward behaviour that it gave rise to the most extraordinary rumours. A few months after Francis's death, for instance, it was confidently reported that the smooth-talking Bishop of Oxford, 'Soapy Sam' Wilberforce, had coaxed her into returning to 'the bosom of the English communion.' The gossipy *Court Journal* even hinted that she was about to join an Anglican sisterhood. None of this was true, of course, but it did reflect her troubled state of mind. She was indeed seeking an outlet for her pent-up emotions but she was not to find it in a change of religion. Her release, when it came, was of a very different order.

Queensberry's conflicts were more easily allayed. Profoundly distressed as he undoubtedly was, he was not one for sustained introspection. His experiences in Switzerland, although not forgotten, were soon pushed to the back of his mind. He was consoled in a more conventional manner. Either before or shortly after Francis's death he had become engaged to a pretty, sweet-natured, sympathetic girl. She was able to nurse him through his grief. Her name was Sybil Montgomery and they had known each other for over a year. Their marriage had been planned for the following February and, despite the tragedy, the arrangement still stood. The wedding was to be a very grand affair.

Chapter Four

The Marquess's Marriage

Queensberry's sons always prided themselves on being thorough-going Scotsmen. Not only, they liked to claim, were they Douglasses but through their mother they were descended from 'the Scottish Mont-gomeries of Eglinton (a princely Norman family, nearly as old in Scotland as the Douglas family).' While this is true enough, it tells only part of the story. Their mother Sybil Montgomery, was indeed a descendant of the Scottish Montgomeries but her particular branch of that family had long since severed all ties with Scotland. For centuries they had been settled in northern Ireland, had married into Irish families, owned extensive lands in Donegal, Down, Fermanagh, Monaghan and Cavan, and were recognised upholders of the Anglo-Irish establishment. If national blood is inherited than Queensberry's children—considering their father's mother was half Irish—had almost as much Irish as Scottish blood pulsing through their veins. For some reason or other this was kept very dark. Only protestingly would they admit to their mother's Irish con-nections; of their grandmother's Irish blood they said not a word.

But Queensberry's wife, Sybil Montgomery, added more than an Irish strain to the family. She was charming, poised, witty, artistic, gentle and quite exceptionally beautiful. Most, if not all, of these qualities she in-herited from her delightfully elegant father. Indeed, to understand Queensberry's children it is necessary to know something of their mater-nal grandfather. Alfred Montgomery was, in many ways, a very remark-able man.

His career, in all honesty, can hardly be described as brilliant. The fourth son of Sir Henry Conyngham Montgomery, a former officer in the East India Company's military service, Alfred Montgomery was born in London in 1814, educated at Charterhouse—where he was a contempor-ary of Thackeray's—worked for a short time as a clerk in the Admiralty and then, at the age of sixteen, became private secretary to the Marquess of Wellesley (elder brother of the Duke of Wellington). That Lord Wel-lesley, a former Governor-General of India and Viceroy of Ireland, should have employed so young a boy as his confidential secretary inevitably started tongues wagging. His Lordship was known to have been very much attached to Alfred's mother, Lady Montgomery, and it was hinted that the boy was their illegitimate son. It was easily believed. Young 'Ally' (as he was known) looked suspiciously like Wellesley and there was undoubtedly a strong bond between them—they were far more like father and son than statesman and secretary. When, in 1832, the Marquess became Viceroy of Ireland for a second term he took Alfred with him to Dublin and from then until Wellesley's death, ten years later, they were inseparable. Wellesley, it is said, positively doted on Alfred Montgomery.

Whether or not they were related is, however, open to question. Wellesley's biographers have pooh-poohed the idea and Alfred, snob though he was, always insisted that he was a Montgomery through and through. Not that this stopped the gossip. The scandalous story lingered on, much to the delight of Queensberry's children. 'It would be interesting if it were true,' smirked one of them, 'and would make me the great-grand-nephew of the Waterloo Duke.'

But bastard or favourite, Alfred Montgomery was happy to be Wellesley's secretary. It suited his talents and his temperament. He was, in some ways, a singularly unambitious young man. He had a good brain, but no professional drive. He was more concerned with the trapping of high life than with its rewards; for him power, wealth and influence were things to be admired rather than acquired. To know the right people, to be confided in, to be accepted by fashionable society was, in his opinion, sufficient in itself. His listening post in the Wellesley household gave him all the prestige, and the contacts, he needed. He loved gossip, adored scandal and revelled in intrigue. He was born to decorate drawing rooms.

And decorative he certainly was. Of all his natural attributes his looks were his greatest asset. With his chiselled, classical features and his keen sardonic gaze, Alfred Montgomery was an exceptionally handsome man. He knew it and dressed the part to perfection. No dandy of the period was more impeccably dressed than the elegant young Alfred.

His popularity was instantaneous. He was admired for his looks, his charm, his wit and his polish; he knew everyone, was asked everywhere and was equally at home with the raffish Blessington-D'orsay set as he was with Wellesley's staid associates. Every bit as accomplished a host as he was a guest, he entertained lavishly at his Chesterfield Street house. His dinners were sheer delight. Everything, from the menu to the table talk, was fastidiously planned. Alfred Montgomery was nothing if not suave. He prided himself on his attention to detail. Any suggestion of boorishness shocked him to the core. He loved to exaggerate his horror of bad manners. Once, for instance, when discussing a murderer who had strangled his host, he threw up his hands in mock alarm. 'I wonder,' he quipped, 'how you would begin murdering a man at his own table? It would seem to me to be taking such a liberty.'

Impromptu remarks like this gave his dinner parties their flavour. 'His conversation,' remembered one of his guests, 'was most amusing, he always gave some quaint turn to everything he said.' Although not memorable, his wit was sharp. He was the master of the throw-away line; his timing was brilliant. With his pronounced lisp he could make the most casual quip seem amusing. How real or how affected his stammer was, nobody cared. It was all part, as one of his friends put it, of 'his bewitching attraction of manner which endeared him to everybody.'

But if his stammer added to his attractions it helped emphasise his fastidiousness. It gave him a somewhat foppish, finicky, old maidish air. There was more than a hint of effeminacy about Alfred Montgomery; so much so that it was doubted whether he would ever marry. His contemporaries were inclined to describe him, euphemistically, as a 'confirmed bachelor.' It was an impression he liked to encourage. 'To marry,' he would yawn, 'is to enter Inferno.'

Yet enter Inferno he did. At the age of twenty-nine—and less than three weeks after the death of Lord Wellesley—he astonished his friends by marrying Fanny Charlotte Wyndham. It is doubtful whether Wellesley's death had anything to do with this seemingly hasty marriage. The Marquess was in his eighty-third year, had been ill for some time and his death was not unexpected. He must, in any case, have known about Alfred's engagement. Nevertheless the marriage was extremely timely. With Wellesley's death, Alfred Montgomery was left without position or employment. To have found, so soon, a bride as well-connected as Fanny Wyndham was a stroke of luck.

Or so, at least, it seemed at the time. The future was to prove otherwise. For they were, in most respects, a very ill-assorted couple.

Fanny Wyndham was the eldest daughter of George Wyndham, the illegitimate son of the third Earl of Egremont. (This made her—as Queensberry's sons never tired of pointing out—a member of the ancient Percy family who, in the twelfth and thirteenth centuries, had been the formidable foe of the Douglasses.) Although Fanny's father was illegitimate he had been recognised as Lord Egremont's heir and had inherited the extensive Egremont estates, which included the stately Petworth House in Sussex. It was at Petworth House that Fanny had grown up. But if her background was distinguished—her mother was a Miss Blunt, aunt of the poet Wilfrid Blunt—she was by no means the socially accomplished wife one would have expected Alfred Montgomery to choose. Her upbringing had been severely limited.

George Wyndham, her father, was a morose, quarrelsome man whose only interests in life were hunting and the long-running feud he conducted with his brother. Painfully conscious of his bastardy, he developed a marked aversion to strangers and—even after he was created Baron Leconfield in 1859—kept Petworth House shut up, only permitting visitors to stay for short periods and at stated times. Solitary himself, he imposed his recluse-like habits on the entire family. His children were rarely allowed out without a chaperone and were strictly forbidden to make friends in the neighbourhood. Nor was the atmosphere of Petworth lightened by Fanny's mother. Shortly after her marriage, the kindly but naturally aloof Mrs Wyndham had been converted to a narrow evangelicalism and had become so pious that, for a long time, she refused to introduce her daughters to London society. When, eventually, she did allow them to attend dances it was on the condition that they did not waltz. That Fanny and her sisters grew up shy, awkward and unworldly is hardly surprising.

Finding husbands for the Wyndham girls could not have been easy. None of them was particularly pretty and, equally discouraging, a distinctly odd strain seemed to run in the family. It was not merely the gloom of Petworth House that was offputting. George Wyndham's misanthropic surliness was hardly normal; his eldest son, Henry, was decidedly eccentric; and one of his younger daughters, Helen, was unquestionably feeble minded. (So erratic was Helen's behaviour that she was never allowed to leave home. For some years she was her father's sole and apparently devoted companion. When George Wyndham died, in 1869, nobody was sure how Helen would take the news. She surprised them all. Smiling sweetly she calmly announced: 'Now at last I can use the downstairs lavatory.') Of the four other girls only one, Blanche, made a spectacular match: she married the future Viceroy of India, the Earl of Mayo. Even so there appears to have been a jinx on the marriage for it ended tragically, in 1872, when Lord Mayo was assassinated while inspecting a penal settlement on the Andaman Islands.

Fanny's own marriage did not end so dramatically but it was just as unfortunate. Her choice of husband—if she did choose—was a grave mistake.

Fanny was quite the wrong wife for Alfred Montgomery. They had no interests in common and were poles apart temperamentally. Where he was social, gregarious and gossipy, she was retiring, domestic and serious minded. For him church going was a social convention; she, like her mother, turned to religion for consolation. He was a somewhat nonchalant Liberal, she was an unyielding Tory. There was no point at which they seemed to meet. Their differences, while not at first pronounced, became more and more apparent as the years went by. As he grew progressively more skittish—he could, claimed the highly tickled Lady Warwick, have made a fortune as 'an actor cast to play "silly ass" parts'—she grew progressively more serious-minded. (Fanny's first two-volume novel, *Bucklyn Shaig: A Tale*, was published in 1865; she wrote four more.) If Alfred Montgomery chose his wife for her family connections, he was given precious little opportunity to exploit them.

Things were hardly improved by the death, in 1855, of their only son,

Wilfred. He was just over six years of age. Although they were both
devoted to their two, delightfully pretty daughters, Edith and Sybil—
Watts painted an exquisite portrait of them—the loss of their son was a
cruel blow to Alfred and Fanny. Not until their Queensberry grandsons
were born was this gap filled; but by then they had drifted too far apart for
any real hope of reconciliation.

Money too was a problem for Alfred Montgomery. For almost four
years after his marriage he appears to have lived on his small (£300) civil
list pension; then, in 1846, he was appointed a Commissioner of Stamps
and Taxes. He slaved away at this dreary, routine job for three years. In
January 1849 he was promoted to the more elevated, but scarcely more
inspiring, position of a Commissioner of Inland Revenue. He remained a
tax-gatherer for the rest of his professional career. 'Having little or no
income of my own,' he sighed, 'I live by collecting other peoples'.' He was
forever pleading poverty.

Strangely enough his family refused to take his penny-pinching seriously. They remained secretly convinced that he was well-off. Perhaps
this was because he carried off his frugality with such aplomb. He might
complain but he never carped; living on little he managed to keep up a
great show. He continued to dress immaculately, statesmen still befriended him, duchesses still confided in him (when the Prince of Wales
was away from London he relied on Alfred Montgomery to keep him
up-to-date with the gossip) and, although he did not entertain as much,
he was still invited everywhere.

As handsome and witty as ever, Montgomery was a god-send to
hostesses who needed to balance their tables. For he was still regarded as
a single man. Fanny rarely accompanied him on his social round. (The
memoirs of the period are peppered with anecdotes about the irrepressible Alfred, but his wife is seldom mentioned.) Indeed, the usually well-
informed Lady Dorothy Nevill—a leading hostess of the day—seems to
have remained under the impression that Alfred Montgomery was a
'confirmed bachelor.'

But if his name was rarely coupled with his wife's, neither was it linked
to that of any other woman. Fanny need have no worries about her
husband's fidelity. Alfred Montgomery's interest in women was, for the
most part, confined to their social standing and their clothes. 'Do not
forget, dear lady,' he once consoled a bereaved acquaintance, 'that b-b-
black is the p-p-paradise of fair women.' And he was probably quite
serious. Appearance mattered more to him than sentiment. To look right,
to behave correctly, to create a favourable impression, was, in his book, of
greater importance than personal indulgence.

This was something he taught his daughters. Edith and Sybil Montgomery grew up very much under their father's thumb. It was from him
that they acquired their grace, their charm and their poise; it was from

him also that they inherited their exquisite good looks. Of the two, Sybil was more of a Montgomery. She was fairer, more ethereal looking, than her sister; there was about her the same pale sculptured look that distinguished her father. People meeting Sybil for the first time were immediately aware of her vulnerability: she tended to arouse the protective instinct in both men and women. 'Her delicate features and creamy complexion,' wrote Queensberry's captivated sister, Gertrude, 'were more suggestive of high breeding than of robust health. She looked, indeed, fragile as a beautiful piece of porcelain, with her pretty turquoise-blue eyes and her lovely little mouth, small as a rose bud and quite as bewitching.'

Gertrude was the only member of the family to approve whole-heartedly of Queensberry's choice of bride. The rest had distinct reservations about Sybil Montgomery's suitability as a future mistress of Kinmount. Florrie, in particular, considered that her brother was making a serious mistake. 'He thought he loved because he saw a beautiful face . . . ' she scoffed. 'He loved—or rather he thought he did. Was that not enough? *I* think not.' Time was to prove her right.

Alfred Montgomery may have shared Florrie's doubts. He was no fool; he must have realised that the hearty, coarse-grained Queensberry was not the ideal partner for his daughter. But whatever qualms he had, he stifled. The overriding plus in Queensberry's favour was his title. Social climber that he was, Alfred Montgomery delighted in the prospect of Sybil becoming a Marchioness.

[2]

Regardless of what anyone thought, the wedding plans went ahead. The date was set for Thursday, 22 February 1866; a ring encompassing the Queensberry seal—'composed of blood-stone enriched with diamonds and rubies'—was designed; Sybil's uncle, the Hon and Rev Grantham Munton Yorke, was engaged to officiate; and Alfred Montgomery threw himself into arranging a sumptuous wedding breakfast to be held at his Chesterfield Street house. There were to be ten bridesmaids, including Gertrude and Florrie, and one of Queensberry's naval friends, Lieutenant Henry Stephenson, was to act as groomsman. The title-studded guest list, if a little weighty on the female side—'the Duchess of Marlborough, the Duchess of Wellington . . .' but not a Duke in sight—was impressive. So were the invitations, which made full play of the fact that George Wyndham was now Lord Leconsfield and that Sybil was his granddaughter. All in all the ceremony at St George's Church, Hanover Square, promised to be one of the great social events of the year.

But it did not work out quite like that. The hoodoo that was to dog the

ill-fated bridal pair, manifested itself before they were married. A few
days before the ceremony one of Sybil's uncles, Colonel Charles Wyndham, died. Not only was the wedding postponed for four days but Alfred
Montgomery's meticulously planned wedding breakfast had to be can-
celled. As a result of the delay some of the more illustrious guests cried off
and the depleted reception, held after the ceremony, was something of an
anti-climax.

The bridegroom's sister, the tomboyish Florrie, hated the whole business from start to finish. It was the first wedding she had attended and
she found it quite sickening. Not only did she disapprove of the bride and
dislike the bride's father—'one of London's beaux and Society's dar-
lings,' she scoffed—but she considered the wording of the marriage
service unctuous, humiliating and hypocritical. The smug looks on the
faces of the congregation enraged her beyond words. She boiled as Alfred
Montgomery fussed over his pompous guests and shocked everyone by
her pert replies to the questions of a simpering duchess. Child though she
was, the triviality of the conversation bored her to tears. 'Modern Babylon,' she snorted, 'feasted and made merry and talked vapid nothings.'
Her only sympathies were for her unfortunate brother. In her opinion he
had entered a world of sycophants and parasites. 'Poor Queensberry,'
she sighed.

Her sympathy was lost on the beaming bridegroom. For once in his life,
Queensberry was blissfully happy and in no doubt that he had made the
right decision. He was wholeheartedly in love with Sybil Montgomery
and immensely proud of his conquest. Later accounts of the marriage
have pictured Queensberry and his bride as the beast and the beauty: the
long-suffering Sybil, it is implied, was snatched from a life of serenity and
dragged to the gates of hell. But this is hindsight. Sybil's girlhood had not
been without its tensions and, whatever happened later, her marriage
gave her a degree of freedom. Like Queensberry she was twenty-one
and, not sharing her father's passion for society, did not particularly mind
leaving London. At the outset of their life together, her husband could
not have been more attentive.

After a short honeymoon at Braxted Park in Essex, they went immediately to Kinmount. Aware of Sybil's sensibilities, Queensberry was
at great pains to introduce her to her new home as gently as possible. To
do this he decided to make a detour. Instead of travelling direct to the
local railway station—about a mile from Kinmount and rather dreary—
they left the train at Annan and drove the last eight miles by carriage. It
was a small but significant gesture. Queensberry was not, as is sometimes
said, entirely oblivious to his wife's finer feelings.

Even so Kinmount, in March, was hardly the most inviting of places.
Sybil, accustomed to wintering in Italy, could not have warmed to the
bleak, isolated house and its leafless surroundings. Whether she took an

instant dislike to it and regretted the life she had chosen is another matter. Her first year at Kinmount appears to have been reasonably happy and active.

Queensberry, now acknowledged as the local squire, was kept fully occupied. Every bit his father's son, he enjoyed his role as Master of the Dumfriesshire Foxhounds and was content to spend most of his days in the field. He was often away from home and even paid a short visit to America, but this does not mean that Sybil was left to mope. She had her own interests. During that first year she busied herself with local charities and found an outlet for her talent in illustrating a book, *A Very Simple Tale*, by her cousin Florence Montgomery (who later became a popular Victorian novelist). There were occasional visits to London, friends came to stay and within the year her first son was born.

They called this boy Francis, in memory of his dead uncle. It was not the happiest choice of names. Even less fortunate was his courtesy title: as the eldest Queensberry child he was known as Viscount Drumlanrig.

[3]

With Queensberry's marriage his mother became the Dowager Marchioness. Then in her mid-forties, she looked every bit the stately, middle-aged matron. Plump, drably dressed and rapidly losing her youthful prettiness, she nevertheless gave the impression of composed assurance. It was an impression well suited to her august rank, but it was deceptive. She was neither assured nor composed. Her change in manner after Francis's death on the Matterhorn had heightened her dignity but had done nothing to resolve her conflicts. Inwardly she was still as highly-strung and as restless as she ever had been.

Immediately after Queensberry's marriage, she set off on one of her continental jaunts. Her three youngest children—Archie and the twins— and their governess, the tenacious Miss O'Ryan, went with her. There seems to have been no special point to the journey. It might have been that Lady Queensberry wanted to give her son and his wife a chance to settle in at Kinmount, or perhaps she hoped to broaden the younger children's education—Archie was whisked from his school at Oscott to join her—but it seems more likely that she was simply restless.

They travelled aimlessly from France to Germany and then on to northern Italy. They stopped at fashionable watering places and sea-side resorts and made a tour of the Italian lakes. They were forever on the move. Archie, now sixteen, had already made up his mind to become a priest and he at least was able to indulge his passion for churches and shrines. The twins had to find their own amusements. Poor Miss O'Ryan was given a rough time. Keeping up with the unmanageable, often elusive, Florrie and Jim was not easy. Florrie, in particular, seems to have gone out of her way to make Miss O'Ryan's life a hell. Quite incapable of behaving in a lady-like way she took a fiendish delight in shocking her excessively prim governess.

But there was another side to the mischievous Florrie. It was a side which her more simple-minded brother, Jim, could not share. Her thoughts were not always on sky-larking and practical jokes. There were times when she would be engulfed by an urge to rush off by herself; to brood, to ponder and to despair. If she is to be believed—for her comments on her childhood are often coloured by hindsight—she was continually tortured by doubts about religion. Her mother's faith was a complete mystery to her. Try as she might she simply could not accept the doctrines of Christianity. In a journal she claims to have kept on this holiday, Florrie attempted to express her misgivings.

'Last night,' she wrote, 'I wondered thing after thing. I wondered why God made us at all, if only to sin. He must have known we would, because if He thought we wouldn't, He can't be that far-seeing God everyone says He is. . . . Then, I wondered if God was always going to be so unkind. Will He punish me for writing this?'

They were disturbing thoughts for a thirteen-year-old girl. But then Florrie was no ordinary child.

The family's homecoming was sad. They arrived back in England in August 1866 to find Lady Queensberry's father seriously ill. A year earlier the doughty seventy-nine-year-old Sir William Clayton had been promoted to the rank of General in the Royal Horseguards. It was an honorary appointment but the old man had obstinately insisted on taking his duties seriously. At a troop review he had caught a chill which turned to pneumonia and, with his daughter at his bedside, he died at Southsea on 19 September.

With her father's death, the Dowager Marchioness lost another link with her childhood. For her, Harleyford was never the same again.

[4]

In his book *My Candid Recollections*, the Duke of Manchester tells an amusing story about his father and the Marquess of Queensberry. The two men, he says, were staying at a ranch in California and one afternoon rode into the nearest town to visit the local saloon.

'Queensberry,' says the Duke, 'must have been an incongruous looking figure among the cow punchers, for he was dressed in the height of Mayfair fashion. . . . He wore a pair of brightly polished leather boots, and the two men had hardly been inside the bar more than a few moments when a gigantic cowboy appeared in the doorway and cast a menacing look around the assembled company, that finally came to rest on that shining footgear. The sight of them proved the final straw. Lolling his six foot of flesh and muscle across the bar counter, he muttered a profane request to the Divinity to consign all Britishers to a hot climate, and spat vigorously on the cause of the offence.

'Queensberry, without a word to the offender, stretched out a hand, pulled out a red silk handkerchief from the cowboy's breast-pocket, bent down and, continuing his conversation with my father, carefully wiped his boots; having done so, he straightened himself and replaced the handkerchief in its owner's pocket.'

The result was predictable. All hell broke loose. Roaring 'like a wounded grisly' the cowboy rushed head-down at Queensberry, hitting out wildly. A space was cleared, a circle formed, and blinding dust clouds rose as the two men slogged away at each other. It was all over in a matter of minutes. When the air cleared, Queensberry was to be seen 'leaning nonchalantly against the bar counter, immaculate as on his first entrance, minus even a scratch.' His opponent, needless to say, lay stretched out at his feet. 'The onlookers,' claims the Duke of Manchester, 'were very much impressed, but Queensberry treated the incident as too trivial to trouble about.'

Although no date is given for the incident, it seems to belong to 1866 when Queensberry, shortly before the birth of his eldest son, first visited America. He was then twenty-two and at the top of his fighting form.

Little is known of this American visit, apart from the fact that it was brief and had more to do with boxing than with brawling. It may have been inspired by Queensberry's old Cambridge friend, John Graham Chambers, who not only accompanied him but had his own reasons for visiting America.

Earlier that year Chambers had founded the Amateur Athletic Club, which met at Beaufort House in Walham Green and was mainly concerned with improving rowing conditions on the Thames. Chambers's interests, though, were by no means confined to rowing. As dedicated an athlete as ever, he was anxious to raise the standard and codify the rules in every branch of sports. (His activities, in time, extended to a wide variety of games and embraced such diverse sports as boat-racing, billiards and cross-Channel swimming.) In 1866 his chief preoccupation was boxing. No fighter himself, Chambers had nevertheless made a thorough study of the ring and was determined to make boxing a respectable sport. This was an aim with which Queensberry fully agreed. Together— Chambers as the theorist, Queensberry the experienced fighter—they decided to draw up a set of rules that would transform rough and ready prize fights into sportsmanlike competitions, demanding skill and technique. This was the purpose of their American visit.

America was the obvious place to study boxing. Unlike England, where prize fights were disreputable, illegal back-alley affairs, America openly encouraged its boxers. This was natural enough. In a country priding itself on its pioneering spirit, its virility and its democratic principles and where boxing bouts were staged for the entertainment of miners, ranch hands, lumberjacks and factory workers, there was little stigma attached to prize fighting. An American youngster who shaped up well in the ring could win more than a generous purse; he could become a local hero. Many a hefty Irish immigrant had made a name—and a small fortune—in the American prize ring. In seeking social acceptance for boxers, Chambers and Queensberry undoubtedly needed to cross the Atlantic.

But if prize fighting was more popular in America, it was no more scientific than in England. The rules governing a fight—the London Prize Ring rules—were much the same in both countries. First used in 1839 (and revised in 1853) these rules permitted all but the most primitive fighting. A bout had to be fought in a roped-off ring; if a fighter was floored he was dragged back to his corner, given 30 seconds to recover and a further 8 seconds to return, upright, to the centre of the ring. Biting, gouging, kicking and head butting were counted as fouls; otherwise anything, including wrestling, was allowed. Spectators often invaded the ring, free-for-alls would develop and referees were lucky to escape alive. It was all very exciting but it was hardly a sport. Stamina, rather than skill, decided most contests.

Chambers and Queensberry set out to change all this. On their return to England they drafted a new code, incorporating the London Prize Ring rules, and added some refinements. They stipulated, for instance, that padded gloves should be worn and heavy shoes discarded; that twenty rounds should be fought, each lasting three minutes, with one minute intervals; that the ring should be kept clear, no wrestling allowed and a knock-out—from which a boxer must recover unaided—should be decided by a ten second count. In all disputes the referee's word was to be final.

Simple in essence, these rules were to prove extremely effective. They gave Chambers satisfaction and brought Queensberry lasting sporting fame.

For, after they had been passed by the Pugilists' Benevolent Association, they were promoted under Queensberry's name. The part played by Chambers in drafting them was rarely mentioned. This was not Queensberry's fault. Chambers, it seems, insisted on them being known simply as 'The Queensberry Rules.' He was shrewd rather than modest. From the outset the intention had been to make boxing more respectable and what, in Victorian England, could be more respectable than a nobleman's name? Aware of this, Chambers was ready to fade into the background and allow Queensberry to take most, if not all, of the credit for framing the rules.

To his credit, Queensberry never tried to hide the fact that Chambers was mainly responsible for working out the rules. When the mood took him, he would frankly admit that his own contribution had been minimal. 'Lord Queensberry assured me,' claims his friend Sir Claud de Crespigny, 'that [Chambers], practically speaking, drew up the Queensberry rules. They were, of course, passed by Queensberry, but scarcely edited at all, save in one or two matters respecting weights etc.' And Amy Menzies, one of Queensberry's more candid admirers, was told the same thing. 'Who is there,' she observes breezily, 'who has not heard of the Queensberry Rules in connection with boxing, yet he did not draw them up; they were drafted by a Mr J. G. Chambers . . . he it was who drew up the rules and submitted them to Lord Queensberry.' Queensberry, in fact, was sometimes embarrassed by his inflated reputation.

One lesson learnt by Chambers and Queensberry in America was the importance of money to boxing. Attendance at a fight depended largely on the size of the purse involved. Promotion was all-important. This put them at a disadvantage; they were unable to offer large prizes. The best they could do to launch the Queensberry rules was to stage a 'grand competition' at Beaufort House under the auspices of the Amateur Athletic Club. To help things along Queensberry presented, at his own expense, three silver challenge cups worth twenty-five guineas each, to be won three years in succession. In this way, it was hoped, the competition would attract sportsmen and become a respected institution. The aim was worthy, but the rewards were totally inadequate. At the widely advertised event, held on 16 July 1867, only fifty people turned up and the evening was written off as a dismal failure. A much greater effort was needed to popularise the Queensberry rules.

Professional boxers scorned the new code. They considered the 'Queensberry style' restrictive and effete. For many years championships continued to be decided by the tried and tested—and decidedly more robust—London Prize Ring rules. But gradually more and more boxers (including Queensberry's father's protégé, Jem Mace) came to recognise the advantage of relying on skill rather than brawn and opted to fight under the Queensberry rules. All the same, it took time. Not until 1892, when the fearless John L. Sullivan lost his heavyweight title to the fleet-footed 'Gentleman Jim' Corbett, were the new rules finally accepted as the test of a champion.

Chambers did not live to enjoy his triumph. He died in 1883, at the age of forty. Acknowledged as a splendid all-round athlete—he became editor of the sporting magazine *Land and Water*—his efforts to reform boxing were quickly forgotten. All too often, when his name is mentioned in connection with the Queensberry rules, he is inexplicably confused with Arthur Chambers, a contemporary lightweight champion. Time and again, on the flimsiest of evidence, Arthur Chambers has been given the credit for collaborating with Queensberry. Although Queensberry might well have known Arthur Chambers—he knew most fighters—there is no reason to think they were particularly friendly. Arthur Chambers, far from being a boxing purist, was probably one of those old-time bruisers who sneered at the Queensberry rules. Most of his fights ran for more than forty rounds and one—an American championship in the 1870s—lasted a full one hundred and thirty-six rounds. How he came to be confused with John Graham Chambers's role is understandable but ironic.

Queensberry himself, once the first flush of enthusiasm faded, did little to promote his rules. He remained interested in boxing, dearly loved a fight, but had little time for the finer points of the game. On the few occasions he acted as referee 'the soundness of his decisions' it is said, 'were questioned.' He was far too hot-headed to give a considered judgement. When it came to fighting, Queensberry was happier with a free-for-all.

Chapter Five

Fenians and Fox Hunting

The police van which trundled through the streets of Manchester late in the afternoon of Wednesday, 18 September 1867, could not help attracting attention. It positively bristled with police guards. There were no less than five huddled on the front box seat, another two stood on the step behind and four more craned out of the windows of an accompanying cab. Obviously the Manchester constabulary was taking no chances with the prisoners being conveyed to the county gaol at Salford.

Excessive as it appeared, this tight security was well advised. For locked inside the van with yet another policeman, Sergeant Brett, were three women, a boy and—in separate compartments—two of the most wanted men in England. It was with the men that the police were concerned. They were members of a secret Irish organisation, known as Fenians, whose declared aim was to overthrow British authority and 'make Ireland an independent democratic republic.' Until recently little had been known of the Fenians but their activities in the past year or so had earned them a fearsome reputation. Organised, in part, by Irish veterans of the American civil war and backed by money raised in the United States, the Fenian 'army' had attempted to create an international crisis by armed attacks across the Canadian border and, when these failed, by staging an uprising in Ireland itself. The Irish insurrection was no more successful than the Canadian raids had been, but it was sufficiently serious to alarm the British Government. An extensive search was launched to find the Fenian leaders who were known to be hiding in England. The two men being taken to Salford gaol—Colonel Kelly and Captain Deasy—had been discovered, almost by accident, in Manchester and were now awaiting trial. That an attempt would be made to rescue them seemed only too likely.

And rescued they were. On reaching the outskirts of the town, the van was ambushed. The police, taken by surprise, fled. Losing no time, the attackers then tried to force open the van doors. When their battering failed they shouted to Sergeant Brett, inside, to throw out the keys. Brett refused. By this time a large crowd had gathered and, led by the police guards, were preparing to close in. The Fenians panicked. While some tried to frighten off the crowd by firing over their heads, others renewed their attack on the van. In the confusion a shot was fired which shattered the van door and killed Sergeant Brett inside. It was an accident for which the Fenians were to pay dearly.

Kelly and Deasy escaped. Once the door was open, they were grabbed and hustled across the fields to safety. Not all their rescuers were so lucky. Several of them stood their ground till the last moment and, in trying to flee, were overtaken by the crowd, beaten up, and arrested. Eventually five were put on trial for the murder of Sergeant Brett. They were found guilty and three of them—Michael O'Brien, William Allen and Michael Larkin—were hanged.

Their trial and its verdict sparked off hysterical demonstrations throughout Ireland and England. Angry meetings were staged protesting against the death sentence (the Fenians had not, argued their counsel, intended to kill Sergeant Brett) attempts were made to petition Queen Victoria for clemency and extremists publicly threatened reprisals. 'For every Fenian judicially murdered,' screamed an impassioned orator, 'the life of some eminent man will be taken!'

Neither the protests nor the threats had any effect. If anything, English opinion hardened. The Fenians, as far as the average Englishman was concerned, were nothing more than political thugs. The arguments on both sides were to become all too familiar.

Yet there were a few Englishmen brave enough to defy the call for vengeance. Liberal politicians like John Bright and John Stuart Mill protested vehemently, Swinburne wrote a moving poem advocating mercy and the *Star* newspaper pleaded for a stay of execution. But these opinions were easily dismissed. What else could be expected from professional agitators? From the radicals and the unorthodox? Decent Englishmen closed their ears as firmly as they closed their minds. Only when a curt report appeared in the London newspapers, the day before the Fenians were due to be executed, was popular opinion outraged.

'The Dowager Marchioness of Queensberry,' announced *The Times*, on 22 November 1867, 'has sent £300 for Larkin's family.'

Brief as it was, the report came as a shock. As far as anyone knew, Lady Queensberry was in no way connected with the Fenians. She was the English widow of a Scottish peer and, as such, had no business meddling with Irish rebels. Admittedly she was a Catholic convert, but that was hardly an excuse for treachery. To most people her impulsive gesture appeared, to say the least, distinctly perverse. She seemed, as one newspaper put it, to be deliberately cultivating a 'unique reputation for eccentricity.'

But they were wrong. There was nothing cultivated or eccentric about Lady Queensberry's sympathy for the Fenians. Her support for her mother's country was as sincere as her acceptance of her mother's religion. So closely linked were her national and religious loyalties that it is impossible to say which came first—the Irish chicken or the Catholic egg. Her Catholicism was very much the Catholicism of St Patrick; she thought of herself as Irish, she spoke of herself as Irish, she regarded the Fenians as her 'brothers and sisters of the Irish household.' If, until now, she had not publicly declared her Irish sympathies it was not because she doubted them. More likely it was out of deference to her father. While old Sir William Clayton had lived she had hesitated to discard her English connections; his death—only months before the Manchester incident—had broken her restraint. The 'Fenian outrage' had provided her with the opportunity to embrace the Irish cause openly.

She entered the controversy with all the fervour of a latter-day Joan of Arc. Not for one moment did she doubt that Ireland's struggle was God ordained and, despite the fact that Fenianism was officially opposed by the Catholic Church, she saw it as her mission to keep the rebels true to their faith. The frenzied letter she wrote to the three condemned men blazed with pious exhortations.

'We have daily Mass for you here,' she assured them, 'and if it be so that it please the good God to permit you thus to be called to Himself on Saturday morning, the precious body and blood of Our Lord and Saviour and our Friend will be presented for you before God, at eight o'clock, on that day—that blood so precious, that cleanses from all sin. May your last words and thoughts be Jesus. Rest on Him, and on His sacrifice on that Cross for you, instead of you, and hear Him say *"Today thou shalt be with me in Paradise."* '

But her concern was not only for the Fenians' souls. Enclosed in her letter, which she sent by special messenger, was £100 (not £300 as reported) to assist their families 'in their approaching irreparable loss.' 'so long as I live,' she added, 'they shall be cared for to the utmost of my power.'

When the letter was read to the three men, Michael Larkin—the only one of them with dependants—burst into tears. His emotions were shared by Irishmen everywhere. 'Surely,' wrote one stunned Fenian, 'never was an act more noble! Never was a woman's sex more exalted—never was woman's mission more beautifully exemplified, than by this glorious act of bravery, tenderness, and generosity.'

But if Lady Queensberry won the hearts of the Irish, she lost the sympathy of the English. As the 'Fenian outrages' continued—in an attack on Clerkenwell prison, a few weeks later, three people were killed and forty wounded—even her more indulgent friends turned against her. She was no longer dismissed as a misguided eccentric, but condemned as a wilful trouble maker, a traitress, an inciter of murder, mayhem and sedition. Her name was associated with every atrocity, real or imagined.

'To think,' gasped a Tory matron, when it was rumoured that the

Fenians were plotting to kidnap Queen Victoria, 'these are the people whom Lady Queensberry supports!'

Unfair as most of the criticism was, it washed over the head of the Dowager Marchioness. Having found her cause she refused to be swayed by hostility. From now on her purse was always open, her pen always ready, to defend the rebellious Irish. She wrote letters to the press, she published pamphlets, she donated money to extremists groups and even, it is said, secretly financed a Fenian newspaper. Any Irish organisation, however subversive, could turn to her for assistance. 'The more audacious their action,' sneered a political opponent, 'the more liberal would be the subscription, the more gushing the letters.'

Her defiance was all very well but it made life extremely difficult for the Queensberry family. More and more they found themselves being cold shouldered, less and less were the children invited out, smaller and smaller became their circle of friends. This may have been why, at the beginning of 1868, the Dowager Marchioness decided to rent a house in the wilds of Norfolk. The reason she gave for the move was that she wanted to introduce her younger sons to 'the mysteries of farming' but it seems more likely that she was seeking seclusion until the Fenian uproar died down.

If she did vaguely hope to interest Archie and Jim in farming, she was quickly disillusioned. Neither of the boys took kindly to the idea. Archie, now eighteen, was more determined than ever to become a priest and the thirteen-year-old Jim precociously announced that he was 'much opposed . . . to the study of the haunches and hams of the fat and lean kine of Norfolk.' In the end Lady Queensberry dropped the pretence. Never the most resolute of mothers, she weakly allowed her sons to have their own way. Archie was packed off to St Thomas's Seminary in Hammersmith to test his vocation; Jim's future was left to take care of itself.

The Norfolk refuge was also abandoned. Shortly after Archie's departure, Lady Queensberry closed up the house and, with Florrie, Jim, Miss O'Ryan and Jim's tutor in tow, again set off for France. Self-imposed exile in a Catholic country seemed, as before, the most sensible answer to her problems. This time they settled in Boulogne. But there was to be no to-ing and fro-ing of the rest of the family. With Gertrude having returned to her convent, Archie at the seminary and Queensberry married, the Dowager Marchioness was left to cope on her own. Not that this bothered Florrie and Jim unduly. They were only too delighted to have their mother isolated.

'The twins,' crowed Florrie, 'were left in sole possession of the now depopulated nest.'

[2]

Years later, when the tenth Marquess of Queensberry came to record the sporting achievements of his family, he was surprised to discover that his notorious grandfather, the eighth Marquess, took greater pride in his horsemanship than in his abilities as a boxer. This, for a man who had given his name to the Queensberry Rules seemed strange indeed. But there was no denying it: Queensberry's enthusiasm for boxing always took second place to his love of horses.

Like his father, he was a keen, almost fanatical, rider to hounds. During the early years of his marriage it was fox-hunting that occupied most of his time. With the management of his estates in the hands of a competent agent, his only other diversion was his token appointment as Lieutenant-Colonel of the Dumfriesshire Volunteers. But having less taste for soldiering than for his naval career, his Colonelcy remained, for the most part, purely nominal. He was far happier riding hell-for-leather across the Scottish moors.

Queensberry was a gutsy, rather than an accomplished, rider. For him—again like his father—a day in the field was an endurance test. He would ride himself into the ground before he would give up. As a young man, his energy was amazing. Even a seasoned hunter like Sir Claud de Crespigny, who prided himself on his staying power in the saddle, stood in awe of Queensberry's stamina. 'After hunting all day with Lord Wemyss' hounds,' he says of one of the indomitable 'Q's more memorable feats, 'he started off across the Cheviots for Kinmount on the Solway *a distance of one hundred and two miles* riding most of the way on the sorriest of posters, and finally, having arrived home at 2 a.m., hunted his hounds the same day.' (Another version of this marathon says that, on reaching Kinmount, 'they had to cut off his boots and breeches.')

Not for nothing was Queensberry known locally as the wild young Marquess.

There were some, though, who saw his wildness as a dangerous symptom. He appeared at times to be far too impulsive and irresponsible. His life seemed to have no purpose; he was without ambition, he had no serious occupation or interests, he played no part in public affairs and showed no desire to live up to his responsibilities as head of his family. There was something frighteningly familiar about the course his career was taking. In short, Queensberry was altogether too like his father for comfort.

His conscientious mother-in-law was among those most concerned. When Fanny Montgomery visited her daughter, in June 1868, she was far from happy at the state of things at Kinmount.

Her mid-year visit was well timed. Dumfriesshire was at its prettiest; the sun shone, the Solway sparkled, the countryside was lush and leafy,

the grounds of Kinmount were a blaze of colour, there was an early
summer gentleness everywhere. Only inside the Queensberry mansion
was the atmosphere less than radiant. Sybil, again pregnant, moped
about the house—bored and neglected; Queensberry, grimly off-hand,
was seldom to be seen. Fanny found it all very depressing. Not that she
blamed Queensberry. Far from it; she fell over herself to excuse his
churlishness. The trouble, she thought, arose from his unfortunate position. 'He is very young; only 23,' she noted sadly. 'With good abilities
and good principles, but suffering from the overwhelming weight of high
rank and nothing to do. His being a Marquis keeps him out of many
occupations *pro bono publico*, which were he less of a great man would be
open to him . . . I am grieved to see a young man kept idle against his
will.'

This, on the face of it, seemed explanation enough. Queensberry's title
undoubtedly debarred him from active politics. Unlike his father who, as
Lord Drumlanrig, had been an elected Member of Parliament, he was a
peer with no right to sit in the House of Commons. On the other hand, he
was a Scottish peer with no right to a seat in the House of Lords. The only
way Queensberry could enter the English Upper Chamber was as a
representative peer of Scotland but his youth made it extremely unlikely
that he would be chosen by his brother peers for one of the sixteen
available representative seats. The opportunities open to him *pro bono
publico* did indeed seem limited.

But Queensberry's position was not as hopeless as it appeared. There
was, he assured his mother-in-law, Fanny, a simple answer to his di-
lemma. His problems could be solved by a wave of the royal sword. All
that was needed for him to enter the House of Lords in his own right was
an English peerage. If he could be given the title denied to his father—not
to mention other members of his family—he would overnight become a
worthy pillar of the aristocracy. His arguments, if hardly novel, were
persuasive enough to impress the sympathetic Fanny. She was determined to do what she could to help him.

She was not without influence. A few months earlier her old friend
Benjamin Disraeli had become Prime Minister and, after leaving Kinmount, she decided to write to him.

'You will know my political views,' she stoutly assured Disraeli, 'and
will readily imagine how anxious I am to keep my son-in-law in the
straight path. . . . His father, the late Marquis, was a supporter of Sir
Robert Peel and Master of H.M.'s household. He had been promised [*sic*]
an English peerage under the title of Baron Solway. But, as you know, he
died a year & half after becoming Marquis of Queensberry. Now if your
kind influence could obtain for the son the realisation of the promise
made to the Father, all that makes me anxious would be averted. Queensberry would find in the House of Lords occupation and interest, and a

path open to public usefulness. And receiving the favour through your mediation I should have full assurance that he would remain "a good man and true", and would not in his youth and inexperience be cajoled by the other party.'

If her facts were a little hazy, her intentions were crystal clear. All the same, to drive her point home she took the opportunity of having a swipe at her perfidious husband, Alfred Montgomery. Queensberry, she warned Disraeli, was already in danger of succumbing to 'the machinations of our enemies. Amongst whom his father-in-law is always working to draw him from his Conservative allegiance—happily quite in vain hitherto.' For Fanny Montgomery 'the other party' in public, as well as domestic, politics was always Alfred Montgomery.

This particular threat could not, however, have worried the astute Disraeli. He could have faced Alfred Montgomery's machinations without turning a hair. As it happened he was not put to the test. A couple of months later the Tories were defeated in a general election and their removal from office put an end to any slight hope there might have been of Queensberry becoming an English peer.

The hope of things improving at Kinmount was equally dismal. Fanny Montgomery had good reason to despair about her daughter's marriage. It was rapidly becoming apparent that Queensberry and his wife were drifting apart.

There were faults on both sides. What Queensberry needed was a hearty, sociable, sports-loving wife; a wife who would join him in the field and act as hostess to his horsey friends. Sybil was none of these things. She was far too sensitive, urbane and discriminating to be a country squire's jolly wife. Her interests were those of a genteel Victorian Miss: she loved poetry, music and fashionable novels; she was an accomplished artist; she spoke Italian and French and enjoyed civilised conversation. Neither sports-loving nor domesticated, she was bored by housekeeping and never mastered the running of Kinmount.

Before her marriage, as Sybil Montgomery, she had led a pampered life. Spoiled by both her parents and cosseted by governesses, she was far from self-reliant and, in these early days at least, was inclined to sulk when left to cope on her own. There were times when Queensberry, returning home at midday from a morning's hunt, would find her in bed reading, not having bothered to order lunch, even when friends were expected. Such things did not make for a happy home life.

The rot seems to have set in shortly after the birth of the Queensberrys' first son, Francis. By then the novelty of married life was wearing decidedly thin. Once his son and heir was born, Queensberry's attitude towards his wife changed. He no longer felt the need to indulge her 'artistic sensibilities,' to excuse her incompetence, to jolly her along. Naturally short tempered, he became increasingly impatient, resentful and fault finding. They were forever bickering. Almost inevitably he took to his horses and she took to her bedroom; both, in their own ways, became more self-indulgent. There was no give and take. The only thing they seem to have in common was a growing irritation with each other.

The birth of a second son, Percy Sholto, in October 1868, did not improve matters. If anything, things became worse. According to Queensberry's grandson, it was after Percy's birth that Sybil's attitude towards her husband turned from indifference to active dislike. They grew even further apart. There were more scenes, more sulks, more stormings out, longer absences and fewer reconciliations. The atmosphere at Kinmount became unbearable.

Queensberry at least was able to escape. Up at dawn and out with his hounds, he was away most of the day and often most of the night. He would ride miles to a meet and would sometimes disappear from Kinmount for weeks on end. Nothing was allowed to stand in the way of his hunting. Bad weather, rough country, minor injuries and the occasional fall were taken in his stride.

To him, it was all the greatest possible fun. He loved to attract attention, to be talked about, applauded, flattered, envied and admired. He was a born exhibitionist. With him bluster and bravado made up for a multitude of weaknesses. Surrounded by cheering sportsmen, it was all too easy to forget the carpings of his wife and to ignore his responsibilities. The further he was away from Kinmount the more cocky he became.

Queensberry was happiest in England. Every year he would spend at least part of the season in the Midland hunting shires. Here he was in his element; among the fashionable hunting set he could match himself against expert horsemen, talk nothing but sport, and show off to his heart's content. His only regret was that, away from Dumfries, he was deprived of his own pack. Never at his best under orders, he particularly resented being overruled in the field. This is probably why he decided to move his stables from Scotland. At the end of 1869 he closed Kinmount and settled his family in a house called Ham Hill near Worcester. The following year he became Master of the Worcester Foxhounds.

The move made no difference to his relationship with his wife.

During the two years that he acted as Master of the Worcestershire pack, Queensberry's proudest boast was that he never missed a day in the field. It was about all he could boast—'He was not altogether popular from all I can gather,' admitted one of the hunting set—but it was true enough. He still left the house at first light, returning home exhausted, tetchy and mud-bespattered in the evening to prepare for the following day's hunt. His family saw even less of him at Ham Hill than they had at Kinmount.

Sybil's sole consolation during these two years was the birth, on 22 October 1870, of her third son—Alfred Bruce. The arrival of this boy, at a period of intense loneliness in her life, was to be of special significance to her. Deprived of affection, all but deserted by her husband, living among strangers in a rented house, Sybil clung to her new child with a fierce, all-consuming possessiveness. He became the centre of her world, her refuge from her husband's neglect, the solace for her frustrated emotions. He was named after his grandfather, Alfred Montgomery, and his god-father, Lord Robert Bruce (a friend of Queensberry's Royal Navy days) but, almost from birth, Sybil called him Boysie—a pet name which, shortened to Bosie, remained with him throughout his life.

From the time Bosie was born, it is said, virtually no one else mattered to Sybil.

[3]

The Dowager Marchioness's second exile lasted two years. She and the twins remained in Boulogne until they were forced home by the outbreak of the Franco-Prussian war in 1870. The twins were then fifteen and still as harum-scarum, as cheeky and as unmanageable as ever.

Some attempt had been made to discipline them. Their hopes of getting the better of their mother had not been entirely realised. Jim had been taken firmly in hand by his tutor and Florrie, to her exasperation, had again been sent to boarding school. This time she was lodged at a fashion-able convent in Paris, but she was not there long enough for the nuns to tame her. Delighted by her unexpected release, she returned to England determined to resist any further attempts to send her to school.

As it happened, no further attempts were made. After the family had settled in at Glen Stuart on the Kinmount estate, it was Jim who was sent away to college while Florrie stayed at home. Lady Queensberry, evi-dently recognising the futility of trying to turn her hoydenish daughter into a sedate young lady, decided instead that she should be given a more worldly education. Later that year she arranged for friends to take Florrie on yet another tour of Europe.

It was not the happiest of holidays for Florrie. Separated from Jim—and spending several months in Switzerland, where she was haunted by memories of her adored brother Francis—she found it all a far cry from those earlier, carefree family jaunts. More and more the introspective side of her nature took over. She became moody, apathetic, self-absorbed and indefinably sad. Her age probably had something to do with it, but so too did her romantic nature. Whatever it was, her fretfulness was only too evident. On one occasion, Florrie was discovered by the ageing Bulwer Lytton sitting disconsolately by the shores of Lake Leman. He stopped to comfort her and wrote her sonnet—*To Little Florrie Douglas*—in which he spoke of 'that pensive fair-haired child' with the 'dreamy face, and earnest eyes.' He was the first person to sympathise with her emotional isolation; she never forgot the incident. Many years later, when she published her book of poems, *The Songs of a Child*, she dedicated it to the memory of the old novelist. In him, she said, she had found 'a kindred spirit born'. Such spirits were to come her way all too seldom; most people saw no further than the devil-may-care facade.

Florrie was an attractive, rather than a conventionally pretty girl. Tiny, with a neat, lithe figure, she had the fine Douglas features—high cheekbones, intense green eyes and, until she cropped it, a mass of auburn hair. But she took no interest in her looks. She dreaded the thought of growing up, of having to wear fashionable clothes and of mixing in conventional society. Her childish dislike of drawing-room gossips became even more pronounced as she grew older. In a description of London society in 1873, she claims she was completely at odds with the fashionable world because of her 'socialistic' views.

When the time came for her to be presented at Court, she rebelled openly. To the anguish of everyone concerned, she refused to grow her hair long enough to be 'put up' and stomped into the Royal drawing-room without the obligatory lace and feathers. The following day the Lord Chamberlain wrote her a sharp note asking her to observe the rules in future. 'Since then,' she wrote later, 'I have preferred to keep my hair short and forgo the pleasure of attending drawing-rooms.' But this did not prevent her critics from claiming that she had been expelled from Court because of her outrageous conduct.

The only social occasions at which Florrie really felt at home were the county hunts and race meetings. Very much a Douglas, her passion for sport was every bit as lively as that of her brothers. There was hardly a sporting skill that she had not mastered. 'I can handle gun and rifle,' she boasted, 'as well and efficiently as most "sporting folk" and few women, and not many men, have indulged in a tithe of the shooting and hunting in which I have been engaged.' Fearless, tough and excitable, she was as reckless in the field as any member of her family. Despising the side-saddle, she rode astride her mounts like a man and was said to be one of the first women in England 'to advise her sisters to adopt the masculine position and saddle.'

It was probably at a hunt that Florrie met Sir Alexander Beaumont Churchill Dixie—or Sir A.B.C.D. as he waggishly called himself—the tall, good-looking, seemingly phlegmatic young man who became her husband. One imagines that it was sport that brought them together for they had very little else in common. Beau Dixie, as he was known to his friends, was hardly a catch for the lively, honest-to-God young Florrie. Admittedly he came from a highly respected county family. The Dixies had been established at Bosworth Park, on the edge of the famous Bosworth Field in Leicestershire, since the middle of the fourteenth century. One of Beau Dixie's ancestors, Sir Wolstan Dixie, had been Lord Mayor of London in the 1500s and a baronetcy had been conferred on another Sir Wolstan Dixie by Charles II in recognition of his loyalty to the Stuarts. Later Dixies had distinguished themselves in the Royal Navy, several had married clergymen's daughters, and Beau's father, the tenth Baronet, had served as Deputy Lieutenant of Leicestershire. But having said that, one has said about all there is to say in favour of Beau Dixie. As a personality he was pitifully weak and irresolute and, where money was concerned, shockingly irresponsible.

He had only recently inherited his title when he met Florrie. His father had died young (in his early fifties) and unexpectedly in January 1872 leaving Beau, at the age of twenty, master of a large estate and a considerable fortune. It proved a fatal inheritance. Already, as a youngster, Beau had begun to display those incurable weaknesses that were to bring him near to ruin: he was a spendthrift, a hopeless gambler, a heavy drinker. With the family fortune at his disposal he was able to indulge these foibles to his heart's content. He mixed almost exclusively with an extravagant, high-living racing set, entertained lavishly, was a friend of the rakish Prince of Wales, gambled rashly and speculated unwisely and far beyond his means. Within a matter of years he had made a large hole in the family fortune.

Florrie appears to have been blissfully unaware of all this. On the surface Beau Dixie must have seemed to her to be no better and no worse than most of the stolid, unimaginative young sportsmen whom she met in the hunting field. She was, after all, very young.

However it came about, when Beau Dixie proposed, Florrie accepted. They were married quietly in April 1875. He had just turned twenty-three and she was almost twenty. Neither of them was fully aware of what they were letting themselves in for: they had a great deal to learn about each other. Florrie, still a young girl, was to find herself saddled with unlooked for responsibilities and Beau was to face tremendous upheavals. But it was Beau who was in for the greatest shock. Following in Florrie's erratic footsteps, accommodating her wild enthusiasms and falling in with her hare-brained schemes was to prove quite a handful for the feckless and unsuspecting Sir A.B.C.D.

[4]

With the Worcestershire experiment over, Queensberry and his family returned reluctantly to Kinmount. Here they were to live for the next ten years. Or, rather, Sybil and the children were to live at Kinmount while Queensberry rushed about the country in pursuit of foxes, sporting glory and, perhaps inevitably, other women.

These ten years saw the final break-up of Queensberry's marriage. Two more children were born; a son, Sholto George, in 1872 and a daughter, Edith Gertrude, in 1874. But Edith's birth ended all pretence of a settled relationship between Queensberry and his wife. From then on Sybil was left alone. She adamantly refused to have anything more to do with her egotistical, self-centred, self-indulgent and faithless husband. She could no longer bear to have him near her. They met only to quarrel.

Their disputes were usually over the children. The longer Sybil was left alone, the closer she drew the children to her and the more Queensberry resented her possessiveness. A tug-of-war developed between them for the children's affections; it was a struggle in which Queensberry was quickly overpowered. He lacked the leverage for a sustained fight. He was never at home, spent little time with the children, and was far too preoccupied with his own concerns to interest himself in their upbringing. 'He did nothing for us boys,' complained Bosie. 'When he saw us he was generally good natured and kindly, but he never lifted a finger to teach, admonish or influence us in any direction.' One of Bosie's greatest regrets was that, although his father bought him a pony, he never taught him to ride; he and his brothers acquired what sporting skills they had from the servants.

But none of this prevented Queensberry from thinking he could win over the children. He was lenient, he was generous and, as their father, he considered he had a natural right to their affection. He viewed human relationships on the most primitive level. He could never see that his bouts of kiss-and-run fatherliness were no match for Sybil's pervasive and ever-present love. There was little chance of his gaining the children's sympathy, let alone their affection. Nor did he. From their very earliest years the children regarded their mother as the ill-used partner and ranged themselves firmly behind her.

How much Sybil cultivated this support and how much it was a matter of instinctive loyalty is difficult to say. Years later, in his endless tirades against his wife, Queensberry was to accuse Sybil of turning the children against him. But Bosie claims that, as a child, he adored his father, was proud of him as a sportsman, and looked up to him as 'a wonderful man.' This was probably true. Queensberry certainly shone brighter as a sports idol than he did as a father. The difference was one of personal involvement. To admire is not necessarily to love and while the children were not prevented from admiring their father they found it impossible to love a comparative stranger.

To his family the eighth Marquess of Queensberry was a distant but dashing figure, a name that flitted tantalisingly through the pages of *The Field* and other sporting journals. He hunted with the Quorn and the Cottesmore, he rode his own horses in county and national racing events, he bred splendid steeple-chasers, and occasionally featured as referee at boxing tournaments. His sporting accomplishments were nothing if not varied.

Of all his activities, steeple-chasing soon became his favourite. He was inordinately proud of his successes as a gentleman-jockey. For years he competed regularly at the Dumfriesshire Hunt Club. Dressed in the traditional Queensberry colours of green with salmon sleeves—which he later changed to crimson and a black cap—he won his first steeplechase in 1865 and repeated his success in 1869 and 1870. After retiring as Master of the Worcestershire Foxhounds he took to racing more seriously. He became a member of the Grand National Hunt commitee and rarely missed an English county event. His greatest ambition was to win the Grand National but, despite several valiant attempts, he never succeeded. His failure to take this top prize was probably the biggest disappointment of his sporting life.

Where racing was concerned, Queensberry was not a good loser. It was the one sport in which he could accept nothing less than an outright win. Even coming in a good second left him fuming; the merest suggestion of criticism sent him berserk. Once, for instance, having finished second at Warwick, he was walking off the course carrying his saddle and weight-cloth when a huge bookmaker in the ring shouted out: 'Well pulled, my lord.' If the man was joking, the seething Queensberry was not amused. 'Down went the saddle,' reports a startled spectator, 'and bang went the fist between the bookie's eyes. . . . What made the incident the more remarkable was that the man was about the best pugilist in England, and in training to fight the following week.'

In this case, his victim proved the better sportsman. The following day, after Queensberry was thrown by his horse, the bookie rushed to his rescue, saw him safely home, and kept him supplied with 'bone oil' to help his recovery.

Queensberry's fall was one of many. For all his enthusiasm, his skill in the saddle was by no means masterly. 'His ambition as a rider,' admits one of his friends, 'was greater than his abilities.' Time and again he was thrown at a hurdle and forced to lie flat while the other riders thundered over him. Nor did he always escape so easily. On more than one occasion he was knocked unconscious and he is known to have fractured both arms and both legs as well as having his collar bone broken twice.

Could it have been these accidents, asks his grandson, that caused 'those fits of insensate rage that marked the latter years of his life?' Or was it, perhaps, the other way round: could his excitable temperament have caused the accidents? Whatever the truth, those violent spills produced a curious result. He was to give a great deal of thought to the effects of concussion and the state of unconsciousness.

Queensberry's long absences from home and neglect of his wife did not mean that he was without female companionship. Far from it: his triumphs as a skirt chaser were almost as notorious as his exploits in the hunting field. In London he was invariably to be found, with a woman on his arm, in the more disreputable supper-rooms and restaurants of the West End. And some time during these years he took rooms—a sitting room, bedroom and dressing room—at 24 James Street for the sole purpose of entertaining his mistresses. The furtive scurryings up and down stairs, the tête-á-tête dinners and the locked bedroom doors at this London love-nest were later described in sordid detail by his valets. His Lordship, they said, was never 'at home to anyone else' once a young lady had arrived for dinner and had often disappeared into the bedroom with his guest before the second course could be served.

Opinionated and obstreperous, Queensberry had neither the tact nor the temperament to conduct a discreet affair. He liked to brag about his conquests, to flaunt his mistresses; he was always ready to punch it out with a rival or to crow over a jealous husband. It was a rash man who tried to cross Queensberry in love. Not many dared. One furious husband, frightened to take on the battling Marquess himself, is said to have paid a professional thug to beat up Queensberry.

'My Lord,' said the hired bruiser, cornering Queensberry in a cul-de-sac in Maida Vale, 'I've got to give you a hiding.'

'Right,' said his lordship cheerfully. In less than three rounds Queensberry had floored his opponent.

This sort of thing delighted Queensberry's friends. An occasional fist fight added spice to the Marquess's bedroom antics. 'Nothing came amiss to him,' enthused a female admirer, 'he did not know the meaning of the word fear and would tackle people stones heavier than himself.' In fashionable circles, Queensberry's promiscuity was accepted as a matter of course. His womanising might have caused a little scandal but it did not, as was later claimed, make him a social outcast.

What set Queensberry apart from his fellow philanderers was his callous neglect of his wife. Where most unfaithful Victorian husbands felt compelled to keep up appearances, to pay token attention to their families, Queensberry considered nobody but himself. Sybil was not merely cast aside, but was seen to be cast aside. This was the unforgiveable sin. It was humiliation, rather than loneliness, that finally broke Sybil and turned her contempt for her husband into unrelenting hatred.

She was fully aware, even in these early days, of Queensberry's infidelity. Although she rarely visited London, she knew of the rooms in James Street and of the actresses and ballet dancers entertained there. Her father made sure of that. Gossip was Alfred Montgomery's stock-in-trade and when the gossip concerned his son-in-law his ears were well-tuned. Even had Queensberry been a little more discreet it is doubtful whether he would have deceived his wife for long.

Not surprisingly, Queensberry came to loathe Alfred Montgomery.

The two men had never really hit it off. For all his versatility, Alfred Montgomery had never warmed to his hearty son-in-law. They had absolutely nothing in common. Their interests, their tastes, their politics, the people they mixed with, were poles apart. There could be very little rapport between Alfred Montgomery's world of fluttering fans and tinkling teacups and Queensberry's horsey milieu. Yet, in the early years of Queensberry's marriage, they had managed to rub along well enough. They seldom met and when they did it was on polite family occasions. Their relationship was one of necessity. It was not until Queensberry abandoned his wife that they allowed their mutual dislike to surface. From then on they were at daggers drawn.

There is reason to believe that Queensberry, like others, suspected that Alfred Montgomery was homosexual. He later hinted as much and he may have been right. Certainly he held his father-in-law responsible, directly or indirectly, for all his domestic troubles. The very name of Montgomery became, for him, a term of abuse. He blamed all his wife's faults on her Montgomery blood, he traced all his children's weaknesses to their Montgomery inheritance and he saw all attempts to defy his authority as coming from the Montgomery influence. There were times when he would dismiss his entire family as the 'Montgomery lot.' Worse he could not say.

His accusations were not without foundation. Alfred Montgomery was a compulsive meddler. He undoubtedly tried to take Queensberry's place as head of his daughter's family. It was to their grandfather that Sybil's children looked for paternal affection and guidance. Alfred Montgomery spoiled his grandsons outrageously. He watched over their education, directed their careers, indulged their every whim. The eldest boy, Francis—or Drumlanrig as he was known—was the favourite, but the other boys were equally petted and pampered. To them all, Alfred Montgomery was 'the ideal grandfather, the sort of grandfather whom a boy might dream about and hope to find in Paradise.'

And Alfred Montgomery needed his grandchildren. He no longer had a family of his own. His only son had died, his daughters were married and, after years of bickering, he and his wife had finally parted. According to family legend, the break-down of his marriage was largely the result of his intolerance. His wife Fanny had been converted to Catholicism by Cardinal Manning (whom she had known since she was a girl) and this had so enraged Montgomery that he had forced her to leave home.

How true this is one does not know. The Montgomery marriage had never been happy and a break might well have been inevitable, conversion or no conversion. But, however it came about, Fanny had not only left home but left England. Like Lady Queensberry she sought refuge in a Catholic country and eventually settled in Naples where she lived for more than twenty years. Once again the Catholic Church was indirectly responsible for a significant shift in the Queensberry family.

Not only the Catholic Church, but Cardinal Manning, had a further role to play in the unfolding family drama. It was Manning who, on 10 June 1876, ordained Lord Archibald Douglas as a priest and placed him in charge of St Vincent's Home for Boys in Paddington. Innocent as Archie's appointment seemed at the time, it produced some very curious results.

Part Two

Chapter Six

Across Patagonia

For Florrie married life proved an amusing diversion. Her change of status made little difference to her way of life; it merely meant that she hunted at Bosworth Park, Beau Dixie's estate in Leicestershire, as well as in Scotland. She enjoyed it all enormously.

Every year they rented a house in Scotland for the shooting season and had a high old time clambering about the moors dressed as Highland chiefs. They both adored dressing-up. Florrie was particularly proud of her specially designed grey tweed jacket, kilt and jaunty bonnet which made her look every bit the rugged Highlander. A photograph of her in Highland costume, 'standing erect and firm beside a tree with a gun in her right hand and some dead grouse lying at her feet' became her favourite *carte-de-visite*. One needed to look at it twice to realise that the kilted sharp-shooter was, in fact, a woman.

But it was in Leicestershire that Florrie really came into her own. In a county renowned for its spirited horsewomen, none were more so than the young Lady Florence Dixie. Once she started to hunt regularly with the same pack, her popularity soared. It was on the strength of her horsemanship that, in January 1877, the fashionable *Whitehall Review* featured her as one of its 'Leaders of Society.' That Florrie, always the rebel, agreed to appear in this snobbish series was surprising enough; that she allowed herself to be sketched, in bowler hat and full skirt, seated side-saddle on her horse was nothing short of astonishing. But then Florrie was always unpredictable.

'Lady Florence Dixie and her favourite hunter "Remorse",' gushed the accompanying article, 'are as well known in Leicestershire as any master of hounds. Mounted on "Remorse", a bright bay with black points . . . Lady Florence Dixie, even if she does not lead the way, is never far off at the finish. She is a fearless horsewoman.'

It was probably at Florrie's insistence that the article went on to praise her other talents. 'To her equestrian accomplishments,' it explained, 'Lady Florence adds no inconsiderable skill in literary pursuits, and is by no means appalled by the lofty diction employed by *savants* both in conversation and in print to explain theories which to the uncultured mind are nearly as intelligible as a page of Chinese.'

This was very much as Florrie saw herself; sportswoman, scholar, thinker and author. It was also how she wanted others to see her. Her ambitions were not confined to the hunting field. Although her claim to literary distinction was slight, she could at least boast one published work. This was a turgid, completely unactable, blank-verse play entitled *Abel Avenged*. She had written it, she claimed, when she was fourteen years old and had sent it to the editor of an Edinburgh magazine who had promptly returned it. (Later she learned that it was thought 'too un-orthodox.') Nothing daunted, she had continued to badger publishers and, shortly after her marriage, had succeeded in having it published. The play had made little impact on the reading public, but the thrill of seeing herself in print had made a tremendous impression on Florrie. Come what might, she was determined to be recognised as a writer.

During the next couple of years, though, she was far too busy to think about writing. There was the constant round of hunt and race meetings, there was shooting in Scotland and yachting in Norfolk and there was the tiresome inconvenience of her pregnancies. Her first son, George Douglas, was born on 18 January 1876 and two years later she again fell pregnant. She found it all rather a bore. Child bearing neither interested nor amused her and while waiting for her second son to be born she became distinctly restless. She began to look round for a more adventur-ous pastime.

She was not long in finding one. Sometime in 1878 she met Julius Beerbohm—the dapper, but feckless, brother of Herbert Beerbohm (the future actor-manager) and half-brother of the incomparable Max Beer-bohm—who had just returned from an expedition to Patagonia. After listening to Beerbohm's stories of this strange and little-known land, she decided that she had found what she was looking for. If Beerbohm had been the first white man to penetrate those remote regions, she would be the first white woman.

The expedition Florrie planned was very much a family affair. Beau and her brother Jim were included as a matter of course and, more surpris-ingly, Queensberry agreed to travel part of the way with them. Young Julius Beerbohm, who had just published his book *Wanderings in Patagonia*, was to act as their guide and, after some debate, they decided to take a single manservant. 'English servants,' sniffed Florrie, 'inevitably prove a nuisance and hindrance in expeditions of the kind, when a great deal of "roughing it" has to be gone through.'

That they would have to rough it she had no doubt. Indeed the rougher the going was the better it would suit her purpose. She intended to write a book about her travels and she wanted the book to be as sensational as possible. What better way to make her name as a writer than to produce a really stirring book about her adventures in a wild, unexplored country? Travel books by women were having a vogue at the time and she was determined that hers would equal the best of them. Patagonia could provide her with just what she needed. She could hardly wait to get started.

Nor did she wait. Her second son, Albert Edward Wolston, was born at the end of September 1878. He was named after his godfather the Prince of Wales. A mere two months later Florrie and her party crossed to Bordeaux where, on 14 December, they boarded the s.s. *Britannia* and sailed for South America.

[2]

'The sun was rather high in the heavens when I opened my eyes the next morning,' wrote Florrie, a week or so after arriving in Patagonia, 'and pulling aside the flap of the tent, looked upon the scene. All our camp was still wrapt in sleep. . . . The plains below were silent; but the air was noisy with the cries of flocks of geese and wild duck, who were winging their flight from the lake towards the rich fields of cranberries further inland. The sharp quack of the ibis would occasionally startle me, as a bevy of these birds passed seemingly just over my head, but, in reality, far up in the air.'

Nothing could have been more tranquil, more idyllic. On the vast plains of Patagonia, Florrie had found serenity. Her little party had already travelled several miles from the coast and, apart from a visit to an Indian encampment, they had not seen a living soul for days. Now, camped on the edge of a vast inland lake, she was able to enjoy her solitude to the full. Or so she thought. Minutes later she changed her mind. As she stood there breathing in the crisp morning air she was startled by a noise far more alarming than the quack of flying ibis.

'A loud rumbling sound rose on the air,' she wrote, on recovering from the shock, 'and, before I had time to wonder what it could mean, a heaving of the ground, resembling a sea-swell, sent me flying on my back, and, as by magic, the silent camp became alive with shouts of fear and wonder, as everybody rushed out of the tents in dismay. The shocks occurred again and again, but each time weaker, and in about five minutes they had ceased altogether. . . . This was the first time I had ever experienced an earthquake.'

The earthquake was only one of a number of Patagonian surprises. If Florrie was disappointed at not meeting up with cannibals in South America, she could hardly complain that her trip was dull. She found more than enough material for a book on her adventures.

Admittedly the outward voyage had been uneventful. Their fellow passengers on the *Britannia* were not particularly interesting and they were not at all impressed by the coastal ports they visited. Queensberry, with his usual knack for stirring up trouble, had managed to become

involved in a fight with a drunken American shortly after they left Rio de
Janeiro but otherwise they found few shipboard diversions. They were
even to be deprived of Queensberry's antics for, on reaching Monte
Video, he left the ship and, although he was supposed to follow on the
next steamer, was not seen again until they returned to England.

The *Britannia* continued on to the Straits of Magellan where Florrie and
her party were landed—in the teeth of a raging gale—at the bleak little
settlement known as Sandy Point. Here they were met by the British
Consul. He helped them to recruit local guides, servants, hunting dogs
and no less than fifty horses. By the time they left Sandy Point—a
'God-forsaken hole' according to Florrie—they had acquired a sizeable
retinue.

The first few days were hard going and Florrie found the pampas
unspeakably depressing. 'Not a tree or a shrub was to be seen anywhere,'
she complained. It was not only dreary but it was lifeless. Apart from an
occasional hawk and a solitary grey fox there was no sign of animal life
and the shortage of fresh meat soon became a problem; for, although they
had sufficient stores for themselves, they had no provisions for their
dogs. It was in the hopes of bartering for meat that they decided to visit an
isolated Indian encampment.

The camp was nothing more than a dozen or so hide tents and their
arrival there created a considerable stir. They were quickly surrounded by
a crowd of laughing, pop-eyed Indians who were more amused by their
appearance than frightened by their intentions. Not surprisingly, Florrie
was considered a great figure of fun. Wearing a loose, brightly patterned,
cotton ulster over her riding habit, her hair tucked severely into a brim-
med hat, she was quite unlike any white person they had ever seen. They
evidently had difficulty in deciding whether she was a man or a woman.
Her riding boots, in particular, were a source of wonder. This was Florrie's first contact with primitive people and she found them no less
fascinating than they found her.

The further north they travelled the more varied the landscape became.
Leaving the plains behind them, the party entered a stretch of thickly
wooded, hilly country where their hunting began in earnest. The next
few weeks were spent stalking guanaco, panting after ostriches and
taking pot-shots at any duck, geese and water fowl they came across. It
was all very exciting, but quite meaningless. There were times, it is true,
when they needed to kill to eat but for the most part they killed simply for
the sake of killing. Florrie's bloodthirsty account of this senseless slaughter makes sickening reading.

Most of their meals were prepared by a French servant they had
recruited at Sandy Point, but both Jim and Julius Beerbohm fancied
themselves as cooks. They would sometimes spend hours trying to con-
coct a new dish. It was only after Jim had produced a particularly revolt-

ing pudding of 'rice, preserved milk and brown sugar, with a decided taste of burn' that these experiments stopped. From then on Jim's domestic skills were confined to opening kegs of whisky for the heavy drinking sessions that followed the evening meal. Not for nothing did Florrie include 'kegs of whisky' in her list of essential supplies for travellers in Patagonia.

It was during this trip that Beau and Jim became confirmed drinking companions. While Julius Beerbohm contented himself with the local *maté*, they—and often Florrie—sank glass after glass of whisky. Florrie only hints at their drinking, but these hints were to be more than confirmed in later years. Their friendly toasts of whisky and water were, in time, to become a disastrous addiction.

For Jim, drinking undoubtedly provided a much-needed means of escape. Since leaving college his life had been a mess. In 1875 he had joined the West Kent Militia as a sub-lieutenant and two years later had transferred to the Dumfriesshire Mounted Volunteers, but he had shown not the slightest interest in a permanent career. Away from Florrie he seemed hopelessly disorientated, quite incapable of making a life for himself. Florrie's marriage had done nothing to loosen the ties of twin-ship; the twins had simply become a trio. The Dixies rarely moved without Jim. Indeed so close did the bond between Beau and Jim become that, at times, it was difficult to tell which of the twins Beau had married. In Patagonia it was Florrie who, more often than not, was the odd one out.

[3]

By the time they reached the Cordilleras they were feeling distinctly saddle-sore. The weeks of hard riding had begun to take their toll. On their first evening in the mountains, even Florrie was having second thoughts about the joys of open-air living.

But, tired as they were, they were soon revived by the fresh mountain air. The hot rough winds of the plains gave way to gentle breezes, there were clear mountain streams in which they could bathe and, camping beneath the silent snow-covered peaks, they felt refreshed and strangely at peace with themselves. Florrie, in particular, became more reflective, more philosophical.

Her new mood was never more in evidence than during one of their early excursions into the mountain gorges. Florrie led the way and, at one stage, got so far ahead that she decided to halt until the others caught up. It was while she was waiting that she spotted a huge golden-brown antelope, quite unlike any others she had seen. 'He was a fine buck,' she noted, 'with beautiful branching antlers, and large dark languishing eyes.

Close behind him cautiously peered two does.' Not having a gun with her she edged away and then dashed off to meet the rest of the party. As soon as they arrived, she grabbed a gun from one of the servants and then crept back to where the deer were grazing. She was determined to have those horns.

'Anxious to avoid spoiling the head,' she says, 'I took aim behind the shoulder, and fired. . . . Into the glade some half-dozen deer bounded, and like lightning disappeared into the opposite wood. When the smoke cleared away I perceived the one at which I had fired on his knees, evidently unable to proceed. Full of anxiety to place the poor beast out of his agony I fired a second barrel at him, which had the effect of knocking him over. Springing up immediately, however, he walked slowly away, seemingly unconcerned and unhurt.'

She could not bring herself to fire again. Instead, one of the servants rushed forward and shot the animal in the leg. But still the buck refused to die. Limping away it made for an over-hanging rock and sank slowly to the ground. Florrie was appalled. She could hardly bear to look as Beau fired a final shot with his revolver. Even this shot did not kill the buck outright; it continued to breathe faintly until it was put out of its misery with a hunting knife.

'If regret,' she wrote feelingly later,' could atone for that death, of which I unfortunately was the cause, then it has long ago been forgiven; for, for many a day I was haunted by a sad remorse for the loss of that innocent and trusting life, which had hitherto remained in ignorance of the annihilating propensities of man—that man who, directly he sees something beautiful and rare, becomes filled with the desire to destroy.'

They killed no more golden antelope in the Cordilleras.

Their homeward journey was not without its hazards. On the plains they were held up for days by torrential rains and, to make things worse, the nearer they got to the coast the scarcer became the game. The few guanaco they did sight proved infuriatingly elusive and days went by without making a kill. On reaching the place where they had earlier visited the Indians (who had long since moved on) they had very little food of any kind left.

By the time the party sighted the Straits of Magellan they were faint with hunger. So desperate for food were Jim and Julius Beerbohm that they burst into the first farm house they came to and 'without speaking a word rushed to the kitchen and laid their hands on and utterly devoured what was to have been the breakfast of the farmer and his family.' Apparently their behaviour was not considered particularly outrageous for the farmer happily supplied the rest of the party with food. 'No doubt,' remarked Florrie, 'he was used to such strange visits.'

They arrived at Sandy Point looking very much the worse for wear. It was days since they had washed, let alone bathed, their faces were black from the smoke of camp fires, the men were long-haired and unshaven and Florrie's skin was raw from the blistering winds. Their clothes were not only in tatters but stank to high heaven. 'The blood of many a guanaco,' Florrie boasted, 'the grease of many an ostrich-dinner, the thorn of many a *califaté* bush, had left their mark; and, altogether, a more ruffianly, disreputable lot than we looked it would be hard to imagine.'

But it had been worth it. They had come to Patagonia for adventure and had not been disappointed. What were a few discomforts set against the thrill of an ostrich-chase, the excitement of a prairie-fire, the drama of an earthquake or the joy of sleeping in the open with a saddle for a pillow? Their memories would more than outlast their travel stains. Florrie would see to that.

[4]

'I have done little except . . . sit by the fire reading the travels of adventurous ladies,' wrote the Duke of Somerset to a friend. 'Lady Anne Blunt, who nearly lost her husband among the Arabs, Lady Florence Dixie, who nearly starved in Patagonia. . . .'

The Duke was only one of a host of enchanted readers. Florrie's book, *Across Patagonia*—generously illustrated by Julius Beerbohm and dedicated 'by kind permission' to the Prince of Wales—was an immediate success. Her South American exploits provided a novel twist to the currently fashionable sagas of intrepid, button-booted, umbrella-wielding lady explorers. That a young Victorian wife and mother should have left her two-months-old baby to embark on a big game hunting expedition was exceptional enough; to have roughed it the way that Florrie did was considered little short of fantastic. Almost overnight she became a national celebrity.

To add to her notoriety she arrived in England with a pet jaguar which her party had captured in Brazil on their way home. She named this ferocious-looking beast 'Affums' and caused much consternation in the neighbourhood of Bosworth Park by parading it about on a leash. 'I shall never forget her walking about with a tame jaguar in attendance,' wrote Lady Warwick. 'It required more than a little nerve to approach her when she was in the company of her pet, in spite of her assurance that it was as friendly as a kitten.' (Considering that Lady Warwick, in later years, kept a tame elephant, she was hardly in a position to criticise.)

'Affums' remained Florrie's pet for several years. When she and Beau eventually moved from Bosworth Park the jaguar went with them and was kept chained to a tree on the lawn of their Thames-side house near Windsor. Florrie continued to protest that the animal was not dangerous but, at the same time, warned any visiting children to keep well clear. 'Of course he wouldn't hurt you if you did pat him,' she once told the terrified Bosie, 'but perhaps you had better not, as I don't think your dear mother would like it.' It was only after 'Affums' managed to escape and, to the intense annoyance of Queen Victoria, killed several deer in Windsor Park that Florrie was persuaded to part with her pet. The jaguar was sent to the Zoological Gardens where, from time to time, Florrie and Jim would astonish visitors by climbing into its cage for a cosy chat.

But the most important effect of the Patagonian adventure was that it made Florrie more restless than ever. She had hardly returned to England than she was off again; this time to California. Her tour of the United States turned out to be a disappointment. Although she managed to bag 'a couple of grizzly bears' in the Rockies, she found the Wild West far too tame for her tastes. North America, at this time, was very popular with the British aristocracy—many of whom owned land there—and Florrie's visit was in no way exceptional. It did not even provide her with the material for another book. Sitting in the library of Bosworth Park with the skin of a nine-foot puma at her feet and Affums chained up in the garden, she began to cast about for a more exciting expedition.

She thought at first of Africa, and of South Africa in particular. While she had been in Patagonia, South Africa had been very much in the news. January 1879 had seen the outbreak of the Zulu War and the shattering defeat of British troops at Isandhlwana—a defeat which resulted in one of the most devastating massacres in the annals of British colonial warfare. The next few months had brought more shocks and set-backs. By the time she reached England, though, the war was over. On 4 July the Zulu were finally defeated at the battle of Ulindi and a few weeks later the Zulu King, Cetshwayo, was captured and imprisoned at the Cape.

For all that, South Africa remained in the news. The settlement of Zululand was a protracted and complicated business and stories of the war continued to fill the newspapers. South Africa might not be another Patagonia but it undoubtedly had its attractions. Indeed, Florrie was sufficiently attracted for the South African papers to announce that she would be visiting the Cape. Then, at the last minute, she changed her mind. With the Zulu War over, she decided, Africa was not quite exciting enough. She wanted something more outlandish, something that would top Patagonia.

It was not until the middle of 1880 that she hit upon the idea of ploughing through the icy wastes of Alaska, crossing the Bering Straits and making for 'far-off Tuski Land.' There, she was told, she could study the habits and customs of a primitive Asiatic tribe who would certainly give her something to write about. This, she thought, might well be the answer to her problems.

For problems she certainly had. By this time her need to write another book—a book that would sell well—was not just a matter of literary ambition. She was desperately short of money. Beau's spendthrift habits had at last caught up with him. His gambling debts ran into thousands of pounds, Bosworth Park was mortgaged up to the hilt and the various farms he had inherited had become liabilities. Not that any of this unduly worried the ever-optimistic Beau. Confident that one of his chancy speculations would eventually pay-off, he stubbornly refused to admit that he was facing bankruptcy. 'Beau does not realise it,' Florrie confided to a friend, 'but he will have to soon. He has been so accustomed to have heaps of money that he cannot understand that it is all gone.' She was left to shoulder the family's financial burdens alone.

There was very little that she could do but she was determined to do what she could. At all costs she wanted to avoid taking the drastic step of selling Bosworth Park. While this might temporarily ease their problems it would also shut off any hope for the future. Not only did she want to safeguard the property for her sons, but there was a vague hope that coal might be discovered on the estate and this—as had happened to other impoverished land-owners in the midlands—could mean salvation and perhaps riches. It was a question of holding out for as long as they could and the only way that Florrie knew of holding out was to make money from her writing. Chilly as the prospect of far-off Tuski Land appeared, it was decidedly less chilly than the thought of abandoning the Dixie estates.

She had almost completed her arrangements for the journey when there was a new and unexpected turn of events. In December 1880, South Africa again claimed the headlines. This time it was the Boers of the Transvaal who rose in rebellion. Encouraged by the ineptitude of the British forces during the recent Zulu War, the Boers—whose country had been annexed by Britain in 1877—hoisted their Republican flag in the little town of Heidelberg and declared themselves independent. For three years, with little result, they had protested against the high-handed annexation. Now, tired of waiting, they decided to take things into their own hands. They elected their own government, armed themselves to the teeth, and rose up in rebellion.

For Florrie, the Boer insurrection presented a heaven-sent opportunity. The fact that it was not expected to last long suited her very well. How better to write a short, exciting and topical book than to report a short, exciting and topical campaign? And why confine herself to a book? What was to prevent her reporting the war as a journalist? Why should she not become Britain's first woman war-correspondent? Having established her reputation as an iron-nerved big game hunter, she could now blossom on the battlefield. Surely that would top Patagonia? What is more it would mean that her expenses would be paid by a newspaper. The war in South Africa seemed to have been started for her benefit.

When it was announced that Sir Evelyn Wood had been appointed second-in-command of the British forces in South Africa, Florrie arranged to see him before he left England. Sir Evelyn was more than sympathetic. Not only did he agree to supply her with a tent and rations at his headquarters, but he promised to obtain a commission for Beau in the Irregular force. The only problem now was to find an equally obliging newspaper editor. Unless she did so there was little hope of her going to South Africa. Beau's finances would no longer provide them with the fare, let alone equip an expedition. In a painfully frank letter to the editor of *Vanity Fair,* Florrie made no attempt to disguise her reasons for asking him to commission her as a war-correspondent.

'For some time past,' she wrote in January 1881, 'I have been fighting against the terrible consequences which have followed on my husband's immense losses on the Turf and at gambling. I hoped by strenuous efforts to pull matters round. . . . My efforts I am sorry to say have been in vain and the trouble I took wasted. I received the, to me, most distressing news a few days ago of the complete failure of some big speculation in which, unknown to me, my husband had ventured a large sum. It was a great blow to me to find that the last remnants of a once splendid fortune must at once go to pay this debt. Of course it meant little less than the *word* and *reality*, Ruin. . . . By meeting this debt our rent-roll will be gone.'

All the same, she was not asking for charity. Her idea was a sound one and she was prepared to give value for money. 'It might,' she went on earnestly, 'sound something novel to the public in general if they heard I had gone out as a correspondent and the paper might sell accordingly. I cannot say more than that I will live with the troops, go out with them when they fight and in fact never shirk danger, fatigue or trouble . . . All I ask is for my expenses to be paid out there and back . . . and the few horses I shall require.'

Thomas Bowles, the editor, was very taken with the idea but did not think it quite suitable for *Vanity Fair.* As an old friend, though, he proved extremely helpful and managed to interest Algernon Borthwick of the *Morning Post.* The enterprising Borthwick seized on the opportunity to inject some fun into the depressing South African situation. A woman war-correspondent would undoubtedly liven things up and the way the Transvaal campaign was going some livening up was certainly called for. He lost no time in announcing that Lady Florence Dixie, the popular young authoress, was to act as the *Morning Post's* special correspondent in South Africa.

As Florrie had predicted, the announcement caused a sensation. Women might write for newspapers but they did not go to war for them. But then nobody took the appointment seriously. Why should they? With the war as good as won, the whole thing was seen as nothing more than an elaborate joke.

The comic papers broke out in a rash of articles depicting a dizzy young female struggling manfully to keep up with the troops. Florrie's friends found it side-splitting. For them the humour was double-edged. Quips about fainting females might amuse the general public, but the thought of Florrie giving way to the vapours was the biggest laugh of all. And, of course, they were right. However much she needed the money, Florrie was determined to prove her worth. There was more at stake than her personal problems. An ardent, unquestioning Imperialist, the war in the Transvaal had roused all her flag-waving instincts. She saw herself reporting triumphant British victories, ministering to the sick and comforting the wounded, braving bullets and delivering heroic despatches. Once again she was impatient to get started.

Chapter Seven

New Horizons

Queensberry's travels, though not as adventurous as Florrie's, were no less purposeful. His decision to accompany his sister to South America had not been taken lightly. Precisely why he wanted to visit Argentina is difficult to say but, from his later remarks about participating in a 'public discussion' in Buenos Aires, it is fairly obvious that his visit was connected with his new-found philosophy. He seems, in fact, to have made the journey in his capacity as honorary President of the British Secular Union.

Queensberry's surprising conversion to active agnosticism had occurred two years earlier. In 1876 he had spent his summer holidays in Switzerland and had again visited Zermatt. This was not the first time he had returned to the Alpine town since his brother's death eleven years earlier, but this visit was of particular significance. Throughout his stay in Zermatt, Queensberry was haunted not only by the thought of Francis's bones 'bleaching' on the Matterhorn but by his own mystical experience on the mountain. He had never forgotten the early morning 'revelation' of renewed life that he had experienced after his long night of vigil; now the thoughts that had puzzled him then returned to puzzle him again. He could not shake them off. So pressing were these thoughts that he tried to express them in a long, blank-verse poem which he called *The Spirit of the Matterhorn*.

The poem is long, fanciful and often muddled but its theme is consistent. It embodies his earlier notions of nature's eternal cycle—death is a return to the earth and from the earth's sustenance new life blossoms—and follows them to what, in his opinion, is an inevitable conclusion. His momentary 'revelation' is depicted as a somewhat long-winded 'Spirit of great Truth' which descends on the mountain to unfold life's hidden secrets. 'I am thy love, for I am part of thee,' the spirit tells him. 'Yet hast thou much to learn; come, would'st thou hear?'

What he hears is very much what he wants to hear. The entire universe—including mankind—is ruled by an all-pervading spirit. What man calls his soul is nothing more than this spirit working within him. The spirit never dies but is constantly renewed and by its renewal binds mankind together for eternity: 'All fellow workers with the great Divine, all atoms of that one identity.' Man therefore has a duty towards the eternal spirit, a duty which he all too often neglected. In his ignorance he had broken nature's laws 'and consequently came disease and sin.' But this, as Queensberry's hectoring muse made crystal clear, could be remedied.

> *So man must worship what's in man divine,*
> *To nurse with gentle care, to cultivate*
> *Perfection's germ, which partly dwells in all;*
> *Worship his body, and his intellect,*
> *And thus the blessing to his race bequeath*
> *Of vigorous frames with healthy minds endowed.*

Perfection of mind and body (particularly the body) that was the great secret. Religion, which taught men to cherish their souls and despise their bodies, was the great enemy. The 'superstition of a bygone age' must be replaced by the cleansing doctrines of physical perfection. Only in this way could man 'serve the future of his coming race' worthily and free himself of crippling restraints.

These were the commands which Queensberry, Moses-like, had received on the mountain. If not God-ordained they were undoubtedly nature-ordained and that, he considered, was sufficient for a rational man. He apparently saw no contradiction in the quasi-mystical tone of his poem and his claim to logical thought.

Superficial though they were, Queensberry's conclusions bore a passing resemblance to those of Nietszche (whose life-span, curiously enough, precisely paralleled his own) but he could hardly have been influenced by the budding German philosopher. He read little, other than novels, and knew practically nothing of contemporary theology or philosophy. The only philosophers he was to acknowledge were Herbert Spencer and Thomas Huxley and, according to his son, his reading of their works was confined to an occasional passage. Whether Queensberry actually wrote *The Spirit of the Matterhorn* is also open to question. He showed no real interest in poetry—although he occasionally quoted Milton—and the blank verse is slightly too accomplished for a complete amateur. The poem reads rather like the poems produced by Florrie on similar themes and it is quite possible that she had a hand in the final composition. There can be little doubt, though, that the thoughts expressed in *The Spirit of the Matterhorn* were Queensberry's and that the intention of the poem was sincere.

Certainly it echoes Queensberry's own beliefs. With his love of sport, his hard-riding, his boxing and his daily work-outs—his favourite exercise was a regular session with a punch-bag—he had made a religion of keeping fit. To have evolved a creed which elevated these activities into a

moral code was not as remarkable as it at first appears. He had been
surrounded by religious turmoil in his family since childhood and he
doubtless felt the need to justify his own scepticism. Neutrality was alien
to his aggressive nature; in any controversy he had to make a stand and
The Spirit of the Matterhorn was his stand against conventional religion.
The poem not only glorified his rejection of the supernatural but provided
him with a *raison d'être*; it allowed him to give vent to his innate prejudices. By advocating man's perfectibility, he could decry Christian
dogma and defy Christian morality with a semblance of ethical conviction. From now on he was to bring to his crusade against religious
conformity all the sanctimonious fervour of a convert.

For a crusade it became. Once Queensberry had convinced himself he
lost no time in trying to convince others. His hostility towards Christianity developed into an obsession. He could talk of little else. He became
both a battler and a bore in his determination to expose the 'false concep-
tions and erroneous ideas' of organised religion. Even his devotion to
sport took second place to his opposition towards what he liked to term
'Christian tomfoolery.'

But if Queensberry's ranting seemed excessive it was not—as his family
implied—a mere pose to draw attention to himself. His sons, particularly
Bosie, had nothing but contempt for Queensberry's agnosticism. Their
father, they claimed, was an ill-educated, semi-literate bigot who was
incapable of understanding any point of view other than his own. Others
have unquestioningly accepted this judgement. But Queensberry's views
cannot be dismissed as simply as that. It is true that his prejudices
influenced his thinking and that his agnosticism was more instinctive
than informed, but this does not mean that he was insincere. His rejection
of religion was no more and no less bigoted than many Christians'
acceptance of faith. Indeed it was the unreasoning attitude of the average
Christian that had inspired the branch of secularism that Queensberry
adopted.

He was influenced to a great extent by George Jacob Holyoake, the
friend of his grandfather Sir William Clayton. Like the rest of his family he
had been friendly with Holyoake as a child and, after his return from
Switzerland in 1876, this friendship was renewed. Holyoake was then
fifty-nine and widely acknowledged as a leader of free-thought in England. Although, as a young man, Holyoake had achieved notoriety by
becoming the last person in England to be imprisoned for alleged
atheism, he was by no means an extremist. Certainly he was not, and had
never been, an atheist. His religious views had been formed when he was
young and were firmly those of an agnostic. Christianity, he contended,
depended largely on the interpretation of scriptural doctrines and these
doctrines 'could never be made intelligible and convincing except to
students of very considerable research.' As most laymen lacked the

facilities for Biblical research—knowledge of Hebrew, Greek and Latin—they could never test the validity of Christian arguments and therefore the Scriptures could not be taken as a guide for human conduct.

'To myself,' he wrote, 'it was not of moment whether the Scriptures were authentic or inspired. My sole inquiry was—Do they contain clear moral guidance which would increase our certainty of aid from God? If they do, I accept that guidance with implicitness and gratitude. . . . If precepts did not answer to this test, they were not acceptable, though all the apostles in committee had signed them.'

From this premise Holyoake had evolved the principles of secularism. These principles neither accepted nor rejected God; they were concerned merely with the betterment of mankind. Secularism, Holyoake insisted, was not atheism but, like mathematics, was independent of theistical or other doctrines. Man's first duty was to do good and doing good meant being good. 'If a God of goodness existed,' he maintained, 'he would count goodness as a merit; and if no such God existed, goodness was the best thing men could do in this world.'

Holyoake's thinking was very similar to Queensberry's and—in theory, at least—Secularism was the philosophy that Queensberry came to accept. It could hardly be described as bigoted or extreme and if, in later years, Queensberry's arguments were regarded as fanatical it was his temperament rather than his basic beliefs that was at fault. In his calmer moments the 'mad Marquess' was capable of reasoned and logical discussion.

It was probably Holyoake who introduced Queensberry to South Place Chapel in Finsbury where the American former-Unitarian minister, Moncur Conway, presided over an extremely unorthodox congregation. The chapel—a severely classical building, wedged among the terrace houses of a London backstreet—had been a centre of religious dissent since the end of the eighteenth century and over the years had housed a variety of discussion groups and societies dedicated to religious and ethical reform. In the 1870s it was the recognised meeting place of London's secularists and it was here that Queensberry first came in contact with the leaders of contemporary freethought. Prominent among those leaders was the forthright president of the National Secular Society, Charles Bradlaugh, and his fiery companion, Annie Besant.

If Queensberry hoped to find harmony and reason among his fellow rationalists he was quickly disillusioned. The freethought movement was every bit as disunited as the Christian Chruch. The degree to which members of the South Place congregation accepted or rejected God varied enormously: atheists mingled with agnostics, fashionable positivists rubbed shoulders with old fashioned deists and a sprinkling of liberal Christians sat alongside unashamed heathens. There were sects and there were schisms, there were political as well as religious dissidents and, perhaps most important of all, there were distinct personality differences. A large body of freethinkers were grouped together in the National Secular Society but even this purposeful organisation was far from united. Political radicals such as Charles Bradlaugh found it difficult to accept the hesitant policies of men like Holyoake and were frankly disgusted by Holyoake's wooing of aristocratic and middle-class sympathisers. Time and again Holyoake—known as the 'professor of polite politics'—had been accused of trying to water-down secularism to suit the prejudices of his titled friends. By many he was considered to be a snob. Queensberry's introduction to South Place Chapel could hardly warmed the hearts of Holyoake's critics.

The threatened break in the National Secular Society came shortly after Queensberry's arrival on the scene. Although he had nothing to do with it, he was very much involved in its outcome. Ostensibly the break was caused by the fierce squabbles accompanying a notorious court case in which Bradlaugh and Mrs Besant were prosecuted for publishing a book on birth control. The case, which became a *cause célèbre*, united the secularists in principle but left them sadly divided on questions of tactics and responsibility. So high did feelings flare that a group of rebels in the National Secular Society, having failed to oust Bradlaugh and Mrs Besant, broke away and formed a rival organisation.

In May 1877, at a meeting chaired by Holyoake in the Cleveland Hall, the British Secular Union was established. The purpose of this new body, it was later announced, was to strengthen 'the ranks of that ever-increasing party . . . convinced that the question of God's existence and the future life of man are insoluble problems.' And it was as President of the British Secular Union that Queensberry came to the fore.

What prompted the rebels to choose Queensberry as their president can only be surmised. It could scarcely have been his popularity—he was still a relative newcomer—and surely not his intellect. More likely it was his title. Holyoake was not the only snobbish secularist and nothing could have emphasised the difference between the moderates and the radicals than for the British Secular Union to have a Marquess as its nominal head. There was also an incidental advantage. For years the secularists had been trying to obtain a voice in parliament and had placed their hopes on Bradlaugh winning a seat as a Radical; but although Bradlaugh had repeatedly contested the Northampton constituency and steadily increased his vote, he had failed so far to gain a majority. Queensberry, on the other hand, while not able to speak in the House of Commons had at least succeeded in becoming a member of the House of Lords.

His membership of the Upper Chamber was not all that he had wished. The longed-for English peerage still eluded him. In 1872, however, Queensberry had managed to be elected as one of the sixteen representative Scottish peers and had periodically attended debates. He had made very little impression. His political sympathies were largely with the Tories and, among the predominantly conservative peers, his views merely echoed those of the majority. Only after he became President of the British Secular Union did he begin to make his presence felt.

Queensberry took his presidential duties very seriously. The public discussions he initiated in South America were part of a militant campaign to whip up support for the British Secular Union. When it was founded, the Union had a limited membership, few branches, and only sixteen corresponding members in various towns. It was to help remedy this that Queensberry embarked on a series of speaking engagements. He saw himself not merely as an iconoclast but as the precursor of a new and vital faith.

'The value of organisation amongst secularists,' he declared when inaugurating a new branch in the north of England, 'must not be underrated. Catholicism has been able to stand through so many centuries through the efficiency of its organisation. Secularism is but the natural outgrowth of the religions of the past. They were mistaken who thought that secularists cherished a blind animosity to Christianity and its doings. All that secularists had against Christianity was that it had served its cause and performed its functions. It had succeeded other religions, and in its turn must make way for its successors.'

The need for organisation and propaganda was the theme of most of his speeches. Only by a planned and determined onslaught on conventional prejudice, he claimed, could secularists get their views across; any means they employed to this end was fully justified. 'Everything,' he thundered on another occasion, 'is fair in war; and this is war. We Secularists and other bodies of Freethinkers are fighting now tooth and nail to be recognised as a body of people who have a religion and who have a faith. . . . Our great difficulty at the moment is to get a hearing from our orthodox opponents. . . . I myself shall never scruple to use any artifice I can to get at them, and bring them to bay.'

He got few hearings, however, in the House of Lords. Rarely was he called upon to speak and the few speeches he did make were on innocuous subjects. Soap-box oratory came more naturally to him than poker-faced debate. Far more in character was his habit of scattering secularist pamphlets 'over the seats of the Peers spiritual and temporal.' Many an outraged Bishop was seen spluttering over a crumpled tract of the British Secular Union. There were few members of the Upper House who were not aware of the Marquess of Queensberry's views.

Whether he publicly announced his intention of refusing to swear the customary oath of allegiance on a Bible is another matter. Bosie claims he dismissed the oath-taking as 'Christian tomfoolery'; but Bosie—never over-scrupulous about facts that did not suit his prejudices—was writing from hearsay many years later. His claim was probably coloured by later events. The fact is that Queensberry, once he had become President of the British Secular Union, was never required to take the oath. So well did he make his views known that his fellow peers, meeting at Holyrood Palace in 1880, refused to re-elect him to the House of Lords. On a motion introduced by Lord Lothian, it was unanimously decided that the Marquess of Queensberry 'held as a negation all that his brother Peers regard as most sacred' and could no longer be considered a representative peer of Scotland.

No one was more flabbergasted than Queensberry.

[2]

Queensberry's reaction to his expulsion from the House of Lords was typical. In a fit of pique, he cut all his immediate ties with Scotland. Almost overnight his bewildered family was uprooted from Kinmount and planted in a rented house, 67 Cromwell Road, in London. They never lived permanently in Scotland again.

For Queensberry's children the upheaval was a traumatic experience. Kinmount was the only home they knew and, despite family tensions, their years in Scotland had been happy ones. That they had rarely seen their father had not bothered them unduly. Sybil had seen to it that they were protected, that they had wanted for nothing. Their memories of Kinmount remained rose-coloured: they were of woods and glens, of pony rides, of church services at Cummertrees, of visits to Ecclefechan where the village shop sold the toy swords and gold leaf paper which they used in their mock-battles and, perhaps most affectionately of all, of the servants who were their friends. Almost fifty years later a pensive Bosie was still trying to recapture the delights of his childhood and still dreaming of returning to Kinmount. He never did.

The move probably affected Bosie more than his elder brothers. At ten years of age he was a delightfully pretty boy—he had Alfred Montgomery's looks as well as his name—and he still lived at home, hopelessly spoiled by his mother and the rest of the family. It was a tremendous wrench for him to leave the security of Kinmount, with its cosy family atmosphere and endearing Douglas traditions. (Even when they grew older the boys, like their uncles and aunts before them, still called each other 'darling.') All the same, Bosie's days in Scotland were numbered. Move or no move, he was due that year to join his eldest brother, Drumlanrig, who was then completing his last year at a preparatory school called Lambrook, near Windsor. It was not merely the thought of leaving home but the possibility of never seeing Kinmount again that so upset Bosie. One of the 'great misfortunes' of his family, he claimed, was that they lived so short a time in Scotland. Perhaps he was right.

The part played by Queensberry in his children's education was minimal and, for the most part, obstructive. He was still highly suspicious of formal education. He agreed to allow Drumlanrig to attend Lambrook but opposed all suggestions of the boy going to Harrow. English public schools, he insisted, merely turned out 'Belgravian loafers'; his eldest son must be sent to a Scottish school. His obstinacy led to another of those long drawn-out family rows. Drumlanrig was the firm favourite of his grandfather, Alfred Montgomery, and it was probably the stand taken by the 'Montgomery lot' that eventually resulted in Queensberry capitulating by allowing his heir to become a Harrovian.

With the second boy, Percy—Lord Douglas of Hawick, as he was styled—Queensberry's word carried more weight. A high-spirited, good natured and extremely likeable boy, Percy was more ready to fall in with his father's plans. When it was decided that he should follow Queensberry's example and join the Royal Navy there were few objections. So, in 1880, shortly after the family moved to London, the twelve-year-old Percy was packed off to a naval school at Portsmouth in preparation for training on the *Britannia*.

This, as far as guidance was concerned, was the extent of Queensberry's interest in his son's upbringing. From time to time he would visit the boys at school, lavish them with presents and provide them with generous allowances—Bosie always boasted that he had more pocket money than any other boy at his school—but for the rest they were left to the care of their mother and their doting grandfather. Leaving Scotland was purely a whim of Queensberry's; it did nothing to bring him closer to his family.

Sybil was as lonely as ever. From Cromwell Road she soon moved to 18 Cadogan Place, which was to be her home for many years, but she saw no more of her husband in London than she had seen of him in Scotland. Even with his family settled on his doorstep, Queensberry continued to live in his rooms at James Street, to entertain his mistresses and to lead a thoroughly dissolute life. Sybil made no attempt to disguise her unhappiness. Her contempt for her husband became increasingly obvious. Even with a slight acquaintance like the gossipy Amy Menzies, Sybil would sit for hours talking about 'her sorrows and many disappointments.' She did no more than talk. Miserable as she was, Sybil never seems to have considered divorcing Queensberry. She looked instead for more conventional forms of escape.

During the summer months, Sybil was able to take refuge in the country. She rented a large, rambling house, deceptively called The Hut (it could sleep twenty-five at a squeeze) near Bracknell in Berkshire and here, away from the embarrassments of London, she led a reasonably happy domestic life. The children would join her during the school holidays, there were visits from friends and relatives, ard her neighbours—

including her 'landlord' Lord Downshire—were sympathetic and helpful. To all intents and purposes, The Hut, although not another Kinmount, became the new family centre.

But it was a house without a head. Queensberry never spent more than one or two nights at a time—usually during Ascot Week—at The Hut. Sometimes a year or more would pass without his family seeing him. Bosie was to claim that he could count the number of occasions he slept under the same roof as his father 'on the fingers of both hands.' Perhaps it was just as well. A visit from Queensberry invariably meant trouble for his family; if his absences did not make their hearts grow fonder they at least helped them to beat more easily.

In any case, there was no need for Queensberry to keep his family informed of his activities. They could read all they needed to know in the newspapers. During the early 1880s, the name of Lord Queensberry, when not featured in the sporting columns, was frequently to be found in news items. Secularism had suddenly become topical.

[3]

'I think it right to inform you,' Sir Henry Drummond Wolff wrote to the Speaker of the House of Commons on 18 May 1880, 'that if Mr Bradlaugh presents himself to take the oath, I shall move that he is incapable of doing so.'

Drummond Wolff, a Conservative MP for Portsmouth, was one of a group of Tories who were determined to prevent Charles Bradlaugh from entering Parliament After a struggle lasting twelve years, Bradlaugh had finally succeeded in being elected as one of the Radical Members for Northampton. His victory—hailed by his fellow secularists as a tremendous success for freethought—had sparked off a widespread controversy. Almost from the moment that the Northampton results had been announced, there had been considerable speculation about whether he would be admitted to the House of Commons. Ostensibly the dispute revolved round parliamentary procedure.

For an MP to take his seat it was necessary for him to swear the oath of allegiance on the Bible. As Bradlaugh was probably the best known atheist in Britain, it was considered highly unlikely that he would be prepared to do this. Nor, initially, was he. On his first appearance in the House, at the beginning of May, he let it be known that he would make a simple affirmation rather than take the formal oath. The right to affirm was permitted in certain cases and he intended to claim this right. His opponents argued that the Act of Parliament which allowed affirmations did not include professed atheists. As it happened, the matter was not put to the test. The swearing in procedure was stopped before Bradlaugh's turn came and the question of his admittance was referred to a Select Committee.

Two weeks later the Select Committee reported their finding and, by a majority of one, ruled against Bradlaugh. This in no way deterred the Member for Northampton. If he could not affirm, Bradlaugh declared, then he was prepared to take the oath. After all it was a mere formality. The Bible meant nothing to him one way or the other; if swearing on a book allowed him to take his seat then he would swear on a book.

It was at this stage that Sir Henry Drummond Wolff stepped in. Insisting that 'an oath by an infidel had been decided by a court of law to have no value' he objected to Bradlaugh's façade. He was loudly supported by other Tories, including the boisterous Member for Woodstock, Lord Randolph Churchill.

Things reached a climax on 23 June 1880 when a majority in the House of Commons decided that Bradlaugh could neither affirm nor take the oath. When Bradlaugh refused to accept this verdict, the House divided again and voted for his withdrawal. Still he refused to budge. Finally the Sergeant-at-Arms was sent for and Bradlaugh—loudly protesting his 'right as a member'—was hustled from the Chamber and placed in custody. He spent that night in the Clock Tower.

This was the first of many tussles—both inside and outside Parliament—which were to take place over the next five years. Whatever else he may have lacked, Bradlaugh did not lack supporters. Not everyone agreed with his religious views, but there was no shortage of those who were prepared to defend his right to represent the electors of Northampton. The constitutional wrangle developed into a national debate. Committees were formed, meetings were held, demonstrations were staged, newspapers thundered—both for and against Bradlaugh—and the issue was contested in the courts of law. Everything Bradlaugh did or said became news.

The secularists were delighted. If nothing else, the 'Bradlaugh Affair' provided a rallying point for the freethought movement. Here was something that freethinkers, of all shades of opinion, could support. For a while old squabbles and former differences were forgotten.

The annual convention of the National Secular Society, held in May 1880, took on the appearance of a victory jamboree. Several seccessionists returned to the fold and, at a banquet held on the last night, Bradlaugh was cheered by a mixed crowd of three hundred supporters. Even members of the hostile British Secular Union could not stand completely aloof. Much as many of them disliked Bradlaugh, they were forced to support the cause, if not the man. They really had no option. With many practising Christians—including the Prime Minister, Mr Gladstone—upholding Bradlaugh's democratic right, it would have been petty minded and churlish of any freethinker not to join the battle.

All the same, the President of the British Secular Union was not, at first, over-zealous in his support. This was not because of any personal enmity between Queensberry and Bradlaugh. As far as is known, Queensberry had never been a member of the National Secular Society, had played no direct part in the rebel break-away, and his acquaintanceship with Bradlaugh at this stage was slight. Queensberry's attitude towards the 'Bradlaugh Affair' was conditioned by very different considerations. What he resented was the publicity given to Bradlaugh's martyrdom and the complete neglect of his own. After all, he had also lost his seat in Parliament because of his religious opinions. This, as far as the general public was concerned, seemed to count for nothing. As always, Queensberry's resentment at being ignored was stronger than his dedication to a cause.

That his expulsion from the House of Lords was being ignored was certainly not his fault. Admittedly there had been little to attract attention to his rejection by the Scottish peers. The proceedings at Holyrood Palace had been brief and unspectacular, Lord Lothian's motion had been carried unanimously and Queensberry had been allowed to make only a short statement in reply. Taken by surprise, he had had no opportunity to prepare a defence. What he had had to say had captured no headlines.

But since then Queensberry had tried to make up for this lack of publicity. Determined to have his say, and to broadcast it as widely as possible, he decided to publish *The Spirit of the Matterhorn*. The poem summarised his beliefs. What could not be said in blank-verse he was at pains to explain in the plain prose of a lengthy preface. More perhaps than anything else, he was determined to refute the accusation that he was without faith and that he despised the faith of others.

'I have never at any time,' he declared in the opening paragraph, 'denied the existence of God, or ventured to express a decided opinion on the matter. In private I have always objected to give a name, such as God, to a Power which to me appears undefinable by man, and which I have therefore preferred to speak of as the Inscrutable. . . . I leave those who may read this poem to judge for themselves whether my sentiments therein expressed do not breathe forth a great hope, and a sincere belief in all that is highest, and therefore most sacred, for the present and future of mankind.'

For the rest, the preface merely attempts to rationalise the allegorical trappings of the poem. One point he makes, though, is not without interest. The poem concentrates on the revelation he received on the Matterhorn. But this, apparently, was not his only source of inspiration. In arguing that conventional religion assumes the 'so-called Soul' to be 'distinct and separate from the body' he gives various reasons for rejecting this. One of the more important of these reasons was derived from his own experience. What, he asks, happens to the soul when the body is damaged? When, for instance, a man receives a violent blow on the head, he suffers a loss of consciousness, and what 'is called the Soul stops like a clock.' If the soul is distinct and separate from the body, why is it so affected? What happens to it at a time of unconsciousness? One must either accept that it is separate from the body or that it is an extension of the body. He had his doubts.

'To those who have never themselves been unconscious through concussion of the brain,' he contended, 'this argument will not perhaps appear of great weight; but to those who, like myself, have had a severe one, and who have realised what an absolute annihilation to one's individuality it is, the argument cannot, I believe, seem other than proof positive of the truth of the second of these theories.'

Queensberry was essentially a man of action. He only indulged in introspection on rare occasions. One such occasion had been that night on the Matterhorn; the only other times he had been forced into self-examination were those periods of convalescence after bad falls in the hunting field. But it was obvious that, when he did think his thoughts invariably led him to the same conclusions. However superficial those conclusions might appear there can be no doubt that they were arrived at sincerely.

Published privately, *The Spirit of the Matterhorn* was read by only a handful of his friends—most of whom were not remotely interested. His attempts to equate his own position with Bradlaugh's made very little impression. Certainly not on Bradlaugh and his associates. Had Bradluagh been asked for an opinion, he would probably have congratulated rather than condoled with Queensberry. Radical and republican that he was, Bradlaugh had little time for the House of Lords. 'Who are the Lords?' he had once demanded. 'If we answer honestly, the reply must be that the Lords are, in chief, the outgrowths of ages of ignorance, crime and folly, scarcely in any sense redeemed by the few who are on the other side, who have deserved the peerage by their nobility in thought and conduct. . . . The Lords are not necessary to the welfare of the state.' There was not much chance of Lord Queensberry riding in harness with Charles Bradlaugh.

It took some time for Queensberry to realise this. Not until May 1881 did he recognise that the next best thing to pulling the band-wagon was to jump on it. By then the publicity surrounding Bradlaugh's efforts to claim his seat had reached a new peak. Earlier that month Bradlaugh had again presented himself to the Commons and the Sergeant-at-Arms had again escorted him from the House. This time he went quietly. But immediately afterwards he issued an 'Appeal to the People' which sparked off a new round of protests, mass meetings and newspaper debates. The excitement, sometimes bordering on hysteria, proved too much for Queensberry. His love of a fight got the better of him. The time had come, he decided, to wave a Bradlaugh banner.

He was on one of his rare visits to Kinmount at the time and from there he sent a cheque for £50 to Bradlaugh's 'Fund to Fight the Bigots.' The donation, he explained, had been prompted by a semi-literate letter he had received asking him to 'supplicate with us Divine Providence, the Great first Cause . . . to expell Mr Bradlaugh from the Houses of Parliament.' He did not name his correspondent but enclosed his reply to the letter. It was published, on 29 May 1881, in the National Secular Society's journal *The National Reformer*.

'. . . allow me to tell you,' it starts, 'that I long ago gave up the absurdity (to me) of prayers. I know nothing about a "first Cause." It is perfectly unthinkable to anyone, and, therefore, I decline to waste time in discussing such a subject. It amazes me that you orthodox people should have the conceit to define such a "Cause", and to call it "Him." Why not "Her"?'

These somewhat startling feminist sentiments sound more like Florrie —certainly Florrie in later life—than Queensberry. But as Florrie had already left for South Africa, she is unlikely to have had a hand in concocting the letter. Concocted, however, it appears to have been. That anyone should have written to Queensberry, whose views were well known, asking for his prayers seems highly unlikely. His published reply merely served as an excuse for him openly to support Bradlaugh. This he did in no uncertain terms. 'I believe,' he informed his mysterious correspondent, 'Mr Bradlaugh to be an honest and sincere man, whose highest hope is the welfare of mankind. He has my warmest sympathies. . . . I glory in this great battle which he is successfully fighting. . . . I hope myself someday to be foremost in the van, and where the battle is thickest, fighting to the death against all ignorance and superstition, where Mr Bradlaugh now so nobly stands, for the freeing of mankind.'

Queensberry was as good as his word. Within a matter of days he was back in London attending a mass meeting of the 'League for the Defence of Constitutional Rights' at the St James's Hall. According to press reports it was a 'magnificent' affair. On the platform were not only Bradlaugh and Annie Besant but Bradlaugh's fellow MP for Northampton, Henry Labouchere, and Admiral Frederick A. Maxse. Not all the speeches were reported but few papers could resist mentioning that the vote of thanks to the Chairman was proposed by the Marquess of Queensberry 'who said he had lost his seat in the House of Lords on religious grounds.'

From now on the sprightly Queensberry, with his distinctive long sideburns and his hat—'invariably a size or so too small'—tipped rakishly over his black wiry hair, was to be a familiar sight at the Bradlaugh protest meetings.

Chapter Eight

The Land of Misfortune

When the s.s. *Melrose* arrived in the Durban roadsteads early on the morning of 18 March 1881, a dangerous swell made it impossible for her to enter the harbour. Durban's natural bay was beautiful but hazardous; a treacherous sand bar blocked its mouth. Even under ideal conditions crossing this bar was a precarious business, in a storm, it was unthinkable. The passengers of the *Melrose* were told there was no possibility of the ship reaching the harbour until the following day. They were given the choice of staying on board for the night or of taking their chance in a tug which would be coming out at noon. It was very much a matter of the devil and the deep blue sea. To remain on board the pitching ship required a cast-iron stomach, to be lowered into the storm-tossed tug demanded nerves of steel. The majority opted to remain on board. Only when it was learned that Sir Beaumont and Lady Florence Dixie would be leaving by the tug did a few of the hardier passengers decide to follow their example.

For Florrie there was no question of spending the night on the ship. Even the short delay of waiting for the tug was irksome to her. From the time she had arrived at the Cape a week earlier, she had met nothing but delays and disappointments. Her South African venture had begun to look like a ghastly mistake.

The first blow had fallen the day after they docked at Cape Town. Here they had learned of the stunning British defeat at Majuba Hill. Instead of waiting for reinforcements, Sir George Pomeroy-Colley had taken it upon himself to launch an attack against the Boers at the Natal–Transvaal border. Hopelessly outnumbered, his force had been decimated at the summit of what should have been an easily defended hill. When the news reached them, says Florrie, it was greeted by a dazed silence. 'All over the ship a pin might have been heard to drop. . . . It was broken after a long and painful pause by whispered exclamations of horror and amazement.' Almost as staggering was the news that Florrie's friend, Sir Evelyn Wood, had been instructed to sue for an armistice. In a matter of weeks, it was rumoured, the British would relinquish the Transvaal. To Florrie such an idea was unthinkable. She refused to entertain it. The only reason for the armistice, she persuaded herself, was to give Wood time to organise his forces. In spite of all evidence to the contrary, she clung to this belief with every fibre of her Jingoistic soul.

But she was wrong. After sailing round the coast and reaching Natal the news was every bit as discouraging. According to a newspaper that had come aboard the *Melrose*, the peace negotiations at the front were still proceeding. The Transvaal War, in fact, looked like ending without her.

Her depression was not lifted when at last the tug arrived. Suffering from acute claustrophobia, she begged to be allowed to remain on deck. The captain would not hear of it. With the rest of the passengers she was battened beneath the suffocating hatches. Surrounded by a crowd of screaming, vomiting women and children, she became almost hysterical. When the hatch was removed she rushed up on deck gasping for fresh air. The romantic notions with which she had left England were being sorely tested.

Once out in the veld, however, Florrie's confidence returned. The vast open country, the clear antiseptic air and the balmy warmth of the sun lifted her spirits and spurred her on. All along the way they passed convoys of lumbering ox-wagons loaded with supplies for the front. The dirt tracks became more deeply rutted, the farmhouses less frequent. Civilisation with all its timorous rumours was left behind.

It was not until they reached the small town of Estcourt that the truth caught up with them. Here they received a telegram from Sir Evelyn Wood telling them that a peace treaty had been signed. Florrie found the news almost impossible to believe. 'Suffice it to say,' she wrote bitterly, 'we echoed the voices of the condemning millions and blushed for shame and dishonour. . . . Heart-sick and disgusted we continued our journey; we felt in no mood for conversation, and the next twenty-two miles were performed in silence.' They were still in a sullen mood when they arrived at Sir Evelyn Wood's headquarters at Newcastle. The news of peace had not only shattered Florrie's patriotic pride—and ended Beau's hopes of obtaining a commission—but had been a sore blow to her career as a journalist. A war-correspondent without a war to report was not only superfluous but frankly ridiculous. All she could hope for now was some inside information on the Royal Commission that had been set up to investigate the Boer grievances.

The Commission which was meeting at Newcastle was to continue its deliberations at Pretoria—the capital of the Transvaal. At the same time the 94th Regiment was to march through the Transvaal to show the flag. Florrie and Beau decided to accompany the troops on their march and then join the commissioners at Pretoria.

For Florrie it was her first experience of travelling with the army. She found it a painfully slow business. The convoy extended in a line of over three miles and moved at the pace of an ox. Once they entered the Transvaal civilised amenities were few and hotels practically nonexistent. Not that this troubled Florrie. She preferred sleeping under canvas and threw herself into the rough and tumble of camp life with gusto. For her, playing at soldiers in the Transvaal was simply an adult version of the rowdy games she had so enjoyed as a child.

In next to no time she had worked out a routine which must have struck the conventionally minded soldiers as distinctly bizarre. Leaving Beau to attend to the cooking, she took charge of the horses and the packing. Up at the crack of dawn, she dragged her bed out to air and brushed down the horses before anyone else in the camp was awake. Her most difficult morning task was to get her husband out of bed. Sluggish at the best of times, and often suffering from a hang-over, Beau dearly loved his bed and his tendency to fall asleep at the most unlikely moments proved a sore trial to her. She usually solved the early morning problem by letting the tent down around him. He would then grope his way out of the tangle of ropes and canvas and grumpily prepare breakfast. Once they had eaten, they would pack their wagon and be ready to start long before the laggardly soldiers got themselves organised. In the evening they were usually invited to the officer's mess, or on special occasions, treated to a champagne supper in the commander's tent. If all else failed, Beau would rustle up a meal of thick soup and army ration biscuits.

On arriving at Pretoria, Florrie and Beau were invited by Sir Evelyn Wood to stay at Government House. As this was where the Transvaal Royal Commission was sitting, it gave Florrie a distinct advantage over rival reporters. If she could not actually penetrate the Conference Room, she got as near to it as she could. As soon as the morning session started she would saunter along the veranda and sit shamelessly under the open windows. It made life very trying for the Commissioners. As none of them had the courage to order her away, they were forced to close all the windows whenever the discussions became at all angry. This, in the stifling heat of Pretoria, was not a very satisfactory solution. Within a few moments someone would demand some fresh air, the windows would be opened and the conference reduced to whispers. While the windows rattled up and down, the correspondent of the *Morning Post* would sit gazing nonchalantly down the carriage-way. 'A few hours so spent,' she wrote, 'were decidedly pleasant.' Once the meeting was over, she would make a bee-line for the Boer Commissioners. She delighted in reporting their unguarded statements with a malicious twist.

For all her brazen eavesdropping, Florrie found the business of the Royal Commission boring. The routine committee-work left her cold; she liked her politics more controversial. More to her taste was the arrival of a deputation of African tribesmen. They had come to petition the British authorities. Sitting beside Sir Evelyn Wood on the veranda of Government House, Florrie followed the interview with an avid interest. It was her first real encounter with the Africans as people. Like most other visitors to the country she had been aware of their presence but partially blind to their personalities. They had remained unobtrusively in the background; the silent spectators, or when it suited, the convenient pawns in the white man's drama. Now for the first time they were brought sharply into focus.

The deputation consisted of about three hundred tribesmen. They were ushered into the carriage-way and squatted on their haunches under the shady trees. As soon as all the officials were assembled on the veranda, a spokesman for the Africans started a long harangue. The substance of it was that the deputation had come to protest against the restoration of the Transvaal to the Boers. He warned the British authorities that such an act would lead to trouble among his followers. If British protection was withdrawn, he said, it would lead to bloodshed and anarchy. When he had finished speaking Sir Evelyn Wood rose to reply. In a few soothing words he told them that the outcome of the Commission was, at that stage, still uncertain. If they would return in a month's time a more definite and more comprehensive answer would be given to them. 'This,' says Florrie,' 'filled the poor fellows with hope, and, still trusting in the good faith of the country for which they entertained both affection and respect, with the salutation "Inkos" they took their departure.'

It is not possible to pin-point the moment of change that came over Florrie while she was in South Africa. Like all such changes it was gradual and largely sub-conscious. There can, however, be no doubt that this meeting of African chiefs opened her eyes to a new dimension on the South African scene. From this time forward she was to pay more attention to the wayside kraals, to the condition under which the Africans lived, and to the attitude of her fellow countrymen towards them. At first she was to regard them as yet another weapon in her anti-Boer armoury, but the impression they made upon her went much deeper than that. There was probably something atavistic about the kinship she felt for them. There was a great deal about the tribal structure which reflected the clan-spirit of the Scots. The natural dignity of the chiefs and the respect of their followers displayed towards them must have appealed to her aristocratic instincts. Her sympathy with the Africans was always to have aristocratic undertones; her attitude was typical of nineteenth century paternal benevolence. But if her approach was not revolutionary, it was certainly enthusiastic and the first spark of that enthusiasm was now beginning to glow.

[2]

One of the effects of Sir Evelyn Wood's meetings with the chiefs was to remind Florrie of a promise she had made in Cape Town a few months earlier. It was a promise hastily given and half-forgotten. It had been made in a moment of sympathy to Cetshwayo, the vanquished Zulu King, and half-forgotten because, at the time, she had never thought she would be able to keep it. The memory of it returned to her now in a new light.

Her meeting with Cetshwayo had been almost a matter of routine. During their few days stay in Cape Town, Florrie and Beau had been guests of the Governor and his wife, Sir Hercules and Lady Robinson. On learning that Cetshwayo was a prisoner at Oude Molen, a farm outside Cape Town, Florrie had asked permission to visit him. Her request was not unusual. Most English visitors to the Cape wanted to visit the Zulu King. The name of Cetshwayo was well-known to the British public; it had been dramatically brought to their attention during the Zulu War. In his despatches, Sir Bartle Frere, the former Governor, had described Cetshwayo in no uncertain terms. He was, said Frere, 'an ignorant and blood-thirsty despot . . . a sanguinary tyrant . . . a ruthless savage . . . whose history is written in characters of blood.' Such language appealed to Florrie; it was the sort of thing she might have written herself. She was naturally eager to see the ogre who could inspire such spirited prose. She was in for some surprises.

She had gone out to Oude Molen with a party from Government House; it had included Lady Robinson and Prince Louis of Battenberg. The room in which they had interviewed the King had been dark and dismal, furnished with only a few rough kitchen chairs. Expecting Frere's monster, they had been staggered to find Cetshwayo was a fat, jovial old man whose natural dignity completely disarmed them. Seated on one of the rickety chairs and speaking through an interpreter, he had turned the visit into something approaching an audience. The conversation had been largely taken up with banter and small talk. The only time that Cetshwayo had shown a serious interest was when he heard that Florrie was on her way to Natal and the Transvaal. This was country he knew—both territories bordered on Zululand—and he was full of questions about the places she would visit. As the party was leaving Florrie snatched a few minutes private conversation with the King and it was then that she made her promise. Cetshwayo asked her to visit Zululand while she was in Natal and bring him news of his country; she had said that if the opportunity arose she would try to do so. That was all there had been to it. With peace only a rumour and the prospects of an exciting campaign before her, it had seemed unlikely that she would find time to visit Zululand.

Now, of course, things were different. Not only had peace been signed and practically sealed—the Royal Commission was still sitting when Florrie left Pretoria—but on returning to her old camping grounds at Newcastle she found herself with time on her hands. She was looking for new excitements. A trip to Zululand would enable her to keep her promise and provide a fitting finale to her sojourn in South Africa.

Having made up her mind, she began making preparations for the journey. A few days before they were due to leave, however, they came up against an unexpected obstacle. News was received of a serious rising among the discontented Zulu and the acting Governor of Natal sent word that her party would not be allowed to enter Zululand. Florrie, of course, was furious. Having been cheated of her Boer revolt she felt she should at least be allowed a Zulu rising. She immediately sent a telegram to Sir Evelyn Wood asking him to authorise her journey. But Wood agreed with the Natal authorities and ordered her to postpone her trip. This, said Florrie sulkily, 'left me no choice.' To fill in the waiting period Florrie and Beau decided to visit the Kimberley diamond fields. They travelled by mail cart and the journey took the best part of three weeks. By the time they arrived back in Natal they were completely exhausted.

Florrie's first concern was to find out whether it was now safe for them to enter Zululand. On this point her army friends had good news for her. Not only was it safe but Sir Evelyn Wood, having wound up the Royal Commission, would soon be setting out for Zululand himself. There was to be an *indaba* (meeting) with the Zulu chiefs at the Inhlazatshe mountain to enquire into the cause of the Zulu unrest. There was no reason why the Dixies should not accompany the General. For once it seemed that things had turned out for the best. For once it looked as if Florrie would be in the right place at the right time.

[3]

And so at last she was off to Zululand. Early on a cold, damp August morning the bulging wagons, accompanied by two squadrons of cavalry, set out in the drizzling rain towards the land of Cetshwayo. The South African winter had set in and it was proving a particularly bitter one. All along the way the silent Zulu, wrapped in coloured blankets, stared at them with dark impassive eyes. The further they travelled, the more fascinated Florrie became with the wayside kraals and their inhabitants. At one of their overnight stops a party of Zulu called to see Sir Evelyn Wood. They were asked whether they were satisfied with the way their country had been divided after the Zulu War. They decidedly were not. The only advantage they could think of was that now they were allowed to get married when they pleased and have as many wives as they wanted. Previously such matters had been subject to the King's approval. As they were leaving Florrie tried to put a question to them. Grabbing the interpreter's arm, she asked him to enquire whether they wanted Cetshwayo to return to Zululand. There was immediate consternation among the officials. The interpreter was told sharply that the question was not allowed; it must not be asked. Rather taken aback, Florrie decided to hold her tongue.

But the incident had banished all doubt from her mind; she determined there and then not to leave Zululand until she had satisfied herself about Cetshwayo's exile. Was he the ruthless tyrant who was hated by the people he had oppressed? This is what Sir Bartle Frere had claimed. Was he also an irresponsible savage who was only safe in captivity? This was the reason given for keeping him at Oude Molen. The more she saw of the Zulu, the less convinced she was of the stories told about them.

The so-called settlement of Zululand had obviously failed. Discontent and faction fighting was rife throughout the territory. How much was this due to the fact that the people had been deprived of a central authority? Of their hereditary ruler? She had seen enough of Africans to realise the importance of the tribal structure. She was fully aware of the role of the chiefs. Above all she remembered the grave dignity of Cetshwayo. Nothing of what she had seen or heard seemed to fit the accounts given her in Cape Town. She was determined to get a more realistic picture of 'Native policy' in South Africa before she left.

As the time approached for Wood to meet the Zulu chiefs, Florrie paid more and more attention to the way-side kraals.

The great *indaba* at Inhlazatshe (the Place of Green Stones) had been fixed for the end of August. For days before the meeting, torrential rains kept the Government party bogged down in their tents. The weather grew colder; snow started whitening the tops of the surrounding hills. The trek-oxen began to die at an alarming rate. Bored and impatient, Florrie moped about the camp. Unable to change her clothes, sleeping in her sodden boots and sickened by the dying oxen, she waited for the rains to stop.

At last, rain or no rain, Sir Evelyn Wood decided to push on. Thankfully they followed his wagon tracks through the slippery mud.

About noon on the day they arrived at Inhlazatshe the clouds began to break up. The mist lifted from the great flat-topped mountain and a weak, watery sun filtered through. Out of the thinning mist appeared crowds of Zulu. Muffled in dank, body-clinging blankets, they converged on the camp and began bartering with the soldiers. In the general confusion which followed their arrival, Florrie managed to escape the eye of officialdom. Accompanied by an interpreter she mingled freely with the Zulu asking them questions and listening carefully to their answers. Among them were the Usutu—the followers of Cetshwayo—who had come to learn the fate of their King. At the meeting the following day they hoped to hear that he was to be restored to them. 'Many a wholesome truth I learnt that day from the lips of chiefs, indunas, and common men,' reports Florrie. 'From those lips the English method of viewing a Zulu received in my mind its greatest shock. . . . Where was the fear, the hate, and the terror for this tyrant, this despotic savage, this man-slaying machine of Sir Bartle Frere's, which we in England had been taught and encouraged to believe existed? Where indeed?'

As the sun set over the stately Inhlazatshe that evening she considered it one of the most beautiful sights she had ever seen. It gave her, she says, that rarest thing—a new sensation.

The following morning broke bright and clear. From the first light small bands of tribesmen could be seen threading their way across the open country towards the huge Union Jack which marked the meeting place. Gradually they formed a semi-circle with the chiefs in the front. Big as the gathering was it was not as big as had been expected. The rains had made it impossible for them all to get there and many did not arrive until days later when everyone had packed up and gone.

At nine o'clock the band struck up. With pith helmets gleaming and sword hilts a-glitter, the soldiers of the Great White Queen marched into the arena. Leading them, mounted in 'full pontificals,' was Sir Evelyn Wood. Behind him in all the glory of her stained serge suit rode Florrie; it was claimed that her high-pitched, questioning voice could be heard above the full blast of the band. They dismounted and made their way to the chairs and benches facing the tribesmen. The Royal Standard was unfurled and the soldiers unsheathed their swords. Florrie tingled Britishly. The Zulu looked apprehensive.

The proceedings were opened by one of the aides-de-camp barking out a long-winded explanation of British intentions in the Transvaal. Florrie, sitting beside Sir Evelyn Wood, noticed that the Zulu seemed neither convinced nor interested. Imperial policy was then laid down. There would be a hut tax of 10s a hut which would be collected by the chiefs. They would pay part of this revenue to the British Resident. They would build roads and repair roads. They would pay for border patrols. They must combine to prevent the importation of liquor into the country. The chiefs should convene a regular assembly. . . . And so it went on. The Zulu listened and waited, but they waited in vain. The subject uppermost in their minds was not mentioned. Cetshwayo's name did not feature in the official proclamation.

The Government propositions at an end, the time came to settle local disputes—the cause of the recent unrest. While the first case was being heard one of the Usutu leapt to his feet and shouted at his fellows. Why, he wanted to know, were they wasting their time on their own concerns? 'And your King? I thought your intention in coming here was to pray for him? What wrong has he ever done?' The resulting murmur was ignored by the officials. When the disputes had been adjudicated the Usutu tried again. They asked for permission to reply to the white chiefs. The white chiefs dealt with them in no uncertain terms. 'What should you answer? . . . You are always saying that you want the bone of that scoundrel (*ishinga*) whom we have done away with. . . . We do not wish to answer; we are laying down the law to you.'

The National Anthem was played; the troops formed up and marched away; the gathering was over. 'So ended the great Inlazatshe meeting,' scoffed Florrie, 'one which accomplished no end but to disappoint many a loyal and hopeful heart, which, coming filled with the latter, returned to its home angry and discontented.'

And, with the meeting over, the time came for them to separate. Wood and his staff were due to leave the following day for Swaziland but Florrie and Beau, who should have been making for Durban, postponed their departure a little longer. She was still not satisfied. The Inhlazatshe meeting had cast out any doubts she might have had regarding British justice in Zululand but she was still hungry for further evidence. She was determined to find out all she could before leaving the country.

[4]

The important 'pilgrimage of enquiry,' as she chose to call it, is the most scantily documented part of Florrie's wanderings in South Africa. Although she claimed her findings would fill a book, she presents them in vague generalities. There was probably good reason for this. When she wrote her account, things in Zululand were still very uncertain. She had already caused a great deal of trouble with her indiscretions and was no doubt wary of naming names and citing cases.

She toured the Zulu battlefields and describes them in her usual breezy manner. She deplored the slaughter and sighed at the graves of the British dead. But she leaves the details of her talks with the Zulu to a brief summing up. 'That information,' she says sweepingly, 'consists in an almost universal desire on the part of the Zulu nation for their King's return.'

Florrie kept her promise and saw Cetshwayo again at the Cape. She and Beau arrived at Cape Town on their old coaster the *Melrose* and were delighted to find her twin brother Jim waiting for them. Always at a loss when separated from the Dixies and having time on his hands—he had recently resigned from the Dumfriesshire Volunteers—Jim had hurried out to join them in Zululand but had arrived too late. For the past three weeks he had been the guest of Sir Hercules and Lady Robinson at Government House. 'We found him flourishing,' says the joyful Florrie, 'and the whole household in the same condition.'

Jim accompanied Florrie and Beau when they drove out to see Cetshwayo at Oude Molen. The place was just the same. It was as bleak and as formidable as ever. The room in which Cetshwayo lived was just as bare and its crude kitchen chairs just as hard. But the King himself had changed. They had been warned what to expect but it came as a shock nevertheless. He met them at the door and greeted them with a hearty handshake and a sad, fleeting smile. He looked pinched and hopeless and his forehead was deeply wrinkled. He had aged terribly.

Speaking through an interpreter, she told him all she had seen and heard. When she came to the Inhlazatshe meeting the King perked up. He was full of questions. Which chiefs, he wanted to know, had been there? What had they said? To whom had she spoken? She gave him the names of the chiefs. She told him how they wanted him back. 'Yes, yes,' he said, 'they wish me back and so do the Zulu people. All I love is in Zululand; my heart is there where lies my father's grave. I am heart-sick and weary with waiting. When will England be just and let me return?' He had recently peitioned the British Government and clung desperately to the hope that he would be allowed to go to England to put his case to the Great White Queen and her ministers. But so far he had received no reply. How much longer would he have to wait?

Florrie knew the answer but could say nothing. That morning Sir Hercules Robinson had told her that he had some definite news about the King's petition. He had received a telegram from London. Cetshwayo was to be granted his request, but not for some months. Not, in fact, until the following summer. This was something the Governor would have to tell the King himself. In the meantime, Florrie tried to console him. England was slow, she said, but England was just. Public opinion was rising in his favour. He had many friends working for his cause. Winter in England was cruel, she pointed out, he must not think of going then. He must wait for the summer when many influential people would be gathered in London.

The following day Cetshwayo was summoned to Government House and told about the telegram. Florrie was not present when the news was broken but she heard later that the only sign of disappointment he displayed was a slight contraction of his face and a nervous movement with his hands.

She met him later in the day and tried to cheer him up by showing him over Government House. He was greatly impressed by the bedrooms and fascinated by the electric bells. If he were ever returned to Zululand, he said, he would build a similar house and entertain his white friends. When the time came for him to leave, he took her hand. He asked her not to forget him and not to forsake his cause. She gave him her promise.

They returned to England on the s.s. *Durban*. On the day of their departure they were driven to the quay by Lady Robinson and her daughters. A great crowd had gathered to see them off. The deck was gay with brilliant uniforms and feathered hats. As the ship slid slowly out of port, a chorus of goodbyes rose from the shore.

[5]

Before leaving South Africa Florrie had written an account of her interview with Cetshwayo for the *Morning Post*. To it she had added an impassioned plea for his restoration. It was published shortly after she arrived in England and caused quite a stir in the London clubs; particularly the military clubs. She followed this up with a stream of articles, booklets, pamphlets and letters to the press attacking the British authorities—both in England and South Africa—for their inept handling of the situation in Zululand. Although she was no longer the *Morning Post*'s 'special' (her assignment had ended with her return to England) the newspaper's editor gave her all the space she needed to air her controversial views. Her emotional outbursts were backed up with a mass of facts and figures taken from the official Bluebooks on the Zulu War. She was answered with equal vehemence by almost everyone who had been to Zululand—and a great many who had not. Soon there was hardly a newspaper reader in Britain who was not aware of the issues surrounding Cetshwayo's possible restoration.

The results of Florrie's impassioned activity provided a much needed fillip to Cetshwayo's flagging spirits. His cause, which had been bogged down in the labyrinths of Whitehall, suddenly leapt into prominence. It seemed as if he had at last found an ally who could bring influence to bear in the right quarters. His interpreter, Mr Samuelson, wrote to tell her how he had cheered up when he heard of the fight she was waging on his behalf. Mr Samuelson became a very useful source of information to her. He not only gave her news of the King but kept her informed of developments in Cape Town. In the middle of December she received a letter (signed, it seems, by Mr Samuelson) telling her that a Mr Henriques Shepstone had been appointed as interpreter for Cetshwayo during his forthcoming visit to England. According to this letter the King was greatly upset by the appointment. He did not think he could trust Shepstone and wanted his own interpreter (Samuelson) to accompany him.

Florrie had no difficulty in believing this. She had heard a great deal about the Shepstone family from her Natal sources and what she heard had not disposed her favourably towards them. Until 1877, Henriques Shepstone's father, Sir Theophilus Shepstone, had been the secretary for Native Affairs in Natal. He had been regarded with great respect and affection by the Zulu and was known to them as Somtseu—the mighty hunter. It had been Shepstone who had crowned Cetshwayo—with a cardboard crown—at the time of the King's coronation. Then, in 1877, he had been chosen by the Colonial Office to act as its representative in its dealings with the Transvaal. From that time his sympathies appear to have undergone a radical change. In disputes between the Boers and the Zulu he was inclined to take the side of the Boers. This had led to a cooling off of his former friendship with Cetshwayo. In the eyes of the King his every action had become suspect and the actions of his family had been included in this suspicion. The news that his son was to act as interpreter for Cetshwayo convinced Florrie that a colonial plot was afoot to undermine the King's visit. She was determined to foil it.

An opportunity came a few days later. Encouraged by Samuelson, the King sent her two letters to pass on to Queen Victoria and the Prince of Wales. The delivery of the Prince of Wales's letter did not present any problems; as a personal friend, Florrie sent it to him direct. The Queen's letter was another matter. Her earlier behaviour at Court made personal contact impossible. In any case, she was informed that such communications had to be sent through Lord Kimberley, the Colonial Secretary.

Thwarted in one direction, she embarked on another. She had copies made of the letters addressed to the Queen and the Prince and sent them to the *Morning Post*. Together with these letters she also published the letter Cetshwayo had written to her. In the middle of it, however, she inserted the extract from Samuelson's earlier note concerning Henriques Shepstone: 'I hear that one I cannot trust is to be my interpreter to England. I pray it is not so. Why is my present interpreter taken from me? . . .' Afterwards Florrie claimed that she had inserted part of the one letter in the other for convenience's sake, to save publishing a whole series of letters. She had in no way misrepresented the King's word—she had merely edited the notes she had received. It was a fairly harmless deception but, as it turned out, it caused a terrific rumpus. When the entire correspondence concerning the incident was published it practically filled a Government Bluebook.

The main cause of the trouble was that, unbeknown to Florrie, there had been a shift in the relationship between Shepstone and Cetshwayo. Sir Theophilus, no longer the Administrator of the Transvaal, was returning to his old loyalties. Unfortunately the time lag in letters reaching England from South Africa prevented Florrie from knowing this. Now, when Henriques Shepstone read her letter in the *Morning Post*, he was naturally incensed. He wrote to Sir Hercules Robinson for an explanation; Sir Hercules wrote to Lord Kimberley, Lord Kimberley wrote to Florrie. Explanations were advanced and refuted. Cetshwayo was interviewed. He knew nothing of the objection to Shepstone. He had seen Shepstone twice and agreed to his coming to England but, he pointed out, he would like Mr Samuelson to come as well. When Samuelson was interviewed he said he knew nothing of the offending passage. Florrie said she was prepared to accept his word but that if this were the case someone must have sent her a forged letter with the intention of undermining the King's visit.

The more it was thrashed out the more involved it became. It had two disastrous consequences. The King's visit was postponed and Samuelson was dismissed.

[6]

When, a few weeks later, the Bluebook setting out the affair was published, Florrie's opponents were triumphant. 'We have had various instances of late of Government by "private agitation",' commented one newspaper, 'but the inherent dishonesty and resulting mischief of this new mode of influencing national affairs have seldom been so clearly revealed as in this interesting Bluebook.'

The flood of criticism, when it came, washed over Florrie. The only action she took was to have a pretty drawing of herself interviewing Cetshwayo published in the *Graphic*. In the article accompanying it she reproduced Cetshwayo's signature without comment. It was her answer to those who doubted whether she had received any letters from the King at all. After that she returned to the attack as if nothing had happened. When rumours of a new outbreak of fighting in Zululand reached England, she announced grandly that she had despatched a special messenger to stay the rising and influence peace for a time longer if it were possible.

'Undaunted by the effects of exposure, and cruel criticism of an un-chivalric press,' gasped a South African newspaper, 'Lady Florence once more enters the arena and . . . puts forward pretensions that almost take one's breath away.'

But it paid off. At the beginning of July it was announced that Cetshwayo was about to leave Cape Town for England. In spite of all the bungling, all the criticism, and all the opposition, the visit was to take place.

Cetshwayo arrived at Plymouth on board the s.s. *Arab* on 5 August 1882. To coincide with his arrival, Florrie had written an article for the August edition of *The Nineteenth Century*. It contained very little that was new and dealt mainly with the recent rising in Zululand. There was now an uneasy peace in the country, she said. The people were merely waiting to see the outcome of Cetshwayo's visit to England. Only if the King was restored would peace become permanent. At the end of the article, however, she wrote: 'When this appears in print I shall be in all probability on the north shores of Africa and can therefore only learn at a distance the outcome of Cetshwayo's visit. . . .'

The reason for the proposed trip was entirely belligerent. Trouble was looming large in Egypt. A British Expeditionary Force had been sent to North Africa (Sir Evelyn Wood was among the officers of this force). Florrie had immediately seized upon the idea of joining the troops. But she did not go. What made her change her mind is not certain. It might have been that she was unable to obtain another newspaper commission and was unable to finance herself; or she could have been held back by a new interest that was shortly to manifest itself. But, whatever the reason, she was reluctantly forced to abandon the idea of campaigning in North Africa.

Shortly after her article in *The Nineteenth Century* appeared, it was announced that Lady Florence Dixie had decided to remain in England. She was living quietly at her estate in Leicestershire and completing her account of her travels in South Africa. The book, for which it was said she was to receive a handsome sum, was dedicated to 'the late Charles Darwin' and called *In the Land of Misfortune*. ('Those who know the land most intimately,' quipped a Cape paper, on learning the title, 'may think that not one of its least "misfortunes" was Lady Florence Dixie's visit.')

Her sudden retirement into the country at this time mystified her opponents. Those who considered she was nothing more than a sensation-monger could not understand why she should bow herself out of the limelight now that it was at its brightest.

There were plenty of others who were not so reticent. From the moment Cetshwayo arrived he was dogged by newspaper reporters and crowds of curious sightseers. His every word, his every move was reported in detail. What he ate, what he wore, how he slept, were all listed for the public's benefit. Every day the pavement outside the house in Melbury Road where he was staying was crowded with people trying to catch a glimpse of him. The road leading to his house was permanently jammed with carriages.

But, for all the excitement, Cetshwayo's official visit proceeded as planned. He was received at Marlborough House by the Prince and Princess of Wales where he exchanged walking sticks with their Royal Highnesses. He went to Osborne to visit the Queen. Later Victoria presented him with an inscribed silver mug and a photograph of herself; in return (persuaded it is said by Florrie) he sat for a portrait of himself in national costume, painted by the Queen's artist, Carl Sohn. Reproductions of this portrait were soon to be seen in every stationer's shopwindow in London; in it Cetshwayo, says one report, looked 'like a fat, black edition of Henry VIII.' He was taken over Woolwich Arsenal and was duly impressed by Britain's might.

And he attended three important interviews at the Colonial Office with Lord Kimberley. The upshot of these interviews was that his return to Zululand was assured under certain conditions. He must disband the Zulu army. He must agree to a British Resident acting as his adviser. He must observe the boundaries laid down by the British authorities. He must agree to a portion of his country, to be later defined, being allocated to those Zulu who did not wish to live under his rule. To all these conditions, with the exception of the last one, the King agreed. When he protested against part of his country being taken from him, Kimberley advised him to wait and see how much was lopped off before refusing to agree to the division. After repeating his misgivings the King accepted this advice. It was a mistake. When the country was eventually divided it was a great deal worse than he could possibly have imagined. Under terms worked out at Cape Town, two large slices of Zululand were handed over to Cetshwayo's most bitter enemies. It made a lasting peace impossible. A little over a year after his restoration, the King was a fugitive in his own country. Worn out and desperate, he died on 8 February 1884 amid rumours that he had been poisoned.

It was very much what Florrie had predicted. She was far from happy with the idea of Zululand being divided. It was she thought a deliberate spoilation of the King's property and an arbitrary assumption of his rights. She warned that it would result in trouble. Still, at the time, she accepted it as a step in the right direction.

She was probably glad that this particular crusade was over. It had been an exhausting business. For, in the midst of her political entanglements, she was still battling to retain Bosworth Park. Her various writings—her newspaper articles and her books—had helped, but had certainly not solved, her financial problems. Things had reached a stage where, if not actually forced to sell the family property, Beau and Florrie could no longer afford its upkeep. As a temporary solution they decided to rent a house some three miles from Windsor. Standing on the banks of the Thames, and known as The Fishery, this flamboyant, pseudo-rustic villa was a far cry from the stately Bosworth Park; but it was big and it was comfortable and for the next few years it served as a permanent base for Florrie.

It was the only permanence there was in her life. Beau remained as weak-willed and shiftless as ever. There seemed no question of his making an effort to support his family; what little effort he did make was confined to the race-course and the card table. Even now, when his fortune had practically disappeared, he continued to pin his hopes on a lucky win or a chance investment. Any decisions that had to be made were invariably made by Florrie.

And when Beau was not gambling he was drinking. Florrie's twin, Jim, became a regular visitor at The Fishery and he and Beau would spend most of their evenings in a drunken stupor, reminiscing about their adventures in Patagonia and South Africa. All too often Florrie was persuaded to join them. Whether it was the strain of her never-ending battles, or a habit acquired round the camp-fire, that made her reach for a glass, Florrie's nightly tippling became all too obvious. To their more knowing friends, Sir Beaumont and Lady Florence Dixie were now referred to jokingly as 'Sir Always and Lady Sometimes Tipsy.'

Chapter Nine

Theatrical Events

While Florrie was busy boosting Cetshwayo's right to his throne, her brother Lord Queensberry was no less busy supporting Charles Bradlaugh's right to a seat in Parliament.

The 'Bradlaugh Affair' was still very alive. August 1881 had seen the most determined effort yet made by the undaunted Member for Northampton. At the beginning of that month, after a spirited mass meeting in Trafalgar Square, Bradlaugh—cheered on by hundreds of his supporters—had again marched to the House of Commons and demanded admittance. This time he had been met by a posse of ushers and policemen who, after a frantic struggle, had hurled him into the Palace Yard. When his supporters reached him the badly bruised Bradlaugh was standing, ashen-faced, motionless, with his coat torn, staring at the doors of the House. That evening, when he addressed a meeting at the Hall of Science, both his arms were swathed in bandages.

This violent change of parliamentary procedure had not deterred the Bradlaughites. If anything, it spurred them on. They looked around for new targets and soon found them. With Bradlaugh's opponents outnumbering his supporters the field was wide open. Anyone and everyone remotely opposed to freethought came under fire. Not the least to suffer was the unsuspecting Poet Laureate.

Alfred Tennyson was a man of sound religious beliefs. The idea of a Godless universe horrified him. It was this horror, rather than opposition to Bradlaugh, that inspired a poem called *Despair* which he published in *The Nineteenth Century* in November 1881. The poem had been suggested by a newspaper report of a suicide pact between a man and wife. Having lost faith in God, the couple had tried to drown themselves but the man had been saved. The poem explored his hopelessness. To secularists it appeared, as Queensberry later pointed out, 'to caricature and misrepresent what the outcome of freethought has led to in its secession from orthodoxy.' This had not been Tennyson's intention. He was more concerned with the type of hell-fire preaching that made men afraid to accept God than with the arguments of rationalists. But that was thought to be beside the point. That Tennyson spoke of the 'Godless gloom' of a life 'without sun, without health, without hope, without any delight,' was enough for his poem to be damned by Bradlaugh's supporters. However, apart from the odd sneer, there was nothing they could do about it. *Despair* had been published and praised and that was that. Not until the following year, when it was learned that a play by Tennyson was to be staged at the Globe Theatre, did they see a chance of making themselves heard.

The play was called *The Promise of May*. Described as a 'village tragedy' it was the only complete prose work of Tennyson's ever performed. It was also one of his greatest disasters. Even his most ardent admirers found it embarrassing.

The trouble started on the opening night. Hardly had the curtain gone up than the hissing began. Appropriately enough it was sparked off by the villain of the piece, Philip Edgar. The preposterous, but seemingly sinister Edgar was meant to personify the encroaching evils of the mid-Victorian period, as seen by Tennyson. He was a freethinker, a radical and a hedonist. What was perhaps worse, he was also a completely humourless, long-winded bore. Much of the first act of *The Promise of May* is taken up by Edgar airing his views on heredity. Man, he concludes, is nothing more than a 'willy-nilly bundle of sensations.' Not surprisingly the Bradlaughites found this highly amusing. Their hisses soon turned into cat calls and laughter. A climax is reached when the ill-used heroine pleads with Edgar to marry her and is solemnly spurned. Poker-faced, Edgar tells the tearful girl to observe the birds of the air 'which pair for a season and then part.' This proved too much for the hecklers. The uproar which followed almost brought the play to a halt.

Most critics were inclined to dismiss the cat calls as misplaced theatrical protest. The fault, in their opinion, was not Tennyson's heavy-handed morality but his unconvincing dialogue. 'The moment that the play,' observed the *Morning Post*, 'had—doubtless by its own intrinsic faults—lost its grip of the house, there were audible those ill-bred interruptions and that needless laughter which constitutes the process known as "guying" a piece.' Outside the theatrical columns little notice was taken of the demonstration.

This was not what Bradlaugh's supports had been hoping for. Having gone to the theatre to protest, they were furious at being shrugged off as first night rowdies. Obviously it would take more than conventional heckling to expose Tennyson. Something far more sensational was called for, something that would leave no doubt as to their intentions. Luckily the man to create such a sensation was at hand.

On Tuesday 14 November 1882, the Marquess of Queensberry was seated at the front of the stalls in the Globe for the third performance of *The Promise of May*. He did not remain in his seat long. As soon as Philip Edgar appeared and began to speak he leapt to his feet.

'These,' he shouted, 'are the sentiments that a professing Christian has put into the mouth of his imaginary Freethinker, and it is not the truth!'

At least, that is what he claims to have shouted. It was almost impossible for others to catch a word. Once he was on his feet all hell broke loose. There were shouts for him to sit down, shouts for him to speak up, shouts for him to be thrown out and a good many shouts for the sake of shouting. Only the actors were silent. It took several minutes for things to quieten down. Eventually, however, Queensberry resumed his seat and the play continued to the end of the first scene.

As the curtains closed the shouting began again. From all over the theatre there came calls for Queensberry to explain himself. He was only too willing. 'Apparently under the influence of considerable excitement,' says one report, 'he announced himself as a professing Freethinker, and once more accused Mr Tennyson of presenting a travesty of the sentiments of the party to which he avowedly belonged.' But this time it was Queensberry who was rudely interrupted. Attendants rushed down the aisle and, as the struggling Marquess put it, 'I was forcibly but kindly removed while endeavouring to explain myself.'

Queensberry could not have been more delighted. To have actually been thrown out of the theatre was probably more than he had dared expect. There could be no doubt that he had created a newsworthy sensation. His only fear was that his motives, like those of the first night hecklers, might be misinterpreted. This he was determined to prevent. Hurrying back to his rooms in James Street, he dashed off a letter to the *Daily Telegraph*. He was quite sure, he informed the editor hopefully, that an 'incident that occurred tonight at the Globe Theatre will find its way into the daily papers.' So that there should be no misunderstanding, he explained what had happened in detail. 'My statement of the facts,' he concluded, 'will I presume explain my motives. I am a Secularist and a Freethinker and, though I repudiate it, a so-called Atheist, and as president of the British Secular Union, I protest against Mr Tennyson's abominable caricature of an individual whom, I presume, he would have us believe represents some body of people, which, thanks to the good of humanity, most certainly does not exist amongst Freethinkers.'

That, he had every reason to feel, should have made his position crystal clear.

[2]

It did nothing of the sort. Few incidents in Queensberry's career have been more wildly reported than his much publicised protest at the Globe Theatre. At various times he has been said to have jumped on the stage, to have assaulted the leading actor, to have flung a bouquet of vegetables at the cast, to have confronted Tennyson personally and to have been hurled headlong from the foyer. But perhaps the funniest account was that which appeared at the time in a theatrical paper. Tongue-in-cheek, one hopes, it reported that the Marquess's fury was perfectly understandable. His moral susceptibilities had been outraged, not by Tennyson's religious views, but by an unintentional *double-entendre*. At a dramatic moment in the play the dastardly Edgar is said to have burst into the heroine's bedroom and found it unoccupied. 'She must be gone!' he snarled. 'Her bed has not been slept in. Her little chamber is empty!' It was this 'equivocal expression,' insisted the paper, that had shocked not only Queensberry but half the audience.

One hopes that Queensberry enjoyed the joke. Certainly he enjoyed the publicity. His letter to the *Telegraph* was only the first of a stream of letters that he wrote over the next few days. There was hardly a newspaper that did not comment on the incident and few of the comments went unanswered.

For the cast of *The Promise of May*, Queensberry's protest came as a God-send. The play had been unanimously panned by the critics and its only hope of survival was a well-publicised controversy. It was just possible that curiosity might succeed where Tennyson's prose had so dismally failed. No one was more aware of this than Hermann Vezin, the American-born actor who played Philip Edgar. Vezin, a University graduate, was a man who took both himself and his work very seriously. For him the failure of the play had been a double disaster. Having established himself as a London actor some twenty years earlier, he was now in his fifties and his popularity was declining. The offer of a leading role in a play by the Poet Laureate had seemed his only hope of salvaging his career. That the play, and his role in particular, had been such a failure was a bitter disappointment. He was determined not to give up without a struggle.

On 20 November 1882, the *Globe* newspaper published a letter from Hermann Vezin, written from the Globe Theatre. With a triumphant flourish he pointed out that *The Promise of May* had created 'much confused excitement.' First there had been the first night heckling which, he slyly claimed, had come from 'professing, orthodox Christian Church and State people' and then had come Lord Queensberry's protest on behalf of Freethinkers. The play, in fact, had aroused the fury of extremists on both sides.

It was a valiant effort but it misfired. The following day Queensberry replied in no uncertain terms. He had no intention of allowing Vezin to claim impartiality on the part of Tennyson. The first night heckling, he insisted, originated from 'the mouth of some Freethinker impelled by the same feeling which two days later on was the cause of my making the interruption I did at the Globe Theatre.' Why, in any case, was it left to Vezin to explain Tennyson's meaning? Why could not Tennyson answer for himself? 'My object the other night,' continued Queensberry, ' . . . . was not to make a protest against the sentiments of a Freethinker (on marriage) but to attract attention to that protest, and I consider that the end justified the means.'

In fact, Vezin had not mentioned Edgar's views on marriage. This was something Queensberry felt compelled to drag into the argument himself. Doubtless aware of the talk about his own marriage, he made a point of defending himself against Tennyson's accusation that Freethinkers 'pair for a season and then part.'

'Marriage,' he told the editor of the *Daily News*, 'ought to be, and is, a human institution; not a Divine one—a law of man we know of, not of God we do not know; that therefore, like all laws of mankind, it is open to reform. Keep your marriage law much as it is, and reform your divorce law; only let it—the marriage law—be a law of man and not bolstered up with the unnecessary falsehood that any Supreme Being has bound two unfortunate people together for life, however, unsuitable they may turn out to be to one another. If this falsehood is retained, why have the ridiculous anomaly of a divorce law? To separate those whom God has bound together until death let us have a human law and a just law of divorce in the place of a supposed Divine marriage law, with a necessary ridiculous and, as it stands, most unjust law of divorce. These, Sir, are some of my sentiments as to marriage.'

Whether these sentiments were read by Sybil one does not know. If they were, they could hardly have come as news to her. Queensberry's views on the marriage laws were undoubtedly coloured by his own experience. Much as he wanted to divorce Sybil he had no grounds for doing so. Had the divorce courts recognised incompatibility he would have had no difficulty in bringing an action but, as it was, he could do nothing. Sybil, although not overly religious, was conventional enough to regard marriage as indissoluble and, despite Queensberry's rantings, had so far refused to consider divorcing him. As so often happened, Queensberry's campaign against Tennyson quickly became linked with his campaign against his wife.

For the next few weeks, Queensberry was cock-a-hoop. Requests for him to address public meetings poured in. He rarely refused them. Having literally leapt into the limelight, he was determined to bask in it. All the same, he had little but his personal grievances to offer. The speech he made when inaugurating a branch of the British Secular Union at Stockport at the end of November 1882 was typical of many others. It was incredibly boring.

'He had himself been excluded from the House of Lords for his opinions. . . .' noted a weary reporter. 'He was actually expelled from the House of Lords. . . . It was not widely known he was excluded from the House of Lords on account of his secular belief. He should, however, take every opportunity until he regained his seat in that House to remind the public of the fact, and to call their attention to the injustice done. . . .'

That was his main concern. To be recognised as a rebel was, for Queensberry, far more important than the rebellion. Not surprisingly his moment of glory soon passed. Indeed his attack on Tennyson might have been forgotten sooner had it not been for the sensation caused simultaneously by another member of his family. As it was, the names of Queensberry and Douglas continued to feature in the newspapers for several weeks.

[3]

The Reverend Lord Archibald Douglas was a conscientious, if somewhat unorthodox, Catholic priest. Like the rest of his family, Archie had a marked streak of independence which, at times, must have caused his superiors some concern. This, however, was not noticeable during the early years of his career. As long as he remained in charge of the St Vincent's Home for Boys—the post to which he had been appointed by Cardinal Manning after his ordination—his career appears to have been conventional enough. That St Vincent's became the centre of what many people considered a 'scandal' was not his fault.

St Vincent's Home was in Woodfield Terrace, a dingy side-street off the Harrow Road in Paddington. By Victorian standards, it was an extremely worthy institution. Largely self-supporting—although aided by various Catholic lay·societies—its main concern was in rescuing orphaned and destitute Catholic boys from the streets, teaching them a trade and finding them employment. (In time the work of St Vincent's was to develop into a well-known Catholic organisation known as the Crusade of Rescue.) In 1882 a substantial portion of its income came from the sale of bread which, baked on the premises, was sold to local Catholic families. The brightly coloured, hand-pulled carts marked 'St Vincent's Bread' were a familiar sight in the Paddington Streets. There were between 70 and 80 youngsters resident in the Home and for several years they ran the establishment themselves under the supervision of Archie and a married couple who acted as caretaker and housekeeper. It was a highly commendable but somewhat spartan arrangement. Only by rigorous cheese-paring and by his talent for improvisation was Archie able to keep the Home going.

But keep it going he did. During his first few years as priest-in-charge he was able to chalk up a number of successes. Several of the St Vincent's boys were trained as skilled craftsmen, others were found employment as artisans and a scheme was initiated for settling the less able in jobs in the British colonies. But perhaps Archie's greatest single achievement was in training a sixteen-year-old lad, named Thomas Henry Stock, as the chief baker at St Vincent's. By all accounts young Tom Stock was a model pupil. Handsome, hard-working and intelligent, he had been placed in the Home by his dissolute father and had quickly developed into an accomplished baker and pastry cook. It was largely due to Tom Stock's efforts that St Vincent's bread had become so popular in the neighbourhood. Not only did young Stock become a favourite of Archie's but was acknowledged as a tower of strength in the running of St Vincent's.

The same, unfortunately, could not be said for the caretaker and his wife. In an institution geared to economy, this slovenly pair became notorious for their extravagance. Things got so bad that the long-suffering Archie was eventually forced to sack them and look for more competent assistance. Luckily he did not have to look any further than his own family. Indeed it may well have been the availability and enthusiasm of his eldest sister, Gertrude, that prompted him to make the long-delayed change.

He could not have found a more suitable housekeeper than Gertrude; or so it seemed at the time. Having twice tested her vocation as a nun, Gertrude had finally decided that she was not cut out for the enclosed life of a religious order. After an agonising period of doubt and despair, she had applied to Rome to have her vows annulled. Her request (a rare thing at that time) was granted and in the early 1870s she was released from her convent. Returning to secular life after ten years of religious confinement had not been easy. Gertrude was then in her thirties and by no means the charmingly shy girl who had once been so eagerly pursued by Queensberry's shipmates. Reserved and introspective by nature, she had been made more so by the disappointments of her unresolved life.

For a while, Gertrude found release of a sort in writing. In 1874 she published her first three-volume novel, *Brown as a Berry*. She wrote under the name of George Douglas but the masculine pseudonymn could not have fooled anyone; both in style and plot the novel is unmistakably feminine. It tells the story of a young orphaned governess, exotically named Thyrza, who becomes involved in sedate love affairs with two older men. After being tricked into a disastrous marriage, she dutifully dies on the last page. Over-long, cloyingly sentimental, full of incredible coincidences and timely quirks of fate, it was no better and no worse than the average Victorian novel.

Unlike her sister Florrie, Gertrude had no taste for crusades and causes. Lacking Florrie's rebellious streak, Gertrude openly despised what she termed 'the Woman's Rights mania' and had no desire 'to expatiate on a platform in public under the impression she was born to set the world as it ought to be, and remedy the grievances of society.' Her strong emotions could never be sublimated in politics. Escape from the cloister had not freed her from the teachings of the Catholic Church. As a good Catholic,

Gertrude passionately believed that a woman who had no religious vocation was destined to become a wife and mother. Despite her conviction that there was 'a mate for everyone' it did not make her quest for fulfilment easier.

In the meantime she continued to write. *Brown as a Berry* was politely enough received to encourage her to further efforts. Two more three-volumed novels, this time under her own name, were published in 1876; another appeared the following year. Somewhat more accomplished—but no less sentimental—than *Brown as a Berry* they were, as reviewers remarked, spoiled by their obvious Catholic bias. Far from resolving her spiritual conflicts, Gertrude's literary outpourings seemed to emphasise them. The tortured tangle of religious and sexual repression was only too apparent.

But release of a more practical kind was at hand. As it happened, the publication of her fourth novel coincided with Archie's first year as priest-in-charge of St Vincent's and, from the very outset, Gertrude involved herself with her brother's work. Catholic charity was a very different thing from political agitation; she had no hesitation in championing the waifs and strays of St Vincent's. Both as helper and as a fund raiser she proved invaluable to Archie. There can be no doubt that the work helped to solve some of her own problems. Mothering a houseful of boys was probably the next best thing to having a family of her own. When Archie decided to get rid of the caretaker and his wife, it was inevitable that Gertrude should take over as housekeeper.

Precisely when Gertrude moved into St Vincent's is not certain, but the results of her appointment soon became noticeable. From that time on, it was reported, 'matters have been on a much more satisfactory basis.' Never one to do things by half, Gertrude threw herself into the work with gusto. She saw herself not so much as a supervisor as an example to the boys. Scrubbing floors, making beds, cooking and nursing, there was no job that she was not ready to tackle. Visitors to 'that admirably-kept house' were often startled when the maid-of-all-work who answered the door—her arms covered in soap-suds—announced herself as Lady Gertrude Douglas. Different as she was from Florrie in many ways, Gertrude shared her sister's contempt for social pretensions.

It was probably Gertrude's bustling efficiency that encouraged Archie to embark on his most ambitious project. His scheme for settling boys in the colonies had got off to a slow start; as far as one can tell, it had never amounted to much more than finding employment for the odd individual. Not until the beginning of 1882 was he able to widen the scope of the scheme. Then it was that he arranged for no less than forty boys to be settled in the west of Canada. As this was the largest contingent to leave the Home, Archie decided to accompany them himself and see them safely established. He could have had no qualms about leaving Gertrude in charge while he was away. By that time she had proved her worth, was popular with the boys, and was quite as capable of running the day-to-day affairs of St Vincent's as Archie himself. And she could always rely on the help of the equally capable Tom Stock. Between them Gertrude and young Stock were as excellent a team as Archie could have hoped for.

That, at least, is what he must have thought. He had not bargained for just how well matched his sister and his prize pupil were. He quickly found out. He had hardly arrived in Canada than he received a letter from Gertrude announcing that she and Tom Stock were about to be married. How long the affair had been developing is not known; it evidently took Archie completely by surprise. 'His Lordship,' it was reported, 'was greatly taken aback by the news, and telegraphed and wrote to his sister at any rate to delay her intended marriage until his return.' He was too late.

[4]

Lady Gertrude Georgina Douglas and Thomas Henry Stock were married at a quiet ceremony in the Catholic Church of the Holy Trinity, Brook Green, Hammersmith on 3 October 1882. The registrar recorded the bride's age as thirty-six and the bridegroom's as twenty. In fact Gertrude had recently turned forty and Tom Stock could have been no more than seventeen or eighteen. Archie returned a few weeks later to find himself caught up in yet another embarrassing family scandal.

It took the press sometime to uncover the misalliance. Not until the middle of November—when the furore over Queensberry's outburst at the Globe Theatre was at its height—did tantalising paragraphs about the 'sister of a well-known Marquess' marrying 'a man not only much younger than herself, but lower in the social scale' begin to appear in the gossip columns. The full story was eventually broken by the *Manchester Guardian* which, after outlining Gertrude's history, gave a detailed account of the events leading up to the marriage. 'It is needless to say,' it added gleefully, 'that the Roman Catholic community in London has been not a little agitated by this marraige. The lady is related to some of the most aristocratic families in the country, dating back hundreds of years. Her husband is barely 21 years.' The story was immediately seized upon by the national press.

The sensation it created was out of all proportion. There was not a newspaper that did not find an excuse to pontificate on the eccentricities of the aristocracy and of the Queensberry family in particular. Only a few weeks earlier the daughter of an earl had caused a mild stir by running away with her music master but, as *The World* pompously pointed out, her elopement was quite 'outdone by that of the marquess's daughter.'

Few could resist linking Gertrude's Catholic background to Queens-berry's passionate defence of freethought. 'The mutations of opinion in the Queensberry family,' sighed one columnist,' are, indeed, somewhat singular. . . . This is a strange passage in the history of the Peerage.'

Nor could Gertrude escape comparison with her sister Florrie. To some it appeared that she was following Florrie's example: defying convention to further her radical convictions. The *Pall Mall Gazette* became quite heated on the subject. 'The marriage,' it sniffed, 'was an experiment in a sort of Christian socialism; but it is not likely to be quoted as a precedent by persons who think such alliances promising.' Nothing, of course, could have been further from the truth. Gertrude's motives for rushing into marriage were anything but political. She must have been highly embarrassed when the radical *Reynolds News* sprang to her defence. 'The society organs,' it remarked, 'made a lot of unnecessary fuss, for, since she was forty, her ladyship was quite old enough to choose a husband for herself.' It was the first time her age had been reported; the fact that it was reported accurately was no more comforting than the suggestion that she had chosen her husband rather than the other way around. It may have been this report that gave rise to the taunt that she had gone to St Vincent's to find a husband, picked out the 'best-looking boy in the school' and married him.

In face of all the snide remarks—one paper even suggested that she had escaped from her convent and run off with the baker—Gertrude kept a dignified silence. She had none of her family's love of publicity and resolutely refused to give interviews to reporters. The only statement she made was to the London correspondent of the Irish *Freeman's Journal*. This was aimed more at her former friends than at the gossip columnists. Lady Gertrude, the correspondent claimed, had no intention of being 'turned from carrying out her purpose by the sneers or jokes of her fashionable acquaintances. She and her husband have now opened a bakery business in Hammersmith.'

Chapter Ten

Curious Happenings at Windsor

The Queensberry family were said to be unhappy about Gertrude's marriage. No doubt they were. However unconventional their religious and political opinions might have appeared, they remained very conscious of their social position. Never for one moment did they forget that they were members of one of the most distinguished families in Scotland. Their support for unpopular causes owed more to egoism than to egalitarianism. But they were, if nothing else, adaptable. Whatever their initial reaction, their objections to the marriage did not last long. Gertrude was soon forgiven and her husband, if not welcome, was at least accepted by the family.

This softening of attitude was due, in no small part, to the Queensberry family's many preoccupations. They were all far too wrapped up in their own concerns to harbour petty resentments. Archie, having lost his housekeeper and his chief baker, had his hands full at St Vincent's; Queensberry was still stomping the country as President of the British Secular Union; Florrie was caught up in a new political crusade; and Jim was entangled in a highly unsuitable love affair.

The Dowager Marchioness's activities are slightly more obscure. Sometime earlier she had moved to a house in the Maidenhead district and it may have been a need to be near her that decided Florrie and Beau to rent The Fishery. Whenever Florrie was away from home, her mother was at hand to care for the children. What is more certain is that Lady Queensberry's adherence to the Irish cause was as passionate as ever. Her 'gushing letters' advocating Home Rule for Ireland continued to appear in the English and Irish press; some of her more provocative articles were republished in America.

The early 1880s—the time of Gladstone's second term as Prime Minister—were very tense years for Ireland and England. The trouble resulted mainly from the long-standing conflict between the Irish tenants and their English landlords. Ireland had never recovered from the disastrous famine, caused by the failure of the potato crop in the 1840s; the continuing agricultural depression had deprived the peasant farmers of any semblance of security. Those who could not pay their ever-increasing rents were often ruthlessly evicted. Land speculation was rife. The hardships suffered by the peasants had contributed largely to the rise of the Fenians and other nationalist organisations. One of the most powerful in the 1880s was the Land League, with Charles Stewart Parnell as its president. This organisation, formed in 1879, was dedicated to freeing Ireland from its hated overlords. Not all of its methods were peaceful and, rightly or not, it became associated with the outbreak of rent strikes, rick burnings and assaults which plagued Gladstone's second administration. A culminating point was reached in May 1882 when the new Chief Secretary for Ireland, Lord Frederick Cavendish, and the Under-Secretary, Mr Burke, were attacked and murdered in Dublin's Phoenix Park. The Land League was not responsible but, inevitably, it came under suspicion. Both in Ireland and England, people were horrified by the news of the assassination.

It appears to have been the Phoenix Park murders, together with her mother's sympathies, that first attracted Florrie's attention to Ireland. Always on the look-out for a well-publicised cause, the Irish situation seemed to demand her intervention. Cancelling her plans to sail for Egypt she set off for Ireland.

If Lady Queensberry helped to influence Florrie's decision, she certainly did not shape her views. Florrie had none of her mother's admiration for Parnell; from the very outset she was suspicious of the Land League. In the letters and pamphlets which she now began to churn out Florrie assured the Irish that she was neither a Conservative nor a reactionary. She stood for Home Rule. But she insisted that the solution to the Irish problem could not come from the Land League. The people behind the Land League, claimed Florrie, were using the sufferings of the peasants for their own ends; in letter after letter she accused the Land League of misleading the people and serving vested interests.

Her own solution to the trouble was simple. Only the Irish could help the Irish. The Irish people must set an example in self-sufficiency and shame the landlords into paying up. She was by no means the first person to think that a radical political ill could be cured with a coating of charity.

To prove her point, Florrie set to work with her usual vigour. Within weeks of establishing herself at Ballycastle, County Mayo, she was writing home triumphantly. 'I have been successful,' she claimed, 'and during one week have collected £3,000 with £1,700 promised. . . . The Land League is furious but that does not matter. One of my best triumphs in this is the fact that the gross amount of the subscriptions have come from Ireland and the Irish people. This demonstrates what may be accomplished without noise or agitation and without the machinery of paid agents.'

There was one serious drawback to Florrie's otherwise successful campaign: it failed to attract the publicity she hoped for. Without the *Morning Post* to back her, she found it impossible to rouse any real interest in England. What she was doing was far too commonplace. For an adventurous woman journalist to meddle in the affairs of far-off Zululand was one thing, for a titled lady to embark on charitable work in Ireland was quite another. Some newspapers dutifully published her letters, but they did so without comment. Only occasionally did a paragraph praising her work appear in the columns of the more fashionable journals. For the first time in her life, Lady Florence Dixie found that her activities were not considered newsworthy. She returned to England exhausted and not a little disappointed.

She need not have worried. If the English public was not interested in her, the Irish rebels were. Hardly had she arrived back in England than things took a sinister turn. Before returning permanently to The Fishery she decided to spend a few days at Bosworth Park. It was there, she claimed, that her opponents first showed their hand. One day, while she was walking in the estate grounds, a threatening letter was thrust into her hands. The writer, who signed himself 'Liberty', said that he had been deputed to warn her that the ideas she was spreading among the Irish people were not in conformity with those held by 'the party to which I belong.' The letter went on to say that if she continued with her activities she would be assassinated. 'The hand that writes this,' it ended dramatically, 'killed Lord Fred. Cavendish. It has £20,000 offered for its discovery, and we defy discovery.'

If anything was needed to encourage Florrie this letter would certainly have done so. The fact that it was rightly considered a hoax made no difference to her determination. By the end of the year she was back at The Fishery bombarding the press with letters attacking the Land League. She began to amass facts and figures related to the Land League's finances. This time she had no Bluebooks to work from but she was able to make use of the details published in the *Freeman's Journal* concerning money collected from various funds. There was, she found, a 'Fair Trial Fund,' a 'Distress Relief Fund', a 'Parnell Relief Fund' as well as various funds of the Land League and the Ladies Land League. By adding the receipts of all these funds together and subtracting the known expenditure, she came to the conclusion that something like £152,000 was not accounted for. This provided Florrie with all the evidence she needed.

She was quick to put it to use. When in March 1883, Parnell made a powerful speech in the House of Commons deploring the poverty of the west of Ireland, Florrie answered him in no uncertain terms. So impressive did her facts appear that *The Times* published her letter the following day.

Parnell did not answer her directly. However, a few days later, he claimed in the House of Commons that the Land League's funds amounted to a mere £27,000. 'It was raised,' he explained, 'not to relieve distress, but to check the tide of landlord oppression.' Florrie was triumphant. She had at last drawn fire, even though the bullets were a little off target. Determined to put herself firmly within Parnell's sights, she launched a second blistering attack in *The Times*.

But Parnell refused to do battle. Interviewed about Florrie's second letter, by a correspondent of *The Times*, he waved it airily aside. He did not, he said, 'intend to take any notice of the matter, as the accusations were unfounded and only amounted to a repetition of an old charge which the same lady had previously brought against the whole of the Parliamentary members of the Land League.'

Florrie's little skirmish was, to all intents and purposes, over. If she had not actually been defeated, her guns had been spiked. Without a prominent target like Parnell to attack, any weapons she wielded were useless. *The Times* had published her letters but had shown no inclination to support her editorially; the rest of the press had ignored the correspondence. What, she must have asked herself, would it take to bring her message home to the British public?

[2]

Florrie's second letter was published in *The Times* on 14 March 1883. At nine o'clock the following evening a tremendous explosion occurred in the office of the Local Government Board in Charles Street, Westminster. Fortunately the office was empty and nobody was hurt but the damage to the building, which also housed the Home Office, was extensive. 'The window to the right of the main entrance,' it was reported, 'has been totally destroyed, the stone copings and balustrades completely shattered, and a portion of the stone work, weighing 2 cwt was blown to a distance of 50ft or 60ft with such violence as partially to destroy a blank brick wall. . . .'

So severe was the blast that it shook the floors of the nearby House of Commons where a debate on Naval Estimates was in progress. There was immediate panic. The Duke of Edinburgh—Queen Victoria's second son—was in the Peers' Gallery at the time and he joined the rush of MPs to the scene of the explosion. Bomb experts were sent for and they promptly announced that the explosion had been caused by dynamite planted in the office earlier that evening. Almost as alarming was the discovery of a similar bomb that had been placed in the window of *The Times* office that same night, but had failed to explode. Both incidents were said to be the work of the Irish Invincibles who had earlier murdered Lord Frederick Cavendish.

The newspapers bristled with speculations. Some claimed that the first bomb had been meant for the Home Office and was aimed at the Home

Secretary, Sir William Harcourt. Others were equally certain that Charles Street had been mistaken for Downing Street and that, as Mr Gladstone was at home suffering from a slight cold, it was the Prime Minister who was the intended victim. There was little doubt as to why *The Times* had been selected; the newspaper was one of the most vociferous critics of Irish nationalism. Nobody, however, connected the attempt on *The Times* office with Florrie's recent letters. Only Florrie herself would have imagined this.

She may well, in fact, have been pondering such a link when she set off on her afternoon walk, on St Patrick's day, two days later. The newspapers that morning had been full of the bomb scares. There was plenty for Florrie to think about as she strolled towards the Thames with her huge St Bernard dog, Hubert. How much time she had to think is another matter. One has only her own extraordinary account of what happened on that walk.

Beau was the first to hear it. He had just settled down with the evening paper when the butler burst into the room. 'Sir Beaumont,' the man gasped, 'something terrible has happened to her ladyship! For God's sake, come at once!' Beau's first thought was that one of the children had fallen into the Thames. On dashing into the hall, however, he found Florrie sitting there deathly white, her hands bleeding, her dress ripped and her face spattered with mud. She told him she had been attacked by two men dressed as women. She had met them on her walk. They had first approached her and asked her the time; not having her watch, she had told them she could not help and had walked on. She had then become aware that they were following her but, thinking they were women, she had not been unduly concerned. They were still behind her when she turned off the road through a wicket gate. It was not until she reached a stile, a little further on, that they suddenly rushed at her and threw her to the ground. Then, while one held her down, the other lunged at her with a knife.

'The knife came straight down upon me,' she said, 'driven by this person's hand. It struck through my clothes and against the whalebone of my stays, which turned the point, merely grazing the skin. The knife was quickly withdrawn and plunged at me again. I seized it with both hands, and shouted as loudly as I could, when the person who first pulled me down plunged a large handful of earth into my mouth and nearly choked me.'

She was still wrestling with the knife when her dog, Hubert, bounded from the trees. She saw him pull the man with the knife backwards and then fainted. Just before she passed out she heard the rumble of wheels: when she came to she was alone. Staggering back to the house she met a neighbour's servant, fell into his arms, and gasped 'Two men have been trying to do for me.'

The startled man, alarmed at her condition, asked no questions. He helped her back to The Fishery where she was met by her brother Jim and the butler. (Afterwards Jim was to say 'he had seen his sister after falls in the hunting field, but never saw her so unnerved and frightened before.') Only when Beau arrived did she pull herself together sufficiently to explain what had happened.

She was sure the persons who attacked her were men, not women, because she saw their faces were shaved, though one had a thick veil, reaching below the mouth. The other was unveiled, but she had hardly noticed his face. They had both, she said, 'very dark eyes, dark complexions and dark hair. Neither of them spoke with any brogue, but like ordinary Englishmen.'

The next day (Sunday) there was hardly a newspaper which did not carry the story. Most of these accounts were hopelessly muddled. Florrie was said to have been attacked by gypsies, by poachers, by tramps, by escaped convicts and even a group of 'Eton boys'. One paper had it that the outrage had occurred on the terrace of Windsor Castle and another located it at Barnes Bridge, but there were enough accurate reports to cause genuine alarm.

As was only to be expected, the attack was quickly associated with Florrie's campaign against the Land League. This gave the daily papers a new slant on the story. By Monday morning they were in full cry. The fact that the attack had occurred near Windsor—practically on the Queen's doorstep—made it appear all the more sinister. It seemed to many to be little short of a direct blow at the throne itself.

Somewhat uncharacteristically, Florrie refused to communicate directly with any newspaper but *The Times*. Her first statement was, of necessity, brief and to the point. She confined herself to the bare facts. 'The particulars are short,' she explained, 'and I can write little because my hands are cut. . . . This is all the information I can give. My head is very confused and painful, and I expect they must have stunned me.'

The rest of the press were left to ferret out what details they could. They came up with some tantalising stories. Tradespeople in Windsor reported seeing tall, heavily veiled women striding about the town like men; a soldier claimed to have seen two huddled figures in a dog-cart near the scene of the attack; and a young girl, walking near The Fishery, said she had passed a woman who had 'very large feet' and wore a linsey dress. The butler at The Fishery was particularly helpful. On the day of the attack he had seen two women in a nearby field picking flowers and had pointed them out to Lord James Douglas's manservant. They wore 'light loose clothes,' he said, and 'were constantly looking at the house. . . . In order to see them better I jumped on the dustbin. They seemed to be rather stout and elderly. They certainly were not young people.' A page boy also claimed he had seen the women and that one of them was wearing a green dress; and a servant of a neighbouring house said he had met two women of 'unusual stature' near the spot where Florrie was attacked.

The following day Florrie roused herself to speak to *The Times* reporter. She felt it necessary to clear up some misunderstandings. 'I have never said it was a positive attempt on my life,' she insisted, 'though I must admit I thought it was at the time. It stands to common sense that two strong men could easily have killed a woman lying helpless on the ground if they chose. It must have been simply a matter of intimidation to show me what they could do if they liked. I never saw, nor have I said I saw, a woman in green. Neither of my assailants wore a dress of that colour. . . . It may have been intended for intimidation, but they will not stop me from doing anything I intend to do. They do not know me if they think they can.' She had no intention of explaining herself further. She was far too busy for that. 'I have had a lot to do,' she said, 'in opening and answering letters, for I do not like to leave that to anyone else. Letters and telegrams are still coming in from Ireland and all over the world. In fact I have had hundreds of letters from England, and still more from the Irish people.'

Nor was it only the general public who were concerned. Among those who wrote or telegraphed were the Prince of Wales, the Duke of Edinburgh, the Duke and Duchess of Albany, Prince and Princess Christian and the ex-Empress Eugénie of the French. No one, though, was more sympathetic than Queen Victoria. On the day following the attack she sent Sir Henry Ponsonby, Lord Methuen and the Marchioness of Ely to enquire after Florrie's health and shortly afterwards the Queen's celebrated ghillie, John Brown, arrived with a police inspector to make a detailed investigation. They came in an open dog-cart and Brown was immediately shown to Florrie's boudoir. After she had told him her story—and the part played by her St Bernard dog—he is reported to have said: 'What a thing to be happening to a lassie. Have ye got a picture of the dog for I'd like one for mysel'. If ye canna spare one, I'll be wulling to pay for it.'

When he was taken to the spot where the attack had taken place, though, John Brown seems to have changed his tune. After stomping about the ground, he grunted something about there being no evidence of a struggle in spite of the fact that the soil was soft. Both by his tone and expression, he was said to convey 'an unmistakable meaning.' There was a keen wind blowing when Brown carried out his inspection; when he got back to Windsor Castle he was chilled to the bone. The following day the Queen advised him to go to bed and, for once, he followed her advice. But it was too late. Erysipelas set in overnight and within a few days the Court favourite was dead. Florrie sent the promised photograph, signed by herself, to the Queen.

John Brown was not the only one suspicious of Florrie's story. When, after a two day search, the police could find no trace of the attackers even the more sympathetic newspapers began to have second thoughts. Stories of mysterious veiled women and disappearing dog-carts gave way to more critical accounts. Witnesses were found who threw doubt on the entire affair. A gardener who was working within a few yards of the attack, and had often heard Beau and Florrie talking behind a hedge, had neither seen nor heard anything unusual that afternoon; and the proprietor of a nearby hotel, who was also within earshot, said the same thing. Even the soldier who had reported the dog-cart admitted that he had not heard Florrie's cry nor, for that matter, had the young girl who was passing. Lock-keepers along the Thames were adamant in refuting Beau's suggestion that the attackers had escaped on the river. What then had happened to them? Perhaps, quipped a columnist, the heroic Hubert had not merely frightened but eaten Florrie's assailants.

To Florrie's neighbours, the whole incident seemed typical of the bizarre Dixie household. From the time Beau and Florrie had moved to The Fishery, their behaviour had appeared distinctly odd to the locals. Florrie was seen as a prime example of the New Woman and her popularity had not been helped by a report that she had physically attacked a man for encroaching on her fishing rights. 'She was certainly very eccentric. . . .' says Mrs Harriet Ward, an artist who lived close to The Fishery and never ceased to be amazed by the goings-on there. 'Her favourite headgear was a polo cap and I have watched her at a respectful distance sporting on the lawn with a strange pet, a large jaguar, which thoroughly alarmed her household and myself. . . . Her husband was as unconventional as his wife. I once saw him dressed as a harlequin reading a paper on his lawn. The gong sounded for dinner, and he sprang up like a typical one, and leaped off to the house.' With such antics on the lawn, who could tell what happened behind the bushes? Mrs Ward was among those who dismissed the alleged attack as 'an hallucination emanating from an hysterical woman.'

As the criticism rose, so did Florrie's spirits. 'I am not a person given to exaggeration,' she retorted angrily. 'and people do not know me if they think my statement is exaggerated. On the contrary, instead of exaggerating I should rather try to minimise the affair. Indeed, I should have preferred that it had not been made public at all. . . . So many things have been placed in my mouth that I have not said, that I really cannot take the trouble to contradict them.'

Her shy violet pose was unconvincing. She was not exactly noted for her reticence. She, it was thought, was the last person to complain of having words put in her mouth. Inevitably her 'editing' of Cetshwayo's letters was dug up; the fact that she had deliberately inserted a false accusation into the correspondence was seen as further proof of her unreliability. As for her claim that she was not given to exaggeration, how could this be accepted from a member of the Queensberry family?

'The Queensberry family,' sighed the *Echo*, 'enjoy an almost unique reputation for eccentricity. Every member of it is distinguished by some startling singularity.'

The divisions in the Queensberry family were also seized upon by officials of the Land League. Although Parnell refused to be drawn into the controversy, others were quick to deny that the Land League was involved. In America the League's treasurer, Patrick Egan—who was on a fund-raising tour—emphatically dismissed the suggestion that the attack was of political significance. 'The family,' he snorted, 'is a peculiar one, and the assault was probably the result of a family feud.' Whether he thought that the Dowager Marchioness had hired thugs to attack her disloyal daughter he did not say. Mr Gallagher, the president of the Land League in New York, came up with a more ingenious suggestion. After branding Florrie as a 'crank' and a liar, he hinted that the affair was probably manufactured by the Gladstone government 'for a purpose against Mr Parnell.' It may have been this kind of talk that prompted Captain O'Shea (the then unsuspecting husband of Parnell's mistress) to call for an official enquiry.

When Florrie heard that O'Shea intended tabling a Parliamentary question concerning the attack, she was appalled. This was the last straw. That her word should be doubted by the newspapers was bad enough; that it should be officially investigated was downright insulting. Whether, as one paper reported, she threatened to arrive in the lobby of the House of Commons with a horsewhip and 'inflict personal chastisement on Captain O'Shea' is not certain; but there was no mistaking her anger.

[4]

The debate was held on the last day of the parliamentary session before the Easter recess. Members were in an end-of-term mood; by question time they had become distinctly rowdy. The mere mention of Florrie's name was sufficient to send both sides of the House into convulsions. Even the habitually poker-faced Mr Gladstone was seen to be grinning broadly as he took his place on the Treasury bench.

The first question came from a Tory MP who solemnly asked the Prime Minister whether he could provide any information about 'the reported attempt to assassinate Lady Florence Dixie?' Before Gladstone replied, the Home Secretary leant forward and whispered something to him which obviously amused him enormously. He was still smiling when he rose to answer the question. 'Having consulted my right honourable friend,' he beamed, 'I do not think that he is in a position to give any information which would be of value to the house.' Once again the House was convulsed. 'It was evident,' observed a reporter, 'that whoever else has doubts on the Dixie mystery, the "faithful Commons" are not to be numbered among them.'

But the fun was not over. Hardly had the laughter died down than Captain O'Shea was on his feet with a question for the Home Secretary. 'I wish to learn,' he insisted, 'if the police have come to any definite conclusion as to the alleged attack on a lady at Windsor; and whether, considering the gravity of the comments by the Press, Her Majesty's Government are prepared to institute a public inquiry into all the circumstances of the case?' The Home Secretary, still struggling to keep a straight face, assured him that the matter was being investigated and that he saw no reason to interfere with the investigation. This was too much for the waggish Henry Labouchere who, shouting above another roar of laughter, demanded to know whether a reward was being offered to find out 'who is the guilty party.' As few members had any doubt about the 'guilty party' this was considered the height of wit. The Home Secretary could hardly be heard as he begged the House to leave the matter in the hands of his department.

Florrie became convinced that she was the victim of a devious political plot. For reasons best known to themselves the police, the press, the Government—and presumably the Land League—had joined forces to discredit her. 'Innuendo, insinuation, and deliberate falsehood,' she fulminated, 'have been shamelessly employed for this purpose'. She was particularly incensed by the accusation that she was responsible for John Brown's death. The ghillie, she claimed loftily, had caught his fatal cold elsewhere. But it was no use. Her protests were ignored. Finally she was forced to give up. In a huff, she retired to Bosworth Park where her last act of retaliation was to enter Hubert as a special exhibit in the local dog show.

The truth behind the 'Windsor outrage' was never revealed. A final attempt to defend Florrie was made in a privately printed pamphlet, *Lady Florence Dixie Vindicated*, published later that year. The arguments put forward were not altogether convincing. In any case, they came too late. By that time most people had accepted the Home Secretary's more pointed remarks. Presenting the results of the official police investigation to Parliament, Sir William Harcourt had more or less dismissed the affair by emphasising that it rested entirely 'on her ladyship's own statements, the police having discovered nothing.'

Chapter Eleven

'Your Uncle Certainly'

When, in July 1884, the eighth Marquess of Queensberry turned forty, his position was not unlike his father's at the same age. Having devoted himself to sport and self-indulgence there was little he could boast about. His life, in most respects, had been fashioned by his bungling ineptitude. He had failed to make a career for himself; he had done nothing to improve his fortune; he had neglected his estates; he was barred from the House of Lords; and his personal life was a shambles. What small distinction he had acquired had earned him more notoriety than respect. Born into an age of earnest self-endeavour he had lived like an eighteenth-century rake.

True, he had given his name to the rules of boxing. But this was, as he well knew, very much a second-hand achievement; one which many sportsmen found convenient to ignore. In 1884 he was better known as a battling freethinker than as the promoter of fair fighting. Even his questionable reputation among secularists was on the decline. For in that same year, despite his vigorous campaigning, the British Secular Union was disbanded and he was left without a platform for his egocentric views.

Cast adrift by his secularist friends, Queensberry was dejected but not despondent. There was no question of his following his father's example by finding release from disappointed middle-age in a shooting accident. He had other outlets for his frustrations, not the least of these being his relentless vendetta against his wife. If Queensberry had no other use for Sybil, she at least provided him with a target for his spite. So long as he remained married he could ignore his own inadequacies and regard himself as the victim of outmoded convention. Not for nothing had he attacked the unjust divorce laws during the Globe Theatre controversy. His determination to obtain a divorce had developed into a neurotic obsession; now, free from other distractions, he gave that obsession full play.

Queensberry's letters to Sybil became more abusive, more wildly worded, more threatening. He seized upon every excuse to attack her. So impassioned were his letters that at times they were almost incomprehensible. According to Bosie, who later read them, they gave the impression of having been written by a raving lunatic. Nor did he stop at writing. Failing to get any response to his letters, Queensberry took to descending upon his family unexpectedly for the sole purpose of making their life hell. On one occasion he went even further. Arriving at The Hut just before Ascot week, he gave Sybil twenty-four hours to leave the house so that he could entertain a party of his racing friends, including his current mistress. Sybil, who had also invited friends for the week, had no alternative but to pack her bags and return to London.

Sybil was unwise in choosing to live near Ascot. If she wished to escape her husband's attentions she should have kept well clear of a race-course. Of all Queensberry's erratic passions, his devotion to the turf was probably the strongest. When all else failed, he could always find comfort in the thunder of hoofs. Only a growing awareness that his days as a competitor were numbered marred his enthusiasm for horse racing. As he entered his forties he, like his father, took a jaundiced view of his sporting future and became more and more conscious of his shortcomings. What troubled him most was his failure to achieve his greatest sporting ambition: his failure to win the Grand National.

He had repeatedly ridden the event but, despite some promising mounts, had never finished first. The fact that he could claim that he was one of the few riders who had never failed to take the thirty-three daunting jumps and complete the course of the Grand National was poor compensation for not winning the race.

What seemed to be his last chance presented itself in 1886. His cousin, Arthur Johnstone Douglas, had high hopes that year of a horse named *Old Joe* which he had bought for £150 and which had shown its paces by winning a race at Sandown. Queensberry was equally enthusiastic. Having tested *Old Joe* in its training gallops, he was sure that this was the horse on which he could pull off the National. And he might well have done so, had he been given the chance. But his age was against him. At forty-four he was past his prime as a rider and, at the last moment, his cousin decided not to take the risk. He replaced Queensberry with a professional jockey who brought *Old Joe* in as a 40-1 winner.

Queensberry was shattered. He felt insulted at having been passed over; he was convinced that he had been cheated out of a golden opportunity. His hopes of winning the National had been killed. Such was his disappointment that his family firmly believed that it was this, more than any other failure, that soured him for the rest of his life. He never rode in a big race again and, according to his son, once he gave up racing 'his whole character and his brain-power deteriorated.' But this, like so much that has been written about Queensberry, is an oversimplification. The complexities of his deranged personality are not so easily explained.

Obviously the ending of his active career as a sportsman did have a profound effect on Queensberry. The significance of this turning-point in his life—particularly when one considers the circumstances of his father's death—cannot be underrated. He had, after all, deified physical fitness and transformed sport into a means of worship; it had become not only his *raison d'être* but, in a way, his hope of immortality. Only by striving for physical perfection, he had written in *The Spirit of the Matterhorn,* could man ensure 'the future of himself within his race.' To acknowledge the decline of his bodily powers was tantamount to denying his faith; there was no allowance for old age in his youthful ideology.

All the same, it would be a mistake to attribute Queensberry's erratic temperament to a single cause. He was subject to more pressures than were dreamed of in his philosophy. The trouble lay not in his sport but in himself. This had become glaringly apparent long before he was forced to give up racing. Instability was inherent in what Sybil called 'the fatal Douglas temperament.' Queensberry's reactions to a crisis were invariably violent; each crisis left its scars. The wound to his pride at being rejected for the 1886 Grand National was deep and lasting, but then so were the effects of another traumatic event which followed soon after.

At the end of 1886 Sybil finally agreed to a divorce.

What caused this capitulation is not certain. Bosie, who was closer to his mother than anyone, later claimed that Queensberry was solely responsible for the break. The final insult, he says, came when Queensberry proposed that his current mistress should move into Sybil's house and that the three of them should live together. This may or may not be true. Nothing was impossible with Queensberry. But, given his hatred for his wife, the idea of his suggesting a *ménage à trois* with Sybil as the third party takes some believing. And so, for that matter, does Bosie's word. When writing about his father, Bosie never hesitated to pile on the agony; he was quite capable of inventing anything he did not know.

If Queensberry did make such a suggestion, it was not mentioned during the divorce proceedings. Indeed, at that time, Queensberry appears to have been conducting a singularly furtive affair. Sybil had to rely entirely on the word of servants for her evidence.

The case was heard by Lord Trayner in the Court of Sessions, Edinburgh, on 22 January 1887. Sybil was represented by the Dean of Faculty, a Mr Macintosh, and Queensberry did not oppose. The first witness was Major Hugh Montgomery, Sybil's cousin, who simply testified that he had attended 'the marriage of the Marquess and Marchioness' and that he knew afterwards they 'lived together as man and wife.' It was left to Queensberry's valet, Thomas Gill, to supply the more pertinent details. These were mainly concerned with his abortive attempts to serve tea to Queensberry and a young woman who, coming for dinner at James Street, spent more time in his lordship's bedroom than in the dining room. On more than one occasion Gill had struggled upstairs with loaded tea trays only to find the dining room empty and the bedroom door locked. He was quite certain, he said, that Queensberry and his guest were in the bedroom because once, when the door was unlocked, 'he walked into the bedroom and found them both there.' This, and the fact that he had earlier stumbled upon the young woman hiding behind the dining room door, had left him in no doubt as to the purpose of these evening entertainments. His evidence was confirmed by a former valet whose jugglings with tea trays at locked bedroom doors had been equally unsuccessful.

Lord Trayner had no hesitation in granting Sybil her divorce. The hearing, from start to finish, lasted less than an hour.

'It is a pity,' clucked a gossip columnist, deprived of a more titillating story, 'that all divorce cases—since divorce seems to have become in the present state of our civilisation a necessary evil—cannot be conducted with the same decency and despatch as that which has just been brought by Lady Queensberry against her husband.' Whether these worthy sentiments were echoed by his readers is another matter. To have the secrets of Lord Queensberry's love-nest revealed from the wrong side of the bedroom door was not what the public had been hoping for.

[2]

Queensberry's divorce was doubly distressing for his mother. Not only, as a devout Catholic, was she resolutely opposed to divorce but Queensberry was the only one of her sons to have married and his estrangement from his wife effectively cut her off from her Douglas grandchildren. As far as Queensberry's sons were concerned, their paternal grandmother might never have existed: they neither spoke nor wrote of her in later life. It was a gap in the Dowager Marchioness's life which her other sons seemed unlikely to fill. Francis, of course, had died on the Matterhorn before he could think of marriage, Archie was pledged to celibacy and Jim, then in his thirties, had shown no signs of settling down, let alone marrying. Her only consolation lay in Florrie's boys who, though closer to her than Queensberry's children, were members of the Dixie rather than the Douglas family. With her strict sense of hierarchy, the Dowager Marchioness of Queensberry could not but be aware of her isolation from her Douglas descendants.

So it must have delighted her when, a year after Queensberry's divorce and contrary to all expectations, Jim surprised his family by announcing his engagement to a rich, well-established, Catholic widow.

Surprise it undoubtedly was. Of all the family, Jim was far and away the most irresolute. For years he had lived in Florrie's shadow, seeming to have no mind nor will of his own. His personality appears to have been submerged at birth by that of his aggressive twin sister. If Florrie cried Jim sighed, if Florrie coughed Jim sneezed, if Florrie bullied Jim obeyed, and if Florrie travelled to the ends of the earth Jim either went with her or booked a passage on the next ship. It had become very much a one-sided relationship. Fond as she was of her brother, Florrie no longer depended upon him; at least not to the extent that he depended upon her. Florrie had no blanks in her life that needed to be filled by brotherly reassurance. Jim's life, on the other hand, was pathetically empty. He had no profession, no real ambition, no close friends and, apart from Florrie's concerns, no definite interests. By the time he was twenty-five he had abandoned whatever plans he might have had of a military career; by the time he was thirty his family had abandoned all hopes that he might make a life for himself. Jim's existence depended entirely on a small family allowance and his slavish devotion to Florrie.

Significantly enough, his only known attempt to carve a niche for himself resulted from his desire to emulate his sister. In 1882, spurred on by Florrie, he published a two-volume novel called *Royal Angus*. He wrote it soon after his return from South Africa and it was accepted by Florrie's publishers, Richard Bentley and Sons, who were about to bring out Florrie's travel book *In the Land of Misfortune*.

Loosely constructed, repetitive and often confusing, *Royal Angus* reads more like a sporting travelogue than a novel. It tells the story of the aristocratic Lord Royal Angus who, disappointed in love, embarks on a pointless round of hunting, shooting, fishing and gambling adventures in England, Ireland, Norway and Switzerland. As in many first novels, the self-justifying, autobiographical undertones are unmistakable. The hero's extravagant activities are redeemed by his high intentions; his early death in an Alpine accident is reminiscent of Lord Francis Douglas's fatal fall on the Matterhorn. ('With a rapid slash the rope parted, and without a word or a groan Lord Royal fell headlong into the fearful abyss.') Death was the only solution Jim could offer for his hero's wasted life.

For all its weaknesses, *Royal Angus* received several encouraging reviews. There was some criticism of the disjointed plot and the baffling behaviour of some minor characters but, by and large, the book was thought to show promise. 'He will be a very exacting reader who cannot find some pleasure in it. . . .' commented the *St James Gazette*. 'There is so much breezy downrightness in the open air scenes of the tale, that it should be possible for Lord James Douglas to make his next a more important novel.' This was expecting too much of Lord James. What little talent he had had been exhausted in his idealised self-portrait of Lord Royal Angus. He had neither the intellect nor the imagination to write an important novel. Jim's next two books—*Estcourt* in 1883 and *Queen Mab* in 1884—were painfully contrived adventure stories which even the most kindly disposed critics (and his title always ensured a few of these) found difficult to praise. Easily disheartened, Jim retired from the literary field as abruptly as he had retired from the battlefield.

But if he lacked the Douglas push, Jim had his full share of the Douglas temperament. Moody, self-indulgent, overbearingly conceited and given to violent outbursts, he could be as pig-headed as any member of the family. His life, devoid as it was of purpose, was not devoid of passion. This became only too clear during his brief career as a novelist. His relentless pursuit of a young girl at this time landed him in serious trouble. Not much is known of the affair but, if Florrie is to be believed— and she had no reason to lie—it came near to creating yet another public scandal. The girl was under-age and a ward of the Court and when Jim, in a fit of defiance, attempted to abduct her, he was hauled before a magistrate, charged, and locked up in a police cell. Luckily the girl's guardians refused to press the charge and the matter was hushed-up. Released from the police cell, Jim returned to The Fishery unshaven, unnerved and, for all Florrie's merry teasing, distinctly unamused.

It took several months hard-drinking for Jim to recover. Some three years passed before he showed serious interest in another woman. This time he was more careful. Far from being a young, inexperienced girl, the woman he decided to marry was a robust widow of his own age and the mother of a ten-year-old son.

She was Martha Lucy Hennessy, whose family—she was born a Hennessy and had married a Hennessy—was famous in the Cognac region of France as brandy distillers. How and when Jim met her is not known. They undoubtedly had a lot in common and it was probably their mutual interests that brought them together. For besides being a member of the famous Hennessy family—which was attraction enough for a tippler like Jim—Martha was also a keen sportswoman and shared the Queensberry passion for horses. And if sporting interests seemed a flimsy basis for marriage, there was the added enticement of the Hennessy fortunes. Martha might have lacked the charms of youth but with her well-filled purse, her well-stocked stables (she later became the first woman owner of a Derby winner) her house in London and an estate in Scotland, she was not likely to land Jim in the police cells again. All in all, the Queensberry family had every reason to be pleased with Jim's choice of bride.

They turned out in full force for the wedding. The ceremony in the Catholic church at Hawick in Scotland on 4 September 1888 was performed by the bridgroom's brother, Lord Archibald Douglas, and attended by his mother, his sisters, his brothers-in-law, his uncles, his aunts and his cousins. The only notable absentee was the nominal head of the family, the recently divorced eighth Marquess of Queensberry.

[3]

Spineless at the best of times, Jim was quite unable to cope with the responsibilities of marriage. He had none of the qualities expected of a Victorian husband; still less any of those expected of a step-father. Perhaps, had he been allowed to marry the cosseted young girl he had so relentlessly pursued, he might have assumed the role of lord and master more convincingly. Martha Hennessy was used to, and required, more than play-acting. Poor Jim's defects were too deeply ingrained for him to meet the demands of a strong-minded wife; he was not even able to keep up the pretence for long. Almost from the day he moved into his wife's London house, in Kensington Court, he began to display alarming symptoms of instability.

Jim's neurotic behaviour was, at first, put down to crippling attacks of gout. Doubled up in pain, he would sink into fits of depression. These fits, which lasted for days, sometimes weeks, were followed by outbursts of fiendish rage. He would storm about the house, screaming at Martha, snarling at her son and jabbering incomprehensively. Finally, exhausted, he would grab a bottle of brandy and retire to bed to drink himself insensible. Drink only made matters worse: the more he drank the more violent were his tantrums. The local doctor could do nothing. Armed with only a primitive sedative, he was incapable of diagnosing, let alone treating, his patient's condition. Lord James Douglas, he concluded lamely, was 'an exceedingly excitable man.'

Things might have been better had Florrie been at hand to offer advice. She, more than anyone, knew how to handle Jim. She might not have cured his gout but she might, at least, have helped him over his emotional outbursts. Unfortunately, during this critical period, Florrie was in Scotland. Sometime before Jim married, she and Beau—still fighting off their debts—had been forced to give up The Fishery and move to Glen Stuart, on the Kinmount estate, which Queensberry let to them at a nominal rent. They were to live there for the rest of their married life, coming to London only on rare occasions.

So, denied the support of the one person who understood him, Jim floundered even more deeply in his emotional morass. To expect help from his elder brother, Queensberry—the only member of the family still in London—was to expect too much. Queensberry, in his unimaginative way, put all his brother's troubles down to drink. 'I wish your Uncle James did not drink so much,' he would say to his sons, 'he now drinks at least three bottles of brandy a day.' And not only three, or even four bottles of brandy, Queensberry would add, but 'claret and port and champagne.' Later he admitted he was worried by Jim's fits of depression, but his worry stopped short of action. Martha was left to battle with her husband alone.

The battle grew more desperate by the day. There was only one thing certain about Jim's mental condition: it was bound to deteriorate. No cure was possible; the most that could be hoped was that his extraordinary behaviour would not cause a public scandal. It was a forlorn hope. Both Martha and the doctor were convinced 'he might one day commit a rash act.' And there was no telling just how rash that act would be. As it happened, Jim's first public indiscretion was not so much rash as farcical.

At the beginning of 1891 a national census was conducted in Britain. This was the ninth attempt at official head-counting and, as usual, the authorities went to great lengths to ensure that it was as accurate as possible. Detailed instructions on the filling up of the forms were published in the press; the public was repeatedly warned against making false returns. On the whole the campaign was a success. In the London area only two summonses were issued for misinformation. One was against a man who simply stated that he had slept under his own roof with his wife and three children on the night of 16 April and refused to supply any further details. The other was against Lord James Douglas.

The census form returned from 16 Kensington Court was a curious document. Signed in pencil, it gave the householder's name as Lord James Edward Sholto Douglas and described his wife as a 'cross sweep' and a 'lunatic' and his step-son as a 'shoeblack born in darkest Africa.' The handwriting was shaky but sufficiently recognisable for the Registrar General to apply for a summons under Section 20 of the Census Act. The application was granted.

Martha was beside herself. The mere thought of Jim appearing in court was frightening. She was only too aware that, under the slightest pressure, her husband was quite capable of magnifying a rash act with even rasher words. This she was determined to prevent. Steeling herself for an interview with the local Superintendent Registrar, Mr J. H. Rutherglen, she tried to laugh the whole thing off. Lord James, she explained, had been in bed suffering from a severe attack of rheumatism when the census form arrived and, after signing it, had left it to her to fill in the details. She and her son had 'thought it a good joke' to answer the questions with flippant remarks; they had no idea they were breaking the law. This rather lame excuse was supported by Jim. Somehow or other, he was persuaded to write a letter of apology, pay the costs, and fill out another form correctly. As there appeared to be different handwriting on the original return, the summons was withdrawn without Jim appearing before the magistrate.

Only the more sensational newspapers reported the incident; even they dismissed it in a paragraph. The scandal that Martha feared had been averted. But it had been a close thing. Obviously things could not go on as they were. In her desperation Martha turned to Queensberry for advice. The sporting Marquess could only offer a sporting solution. Jim, he suggested, should take a holiday; he should go fishing in Ireland for a week or two and try to forget his troubles. Since he had no idea what those troubles were, it did not occur to Queensberry that it might be dangerous to turn Jim loose on his own. Had he acted more responsibly, had he offered to accompany his brother, things might have taken a different turn. As it was, Jim was left to himself.

Nothing could have been more ill-advised. Melancholy, haunted by nameless fears and tortured by self-doubt, Jim was on the brink of a serious breakdown. It needed only ten days of solitude in Ireland for him to crack-up completely. By the time he returned to Dublin he was a nervous wreck. His behaviour at the Dublin railway station was so strange that an inspector was detailed to travel with him to England. But, by then, Jim was in need of more than one keeper. Pacing dementedly up and down the corridor of the train, he was quite uncontrollable. Shortly after leaving Holyhead, his conduct became even more erratic. During a stop at Stafford, for instance, he suddenly leapt from his carriage, dashed to the telegraph office and sent a wire to the editor of the *Globe* newspaper. It read simply: 'Facts lies—Lord Douglas.' Later the editor was to say that he found the telegram—as well he might—utterly bewildering.

On reaching Euston late that evening, Jim booked in at the station hotel. He was shown to a room in the west wing and, although a waiter claimed that he heard voices coming from the room, he was not seen again.

That same evening both Martha and Queensberry had received telegrams (probably from Ireland) telling them Jim had returned. It was too late for them to do anything then but the next morning they met and decided that Jim should be sent away again—this time to Scotland. Martha contacted the family doctor and both the doctor and Queensberry agreed to go to the Euston hotel. They arrived there shortly after eleven o'clock and were met by the manager who told them that Jim was dead.

His body had been discovered half an hour earlier. A maid had gone to his room with a telegram and, receiving no answer to her knocks, had cautiously opened the door and tip-toed into the room: what she had found there had sent her screaming back into the corridor. Jim was lying in a pool of blood between the bed and the dressing table. His throat was cut from ear to ear.

[4]

The inquest on Lord James Douglas was held at the St Pancras Coroner's Court on 6 May 1891. Queensberry was the first witness. He arrived at the court in a belligerent mood and immediately created a scene. Taking the stand, he pushed aside the Bible and announced that he had no intention

of taking the oath. As an agnostic he insisted upon his right to make a
simple affirmation; not until this had been agreed would he say a word.
Mercifully his testimony was short. He had not, he said, seen his
brother's body at the Euston hotel the day before but had identified it
later. The death had not surprised him because he had long thought his
brother might commit suicide 'as he had shown the greatest depression in
connection with his health.' The doctor said much the same thing. Having examined the body in the hotel room, he had no doubts about the
cause of death. Lord James, he told the court, had 'evidently cut his throat
with the razor found by his side and probably stood in front of the looking
glass while inflicting the wound.' He had been dead for over ten hours.
On the doctor's evidence, the Coroner had no hesitation in returning a
verdict of 'Suicide whilst of unsound mind.'

After the inquest Jim's body was taken to his house in Kensington
Court. Three days later Queensberry accompanied his coffin to Kinmount where he was buried in the family burial-ground.

The funeral was characterised by the customary Douglas blend of the
tragic and the bizarre. The family burial-ground, a wooded knoll across
the fields from Kinmount, was thick with Douglasses, both living and
dead. Notable among the living was Lord Archibald Douglas, who
blithely read the full Roman Catholic burial service over the coffin of a
brother who had taken his own life. Notable among the dead was Lord
Francis Douglas, whose fatal accident on the Matterhorn some thirty
years earlier was commemorated on a marble tablet close to the newly-
dug grave. Notable by his absence was Sir Beaumont Dixie, brother-in-
law and long-time drinking crony of the recently deceased Lord James
Douglas. He was absent for a good reason. With his beloved Jim's death
driving him to consume even more alcohol than usual, Beau had been
packed off to bed by the disapproving Florrie and warned that on no
account was he to attend the funeral in 'that state'. To make doubly sure
that he did not, she hid all his mourning clothes.

But Beau was not to be cheated of paying his last respects. Crawling out
of bed, and having hunted in vain for his mourning clothes, he staggered
off to the village pub where he borrowed a pair of black trousers from a
waiter. That they did not quite reach his ankles bothered him not at all.
Pulling on a dark overcoat, he hired a ramshackle carriage and went
clattering off to the cemetery. He arrived there just as the oak coffin was
being lowered into the primrose lined vault. His family, shocked by the
sight of the unkempt Beau, were more shocked still when, with tears
streaming down his cheeks, he flung himself down by the grave. But he
had one shock still in store.

'My God, how I loved that man;' he shouted, 'we were like a pair of
apes'.

In time, a St Andrew's cross of grey granite came to mark the scene of the day's ceremony. At the foot of the grave was an 'expression of pious hope and solace' from Jim's mother, the Dowager Marchioness, and a strangely moving tribute from Florrie. 'Loved with an undying love by his twin sister Florrie,' runs the inscription. 'Here, where he played in childhood's happy days, he now rests.'

Chapter Twelve

Sons and Lovers

'I have quite given up going out in what is called *English Society*,' Queensberry wrote to his friend Moreton Frewen at the end of 1889, 'they don't understand me and I don't care much about *them*.'

This was typical Queensberry bluster. By saying he had turned his back on society he was trying to make a virtue out of necessity: the truth was, society had turned its back on him. Far from being misunderstood, Queensberry was understood only too well. He was understood to be the guilty party of a divorce and that, in Victorian eyes, was understanding enough. His former sins—his agnosticism, his whoring, his exhibitionism, his appalling conceit and his neglect of his family—had made him socially unpopular, but his divorce turned him into a social leper. If he pretended not to care, it was because pretence was his only option.

But he did care. In matters affecting his self-esteem, Queensberry was very touchy; he could respond violently to the most unintentional slight. To be shunned, even by people he despised, brought all his simmering self-pity to the boil. His black moods, those alternating fits of sullen resentment, towering rage and sulky petulance, which had plagued him throughout his life, became even more pronounced in the years following his divorce. His son, Bosie, whom he occasionally visited at school and university, found it impossible to deal with his father's unpredictable behaviour. Bosie was never quite sure what was expected of him. Lavish displays of fatherly concern and generosity would, for no apparent reason, suddenly sour into bewildering silences. 'He had,' says Bosie, 'a disconcerting way of not listening to and completely ignoring what one said.' Tight-lipped and glowering, Queensberry would sit for hours refusing to answer questions. Bosie had to battle to keep the conversation going. And when the father was prepared to talk he invariably created a scene. 'He was incapable of discussing anything without losing his temper,' claims the equally intolerant Bosie, 'or of understanding any point of view which did not coincide with his own.'

That fatal 'Douglas temperament' which drove his brother, and probably his father, to suicide was no less evident in Queensberry.

His only refuge during these years, the only place in which he really felt at ease, was the short-lived Pelican Club in Gerrard Street. The Pelican

was a popular meeting place for sporting aristocrats—the Dukes of Manchester and Hamilton, Lord Lonsdale and Lord Marcus Beresford were
among its members—but its membership was by no means confined to
the nobility. Actors, journalists, business men and a fair smattering of
chancy speculators were as much in evidence in the Pelican's smoking-
room as any blue-blooded sportsmen. To become a member all one
needed was a lively interest in sport. This not very exacting qualification
allowed many an unfortunate excluded from the more select London
clubs to find a home in the Pelican.

Queensberry was happiest at the Pelican's light-hearted functions.
Proud of his booming baritone voice, he was the star of the rowdy
smoking-room concerts. He would spend hours 'practising' the latest
music-hall songs by hammering out the tune with one finger on the
piano—an accomplishment his family failed to appreciate—and was
never less than word perfect when called upon to sing. One of his more
memorable performances was at a party given by a fellow club member
when, dressed and made-up to look like the popular comedian Albert
Chevalier, he gave a spirited rendering of *Knocked 'em in the Old Kent Road*.
The fact that the party ended with the arrival of the police, after several
champagne bottles had been hurled through the window, in no way
detracted from Lord Queensberry's star-turn.

Fun as it all was, Queensberry's role as a knock-about comic did not last
long. When, in 1892, the Pelican was forced to close, after a scandalous
prizefight, the sporting Marquess was not among those members who
transferred to the more purposeful National Sporting Club. His interest
in sport had become that of a dilettante; he was more in evidence at race
meetings than at gatherings of his fellow enthusiasts. The days when he
was laughingly referred to as the 'patron saint' of boxing had long since
passed.

The same, alas, could not be said for his reputation as a brutish
husband. Sybil had divorced him but she could not escape him. The more
he was shunned by society, the more obsessive became his hatred for his
wife and her family. 'My father,' declared Bosie, 'was a madman, and his
mania was to persecute my mother.'

No longer able to claim his place as the head of his family, Queensberry
changed his tactics. There were still ways in which he could torment his
wife and he exploited them all. His most effective method was to with-
hold the alimony due to Sybil under the divorce settlement. He refused to
pay this until he was threatened with legal proceedings. Time and again
Sybil, who had no other means of support, was forced to resort to lawyers
to get him to pay up and rarely succeeded without a full scale row.
Queensberry was forever complaining that his family was ruining him.

How valid his pleas of poverty were, is impossible to say. He was never
actually short of money but his fortune was decidedly on the decline. In

THE TWINS

1 (a) Lady Florence Douglas (Florrie) in fancy dress as Little Red Riding Hood

1 (b) Lord James Douglas (Jim) in Highland dress

1 (c) Kinmount, seat of the Queensberry family in Dumfries, Scotland, by kind permission of the *Scottish Field*

2 (a) The 18-year-old Lord Francis Douglas, photographed before his fatal accident on the Matterhorn

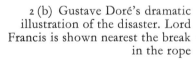

2 (b) Gustave Doré's dramatic illustration of the disaster. Lord Francis is shown nearest the break in the rope

3 (a) The young 8th Marquess of Queens-berry about the time of his marriage to Sybil Montgomery

3 (b) His future father-in-law, the effete and silver-tongued Alfred Mont-gomery

3 (c) His spirited sister Florrie, shortly after her marriage to Sir Beaumont Dixie

3 (d) Phil May's sketch of Lord Queens-berry attacking the punch-bag

4 (a) Florrie in Patagonia 1879
        in full cry at an ostrich hunt

4 (b) The Zulu King, Cetshwayo,
        being interviewed at Oude
        Molen, near Cape Town, by
        Florrie, Beau and Jim

1. The Fishery: Residence of Sir Beaumont and Lady Florence Dixie.   2. Lady Florence Dixie.   3. Wicket-gate where Lady Florence was followed.   4. Spot where the attack took place.

5 Scenes illustrating the celebrated attack on Florrie near the Fishery at Windsor, 1883

6 (a) The Earl of Rosebery at the time of his involvement with Queensberry's eldest son

6 (b) Wilde's 'Screaming Scarlet Marquess', the pugnacious Queensberry in later life

A CASE NOT PROVIDED FOR BY THE "QUEENSBERRY RULES."

"*He the Motive*—and the 'Q' for passion."—*Hamlet.*

"When my 'Q' comes, *don't* call me."
VEZIN'S *Winter's Night's Dream.*

6 (c) A contemporary cartoon of Queensberry challenging Tennyson at a performance of *The Promise of May* at the Globe Theatre, London

7 Oscar Wilde and Lord Alfred Douglas
From a photograph in the William Anderson Clark Library

8 Fighting it out in Piccadilly – the 8th Marquess and his heir, Percy, Lord Douglas of Hawick

1883 it was estimated that his Dumfries estates consisted of 13,343 acres and were worth £13,384 a year. This was considerably less than he had inherited but it was still, for those days, a healthy income. All the same it fell short of his requirements. By 1890 he was so pushed for money that he sold off his Tinwald and Torthowald holdings to a neighbouring land-owner and soon afterwards was seriously considering selling Kinmount. Precisely how he lost so much money is not known. He had no money sense, neglected his estates, gambled, and kept a series of mistresses but he was not exceptional in any of these things. As far as is known his gambling losses were never exorbitant, his mistresses were mostly undemanding actresses and ballet dancers whom he entertained mod-estly, and his spending habits were not excessive. Many a rakish sports-man lived happily on a much tighter budget. One can only assume that, like his ill-starred brother-in-law, Beau Dixie, he was the victim of chancy speculations and chancy business deals.

In any case, Queensberry was never so poor that he could not support his family. The cat-and-mouse game he played with Sybil was inspired by spite, not want. He would use any means to humiliate his wife. Suffering from a form of persecution mania himself, he was driven to persecute others. And, as always, it was his family who suffered most.

Sybil was his first and most obvious target. The children were dragged into his orbit willy-nilly. Their unswerving loyalty to their mother made it inevitable the children should, as they grew older, come under fire from their father.

[2]

Bosie probably saw more of his father at this time than did his elder brothers. When his parents were divorced Bosie was sixteen years of age and at school at Winchester. Although his sympathies during this family crisis were entirely with his mother, he continued to keep in touch with Queensberry after the divorce. This was more a matter of policy than anything else. Whatever his other faults, Queensberry could always be relied on to keep his children well supplied with pocket money. Bosie, never slow in accepting a hand-out, made a point of visiting his father before returning to school.

All the same, Bosie was fully alive to his father's less pleasant traits. He, no less than other members of the family, had been subjected to Queens-berry's tantrums. He had learned to dread those parental rows which reduced his mother to tears and disrupted his otherwise sheltered home life. From a very early age Bosie was made to realise that his pampered existence depended as much on his father's whims as it did on his mother's cosseting. This was never more true than when the time came for him to leave his second preparatory school, Wixenford. At Wixenford he had become passionately attached to an older boy whom he longed to follow to Eton. When his mother tried to arrange this, Queensberry—who until then had shown little interest in the younger boys' education—suddenly put his foot down. Sniffing what he thought to be another 'Montgomery plot' he refused even to consider Eton. He had no intention, Queensberry said, of allowing any son of his to become a 'Belgravian loafer.' That settled the matter. 'His prejudices,' sighed Bosie, 'once formed were as utterly insurmountable as they were unreasonable.'

Bosie could never understand why his father chose Winchester. His first eighteen months at the school were hellish. Victorian public schools being what they were, Bosie would probably have been equally unhappy at Eton but this was something he failed to appreciate. To him Winchester was simply an 'awful place,' a place selected by his father as a form of punishment, a place which destroyed his innocence and corrupted his ideals. He never forgave Queensberry for sending him there.

But if, as he says, he was bullied unmercifully, the fault was not entirely his father's. Bosie had been hopelessly spoilt by his mother and, used to having his own way, was hardly fitted for the boisterous horse-play of the average public school. Nor was he helped by those delicate, somewhat effeminate, good looks inherited from Alfred Montgomery. His bewitching 'prettiness'—his large, limpid eyes, his flaring nostrils, his sensuous mouth, his corn-coloured hair—proved a mixed blessing. On the one hand they made him the target of bullying attacks; on the other they proved invaluable when it came to those activities which he classified as 'neither pure nor innocent.'

In time the bullying ceased. This was partly due to the fact that, despite his delicacy, Bosie proved to be neither a swot nor a sissy. On his own admission, he learned very little at Winchester. And although he never took games as seriously as did most English schoolboys, he excelled at non-team sports such as cross-country running. He even won the two-and-a-half mile steeplechase one year. This sort of achievement was bound to silence the hearties and increase his popularity. Increasing his popularity still further were the visits of his grandfather, Alfred Montgomery. For the elegant old gentleman was always ready—for one reason or other—to take a gang of schoolboys out to tea.

Bosie's more clandestine activities earned him equal popularity. Overcoming an initial reluctance 'to do what everyone else did,' Bosie was soon doing it for all he was worth. Not that his sexual adventures were in any way exceptional at a public school of the period. He was, he protests, in no way 'abnormal' or 'degenerate' or 'wicked' in giving himself over to the pleasure of homosexual love, or rather, play; he reckoned that at least ninety per cent of the boys at Winchester were giving themselves over to the same thing. The only difference was, as time would show, that while most the of boys abandoned such practices once they left school, Bosie's homosexual activities continued into his adult years.

Inevitably, as terms passed, Bosie found himself enjoying Winchester. He made friends (he categorised his friendships as normal, sentimental or impure) he read widely, he gave rein to his growing literary interests by starting a magazine, *The Pentagram*. It had, he boasted, 'a tremendous success.'

So, although Bosie was always to blame his father for sending him to Winchester, when he left there, after four years, at the end of 1888, he could look back on a not unsuccessful period. And Queensberry might well have congratulated himself on Winchester having 'made a man' of his pretty wayward son.

The belief that Bosie had been made a man of, was underlined not long after he left Winchester. Before going up to Oxford, he was sent on a Continental tour with a tutor. It was on this tour that Bosie had his first heterosexual experience. He was staying at an hotel in the south of France and the woman concerned was not only a celebrated beauty but the divorced wife of an earl. This exotic combination proved irresistible to the impressionable Bosie. Without his tutor's knowledge, he embarked on a highly romantic affair with the entrancing countess. Details of this affair are vague—one only has Bosie's word for it—but it ended abruptly one night when the suspicious tutor burst into the lady's bedroom and discovered his tearful 'ewe-lamb' dressed, somewhat disconcertingly, in a hastily borrowed lacy nightgown. Bosie, disgraced but in no way abashed, was immediately sent back to England.

In later years Bosie was to make much of this youthful escapade. Both he, and others, have cited it as proof that his homosexuality was merely a passing phase; his true sexual nature, it is claimed, was late in developing. This, considering his later career, seems highly unlikely.

The fact that some homosexuals can sleep with, and even marry, women, is no proof of late development. More often that not such sexual experiments are simply a gauge of their sensitivity to social pressures. No one welcomes the prospect of living the life of an outcast and, in their desperation to be accepted by society, many homosexuals (particularly Victorian homosexuals) attempt to divert their natural inclinations into more conventional channels. By boasting of heterosexual conquest they offer proof of their 'virility'—both to themselves and others—and disguise a far more complex problem. Such postures are common enough today and were even more prevalent in sexually unenlightened eras. Homosexuality, however, can no longer be thought of as an acquired 'vice' that can be discarded at will or convenience; nor can prolonged homosexual phases—phases independent of artificial environments such as boarding schools or prisons—be dismissed as transitory. The sexual drive is more complicated than that.

In Bosie's case, there can be little doubt that his was essentially a homosexual nature. Whatever the truth of his affair with the countess, it made no difference to his subsequent behaviour. There is no evidence of his conducting a similar experiment or, for many years at least, of his showing the slightest interest in women. It was to require a far more profound experience than a casual heterosexual affair to wean him from his homosexual activities. Even then his apparent 'reform' was never more than superficial. Throughout his life Bosie was happiest in the company of homosexuals.

Bosie went up to Magdalen College, Oxford, shortly before his nineteenth birthday, in October 1899. His life at university differed little from his life at Winchester but, being that much older, he was a great deal happier. Freed from the restrictions of school, he was now able to lead a more relaxed personal life.

He liked to boast that the little learning he acquired at Oxford was come by more or less by accident. His outlook, he says, was mostly sporting. Even allowing for his tendency to exaggerate, this appears to be substantially true. He certainly did not distinguish himself as a scholar but he managed to chalk up a few notable achievements as a runner. In his first year Bosie came second in the two-mile race at the Magdalen College Sports and the following year he won the event outright. Only a clumsily bandaged knee prevented him from realising his cherished ambition of winning the three-mile race in the university sports and getting his half-blue.

As a budding adult he was allowed more freedom during the Oxford vacations, and was now able to indulge his own enthusiasms. These, of course, were mostly sporting. Often he stayed with his mother's sister, Edith, and her husband, George Finch, at their 'glorious' house at Burley-on-the-Hill and from there he kept up the family tradition of hunting with the Cottesmore. He rode well and, though not an expert, was fond of shooting. There was, as one of his biographers put it, 'nothing in the least pansy about him.' During these years Bosie was able to give full rein to his inherited love of sport and gambling.

Social life was every bit as important to him as sport. When he was not staying at country houses, he spent his summer vacations at Homburg with Alfred Montgomery. And Montgomery, proud of his good-looking grandson, made a point of introducing Bosie to his fashionable friends. Not the least of these friends was that regular visitor to Homburg, the Prince of Wales. According to Bosie, the Prince 'made quite a fuss' of him whenever they met for dinner in the Gardens of the Kursaal. Alfred Montgomery was able to open royal doors for him in London as well. Bosie was particulary flattered at being taken to visit the Duke of Cambridge at his house in Piccadilly; one of his more vivid memories was of the elderly Duke slowly nodding to sleep during a dinner given by Alfred

Montgomery at the Travellers Club. If he inherited his love of sport from the Douglas side of his family, Bosie had his 'Grandfather Montgomery' to thank for his love of the high-life.

He was a many-sided, complex young man. Gregarious, lively, given to wild enthusiasms and boisterous friendships, he seemed on the face of things to be the very antithesis of his surly father. But there was more to Bosie than met the eye. His public face in no way reflected his true nature. Left to himself, he could be as sullen, moody and self-obsessed as any member of his family. His sudden outbursts of anger were as frightening as they were unpredictable. Indeed, his mother always maintained that, of all her sons, Bosie was the only one afflicted with the 'fatal Douglas temperament.'

He was also very secretive. There was a hidden part of his life at Oxford which, as his father later discovered, had nothing to do with his sporting activities. At Winchester he had divided his friendships into separate categories and these divisions continued at Oxford. His closest associates were not his sporting cronies but those who appealed to what he called his 'intellectual and artistic side.' Not all, but certainly some of these were practising homosexuals whose proclivities were not confined to the schoolboy fumblings of Winchester. Bosie may have lost his innocence at school, but it was at university that he became worldly-wise. Through his new friends he was put in touch with a classless, far more varied world than any he had ever known.

His initiation into this world was gradual. During his early years at Oxford his 'intellectual and artistic' interests were almost exclusively literary. Encouraged by his success as editor of his school magazine, he continued writing and was delighted when, in 1890, a poem of his was accepted by *The Oxford Magazine*. The poem, *Autumn Days,* immature and derivative as it was, earned him the praise of the Principal of Magdalen College and marked the beginning of his career as a poet.

From these tentative beginnings Bosie advanced, by way of poems published in an undergraduate weekly called *The Spirit Lamp,* to the editorship of the magazine itself. With its glossy, lemon-covered covers carrying more than a hint of daring, even decadence, it is not surprising to find some of the leading homosexuals of the day among its contributors. What is surprising is to find Queensberry's name there. For in one issue Bosie included a poem by his father called 'Lines suggested by Fred Leslie's death.' Occasionally, it seems, Bosie was ready to give his otherwise philistine father his due. He even admitted that Queensberry's poem on another death, *The Spirit of the Matterhorn,* had 'a lot of good lines in it.'

Shining brightest, though, among all the luminaries whom Bosie managed to talk into contributing to *The Spirit Lamp* was that most flamboyant of all contemporary *littérateurs*, his new friend Oscar Wilde.

The two of them had met sometime in 1891. Another homosexual poet, Lionel Johnson, took Bosie to Wilde's house in Tite Street. Johnson, a likeable little man who died of drink a few years later, was one of Bosie's close friends at Oxford and had known Wilde for some months. Whether, as is sometimes said, Johnson was in the habit of introducing Wilde to young men is not certain but he was quick to recognise the advantages of a meeting between Bosie and Wilde. They would, he assured them both, *adore* each other. And he was right.

Wilde, when Bosie first met him, was thirty-seven. He was married, with two sons, and already a dazzling figure in the London world of art, literature and fashion. Although he had not yet achieved fame as a playwright—he was on the point of completing his first theatrical success, *Lady Windermere's Fan*—Wilde was well-known as a poet, essayist and story writer and even better known as a devastatingly witty, outrageously provocative, conversationalist. His audacity had amused fashionable London for years. 'There is only one thing in the world worse than being talked about,' he would say, 'and that is not being talked about.' It was a maxim that had stood him in good stead. In the circles to which Bosie aspired, few men were more talked about than Oscar Wilde.

The claim, made later, that Bosie only agreed to meet Wilde out of curiosity is an obvious understatement. It implies that until he was approached by Lionel Johnson, Bosie was scarcely aware of Wilde's existence. This can hardly be true. If nothing else, Bosie must have known about the controversy which, in June 1890, had surrounded the publication of Wilde's novel *The Picture of Dorian Gray*. This novel, with its thinly disguised homosexual theme, had attracted some severe criticism: criticism to which Wilde had replied in lengthy letters to the press. Given Bosie's literary interests and sexual inclinations it would be surprising indeed if such a titillating public debate had escaped his notice. There can be little doubt that Bosie was as eager to meet Wilde as Wilde was eager to meet him.

Wilde's own eagerness is more easily explained. Bosie was an exceedingly handsome young aristocrat, an undergraduate at Wilde's old university and a dabbler in poetry. With his cult of youth, beauty and art, Wilde could not but respond enthusiastically to Johnson's description of his friend. The fact that Bosie was a lord would have added to his attractions. Wilde, for all his worldliness, could never resist a title.

Their first meeting—despite later colourings—was conducted with great decorum. Johnson introduced them in Wilde's book-lined study, on the ground floor of his Tite Street house, and they chatted politely over the tea-cups. Whatever attraction they felt for each other was kept tightly in rein. But the attraction, according to Bosie, was there. 'Oscar,' he says, 'took a violent fancy—it is no exaggeration to describe it as an infatuation—to me at sight; and although at the beginning of our friendship my feeling for him was nothing like so strong as his for me, I was from the first flattered that a man as distinguished as he was should pay me so much attention and attach so much importance as he apparently did, to all my views and preferences and whims. I adopted the attitude of *enfant gâté* with considerable delight and some amusement.'

Such undertones, however, were not allowed to interfere with conventions when, after tea, Wilde took Bosie to the upstairs drawing-room to meet his wife, Constance. 'I liked her,' remembered Bosie, 'and she liked me.'

There is some confusion about when this meeting took place. Bosie claimed it was in the summer of 1891, but Wilde seemed to think it was earlier that year. Neither of them was very good at dates. For once, though, Bosie may have been right. It is fairly certain that, before Bosie left Tite Street, Wilde invited him to dine at the Albemarle Club a few days later and at that dinner gave him an inscribed copy of *Dorian Gray*. The inscription was dated July 1891.

From then on, according to Bosie, Wilde laid siege to him. Letters, notes and telegrams were accompanied by presents and invitations to lunch or dine; a sonnet which Wilde presented to him in a restaurant was published in *The Spirit Lamp*. It started: 'The sin was mine, I did not understand.' Although there could have been little doubt about Wilde's intentions, it was not until some six months later that, what Bosie coyly calls, 'familiarities' took place. Apparently these were never more than schoolboy gropings: sodomy, Bosie insists, was never attempted. He can be believed. Sexually Bosie and Wilde were incompatible; each was too dominant by nature to submit to the other; theirs was essentially a romantic friendship.

Wilde's version of their early association is somewhat different. He claimed that, far from pursuing Bosie, he saw little of him for several months. During the summer of 1891 he was busy writing *Lady Windermere's Fan*. In the autumn he went to Paris for two months where he completed another play, this time in French, *Salome*. Not until the spring of the following year did Bosie occupy Wilde's full attention and then it was more a matter of necessity than of pursuit. In May 1892 Wilde received 'a very pathetic letter' from Bosie asking him 'to help him in terrible trouble with people who were blackmailing him.' Wilde was taken completely by surprise: 'I hardly knew him at the time,' he says. It was this crisis, Wilde maintained, that brought them closer together.

Why Bosie was being blackmailed has never been revealed. It was undoubtedly a homosexual intrigue but who and what was involved is not known. Whatever it was, Wilde rushed to the rescue. With the help of an eminent lawyer, Sir George Lewis, and a payment of £100, the affair was successfully hushed up. A few years later, however, Queensberry got to hear of it—probably through Sir George Lewis—and it helped to confirm his growing suspicions about his son.

Those suspicions had been quickly roused. The friendship between Bosie and Wilde was soon being talked about. It could hardly not be. For one thing they were such an oddly assorted couple. The huge and paunchy Wilde not only towered above his slightly-built young friend but in manner, dress and presence the two of them were complete opposites. Where Wilde, with his strong features—his heavy-lidded eyes, well-defined nose, thick sensuous lips—was flamboyant and imposing, the dreamy-eyed Bosie had the half-confident, half-diffident air of a gauche undergraduate. Wilde was invariably well-groomed, Bosie was always slightly dishevelled; Wilde wore ornate rings and carried a gold-topped walking stick, Bosie's taste was for straw boaters and white flannels; Wilde radiated good-humour and kindliness, Bosie's expression was often sulky and suspicious. They appeared to be as different in personality as they were in age.

But it was not merely these superficial differences that caused comment. More significant, and more salacious, was the gossip about Wilde's homosexual reputation.

It was gossip which Wilde encouraged. His private life, as Rupert Croft-Cooke has observed, 'was indiscreet to a point of imbecility. He wrote, behaved and talked like a homosexual till his "dining-out" connection became almost a chore from which he escaped to his circle of admirers with relief.' Only among homosexuals did he really feel at home. Fond as he undoubtedly was of his wife, she could satisfy neither his sexual nor his temperamental needs. After the birth of his two sons, Wilde spent less and less time at home.

Far more to his liking were the evenings spent in haunts like the Café Royal where, surrounded by a group of tittering young men, he would hold forth on the delights of male beauty. He made no attempt to disguise his conversation or to discriminate among his listeners. The companions he chose were, considering his position, a very mixed bag. That scurrilous old gossip, Frank Harris—not the most shockable of men—was once astounded to overhear him describing the physical charms of Olympic athletes in ancient Greece to a pair of extremely suspect youths.

Nor was it only hardened muck-rakers like Harris who were scandalised. Oscar Wilde's predilections were discussed in more select circles. When, for instance, he was invited to become a literary member of the exclusive Crabbet Club in 1890—the year before he met Bosie—his 'little weaknesses' provoked some embarrassed amusement. As was usual with the club a devil's advocate was appointed to challenge his membership. The man chosen to oppose him was the future Lord Curzon who, having known Wilde at Oxford, made a point of 'playing with astonishing audacity and skill upon his reputation for sodomy and his treatment of the subject in Dorian Gray.' Sitting next to Wilde was the president and founder of the Crabbet Club, Wilfrid Scawen Blunt, who considered Curzon's attack unfair. 'Poor Oscar,' he noted later, 'sat helplessly smiling, a fat mass, in his chair.' As Wilfrid Blunt was a cousin of Queensberry's former wife, the incident must have been discussed within the Queensberry circle.

It was inevitable that Queensberry, for all his isolation, should get to hear of his son's friendship with Wilde. When he did his reaction was surprisingly subdued. Taking Bosie aside, he told him that he did not think Wilde was a suitable man for him to associate with. His attitude, says Bosie, was light-hearted and 'not unkind or offensive.' Not all Victorian fathers would have been as reasonable; but then Queensberry's relationship with his family was hardly that of a typical Victorian father. Nor, for that matter, was Bosie a typical Victorian son. Headstrong and opinionated, he considered that at the age of twenty-one he was old enough to choose his own friends and wrote to his father saying as much. He pertly begged Queensberry not to interfere. This produced a more characteristic response from Queensberry. He wrote back calling Bosie a fool and a baby who did not know what he was doing. There were further exchanges but eventually Queensberry seemed to tire of the subject and allowed it to drop.

A few months later, probably towards the end of 1892, Queensberry and Wilde met for the first time. The meeting came about by accident and produced an unexpected result. Bosie and Wilde were lunching at the Café Royal when Queensberry walked in and sat at a nearby table. He was alone and does not appear to have noticed his son. However Bosie, with what Wilde called 'great presence of mind,' decided that the opportunity was too good to miss. Going over to his father's table, he invited Queensberry to join him and Wilde. Queensberry at first refused but, after a little pressing from Bosie, he somewhat churlishly agreed. Wilde was delighted. As he well knew, few people could resist him when he set out to charm. Queensberry proved to be no exception. Within minutes the bewitching Oscar had him laughing, smiling and hanging on his every word. The lunch, claims Bosie, was a huge success. Over coffee they got on to Queensberry's favourite topic—Christianity. After that there was no stopping them. So absorbed did Wilde and Queensberry become that Bosie eventually grew bored and left them to it. Wilde later told him that the luncheon went on till past four o'clock and that he had completely won Queensberry over.

And so he had. Two days later Bosie received a glowing letter from his father in which Queensberry confessed that he had been quite mistaken about Wilde. He now thought him a 'charming fellow and very clever' and could fully understand why his son was captivated. His revised opinion had been confirmed by his friend Lord de Grey who knew Wilde and had assured him that he was 'perfectly all right' in every way. There seemed no reason why the friendship should not continue.

Unfortunately, as Bosie ruefully remarked, this 'pleasant state of affairs' was only to last a couple of months.

[3]

Bosie liked to boast that he had 'the Douglas fighting blood and spirit.' The same could not be said for his brother, Francis. As Queensberry's eldest son and heir, Francis held the fatal title of Viscount Drumlanrig and it was his position rather than his personality that earned him the esteem of his family. His brothers always referred to him politely as Drumlanrig and acknowledged his rights as the future head of the family, but that was as far as their respect went. Drumlanrig was incapable of commanding anything more than affectionate regard.

Good looking, conscientious and wholly reliable, Drumlanrig was a singularly unadventurous young man. So timid was he, so little did he stray from the conventional paths, that his mother mistook his caution for earnestness and looked upon him as her one pillar of strength. From the day he was born, she would say, he had not caused her 'to shed a single tear.' This, in the turbulent Queensberry family, was remarkable. But it was a mistaken judgement. If the truth be told, Drumlanrig's qualities were more stolid than solid. He was, as one of his kinsmen remarked, 'a highly nervous boy with considerable charm but no great intellect.'

Neither Harrow, nor Sandhurst, nor the years he spent as a lieutenant in the Coldstream Guards had done anything to improve Drumlanrig's lumpishness. He had a soldierly bearing and was genial and pleasantly mannered, but having said that, one had said everything. He lacked any sort of spark. Why, when he left the army, Lord Rosebery—then Gladstone's Foreign Minister—decided to employ him as his private secretary was something which puzzled many people.

It was certainly not because of his political acumen. His political opinions could, to say the least, be startling. This was something that Lady Paget discovered when they were both guests at Howell Grange, the home of one of his Wyndham relations. At first Drumlanrig's polite, diffident manner impressed Lady Paget. He was always up by eight, writing his letters in the drawing room, and seemed to be 'an excellent, amiable little man.' It was not until they began to discuss politics that she began to doubt his abilities. 'He imparted to me,' Lady Paget wrote incredulously, 'that though he thought Home Rule might turn Ireland into Eden, he knew that the objections to it were so great that it could not become law, and that was the reason his party voted for it!'

Alfred Montgomery seems to have been responsible for introducing

Drumlanrig to Lord Rosebery. Of all the Queensberry children, Drumlanrig was undoubtedly Montgomery's favourite. 'Grandpapa . . . was
absolutely devoted to my brother,' says Bosie. It was Montgomery's
devotion that largely decided Drumlanrig's career. After he left the army
he moved into his grandfather's house in Hertford Street and there he
met most of the prominent members of the Liberal party. The aristocratic
Lord Rosebery (whose sister, Constance, was married to Fanny Montgomery's brother) was very much a man after Alfred Montgomery's heart
and would have been high on his list of suitable friends for his grandson.
That Drumlanrig was hardly qualified to act as Rosebery's private secretary was, in Montgomery's world of political nepotism, of little significance. Had not Montgomery himself, as a young man, been similarly
favoured by the Marquess of Wellesley?

What Queensberry thought of his eldest son's occupation is not
known. They saw very little of each other. The mere fact that Drumlanrig
lived with his grandfather was sufficient to keep Queensberry at bay.
Heir or no heir, his eldest son had allied himself with the 'Montgomery
lot' and that, as far as Queensberry was concerned, placed him squarely
in the enemy camp. Not until he was more directly involved did Lord
Queensberry actively interest himself in the affairs of Lord Drumlanrig
and Lord Rosebery.

This involvement came about almost by chance. In May 1893 Rosebery
decided to seek promotion for his secretary: he wanted Drumlanrig to
become a Lord-in-Waiting to Queen Victoria. This meant, of course, that
Drumlanrig would have to become an English peer. At first Drumlanrig
did not warm to the idea. Knowing how his family had struggled to obtain
an English peerage, and fully aware of how bitterly his father resented
being excluded from the House of Lords, he was not at all happy at the
thought of snatching such a prize from under Queensberry's nose. He
was sure that his father would be furious. According to Bosie, it took the
combined efforts of Rosebery and Gladstone to win Drumlanrig round.
They suggested that he should first approach Queensberry and ask him
tactfully whether he had any objections. Somewhat reluctantly, Drumlanrig made the approach.

Queensberry could not have been nicer. To Drumlanrig's utter
astonishment, he not only welcomed the English peerage but, considering it a feather in the family cap, urged his son to accept. His acquiesence
seemed too good to be true. Drumlanrig remained wary. Only too conscious of how unpredictable his father could be, he insisted that the
agreement be put in writing. He suggested that Queensberry write to
Gladstone giving his consent. Again Queensberry raised no objection.
'He wrote to Gladstone,' says Bosie, 'thanking him and expressing his
great satisfaction at the honour done by Her Majesty to his son.'

That should have settled the matter. But it did not. Within a month

Queensberry had changed his mind and was writing insulting letters to everyone concerned. Sybil, of course, was the first to be attacked. When, on 5 June, Sir Algernon West—Gladstone's private secretary and a great admirer of Alfred Montgomery's—went to see Sybil about the peerage she was very worried. 'Lord Queensberry,' West noted in his diary, 'was for the moment furious, as he himself had not a seat in the Lords as a representative peer and had written a very offensive letter to Mr Gladstone. I promised Lady Queensberry that a soothing answer should be sent.' A soothing answer was sent but it was not soothing enough. Two weeks later Queensberry was still bombarding Gladstone with letters. On 20 June one of these letters was read out at a Cabinet meeting and, according to West, Lord Rosebery strongly advised that it should be ignored. His advice was taken.

Rosebery should have known better. Queensberry was not a man who could easily be ignored. Before long the angry Marquess was hitting out in all directions. Not only Gladstone, but Rosebery himself and even Queen Victoria received inflammatory letters from Queensberry. He informed the Queen, among other things, that he considered Lord Rosebery to be a 'bad influence' on his son. But it was Rosebery who became the main target. It was Rosebery who had initiated the move to make Drumlanrig an English peer and it was Rosebery who came in for the most vicious attacks. Queensberry's hatred for Lord Rosebery is said to have been every bit as intense as his subsequent hatred for Oscar Wilde.

Nor did Queensberry stop at writing letters. A month or so later Rosebery fell ill and his doctor ordered him to take a short holiday at Homburg. He was followed hot-foot by Queensberry. Still beside himself with rage, Queensberry then proceeded to make a public spectacle of himself by prowling about Rosebery's Homburg hotel, threatening to thrash the Foreign Secretary with a dog whip.

Again Rosebery refused to take his threats seriously. Writing to Queen Victoria, he flippantly observed that one of the less pleasant aspects of his labours as a Minister of the Crown was 'to be pursued by a pugilist of unsound mind.' It was not until the Prince of Wales—who was also at Homburg—intervened that Queensberry was persuaded to abandon the idea of attacking Lord Rosebery. That at least is what was commonly believed.

Actually Queensberry's departure from Homburg was arranged in a more forthright manner. The Chief Commissioner of Police was called in to deal with him. 'The Marquess of Queensberry,' the Commissioner pompously informed Rosebery, 'in consequence of the entertainment I had with him, found it advisable to part this morning with the 7 o'clock train for Paris.' Lord Rosebery, it seems, was no longer amused by the Marquess's antics.

This was not the end of Rosebery's involvement with the Queensberry family. The Homburg incident was later believed to have had more sinister undertones. Even at the time there was some confusion about the precise nature of Queensberry's threats. They were said to have little or nothing to do with Drumlanrig's English peerage. Some accounts claimed the two men had quarrelled over the ownership of a horse, others hinted that Queensberry was trying to break up an undesirable friendship. Whatever its cause Queensberry's anger certainly seemed excessive. Could it really have been due to his resentment about the English peerage? This was undoubtedly a sensitive issue but it was an issue he had long learned to live with. Queensberry even took pride in his 'martyrdom' in being excluded from the House of Lords. He frequently boasted about it. The fact that he had originally welcomed Drumlanrig's peerage was not so out of character as it at first appeared. What then had suddenly made him change his mind? Why had a quarrel with the Liberal Government turned into a personal vendetta against Lord Rosebery? Queensberry's motives are never easy to define but later events were to add substance to the suspicions surrounding the Homburg incident.

[4]

Of all Queensberry's sons, his second-born, Percy Sholto—Lord Douglas of Hawick—was far and away the most likeable. An incurable optimist, he had none of those obsessive melancholy traits that so plagued the rest of his family. He was a happy-go-lucky, high-spirited young man, entirely lacking in conceit and blissfully free of the Queensberry churlishness. 'My brother Percy, 'declared Bosie,' 'was the kindest-hearted and sweetest-tempered man I have ever met.' Biased as Bosie undoubtedly was, his judgement is confirmed by others. Most people who knew Percy, loved him.

But, for all his popularity, Percy was no paragon. He had all the failings as well as the virtues of his sunny nature. Generous to a fault, always ready to help others, Percy was quite impractical when it came to handling his own affairs. He lived entirely for the moment, never caring where the next penny came from, borrowing money as easily as he spent it. He had big ideas but no sense of purpose. His hare-brained schemes invariably petered out in a welter of good intentions and unpaid bills. Not that he allowed this to depress him unduly. Failure, for him, was a challenge: it was something he learned to cope with very early in life.

His first failure had occurred in the Royal Navy. At the age of twelve, he, like his father, had been sent to a naval school in Portsmouth and then to the training ship *Britainnia*. Four years later he joined H.M.S. *Triumph*—the flagship of the Pacific station—as a midshipman. He was not to spend long at sea. His naval career ended abruptly in the midst of a carefully hushed up scandal. 'Just what happened,' says his son, 'I have never been able to discover.' It was left to Queensberry to provide the few clues that have survived.

Queensberry, probably because Percy was following in his footsteps, had taken a lively interest in his second son's career. Twice he had travelled to America to visit Percy on the *Triumph*; on one of these occasions he had spent two months aboard the ship. It was then he learned of his son's 'disgraceful' behaviour. 'One admiral,' he was to claim some years later, 'said he [Percy] was not fit to mix with gentlemen, the other that he was damned glad to get rid of him, and when on shore if he was not in hospital I believe bawdy houses were his principal attraction where he used to soak.' From other hints dropped by Queensberry, it would seem that the trouble was caused by a mixture of heavy drinking, bad debts and youthful high spirits. Why this should have shocked Queensberry (of all people) only Queensberry could say; but shocked he claimed to be. He never let Percy forget his disgrace. Nor for that matter, did Percy's senior officers. At the age of nineteen, while still a midshipman, Lord Douglas of Hawick left the Royal Navy with more haste than honour.

But Percy was nothing if not resilient. After returning home for a few months, he launched out in a very different direction. Forgetting the sea, he decided to try his hand at cattle ranching in the north west of Canada. He may have been encouraged by his uncle Archie who, having earlier settled boys from the St Vincent's home in the same area, had a number of contacts in Canada. However it came about, Percy was apprenticed to a wealthy rancher and, optimist that he was, had high hopes of starting a new and lucrative career. His hopes did not last long. Life as a cowboy was more exciting in theory than in practice and the restless Percy soon became bored. Deciding that 'paid work was better than paying to work' he abandoned the ranch for a more rewarding job. He became manager of a roadside canteen on the borders of Alberta and Montana.

Here at least he was his own master. The fact that he was expected to cook, wash-up and clean out the stables, as well as keep order among the rowdy miners, cowboys and whisky-smugglers who frequented the canteen, bothered him not at all. Whatever his other faults, Percy was no snob and had more than his share of the Douglas fighting spirit. He spent several happy months at the canteen and returned to England full of stories about his adventures.

He was then in his early twenties and still without a career. This was nothing unusual in the Queensberry family but for once his father—who seems at this stage to have been fonder of Percy than of his other sons—showed some concern. It was Queensberry who now decided that his second son, having failed as a sailor, should follow his elder brother's example and become a soldier. Willing to try anything once, Percy accepted his father's decision.

Before he could enter the army, steps had to be taken to improve Percy's education. As a naval cadet his schooling had been of the most elementary kind; some intense coaching was required to prepare him for Sandhurst. He was therefore packed off to Cornwall with a suitably qualified tutor. Why Cornwall was chosen was never explained. Queensberry probably hoped that the isolation would encourage his son to study but, if this was his intention, he would have been better advised to send Percy to the outer Hebrides. The attractions of Cornwall proved fatal to Percy's army career. Shortly after he arrived there he met a delightful girl whom he promptly decided to marry.

The girl was Anna Maria Walters, younger daughter of the vicar of Boyton near Launceston. She was charming, pretty and, by all accounts, engagingly modest. Her elderly father, the Reverend Thomas Walters, was a descendant of an 'ancient and gentle' family and in most respects Anna Maria—or Minnie, as she was known—seemed a highly suitable wife for the erratic young Percy. The only objections to the marriage came, not surprisingly, from Queensberry.

Most accounts of Percy's relationship with his father claim that Queensberry took an instant dislike to his future daughter-in-law simply because she was a parson's daughter. Such was his hatred for Christianity, it is said, that he refused even to consider the possibility of his son marrying into a cleric's family. This is only partly true. Queensberry's distaste for the Reverend Thomas Walter's profession undoubtedly intensified his opposition to Percy's marriage but this was not his sole objection. As he was repeatedly to point out, he was genuinely concerned about Percy's inability to support a wife and family. And there can be no doubt that he had reason for his concern.

Percy, after all, was not the most stable of Queensberry's sons. His half-hearted attempts to make a career for himself had proved disastrous; he showed no signs of settling down. Even his decision to marry at this time seemed to indicate that he was not taking his preparations for the army seriously. He was entirely dependent upon an allowance from his father and by marrying Minnie Walters he would be adding to his own, as well as Queensberry's, burdens.

Queensberry claimed that he pointed all this out to Percy in the kindest possible manner. When he heard of the intended marriage he was staying in Monte Carlo—where he had gone after his expulsion from Homburg—and he wrote to his wife saying he did not object to Percy seeing 'his girl' from time to time but there could be no question of marriage. 'I could not have you living down there altogether,' he later told Percy, 'and doing nothing for yourself, thereby hinting that did you do something for yourself and were in a position to marry I should withdraw my objection.'

His hints, unfortunately, were not appreciated. Sybil did not reply to his letter and Percy became more determined than ever to marry. This blatant defiance of his authority incensed Queensberry.

Percy married Minnie Walters at Royston in Cornwall on 11 September 1893. The fact that the wedding attracted a fair amount of publicity did nothing to soothe the absent Queensberry. 'Why indeed,' he exploded in one of his letters to Percy, 'if you were going to marry in this way should you not have married quietly as thousands of other young men have done before?' The entire affair, in his opinion, was just another Montgomery plot designed to hold his authority 'up to the derision of the whole country.'

This was the unpardonable sin. Only a few weeks earlier Queensberry had been made to look a fool at Homburg, now he was again exposed to ridicule. His sons seemed to take a fiendish delight in flaunting their contempt for him. Nothing could be more certain to provoke Queensberry's wrath. The fury with which Queensberry now turned on Percy was every bit as blind and unreasoning as that with which he had so recently pursued Lord Rosebery.

According to Percy's son, a veritable 'cascade of vitriolic letters' poured in upon the hapless newly-weds immediately after the wedding. Percy was roundly abused for his obstinacy and dismissed as a cowardly spoilt child ('white-livered' was Queensberry's favourite epithet for Percy). His young wife was even more viciously attacked. Queensberry saw Minnie Walters as a scheming adventuress who had deliberately trapped Percy into marriage for the sake of his title and possible fortune. He was convinced that she had been encouraged in this by her Christian father. Later he was to write to the Reverend Thomas Walters accusing his 'stuck-up, pauper, impertinent daughter' of 'forcing herself into my family and marrying my son, a mere boy and younger than herself, in defiance of my consent.' As always, Queensberry's uncontrollable temper completely smothered his genuine concern for his son's well-being.

Percy never forgave Queensberry for these attacks. Whatever his other shortcomings, he was not white-livered nor was he a 'mere boy.' He was a spirited young man, almost twenty-five when he married, and fully prepared to stand up for himself. While he might have overlooked the abuse hurled at himself, he could not stand by and have his wife attacked. Ignoring Queensberry's threats to cut off his allowance, he turned his back on the army and struck out in another direction. This time he decided that he could make his fortune as a tea-planter. A few months after his marriage he left England for Ceylon.

Once again, however, Percy's ambition outran his staying powers. Hardly had he arrived in Ceylon than he met the Honourable David Carnegie—the youngest son of Lord Southesk—who was full of exciting stories about the Coolgardie gold rush in Western Australia. It took little to persuade the rainbow-chasing Percy that gold offered a quicker return than tea and he quickly fell in with Carnegie's plan to set off for the new El Dorado. 'All my life,' he was to claim, 'I have been an explorer and prospector; I was one of the first men in the rush to Coolgardie.' This might have been a slight exaggeration but he certainly arrived in Australia when the pickings were good. The fortune he made on the gold fields was the first of his many ill-fated speculations; it was dissipated almost as quickly as it was accumulated.

But, for the time being, it kept him out of his father's clutches. Queensberry was forced to look for other ways to keep the family vendetta alive.

Part Three

Chapter Thirteen

Florrie Resurgent

'Lady Florence Dixie,' commented a newspaper shortly after the alleged attack on Florrie at Windsor, 'will presumably cease to concern herself with public or political affairs confining herself to those spheres of literary activities which are the rightful domain of her sex.'

Nothing could have been wider of the mark. Florrie had not the slightest intention of abandoning her public crusades, let alone of settling down to the life of a genteel lady novelist. Once the furore had died down she bounced back again with all her old resilience. In January 1884 she was featured in *Vanity Fair* as 'a true representative of the great family to which by birth she belongs.' The article appeared in the magazine's 'Men and Women of the Day' series. It was accompanied by a full page illustration of Florrie perched somewhat woodenly on a sofa and looking anything but abashed. She was described in the article as 'generous, chivalrous, warm-hearted, thoroughly loyal, very energetic, and very impulsive and her courage, physical as well as moral, has often been severely tried and never found wanting.' Those who prophesied the eclipse of Lady Florence Dixie were forced to think again.

For a while Florrie remained as active as ever. Her unfortunate confrontation with the Land League in no way prevented her voicing her opinions on Ireland. She continued to advocate self-help for the Irish peasants and to champion Home Rule—in fact she went further and demanded Home Rule throughout the British Empire under an Imperial Federation. The greatest need for any country, she argued, 'is Home Rule. Without it there is a dreary dearth of progress, prosperity or reform. Self-government is a great moral necessity and natural law.'

But she needed more than a brave face to live down the Windsor fiasco. She was now regarded as an amusing eccentric rather than a serious reformer. Comment on her activities was invariably tinged with ridicule. More than ever she found it difficult to get a hearing for her unfashionable views. Even when she did appear to take the advice of her critics by writing a novel—*Waifs and Strays: or, the Pilgrimage of a Bohemian Abroad*—she had trouble in finding a publisher. The book was eventually taken by an obscure Edinburgh firm and passed almost unnoticed by the English press. Her brief spell of notoriety, it seemed had put an end to her literary ambitions.

Things were not helped by her precarious financial position. There was little hope of her launching one of her spectacular crusades in the wilds of Scotland.

Still the move to Scotland was not without its compensations. All her life Florrie prided herself on being a country woman; Glen Stuart occupied a very special place in her affections. It was the house which had provided her with an anchor in her restless childhood; she and Jim had always returned there with undisguised delight.

Life at Glen Stuart meant, if nothing else, a return to the joys of her childhood. There she could recapture the thrills of galloping across the moors, of climbing the tors and wading the streams. She had lost none of her love of the chase; the article in *Vanity Fair* had emphasised her many sporting achievements. 'In horsemanship,' it had pointed out, 'she is magnificent and unrivalled. . . . She is a skilful and admirable whip, a rare shot, and a splendid swimmer.' For some years her preoccupation with politics had caused her to neglect these skills; now she could look forward to days of carefree hunting, shooting and fishing. When all was said and done, she was still very much a Douglas.

And, for some time, a Douglas she remained. She put away her pen, took up her gun and forgot about the politics of Ireland and Africa. She was then in her early thirties and still young enough to spend a full day in the field or, as she put it, 'tramp the turnips after partridges and heather after grouse.' Yet, exhilarating as it all was, her heart was not really in it. There was an element of play-acting about her hunting activities. She did what was expected of her but she did it more and more reluctantly. The truth was, her love of sport could no longer smother her humanitarian instincts; she was beginning to find the meaningless slaughter of animals repugnant.

It was therefore inevitable that, needing a cause that would engage her heart and mind as well as her skills, Florrie should find one in the sporting field. Her growing distaste for the killing of wild life developed into a positive loathing of blood sports.

Her conversion was gradual but not entirely unexpected. As a child she had shuddered at the sight of her dying prey and in Patagonia she had been chastened by the painful, long drawn-out death of a golden antelope. 'The memory of those scenes,' she confessed, 'brings no pleasure to my mind. On the contrary, it haunts me with a huge reproach, and I fain I never had done those deeds of skill—and cruelty.' But, troubled as she was, Florrie had always managed to stifle her misgivings. It was not until she returned to Scotland that she questioned her reputation as a 'female Nimrod.'

A turning point came when Florrie was involved in an incident similar to her experience in Patagonia. She and a 'man friend' (probably Beau) were on a day's hunt in a remote part of Scotland. They were after red deer but had had no luck until they climbed some rocks and spotted a herd grazing on the moor below them. 'There were several stags,' says Florrie, 'but one in particular, a magnificent "royal", evidently the lord of the harem, was feeding broadside on us.' They watched for several minutes until the deer were startled by the sudden cackle and flight of a solitary grouse. Florrie's companion, who had been preparing to shoot, was furious. Leaping to his feet, he took hurried aim and fired. The stag stumbled to its knees, got up, trotted towards a jagged rock and collapsed. At the same moment the man fired a second shot. 'I have wounded another,' he shouted to Florrie, 'see to this one, while I go after the other.' The next moment he was gone.

Florrie ran down to the wounded "royal." She was appalled at what she found. 'He was groaning terribly,' she says, 'his red tongue lolled from his mouth and he rolled about, apparently in agony. Large tears dimmed his dark eyes as they fixed themselves upon me in their terror. I was horrified. I had nothing about me wherewith to end his pain. No knife, no rifle, and I was powerless. It was a scene which filled me with loathing and disgust. How different to the peaceful one we had come to disturb, and on which I had gazed a few minutes since.'

For twenty minutes she sat stroking the terrified animal's head. Then her companion returned. He had killed his second stag and was completely bewildered by Florrie's distress. 'He knew me as a sportswoman; he could not understand my sudden horror,' she later recalled. 'But he came on quicker, and in a few minutes the poor, groaning stag was put out of its pain.'

Florrie's pain was not so easily ended. Although she was not directly responsible for the stag's suffering, she was completely overcome with remorse. Somehow this incident, more than any other, came to symbolise for her the barbarity of what she had once regarded as a civilised pastime.

Laying down her gun, she picked up her pen. In the wilds of Scotland she discovered a new cause, a cause which had nothing to do with politics but which answered her deeply felt need to expose the corruption of human nature. The letters, the articles, the tracts that she now wrote in defence of animals were every bit as intense, every bit as challenging, as those she had written to defend the rights of Cetshwayo and the Irish peasants. They were also every bit as unpopular. For with Florrie the best method of defence was always attack and the attack she now launched was aimed directly at her own kind—the British aristocracy.

Reform was called for; and that reform, she argued, must start with the young. What good could come to a nation whose ruling class encouraged blood lust among its own sons and daughters? 'Much of this barbarous taste and callous indifference to the sufferings of animals,' she wrote in a

pamphlet published by the Humanitarian Society, 'is bred with our childhood and upbringing. Youth, especially of the male sex, is taught to
regard shooting and hunting as manly accomplishments, without which
a man is regarded rather as a "poop" than otherwise. Women, myself
included, are, in many instances, brought up to indulge in sporting
amusements, and it follows, as a natural sequence, that in a large majority
of cases where this is so, a callous indifference to the agony and misery
caused to the victims is imperceptibly engendered. . . . The young must
be taught to be kind and to be merciful, and if they are so taught they
cannot reconcile their consciences to Sport.'

Never one to duck an issue, Florrie was quick to recognise the implications of her anti-bloodsport convictions. To condemn the killing of wild-
life and, at the same time, turn a blind eye to other forms of animal
exploitation was in her opinion not merely illogical but hypocritical.
Cruelty to animals had to be challenged in whatever guise it presented
itself. Acknowledging this, she broadened her attack to include all
practices that involved the suffering of animals. She became a convinced
opponent of vivisection, she denounced the use of skins and furs for
clothing and was particularly incensed by the fashionable craze for dec-
orating women's hats with feathers and stuffed birds. And, of course, she
became a vegetarian.

Her daily diet, she proudly announced in a newspaper interview, was
bloodless. Nothing would induce her to eat produce obtained by the
slaughter of animals. 'For breakfast,' it was reported, 'she had a slice of
melon, a banana or two, almonds and raisins, dates, and a tumbler of milk
with the white of egg whisked in it. She took nothing more till about 4.30
p.m., when she had a slice of pineapple, or some other fruit in season,
bananas, figs, Brazil nuts or almonds, and a little unfermented bread,
with butter and milk and egg as before.' That was all she ate and all she
needed. The consumption of meat, she insisted, was a relic of man's need
to gratify a 'still-lingering savage instinct.'

[2]

With Florrie one enthusiasm tended to kindle another. Her much
publicised journalistic ventures in South Africa had led her to champion
the luckless Cetshwayo; her fight on behalf of the homeless Irish peasant
had developed into a full scale war against the Land League. In the same
way her campaign against bloodsports and all forms of animal cruelty
helped to focus her attention on other injustices—not the least being the
shameful restrictions imposed upon Victorian women. Having battled all
her life on behalf of others, she now emerged as a fervent champion of her
own sex.

Her support for the feminist cause was not entirely a matter of chance.

It was something she had pondered over for years. Like many another educated woman of her generation she was greatly influenced by the publication, in the mid-1860s, of John Stuart Mill's famous book, *The Subjection of Women*, which highlighted the hardships suffered by women under the existing laws of marriage and property. The Victorian wife, Mill argued, was nothing more than the 'bond-servant of her husband, no less so far as legal obligation goes than slaves.' This was a truth that Florrie had taken to heart. The fact that her own husband was singularly un-masterful did not prevent her emphasising the 'slave' theme in her demands for sex-equality. Reform of the law was called for, and she called for it with characteristic vigour. 'Woman,' she thundered, 'submits and acquiesces in her slavery. She is a helot; she has no voice in the framing of the law, no right to assume governing powers, no representation in the councils of the world. Even her own person is denied her. Body and soul she is the property of others. She has no right in herself.'

Once again Florrie found herself at odds with her family. Although her mother—who now lived with her at Glen Stuart—was vaguely sym-pathetic, her sister Gertrude was openly hostile to any suggestion of equality between the sexes. A woman's first duty, Gertrude insisted, was to her husband and family; anyone who spelt Woman's Rights 'in capital letters' was undermining the basis of Christian society. Such arguments merely spurred Florrie on. In her opinion Christian society was so male-orientated, so repressive for women, that it was the duty of all right-minded females to undermine it. 'This religion,' she wrote in her intro-duction to *The Religion of Women* by Joseph McCabe, an apostate Catholic priest, 'dominates many nations of the earth, and, wherever it prevails, the laws governing woman are in accordance with Bible precepts. . . Science owes nothing to Christianity, which has fought against it tooth and nail; yet to scientific reasoning, and not to Bible reasoning, woman must turn to prove her earth-born rights. By religion and ignorance these rights are condemned and ridiculed. By the reasonings of science they are admitted and upheld. . . . It is for men to give Woman freedom, even as it is her bounden duty to demand it as her right. Let reason be her guide and Truth her beacon.'

Yet, passionately as she believed in the need for women to assert themselves, Florrie was reluctant to commit herself to any of the brave but faltering women's organisations that were then working for female suffrage. For one thing her isolation in Scotland prevented her from taking an active part in these organisations, for another she did not see enfranchisement as the sole answer to the plight of women.

It was not that she did not recognise the importance of the vote—indeed, Rider Haggard described her as 'a proto-suffragette'—but rather that her approach to women's rights was broader and more philosophi-cal. Enfranchisement, desirable as it was, could only produce limited results. The most recent extension of the male franchise—the Reform Bill of 1884—had given the vote to every householder, including agricultural labourers, but it was still based on property and, as few women were property owners, the benefits they would obtain from inclusion were minimal. What was required was an all-out attack on the very structure of male dominated society. Not merely parliament but every bastion of male privilege needed to be assailed. One of Florrie's more revolutionary demands was that the army and navy should be thrown open to women. She preached this incessantly but was given little support. The War Office, it is said, 'thanked her for her suggestion, but left it in their pigeon holes.' As always, her thinking was considered a little too eccentric to be taken seriously. That she was a step or two ahead of the progressive movements of her time did not inspire confidence.

The only organisation she openly supported was the Rational Dress Society. This society, closely allied to the women's rights movement, was formed in 1881 with Viscountess Harberton as its president. Its primary aim was to liberate women from the tyranny of fashion and promote 'a style of dress based on considerations of health, comfort and beauty.' Among the reforms it advocated was the adoption of divided skirts and petticoats and the abandonment of tight fitting corsets, high-heeled or narrow-toed shoes; any type of heavily weighted clothing which interfered with healthy exercise was frowned upon. Many of its members were vegetarians. Worthy as were its aims, the Rational Dress Society was not favoured by all women involved in the struggle for emancipation. Some veteran campaigners, like the redoubtable Lydia Becker, considered loose dresses to be nothing more than an affectation. 'Stick to your stays,' cried Miss Becker, at a dress reform meeting, 'they improve the form, give warmth and assist you. Stick to your stays, ladies, and triumph over the other sex.'

For Florrie, though, the Rational Dress Society provided the means by which she could proclaim her convictions. She had never bothered overmuch about appearances. The severely cut serge jacket and short divided skirt she had worn for most of her South African jaunt had become so shiny that Sir Evelyn Wood had jokingly christened it 'the looking glass.' Many of her neighbours at Windsor had been shocked by her mannish style of dress, her short cropped hair, her polo caps and her tyrolean hats. Now she was able to dress as she liked as a matter of principle. By ignoring fashion she could assert her individuality and, at the same time, register a protest against the exploitation of animals for 'mindless female adornment.' Outlandish as her clothes sometimes appeared, she wore them with the authority of a crusader.

'Though she did not take as active a part as Viscountess Harberton,' remembered a journalist, 'in the movement in favour of so-called "rational dress", she was one of its firmest and most consistent supporters.

She held that costume should be suited to the purpose or the occasion, and her own dress was always chosen with this idea in view.' Just how suitable her clothes were on some occasions was, however, open to question. The shapeless white boating dress she wore on one of her rare appearances at Ascot, for instance, so startled the Prince of Wales that he asked her whether she had come in her night-gown by mistake. 'No, sir,' she answered pertly, '—a comfortable dress.'

But it was the publication, in 1890, of Florrie's novel, *Gloriana: or, The Revolution of 1900,* that attracted widespread attention to her feminist beliefs. This novel—a curious mixture of prophetic fantasy and political dialectic—summed up her views on the false position in which women found themselves. She allowed her imagination to run riot. Her tough-minded heroine is the daughter of an army captain who had married after an elopement. The girl wishing to go to Eton, acquires boy's clothes and is admitted to the school as 'Hector d'Estrange.' She becomes an outstanding scholar and, still disguised as a man, goes up to Oxford where she achieves the highest honours in the shortest possible time. ('Never before had a youth risen so rapidly in the scale of success.') Her later accomplishments, both in the hunting field and in parliament, are every bit as remarkable. At the age of twenty-eight, Hector d'Estrange becomes Prime Minister and the people's favourite; his later hair-raising adventures prove his 'manhood' beyond doubt. In the end, however, convention triumphs; the masquerade ends, and the book closes on a happy marriage. The moral is obvious: prejudice alone subjects women to male dominance and equality between the sexes can only be achieved by removing that prejudice.

The relative success of this novel restored Florrie's confidence. Once again she found she could command attention. She became more vocal, more demanding. In articles and letters to the press, and occasionally at public meetings, she campaigned for sex-equality. She advocated co-education. She called for the revision of the marriage service and the divorce laws. She maintained that as regards both the Throne and the peerage, the succession should go to the eldest born, not the eldest son. She never allowed a slight on women's status to pass unchallenged. When Rider Haggard published his novel *Beatrice* she wrote him a long letter criticising the servility of his heroine.

'It is only another book,' she complained, 'in the many which proclaims the rooted idea in men's minds that women are born to suffer and work for men, to hide all their natural gifts that men may rule alone. . . . Great and in many ways does woman err in all paths of life—but is she entirely to blame? You men have made her your plaything and slave: She is regarded more in the light of a brood mare than anything else; and if within her narrow sphere she errs, who is to blame? Not her, believe me, but the false laws that made her what she is.'

As of old, she would allow nothing to swerve her from her course. When, in 1893, she was offered a huge sum—some reports put it as £135,000—to start a new woman's daily paper, she turned it down because the proprietor insisted that 'considerable space would have to be devoted to fashion, fashion's dress, and other rubbish.' 'I told him,' she said indignantly, 'that not all the gold of the Indies would induce me to debase womankind by helping to pander to such degrading tastes.'

Having regained her political stride, nothing could stop her. It was not long before she was hitting out as passionately as ever. Her main concerns were now for the protection of animals and the rights of women, but this did not mean that she had forsaken her old loyalties. She continued to follow events in Ireland and Africa. Africa, in particular, was never far from her thoughts.

Her interest in the Dark Continent, however, was more constant than her loyalties. When, in 1893, white troops marched against the Matabele King, Lobengula—in the country that later became Rhodesia and is now Zimbabwe—Florrie displayed an astonishing change of face. Far from showing sympathy with the black monarch, she was vociferous in her support for the white army. Indeed, the vehemence with which she denounced the hapless Lobengula smacked strongly of the racialism she had once so roundly condemned. 'Who is this Lobengula,' she fumed in one of her endless letters to the press, 'that such screams of pity should rend the air on his account? A clever crafty savage, a bloated pampered autocrat whose life is spent in sensuality and self gratification. A fat, tub-shaped monstrosity, whose word has brought death and desolation and sorrow to thousands.' Admittedly she claimed to despise Lobengula because of his reputed persecution of his black subjects, but then the same accusation had been levelled at Cetshwayo. With Lady Florence Dixie personal prejudice always tended to override political principle.

[4]

Florrie and her mother were not the only members of the family living in Scotland. The late 1880s saw the return of two other Douglas exiles. First to arrive was Florrie's brother Archie who, in 1887, was sent to Dumfries to take up missionary work.

The sensation created by Gertrude's marriage had not harmed Archie's standing as a priest. By and large the rumpus was regarded as a purely family affair and was quickly forgotten. For the next five years Archie had continued with his work of training boys at the St Vincent's Home and settling them in Canada. His dedication had earned him the respect of all concerned. It had not always been easy. Short of staff and money, he had been forced to shoulder most of the work himself and, at times, he had faced some discouraging risks. One of his more spectacular adventures had occurred during a trans-Atlantic crossing, when his ship was wrecked and he and the rest of the passengers were stranded on a rock for several hours before being rescued. But, for the most part, his work entailed more drudgery than danger; after completing ten years at St Vincent's he decided he needed a change. At heart he was still very much a Catholic convert—he was very active in various Church organisations and was an enthusiastic member of the Guild of Our Lady of Ransom— and his proselytising instincts played an important part in his decision to try his hand at missionary work in Scotland. After applying for the transfer, his position at St Vincent's was taken over by a distant cousin, Father Douglas Hope, and he was appointed to the Diocese of Galloway.

Missionary work provided plenty of scope for Archie's love of novelty. Among his many innovations was a 'conveyance like a gipsy van' which he devised for touring the isolated districts and which served him as a portable chapel. Unorthodox as his methods sometimes appeared, his sincerity was never in doubt and soon he became well-known as a preacher and as a catechist for Catholic converts and children. His popularity was undoubtedly helped by his family's romantic reputation. Aristocratic converts to Catholicism were sufficiently rare in Scotland for the name of Douglas to attract attention; a Catholic Douglas, touring the districts where, as one newpaper put it, 'his ancestors had played a less peaceful part in history,' could hardly escape notice.

In all events, Archie's popularity served him well. It eventually led to his being appointed Canon of St Columba's Church in Annan, a few miles from Kinmount. He was to remain as Canon of St Columba's for the next fourteen years.

If Archie can be said to have achieved his ambition, the same cannot be said for his sister Gertrude. Marriage had done little to brighten Gertrude's sad, unresolved life. Her return to Scotland was more a matter of neces-sity than of choice.

The high hopes with which Gertrude and young Tom Stock started their married life quickly evaporated. Neither of them was equipped to make a success of the little bakery shop they opened in Hammersmith. Tom Stock had the skill and Gertrude the enthusiasm, but they both lacked experience and business sense. Before long they ran into financial trouble; their capital—derived mainly from Gertrude's meagre allow-ance—began to dwindle alarmingly. In the end they were forced to look for a cheaper place to live. Resignedly they decided to follow Florrie's example and move to Scotland.

Gertrude managed to scrape together enough money to buy a small property called Barkerland—which she piously renamed Maryland— near Dumfries and they set up as market gardeners. Again their lack of experience proved an obstacle. The training Tom Stock received at St

Vincent's did not extend to gardening and nothing in Gertrude's clois-
tered career had prepared her for life as a smallholder's wife. For a while,
though, they did their best to make a go of things.

To help out the finances, Gertrude began writing again. Under her
married name of Lady Gertrude Stock she published a couple of three-
volume novels. One, *Nature's Nursling*—dedicated to Florrie 'In Memory
of the Past'—was partly autobiographical and contained a poetic description of Kinmount as well as a moving account of her brother Francis's
death on the Matterhorn. But its appeal was limited. 'Embodying, as it
does, some interesting pages of family history . . .' remarked the *Dumfries
and Galloway Standard,* 'and glimpses of the homelife by the Solway,
reproduced under the most transparent of veils, it attracted special
interest in this district.' Unfortunately that interest was not sufficient to
ensure its success. *Nature's Nursling* was notable more for its piety than
for its popularity. It added little to Gertrude's income.

Bleak as were Gertrude's prospects, her husband's were even bleaker.
Tom Stock was a thoroughly disillusioned young man by the time he
moved to Scotland; his marriage had brought him nothing but disappointment. Still in his early twenties, young enough to look forward to an
exciting life, he found himself burdened with an ageing, somewhat prim
wife with whom he had nothing in common. Gertrude at least had her
writing and her family to divert her and she could turn to the Church for
consolation; young Stock, practically penniless in alien surroundings,
had no distractions. It was hardly what he could have expected when he
married into the Douglas family. That Tom Stock became increasingly
bored, discontent and restless is not surprising.

Finally he could stand it no longer. In 1890 the Chartered Company's
occupation of Mashonaland brought southern Africa into the news and
young men everywhere were stirred by visions of high adventure. Tom
Stock was no exception. He decided that Africa offered greater opportunities than Scotland and, not able to afford the fare to Cape Town,
volunteered for the Bechuanaland Police. He left Britain sometime in
1891. Whether he intended to return is not certain but Gertrude seems to
have had no doubt that he had gone for good. His departure was a blow
from which she never recovered.

Unable to continue at Maryland on her own, Gertrude left Scotland
shortly after her husband. Once again she sought refuge in a convent.
This time, though, she did not take vows but merely became a paying
guest at St Joseph's Convent at Hendon, near London. St Joseph's was
run by the Congregation of Poor Handmaids of Jesus Christ, a religious
order that had come to England from Germany in 1876 and ten years later
had opened a guest house for impoverished genteel Catholic ladies. It
seemed to offer, if not a solution to Gertrude's problems, at least an
answer to her immediate needs. Alas, the answer came too late. Within

months of entering the convent, Gertrude contracted a disease of the lungs from which, for all the nursing of the nuns, she was unable to recover. She died on 25 November 1893, aged fifty-one.

Chapter Fourteen

Family Scandals

Shortly before Gertrude's death—two and a half weeks before, to be precise—another important event occurred in the Queensberry family. On 7th November 1893, the divorced eighth Marquess of Queensberry married for the second time.

The Queensberry wedding, at Eastbourne in Sussex, was very much a hole-in-the-corner affair. Not until four days later did the *Eastbourne Gazette* tersely announce: 'The Marquess of Queensberry married on Tuesday. . . . The marriage was by licence and private.' That was all that could be said at that stage. It took a great deal of snooping by local reporters to discover further details, even then their reports were more speculative than informative. For once, and not without reason, the publicity-seeking Marquess was playing his cards close to his chest.

His bride was Miss Ethel Weeden, the youngest daughter of the late Mr Charles Weeden 'a gentleman of independent means.' Not much was known of her father, who had died some years earlier, but her mother had married for a second time and was now Mrs de Courcy Atkins, wife of a well-known member of the local Liberal party. The family lived at Park Villa, College Road, and were highly respected in the prim Eastbourne community. Mrs Atkins was a pillar of the fashionable St Saviour's Church and her two elder daughters were shining lights at the church's weekly 'Penny Readings.' About young Ethel, though, little could be unearthed. Reporters had to content themselves with lyrical descriptions of her undoubted good looks. 'She is tall,' enthused one of them, 'posesses an admirable carriage, has a charming complexion, and a mass of wavy fair hair. She is a well-known figure on the Eastbourne parade, and invariably attracts an admiring gaze.' Just how this statuesque beauty had attracted the admiring gaze of the lecherous Marquess was anybody's guess.

Whether, as was hinted, Queensberry had simply picked up young Ethel on the Eastbourne parade was never clearly established. It seems as good an explanation as any. Queensberry was staying at the Clifton Hotel at the time and the chances of his being conventionally introduced to the daughter of a respectable provincial family were remote. He and Mr and Mrs de Courcy Atkins moved in very different circles. One thing is certain, his courtship of Ethel Weeden was hurried, secret and definitely not encouraged by her parents.

None of Ethel's family was present at her wedding in the Eastbourne Register Office and it seems unlikely that they knew about it. Apart from the Registrar and his deputy, the only witnesses at the furtive ceremony were a Mr J. Hillman and Queensberry's valet Tom Gill (the same Tom Gill who, six years earlier, had provided the evidence for Queensberry's divorce). It was all very different from the fashionable bustle that had accompanied the Marquess's marriage to Sybil Montgomery.

Queensberry's friends thought it quite extraordinary. When news of the wedding leaked out, the gossip columnists were delighted. What, it was asked, was the reason for such secrecy? Could it be that the Marquess, whose views on marriage were notorious, was about to put his bizarre theories into practice? Or was he now settling for a more conventional union? Much of the speculation was based on a lecture he had given at the St James's Hall, Piccadilly, a few months earlier. In this lecture Queensberry had startled his audience by advocating what he called 'a sort of plurality of marriage.' Precisely what he meant by that was uncertain; his reasoning, as usual, was extremely muddled. 'The lecture,' complained one newspaper, 'was expected to be amusing, but it proved to be merely boring.' All the same, it had aroused sufficient interest for it to be remembered and applied to his marriage to Ethel Weeden. Even his sporting cronies confessed to being shocked.

In one of his impassioned diatribes, Bosie was later to claim that his father had married Ethel Weeden when she was only seventeen and, he said, '*on the following day* he deserted her.' Like so many of Bosie's accusations against Queensberry, this is probably an exaggeration. His knowledge of his father's marriage came mostly from hearsay and may well have been distorted. His account, however, could contain a grain of truth. The reports of Queensberry's wedding are vague about Ethel's age—they describe her as 'a young lady just over 21 years'—and Queensberry's marriage certificate puts both bride and bridegroom as being of 'full age.' But it seems fairly certain that Ethel was younger than was claimed. She appears in fact to have been under-age. As she was married without her family's consent, the validity of the marriage was open to question. Whether Queensberry 'deserted' her the following day or whether, as seems more likely, her family stepped in and demanded an immediate separation is impossible to ascertain. Whatever the truth, the newly-weds were soon parted—the marriage may not even have been consumated—and shortly afterwards proceedings were started to have the marriage annulled.

Ethel Weeden's petition to have her marriage to the Marquess of Queensberry declared null and void came before the President of the Probate, Divorce and Admiralty Division on 24 October 1884. The petitioner was represented by Messrs Inderwick and Pollen and a Mr Deane appeared for Queensberry. As the case was heard *in camera* no details of the hearing were published. The following day *The Times* merely reported that 'the hearing resulted in a *decree nisi* for nullity.' The truth about Queensberry's mysterious second marriage will not be known until 1994 when, under the provisions governing *in camera* divorce cases, the legal proceedings can be made public.

There were those, however, who were not prepared to wait 100 years to discover the truth. One was Oscar Wilde who, by then, had every reason to keep a wary eye on the man he called 'the scarlet Marquess.' So curious was Wilde that, a week or so later, he invited one of Ethel Weeden's lawyers to tea and charmed him into revealing what had been said in court. The details, he delightedly informed Bosie, were 'quite astonishing.' It was probably from Wilde's suitably embellished account that Bosie later accused his father of child-snatching and desertion.

Troubles never came singly for Queensberry. This is particularly true of the events surrounding his controversial second marriage. Two and a half weeks after he parted from Ethel Weeden, his sister Gertrude died; and, by an odd coincidence, it was precisely a week before the annulment of his marriage that another untimely death occurred in his family.

[2]

In the middle of October 1894, Queensberry's eldest son, the shy and phlegmatic Viscount Drumlanrig, was spending a few days at Quantock Lodge, near Bridgewater, in Somerset. He was a guest of Mr Edward Stanley, the Conservative MP for Bridgewater, and he had been invited to attend a family gathering. His presence at Quantock Lodge was of special significance. A week or so earlier he had proposed to and been accepted by his hostess's niece, Alix Ellis, and, though the engagement had not yet been officially announced, the house party had been arranged as part of his introduction to the Ellis family. Alix Ellis was the daughter of Major-General Arthur Ellis, an equerry to the Prince of Wales, and she, her parents and her brother Gerald were also among the guests. That such a seemingly cosy get-together should have ended in tragedy was doubly pathetic.

The tragedy occurred on Thursday, 18 October. Shortly after luncheon on that day, the women guests had been bundled into carriages for an afternoon drive while the men went out shooting. Drumlanrig, Gerald Ellis and three other young men made up the shooting party. They set off towards a nearby farm and started shooting when they reached a turnip field some two miles from Quantock Lodge. A couple of pheasants were killed and picked up, but Drumlanrig had no luck until he managed to wing a bird which fell beyond one of the hedges. Unfortunately it could not be found. Leaving one of the keepers to search for the bird, the party moved on to an adjoining field where another pheasant had been seen to fall. It was after they had climbed through a gap separating the two fields that Drumlanrig suddenly decided to turn back. 'I think my bird is in the hedge,' he said to the man next to him. The next minute he was gone.

He was not missed by the rest of the party until they were startled by a shot coming from the field they had just left. Then one of the keepers realised that Drumlanrig had disappeared. 'Where can his lordship be?' he asked. 'I hope he has not shot himself,' laughed one of the young men. 'Oh no,' gasped the keeper, 'we won't think that.'

Gerald Ellis was not so sure. Giving his gun to the keeper, he hurried across the field, climbed through the gap, and then called back to the others. 'I will walk along beside the hedge,' he shouted, 'and see if I can find him.' He did not have far to walk.

Drumlanrig was found 'lying on his back parallel with the hedge and quite dead. The gun was lying across his stomach. The muzzle was toward the hedge and his arms were stretched out on either side.' His head was buried in the brambles and when the rest of the party joined Ellis it was decided to leave the body as it was found. This made it impossible for them to examine the wound but, as one of them later explained, they could see 'that the head was very much sprinkled with blood, as also was the collar. There was a wound in the forehead.'

Like his grandfather, thirty-five years earlier, Drumlanrig was killed by a shot from his double-barrelled gun. The doctor who examined his body found that 'the charge had entered the mouth, fracturing the lower jaw on the right side, and passed through the roof of the mouth on the left hand side.' Death, he said, 'must have been instantaneous.'

At a perfunctory inquest held at Quantock Lodge two days later, the coroner was quick to rule out any suggestion of foul play. Drumlanrig's gun, he insisted, had probably gone off while he was scaling the hedge. There had been no witnesses to the death and there seemed, on the face of things, no reason to suspect suicide. The fact that the shot had, with deadly accuracy, penetrated the roof of Drumlanrig's mouth seemed to bother no one. The jury returned a verdict of 'Accidental Death.'

This verdict was accepted, for the most part, without question. Newspaper reports of the tragedy concentrated on Drumlanrig's promising career. His military service, his appointment as Lord Rosebery's secretary, his elevation to the English peerage, were listed and the pathos of his dying on the eve of his engagement to Alix Ellis was stressed. One or two gossipy journals could not resist recalling the history of violent deaths in the Queensberry family and comparing the circumstances surrounding Drumlanrig's death with those of his grandfather's 'accident', but even these reports were respectfully qualified. 'The young man who has just come to so melancholy an end,' observed *The World* immediately after the inquest, 'had not inherited the peculiarities of his father's family.' It nevertheless made a point of reviewing those peculiarities.

Not until later were doubts expressed. That Drumlanrig had died on the eve of his engagement was seen by some, not as pathetic, but as significant. His life, it was said, had not been blameless; it was thought there was more to his 'accident' than had come out at the inquest. These rumours did not appear in print but they were so persistent that they warrant closer examination. They concern Drumlanrig's relationship with his friend and former employer, Lord Rosebery.

[2]

John Morley, the wily old Liberal politician, once described Lord Rosebery as 'a dark horse in a loose box.' Gladstone called him 'an incalculable man—one of the most incalculable I have ever known.' Both were speaking politically, but their remarks could easily have applied to Rosebery's enigmatic personality.

A cynic whose aristocratic aloofness was belied by his political ambitions, a sportsman who dabbled in the arts, a gifted talker who could lapse into puzzling silences, a leading Liberal beloved by the Tories, an ardent social reformer and a dedicated Imperialist, the 5th Earl of Rosebery was a man of many contradictions. Even his professed distaste for politics, which he claimed to find 'hateful' is open to doubt. His reluctance to assume office was invariably overcome by his love of high position.

As a boy at Eton, Rosebery is said to have confided to a friend that he had three ambitions—'to marry a great heiress, to win the Derby, and to become Prime Minister.' He achieved all three, but not all at once. In March 1878—shortly before his thirty-first birthday—he married Hannah Rothschild, daughter of Baron Meyer de Rothschild and heiress to her father's banking fortune. The marriage, from which there were two sons and two daughters, was a happy one; Rosebery was crushed by his wife's death some twelve years later. His second ambition was not realised until March 1894 when, after serving as Foreign Secretary, he was appointed to succeed Gladstone as Prime Minister. The appointment did not please the radical section of his party and there were further objections when his horse *Ladas* won the 1894 Derby. Even some of his more moderate followers, it is said, 'disliked the thought of a Liberal Prime Minister winning the Derby.'

But suspicion of Lord Rosebery was not confined to his politics or his sporting activities. From the time his wife died, if not before, there were rumours that his private life was not all it should be. Speculation about his sex life was not limited to those gossip columnists who hinted that he was about to make another spectacular marriage to a Royal princess. There were those who were convinced that the suave and witty Lord Rosebery had homosexual tendencies.

Not the least of the rumour-mongers was Lewis Harcourt, son of Rosebery's arch-rival for the Premiership, Sir William Harcourt. Lewis Harcourt, an ardent champion of his father, had his ear well-tuned to any gossip concerning Rosebery and never hesitated to twist such gossip to his own advantage. He was helped by Rosebery's secretiveness about his private life. When, for instance, one of Rosebery's secretaries told Harcourt that the new Prime Minister insisted on opening all his own letters, Harcourt noted in his diary that this was not surprising 'considering some of the things which, to my knowledge, some of them must contain.'

The suspicion that Rosebery was a covert homosexual did not become prevalent until some years later when he bought a villa at Posillipo on the Italian mainland, near Capri—then a fashionable homosexual resort. Stories about Rosebery's activities at Posillipo—mostly unsubstantiated—were common gossip at Capri and were undoubtedly coloured by his recluse-like habits. He was never happier, it is said, than when he was alone, or with a few chosen friends, on his yacht or at Posillipo. This, in itself, would have been sufficient to set Capri tongues wagging. However, it is fairly obvious that the rumours started earlier than that. It is also obvious that they concerned his relationship with Viscount Drumlanrig.

Drumlanrig, as has been said, was an unlikely choice of secretary for a serious-minded politician. He was not particularly bright and he showed precious little aptitude for politics or diplomacy. His private life is something of a mystery; but on the question of homosexuality he was plainly hypersensitive. Bosie was later to claim that Drumlanrig and Oscar Wilde were antipathetic. 'No two men,' he says, 'could have had less in common. . . . On the one hand you had the soldier, with perhaps a bit of the courtier thrown in; on the other you had the overdressed Bohemian.' This was written when Bosie had become disenchanted with Wilde; it was probably intended to counteract the scandalous talk which, as Bosie well knew, concerned Drumlanrig's association with Rosebery. Certainly there is nothing in Wilde's letters to indicate that he was aware of any coolness between himself and Drumlanrig; on the contrary, his few mentions of Bosie's elder brother are extremely complimentary. But coolness or no, Drumlanrig was undoubtedly chary of the notorious Wilde. He refused to be seen in public with Bosie and Oscar and when trouble threatened between Wilde and Queensberry, Drumlanrig 'left London to avoid the possibility of being drawn into the dispute.' Such, apparently, was Drumlanrig's fear of guilt by association.

For Drumlanrig to avoid Wilde was one thing, for him to avoid his father was quite another. It was Queensberry's bizarre behaviour at Homburg, when he threatened to assault Rosebery, that first drew public attention to Rosebery's secretary. Most accounts of this incident are garbled, but there was clearly more than Queensberry's wounded pride involved in the quarrel. Even in his letter to Queen Victoria, the outraged Marquess had mentioned Rosebery's 'bad influence' on his son and it is unlikely that he was then referring to Drumlanrig's elevation to the English peerage. The fuss about the title, it was thought, was merely a smoke-screen. Behind it lay a more sinister accusation. Admittedly Rosebery had appeared to laugh the incident off—it was not generally known that the police had been called in—but what else could he do? To have shown anger or fear would have created greater suspicion. Rosebery had no option but to pretend indifference. But, considering he had been plagued by Queensberry for weeks, and had gone to Homburg under doctor's orders, his 'indifference' seemed a shade too studied.

Once started, the rumours persisted. They may even have influenced Drumlanrig's proposal to Alix Ellis. By that time Rosebery had become Prime Minister and a scandal, whether true or not, would have been disastrous. When Lewis Harcourt heard of the engagement he was astonished. 'Drumlanrig is going to marry General Ellis's daughter,' he wrote incredulously in his diary. 'It makes the institution of marriage ridiculous.'

What all this had to do with Drumlanrig's death is impossible to say. Rumours, by their very nature, are difficult to pin down. They also take some unexpected turns. One of the more curious results of the gossip about Drumlanrig and Rosebery only came to light many years later. In the recently revealed memoirs of that incorrigible old charlatan Sir Edmund Backhouse, an amusing twist is given to Rosebery's alleged homosexuality. Among the many sexual adventures boasted by the imaginative Backhouse—which include affairs with the poet Verlaine and the Empress Dowager of China—are the graphically described romps he claims to have had with Lord Rosebery. At the time, he says, he was acting as the Prime Minister's secretary.

Backhouse was a pathological liar and his 'revelations' cannot be taken seriously; but, as his biographer Hugh Trevor-Roper points out, his fantasies were invariably woven around a semblance of fact. He took great pains to research the lives of his pretended lovers so that his imagined relationship with them would carry at least a gloss of truth. In Rosebery's case his research was nothing if not detailed. He learned enough about the Prime Minister to describe his character, his interests, his habits and his friends; he also appeared to be familiar with Rosebery's houses, rooms and day-to-day life. More interestingly he drew heavily upon the rumours which linked Rosebery sexually with Drumlanrig. By 'substituting himself for Drumlanrig,' says Professor Trevor Roper, 'both as secretary and as alleged ganymede, [Backhouse] displayed himself proudly in the centre, describing, in slow motion, his *nuits d'amour* with the Prime Minister.'

However Backhouse came to conjure up these flights of fancy, they illustrate—if nothing else—the way in which the gossip surrounding Rosebery had spread in certain circles. And it was gossip, in want of fact, that proved so dangerous.

One does not have to rely on Backhouse's doubtful word for the gossip, however. Others, more closely concerned, were fully aware of what was being said. They were also convinced that the rumours contributed to Drumlanrig's death. This, at any rate, seems to be the conclusion reached by Drumlanrig's nephew, the 11th Marquess of Queensberry, who told the writer H. Montgomery Hyde that he was 'positive' that his uncle had 'taken his own life in the shadow of a suppressed scandal.'

What part, if any, Queensberry played in the events surrounding his heir's death is not known. He was unquestionably concerned about Drumlanrig's involvement with Rosebery and it is doubtful whether he would have been frightened off by the Homburg incident, police or no police. More than that one cannot say. Certainly Queensberry was well placed to sniff out any scandal. Homosexual gossip had, over the last year or so, featured prominently in his dealings with his sons.

[3]

'. . . . Your intimacy with this man Wilde,' Queensberry wrote to Bosie on 1 April 1894. 'It must either cease or I will disown you and stop all money supplies. I am not going to try and analyse this intimacy, and I make no charge; but in my mind to pose as a thing is as bad as to be it. With my own eyes I saw you both in the most loathsome and disgusting relationship as expressed by your manner and expression. Never in my experience have I seen such a sight as that in your horrible features. No wonder people are talking as they are. Also I now hear on good authority, but this may be false, that his wife is petitioning to divorce him for sodomy and other crimes. Is this true or do you not know of it? If I thought the actual thing was true, and it became public property, I should be quite justified in shooting him at sight. These Christian English cowards and men, as they call themselves, want waking up.'

Bosie was not impressed. 'What a funny little man you are,' he wired back contemptuously.

Things had deteriorated since that first happy meeting between Wilde and Queensberry some two years earlier. Bosie and his father were now at each other's throats. They were well matched. Each knew how best to wound the other; their insults were as calculated as they were vindictive. Queensberry relied on financial threats, Bosie on studied insolence.

But there was more to Queensberry's outburst than appeared on paper. His aim was not merely to frighten his son but to protect himself. He was careful, for instance, to qualify his accusations against Wilde. He confined himself to what he had seen and heard—things he could defend if necessary—and insisted he was making no charge. Wilde, he suggested, was nothing more than a *poseur*. This, for a man of Queensberry's temperament, smacks more of chicanery than of anger. He was clearly unsure of himself and showed caution in his dealings with Wilde. It was all part of what he liked to call his 'booby trap.'

With Bosie he was less restrained. 'You impertinent young jackanapes . . .' he stormed in reply to his son's telegram. 'I will give you the thrashing you deserve. Your only excuse is that you must be crazy. . . . If I catch you again with that man I will make a public scandal in a way you little dream of; if it is a suppressed one, I prefer an open one, and at any rate I shall not be blamed for allowing such a state of things to go on. Unless this acquaintance ceases I shall carry out my threat and stop all supplies, and if you are not going to make any attempt to do something, I shall certainly cut you down to a mere pittance, so you know what to expect.'

Bosie remained unimpressed. To show just how unimpressed he was, he instructed his lawyers to draw up a letter informing his father that, rather than give up his 'eternal friendship' with Wilde, he was perfectly prepared to forfeit his allowance. The £250 a year was immediately stopped. Bosie liked to pretend that the loss of his allowance did not bother him unduly. But it obviously did. He was a young man of expensive tastes, money meant a great deal to him. Wilde later claimed that he spent over £5000 entertaining Bosie and Bosie himself admitted that he often had to cadge extra money from his mother and grandfather. The prospect of existing on a 'mere pittance' could not have been pleasant. But, in Bosie's eyes, any sacrifice was worth while if it annoyed his father. 'He might have guessed,' he said of Queensberry, 'that I was quite as obstinate as he was.'

His mother did not need to be told this. She was only too aware that Bosie shared his father's cussedness. To her this pig-headedness, this tendency to parade weaknesses as strengths, was all part of an ominous family trait. She said as much to Wilde. 'She saw, of course,' Wilde told Bosie, 'that heredity had burdened you with a terrible legacy, and frankly admitted it, admitted it with horror.'

Sybil was every bit as worried as Queensberry about Bosie's attachment to Wilde. Her fears had been aroused much earlier and had not been helped by her father's open disapproval of their friendship. Incurable gossip that he was, Alfred Montgomery had quickly scented trouble. He had lost no time in making his suspicions known. In the summer of 1892, he had taken Bosie with him to Homburg and was clearly disconcerted when they were joined there by Wilde. Bosie's attempt to bring his friend and his grandfather together proved disastrous. Alfred Montgomery, he says, took a 'violent and invincible' dislike to Wilde and 'declined to meet him again.' Doubtless the elegant Alfred recognised Wilde as a more flamboyant and decidedly less discreet version of himself. But it was probably the gossip about Wilde's sexual tastes that alarmed him most. Alfred Montgomery was always careful to distance himself from any suggestion of scandal.

Wilde, on the other hand, was blissfully unaware of Montgomery's disapproval. He always admired the older man's wit and had no compunction in passing off some of Montgomery's more amusing aphorisms as his own. 'The only thing which I cannot resist is temptation,' says one of Montgomery's friends, 'was shamefully cribbed by Oscar Wilde.' Bosie's touchy old grandfather would hardly have appreciated such a doubtful compliment.

Whatever his reasons, Montgomery's hostility was obvious enough to add to his daughter's fears. Those fears were inspired by more than gossip: since knowing Wilde, Bosie's career at Oxford had gone to pieces. Not only had he abandoned his sporting friends but he had given up all pretence of studying. He prided himself on being an 'aesthete' and was interested only in cultivating his reputation as a literary dilettante. So worried did Sybil become that she wrote to Herbert Warren—the Principal of Magdalen College—for advice. Warren, a notorious tuft-hunter, was friendly with both Bosie and Wilde and was full of reassurance for Sybil. He had nothing but praise for Wilde's scholarship and literary gifts; he even suggested that Bosie was fortunate to have such a friend. This was small comfort to Sybil. She knew how vain and extravagant her son was and she certainly did not see these faults being cured by his friendship with an older man.

She was right, of course. Flattered and indulged by Wilde, Bosie had become opinionated and indolent. What talent he had was spent in editing *The Spirit Lamp*; his energies were squandered on acquiring notoriety. He loved to shock and delighted in his reputation as an *enfant terrible*. His posturing was often embarrassing to his friends. Max Beerbohm, a fellow undergraduate, found him quite impossible. 'Alfred Douglas,' Beerbohm told a friend, 'does not peculiarly fascinate me: he is for one thing obviously mad (like all his family I believe.)' Others thought the same. Queensberry was well aware of his son's bizarre reputation. 'I hear from a man at Oxford,' he wrote in one of his attacks on Bosie, 'that you were thought crazy there, and that accounts for a good deal that has happened.' Later, when he learned that Bosie had been blackmailed by one of his disreputable associates, he became even more convinced of his son's 'infamous conduct at Oxford.'

Bosie's conduct was more than infamous, it was downright dangerous. Being what he was, he might easily have ruined his Oxford career whether he had known Wilde or not; but it was undoubtedly his friendship with Wilde that encouraged his shadier activities. Their association was not as romantic as it was made to appear. Sexually incompatible, each sought other diversions. And the diversions they sought were often hazardous. It was through Wilde that Bosie was introduced to the homosexual underworld—the world of male prostitutes, telegraph boys, messengers and stable hands who hired themselves out for sex and were known, appropriately, as 'renters.' On at least one occasion Bosie and Wilde are known to have spent a night at the Savoy Hotel in London with one or more of these boys. At Oxford Bosie became disastrously entangled with another untrustworthy young 'renter.'

The youngster was Alfred Wood. He was seventeen years old and Bosie was introduced to him by Wilde's friend, Alfred Taylor. According to Rupert Croft-Cooke, Taylor was 'not exactly a professional procurer but he gave tea-parties at which "gentlemen" could meet out-of-work roughs, and other amenable youths.' Apparently young Fred Wood proved amenable enough to accept Bosie's invitation to spend two weeks with him at Oxford. At the end of the two weeks Bosie rewarded Wood with, among other things, one of his discarded suits of clothes. Unfortunately the gift was given with more haste than care: in the pocket of the suit were some letters Wilde had written to Bosie. One of them began:

'My Own Boy, Your sonnet is quite lovely, and it is a marvel that those red rose-leaf lips of yours should have been made no less for the music of song than for the madness of kisses. Your slim gilt soul walks between passion and poetry. I know Hyacinthus, whom Apollo loved so madly, was you in Greek days. . . .'

Wilde was to describe this letter as a prose-poem, but the poetry was lost on Fred Wood. He merely recognised the letter's monetary value and acted accordingly. With the help of two experienced blackmailers, he had it copied and then used it to extort money from Wilde. He was only partly successful. Wilde blandly refused to acknowledge his demands and eventually succeeded in getting the letters back for a token payment. He could not, however, prevent the copies of the prose-poem from being distributed. One of the copies fell into Queensberry's hands. This, and the knowledge he had of the previous blackmailing attempt on Bosie, left Queensberry in no doubt as to his son's behaviour at Oxford.

But this was to happen later. At the time Wilde's intervention prevented Queensberry from learning of Wood's antics. Bosie must have been thankful. He was already in disgrace with his parents for being rusticated from Oxford for a term after failing to pass an examination. He could not have faced another scandal. His mother's patience, as well he knew, was almost exhausted.

So, for that matter, was Wilde's. Infatuated, indulgent and long-suffering, Wilde was finding it difficult to cope with Bosie's tantrums. A crisis in their relationship had occurred shortly after Bosie had been rusticated from Oxford. Instead of spending the term studying (his mother had engaged a tutor to coach him) Bosie had gone to Devon where Wilde had rented a house. It was intended that Bosie, who was accompanied by his tutor, would study while Wilde worked on his play *A Woman of No Importance*. This arrangement did not last long. A few days after his arrival, Bosie quarrelled violently with Wilde. The following morning, still in a temper, he packed his bags and left.

What caused this quarrel is not known, but its effect on Wilde was profound. 'When . . .' he later reminded Bosie, 'you left my house at Torquay I had determined never to speak to you again, or to allow you under any circumstances to be with me, so revolting had been the scene you had made the night before your departure. You wrote and telegraphed from Bristol to beg me to forgive you and to meet you. Your tutor, who had stayed behind, told me that he thought you were quite irresponsible for what you said and did, and that most, if not all, of the men at Magdalen were of the same opinion. I consented to meet you, and of course I forgave you.'

Wilde had an infinite capacity for forgiveness. He needed it. Shortly after their reconciliation came the trouble with Fred Wood. Life with Bosie Douglas was nothing if not testing. But Wilde was incapable of nursing a grudge: his love for Bosie, tortured as it was, invariably triumphed over their petty squabbles. Even his occasional reproaches were softened by his idolatory.

'Bosie,' he pleaded, shortly after their quarrel, 'you must not make scenes with me. They kill me, they wreck the loveliness of life. I cannot see you, so Greek and gracious, distorted with passion. I cannot listen to your curved lips saying hideous things to me.'

By then Wilde was back in London and busy with rehearsals for *A Woman of No Importance*. When the play opened, on 19 April 1893, Bosie was at the fashionable first night. It was a heady occasion. The theatre was packed and Max Beerbohm, whose brother produced the play, claimed there was not a 'single nonentity in the whole house.' The curtain came down to thunderous applause; if a few critics carped, others were lavish with their praise. 'In intellectual calibre, artistic competence—ay, and in dramatic instinct to boot,' enthused William Archer in *The World*, 'Mr Wilde has no rival among his fellow-workers for the stage.' This, for Oscar, was the loveliness of life. To be acknowledged as a playwright of genius made Bosie's tantrums appear insignificant. What, after all, was the occasional tiff compared with such shared delights.

But the delights were deceptive. If Bosie applauded his friend's success, he could claim none for himself. He returned to Oxford that summer for his last term but, dogged by past negligence, he was sent down at the end of term in disgrace and without a degree. His parents' fears were realised, but he showed no contrition. He was not concerned about the future. So long as he had enough to live on he seemed content to drift.

Queensberry, contemptuous as he was of degrees, was infuriated by Bosie's attitude. 'Am I to understand,' he thundered, 'that, having left Oxford as you did, with discredit to yourself, the reason of which were fully explained to me by your tutor, you now intend to loaf and loll about and do nothing? All the time you were wasting at Oxford I was put off with an assurance that you were eventually to go into the Civil Service or to the Foreign Office, and then I was put off with an assurance that you were going to the Bar. It appears to me that you intend to do nothing. I utterly decline, however, to just supply you with sufficient funds to enable you to loaf about. You are preparing a wretched future for yourself, and it would be most cruel and wrong of me to encourage you in this.'

Wilde was equally worried. After leaving Oxford, Bosie went to stay with him at Goring-on-Thames where Wilde was working, somewhat half-heartedly, on *An Ideal Husband*. The holiday started happily. Constance Wilde, who was at Goring when Bosie arrived, left for France with the children and the two friends were alone for most of the time. To give Bosie an interest, Wilde encouraged him to continue working on the translation into English of his French play, *Salome*. But Bosie needed more than encouragement. Neither he nor Wilde worked very hard that summer. Most of their time was spent idling on the river. Inevitably Bosie became bored, restless and moody. There was more 'hideous scenes,' more partings, more telegrams asking for forgiveness, more reconciliations. Wilde found it emotionally exhausting. So distraught did he become that at one stage he told Bosie that they were ruining each other's lives and their friendship must end.

'An irrevocable parting,' he decided, 'a complete separation was the one wise philosphic thing to do.'

Bosie agreed and left—only to return three days later. Their partings were never irrevocable, their separations never complete. When dealing with Bosie, it was impossible for Wilde to be wise and philosophic. In November 1893 he wrote despairingly to Bosie's mother.

'Bosie,' he said, 'seems to me to be in a very bad state of health. He is sleepless, nervous, and rather hysterical. He seems to me quite altered. He is doing nothing in town. He translated my French play last August. Since then he has really done nothing intellectual. He seems to me to have lost, for the moment only I trust, his interest even in literature. . . . His life seems to me aimless, unhappy and absurd.' What he needed, Wilde suggested, was a change of scene. If he remained in England he would continue to drift and his life would be ruined. 'Why not try,' he wrote, 'and make arrangements for him to go abroad for four or five months, to the Cromers in Egypt if that could be managed, where he would have new surroundings, proper friends, and a different atmosphere?'

The suggestion was hardly novel. A similar cure had been sought for Bosie's moody Uncle James, with disastrous results. But this thought did not occur to Sybil. Desperate, she seized on Wilde's advice. The wife of Lord Cromer—the British Consul-General and Agent in Egypt—was a friend of hers and she had no difficulty in arranging for Bosie to be invited to Cairo. Surprisingly Bosie accepted the invitation. This was largely Wilde's doing. He was forever begging Bosie to respect his mother's wishes, to make something of his life. And Bosie, for all his moods and weaknesses, had sufficient common sense to accept his friend's advice. In his more reflective moments, he recognised the dangers of his temperamental outbursts and was determined to conquer them. He made this clear in two long and thoughtful letters which he wrote to his mother from Egypt.

'I have in my blood,' he confessed, 'the love of a scene and a tragedy, but I am convinced it is a mistake, and certainly in our family of all families somebody ought to make a determined stand against it. There is such a tendency to lift everything up on the stilts of tragedy, we are such a theatrical family. Let us cease from this, and become a little bourgeois.'

But nothing Bosie said—and the letters he wrote from Egypt are the most perceptive he ever wrote—could quieten his mother's fears. Before he left England at the beginning of December 1893, Sybil had had a stern motherly talk to him about his friendship with Wilde. She had warned him he was being led astray. Wilde, she argued, was a malign influence and it would be best if the friendship ended. Bosie had refused to listen. He agreed to go to Egypt but he would make no other promise. Whatever others might say, he refused to part permanently from the man he loved and admired.

Thwarted, Sybil tried to enlist Wilde's help. Shortly after Bosie's departure she wrote to Wilde explaining her son's weaknesses—his temper, his vanity, his lack of money sense—and implied that their turbulent friendship was intensifying these weaknesses. She begged Wilde not to meet Bosie abroad. Wilde was only too willing to agree. He, no less than Sybil, was pleased to have Bosie settled at a distance. He had no wish to upset the arrangement. 'I assured her,' he was to tell Bosie, 'that I had not the slightest intention of meeting you abroad, and begged her to try and keep you there, either as an honorary *attaché*, if that were possible, or to learn modern languages, if it were not.' Wilde even suggested that, for both their sakes, he and Bosie should remain apart for at least two or three years.

It may have been Wilde's suggestion that prompted Alfred Montgomery's intervention. Equally anxious to end the friendship, Montgomery pulled strings to have Bosie appointed honorary *attaché* to the British Ambassador in Constantinople. Such an appointment, it was thought, would solve everyone's problems. Unfortunately the plan misfired.

The fault was entirely Bosie's. He was told of the Constantinople appointment by Lord Cromer, but claimed he had no idea that he was expected to take up the post immediately. More likely he had no intention of taking up the post at all. By that time he had been in Egypt almost three months and had not heard a word from Wilde. Oscar's silence made him desperate. He had written and he had telegraphed—not only to Wilde but to Sybil and Wilde's wife—but, apart from a curt telegram saying it was best that they did not contact each other, Wilde had refused to reply. Finally Bosie lost control. In what appears to have been one of his periodic brain storms he left Cairo for Paris, sending Wilde 'passionate telegrams' to meet him in France. Still Wilde remained unmoved. On reaching Paris, Bosie found a brief letter waiting for him at his hotel. It was from Wilde telling him that a meeting was out of the question.

Wilde was resolute, Bosie was desolate. He immediately sent a pathetic telegram to Tite Street, some ten or eleven pages long, begging Wilde to come to him. It ended with, what seemed to Wilde, 'a threat of suicide, and one not thinly veiled.' If this was meant to frighten Wilde, it certainly succeeded. The mere hint of suicide, coming from Bosie, was to be taken seriously.

'You had yourself,' Wilde recalled, 'often told me how many of your race there had been who had stained their hands with their own blood; your uncle certainly, your grandfather possibly; many others in that mad bad line from which you come. Pity, my old affection for you, regard for your mother to whom your death under such dreadful circumstances would have been a blow too great for her to bear . . . mere humanity itself—all these, if excuses be necessary, must serve as my excuse for consenting to accord you one last interview.'

It was far from being the last interview, however. Wilde hurried to Paris and met Bosie in a welter of tears and emotion. That evening they dined at Voisin's and went to supper at Paillard's, with Bosie clutching at Wilde's hand and behaving like 'a gentle and penitent child.' Sentiment triumphed and Wilde crumbled. Faced with Bosie's anguish, he could not but agree to renew their friendship. All thought of Bosie's diplomatic career was cast aside.

The tears and the hand clutching continued in London. Two days after their return from Paris, Wilde and Bosie were still weltering in emotion. And it was now—on their second day home, that Queensberry marched into the Café Royal and saw them in what he called 'the most loathsome and disgusting relationship.' He said nothing at the time, but again joined their table and drank Wilde's wine. This time, however, there was no laughter and no lingering conversation. They spoke mostly about Egypt and Bosie's experiences there. Queensberry went home early to write that blistering attack on Wilde, the attack to which Bosie replied with his impertinent telegram.

Only Wilde seems to have recognised the seriousness of this fatal exchange. When Bosie showed him Queensberry's letter he felt the cold stab of premonition.

'I saw at once,' he said, 'that a terrible danger was looming on the horizon of my troubled days . . . that I in London was naturally much bigger game for him [Queensberry] than a Secretary for Foreign Affairs at Homburg.'

Chapter Fifteen

The Marquess Leaves his Card

The trouble Wilde foresaw came sooner than he could have expected. Later, in his sad apologia *De Profundis,* he was to blame Bosie for forcing the pace of events. He claimed that it was Bosie's insulting letters and telegrams that goaded Queensberry into his mad quest for revenge. But, as always, Wilde was overestimating Bosie and underrating Queensberry.

Bosie's open defiance undoubtedly helped to intensify his father's hysteria, but it was not the cause of Queensberry's neurosis. The 'fatal Douglas temperament,' as Sybil called it, was a genetic defect; it could not be placated by a show of submission. Once aroused it had to find expression. One has only to study Queensberry's past behaviour, particularly his vendetta against Rosebery, to realise that—whatever Bosie might have said or done—he would have continued to hound Wilde. The calculated wording of his letter attacking Wilde is evidence enough of his vicious sense of purpose. He was not a man who was easily deflected. Wilde was wrong to blame Bosie, but he was right in expecting trouble. It was the timing and nature of Queensberry's attacks that took him by surprise.

There was, it is true, a short breathing space immediately following the initial exchange of insults. This was largely Sybil's doing. She, alarmed by Bosie's return to England, immediately contrived to have him sent abroad again. This time—in the middle of April 1894—he went to Florence where he was taken up by a coterie of expatriate homosexuals. Wilde, then battling with his finances, was not able to join him until some weeks later. At the beginning of May, though, they were reunited and remained for a month or more in Florence. Queensberry was forced to bide his time.

He did not wait long. Hardly had Wilde returned to London than Queensberry pitched up, unannounced, at Tite Street. He was accompanied, Wilde claimed, by 'a gentleman with whom I was not acquainted.' Who this man was has never been revealed. The supposition that he was a prize-fighter whom Queensberry had brought along for protection seems highly improbable. There is no evidence for such a claim and every reason to doubt it. Protection was the last thing Queensberry needed: he was quite capable of taking care of himself. One of his proudest boasts was that, although nearing fifty, he could floor any opponent. Had he been expecting a fight, he would have gloried in taking on Wilde single-handed. What seems more likely is that this was another demonstration of Queensberry's cunning. The encounter was bound to be stormy and he needed his own witness. Many of his sporting cronies looked like bruisers; he probably roped one of them in to vouch for what he said.

In the event, this did not prove necessary. We have only Wilde's word for what happened and his word was never challenged.

'The interview,' says Wilde, 'took place in my library. Lord Queensberry was standing by the window. I walked over to the fireplace, and he said to me "Sit down." I said to him, "I do not allow any one to talk like that to me in my house or anywhere else. I suppose you have come to apologise for the statement you made about my wife and myself in letters you wrote to your son. I should have the right any day I chose to prosecute you for writing such a letter."

'He said, "The letter was privileged, as it was written to my son." I said, "How dare you say such things to me about your son and me?" He said, "You were both kicked out of the Savoy Hotel at a moment's notice for your disgusting conduct." I said, "That is a lie." He said, "You have taken furnished rooms for him in Piccadilly." I said, "Somebody has been telling you an absurd set of lies about your son and me. I have done nothing of the kind." He said, "I hear you were thoroughly well blackmailed for a disgusting letter you wrote to my son." I said, "The letter was a beautiful letter, and I never write except for publication."

'Then I asked: "Lord Queensberry, do you seriously accuse your son and me of improper conduct?" He said, "I do not say you are it, but you look it, and you pose as it, which is just as bad. If I catch you and my son together again in any public restaurant I will thrash you." I said, "I do not know what the Queensberry rules are, but the Oscar Wilde rule is to shoot at sight."

'I then told Lord Queensberry to leave my house. He said he would not do so. I told him that I would have him put out by the police. He said, "It is a disgusting scandal." I said, "If it be so, you are the author of the scandal, and no one else." I then went into the hall and pointed him out to my servant. I said, "This is the Marquis of Queensberry, the most infamous brute in London. You are never to allow him to enter my house again." '

As Rupert Croft-Cooke has pointed out, this one-sided account is far from convincing. It reads, in fact, rather like an extract from one of Wilde's plays. Queensberry was to imply that it was Wilde, not he, who took fright. And he may have been right.

Wilde's servant at that time was a puny sixteen-year-old lad, known as 'Ginger,' who could hardly have posed a threat to Queensberry and his friend. Wilde himself was no coward—he had proved his strength on more than one occasion—but even so, the idea of the obstreperous Marquess allowing himself to be called 'the most infamous brute in London' and then leaving without a word, takes some believing. If nothing more he would have shouted Wilde down.

On the other hand it must be remembered that Queensberry was unsure of himself. He had no tangible evidence against Wilde. All his attempts to find informed witnesses—including a visit to the Savoy Hotel where he had heard Wilde and Bosie had entertained 'renters' and created a 'stinking scandal'—had so far failed. People, it seems, were willing to whisper but no one was prepared to talk. Queensberry's accusations were based entirely on hearsay; and hearsay would not stand up in court. Wilde's threat to call the police might well have put him on his guard. It might even have prompted him to leave quietly. He had no intention of being caught in his own booby-trap.

Be that as it may, the interview undoubtedly took place. Wilde escaped physical violence but was left severely shaken by the encounter. So much so that, three days later, he decided to take action. He consulted his solicitors, C. O. Humphreys, Son & Kershaw, with the intention of sueing Queensberry for libel. Not having a witness to the interview, he relied instead on the abusive letters that Queensberry had written to Bosie. Among them were some in which the names of 'exalted personages'—including, presumably, Rosebery—were mentioned. Precisely what Queensberry said in those letters was never revealed, but they were evidently explosive enough to make the solicitors wary. On 11 July they wrote to Queensberry demanding an apology for his having 'most foully and infamously' libelled their client. Wilde, they pointed out, was reluctant to publish the letters because of the names involved and was therefore giving Queensberry the opportunity of retracting his 'assertions and insinuations in writing, with an apology for having made them.' If this was done at once, they concluded, 'it may prevent litigation, but unless done forthwith no other course will be left open to us but to advise our client as to the proper course to adopt to vindicate his character.'

Queensberry was delighted. The door of his booby-trap was about to open and he was ready for the fall. He was then spending a few days at Maidenhead—it was Henley Regatta week—and replied to the solicitors as soon as their letter reached him.

'I have received your letter here with considerable astonishment,' he blustered self-righteously. 'I certainly shall not tender to Mr Oscar Wilde any apology for letters I have written to my son. I have made no direct accusation against Mr Oscar Wilde, but desired to stop the association as far as my son is concerned.'

He then sat back and waited for a summons. It did not come. Wilde, having steeled himself for action, unexpectedly decided not to press the charge. His change of mind had nothing to do with Queensberry; it was brought about by his sympathy for Bosie's mother. When Sybil heard that Wilde had consulted his solicitors she became extremely alarmed. First she wrote to Wilde begging him not to proceed with the case and then sent her cousin, George Wyndham, to talk him out of it. Wyndham, an extremely persuasive Conservative MP—'plausible George Wyndham,' Wilde called him—did all that was expected of him. Not only did he dissuade Wilde from prosecuting Queensberry but suggested that he should 'gradually drop' Bosie. It was sound advice. Unfortunately Wilde listened with only half an ear.

Sybil, however, must have been relieved. She, probably more than anyone, was aware of how delicate the situation had become. She knew her husband and had recognised the danger signals. Only a few days earlier Queensberry had written to her demanding to know whether Bosie had ever stayed at the Savoy Hotel with Wilde. She had wired back saying Bosie denied having been at the Savoy during the past year; she had then asked her father to meet Queensberry and to reason with him. But Queensberry was in no mood for reasoning; least of all with Alfred Montgomery.

'Why should I come dancing attendance on you?' he had replied to Montgomery. 'Your daughter is the person who is supporting my son to defy me. She won't write but she is now telegraphing on the subject. . . . This hideous scandal has been going on for years. Your daughter must be mad by the way she is behaving. She evidently wants to make out that I want to make a case against my son. It is nothing of the kind. I have made out a case against Oscar Wilde and have to his face accused him of it. If I was quite certain of the thing I would shoot the fellow on sight, but I can only accuse him of posing. It now lies in the hands of the two whether they will further defy me. Your daughter appears now to be encouraging them, although she can hardly intend this. I don't believe Wilde will now defy me. He plainly showed the white feather the other day when I talked to him—damned cur and coward of the Rosebery type. . . . But your daughter's conduct is outrageous, and I am now fully convinced that the Rosebery-Gladstone-Royal insult that came to me through my other son, that she worked—I, thought it was you. I saw Drumlanrig [this was three months before Drumlanrig's death] here on the river, which much upset me. It shall be known some day by all that Rosebery not only insulted me by lying to the Queen, which makes her as bad as him and Gladstone, but has also made a lifelong quarrel between my son and I.'

With Queensberry in full flood—dragging in the Rosebery quarrel as well as the Wilde affair—Sybil had every reason to be afraid. The scandal that was brewing threatened the entire family. It had required little prodding on her part to involve George Wyndham in the quarrel. But if Wyndham had managed to quieten Wilde (at least for the time being) he could do nothing to placate the demented Bosie. By that time the slanging-match between Bosie and his father had reached a point of near-hysteria.

There had been plenty of scope for theatrical gestures. Queensberry, always prepared to play to the gallery, had lost no time in finding an audience. Shortly after his visit to Tite Street, he had repeated the tactics he had used against Rosebery, by making a round of the restaurants frequented by Wilde and Bosie and warning waiters of his determination to thrash Wilde if he caught him dining with his son. Word of this soon got back to Wilde who began to have second thoughts about his promise to George Wyndham. 'Your father,' he told Bosie, 'is on the rampage again—been to the Café Royal to enquire for us, with threats etc. I think now it would have been better for me to have had him bound over to keep the peace, but what a scandal! Still it is intolerable to be dogged by a maniac.'

Bosie's reaction was more dramatic. He armed himself with a loaded revolver and then wrote to his father telling him when he would be visiting certain restaurants and inviting him to do his worst. 'If I shoot you,' he warned, 'or he [Wilde] shoots you, we shall be acting in self defence against a dangerous rough.'

These histrionics shocked Wilde. He had no desire to shoot anyone and was thoroughly alarmed when Bosie accidentally fired off his 'ridiculous pistol' on the roof of the Berkeley Hotel. Queensberry, on the other hand, took his son's warning seriously. He immediately rushed to Wilde's solicitors and threatened to call in the police. It took all the efforts of Messrs Humphreys, Son & Kershaw to calm father and son down. 'I have heard,' Queensberry wrote to them on 18 July, 'that the revolver has been given up. I shall therefore not insist on taking the step I threatened. . . . However, if this is to go on, and I am openly defied by Mr Oscar Wilde and my son by further scandals in public places, I shall have no other resort but to do as I have threatened and give information to Scotland Yard as to what has happened.'

Bosie and Queensberry, for all their passion and cries of vengeance, were merely play-acting. At no stage was Bosie seriously worried about his father's threats; his loaded revolver was nothing more than a stage prop. 'If my father,' he frankly admitted, 'had really meant to assault me or Wilde in a restaurant he would have done it first and talked about it afterwards.' And he was right. Queensberry might bluster and threaten violence but he was careful not to push things too far. Certainly he had no intention of laying himself open to a charge of assault: that, as he saw it, would have been playing into Wilde's hands. Anxious as he was for Wilde to bring a charge against him, he wanted it to be a charge he could defend and not—as had happened with Rosebery—one that made him appear the aggressor.

When dealing directly with Bosie, Queensberry was less inhibited. Here at least he could claim to be asserting parental authority: anything he said to his son was, in his opinion, privileged. Even so he was unable to match Bosie's frenzy; finally he sought refuge in refusing to open any letter sent by his son. Undaunted, Bosie then began to bombard him with postcards. One of these reached him in Scotland where, after leaving Maidenhead, he was staying with the agent of his estates.

'I have received your postcard,' he replied angrily, 'which I presume is from you, but as the writing is utterly unreadable to me, have been able to make out hardly one sentence. My object of receiving no written communication from you is therefore kept intact. All future cards will go into the fire unread. . . . I congratulate you on your autography; it is beautiful, and should help you get a living. I don't know what at, but say crossing sweeper. . . I shall keep it as a specimen, and also as a protection in case I ever feel tempted to give you the thrashing you deserve. You reptile. You are no son of mine, and I never thought you were.'

This, from now on, was the line he was to take. Having for years accused Sybil of turning his children against him, he was now to deny having fathered his sons. Before long Percy, as well as Bosie, was to find himself written off as a bastard.

[2]

There was no accounting for Queensberry's moods. Capable of working himself up into a towering rage and persecuting anyone who defied him, he could—quite unexpectedly and without apparent reason—calm down and behave rationally, as if nothing had happened. These lulls were deceptive. They never lasted long but they did occur from time to time. It was largely a matter of time and circumstance. So long as he was not directly confronted, he was able to give the appearance that he was willing to forget and even forgive a grievance. This is what happened in the case of his second son Percy, Lord Douglas of Hawick.

At the time of Percy's marriage to Minnie Walters in Cornwall, Queensberry had appeared unappeasable. His anger at having his authority flaunted, at being ignored and treated—as he thought—with contempt, had been monumental. He had stormed and ranted, stopped Percy's allowance, hurled abuse at his daughter-in-law, and accused the entire family of plotting against him. The break between father and son at the time had seemed to be final.

Fortunately Percy had not retaliated. Angry and hurt as he was, he accepted Queensberry's tantrums philosophically, shrugged off the insults and set out to make a life for himself in Australia. Percy's career on the Coolgardie gold-fields is something of a mystery. Rumour had it that he 'made a fortune by the age of twenty-five' but his son claims that this fortune was illusory and his gold-field speculations were backed by brokers whose exorbitant interest rates eventually ruined him. Certainly whatever gains he made were short lived. The only real advantage of his sojourn in Australia was that it distanced him from Queensberry. In doing so it helped to heal the rift between them.

For healed it seemed to be. Whilst he was in Australia, Percy renewed contact with his father. Within a matter of months they were writing friendly letters to each other. Queensberry withdrew his objections to Percy's marriage but, characteristically, insisted that he had been right in opposing it. 'I was not intending to stand between you two,' he explained to his daughter-in-law. 'All I wanted was some assurance he had some prospects to marry on first. No-one knows better than I how hard it is for young people to wait, but it is often better for them to do so but not too long. I was and am very angry not with you two, but all the others who simply defied my authority and judgement.' That was as near as Queensberry could come to an apology. However, to help matters along, he began sending them small 'tips'—including £100 when their first child, a daughter, was born—and at one stage even toyed with the idea of visiting them in Australia. 'If I go anywhere,' he told Percy, '[I] will come out to you as I shall be able to look forward to meeting you both and shall not feel so terriby, so fearfully desolate as I always do now when I go alone on these travels.'

How long this happy state of affairs would have lasted there is no telling. It was brought to an abrupt end by Drumlanrig's death. Immediately he heard of his brother's death, Percy—who automatically became Queensberry's heir—decided to return home. In doing so he sailed straight into an impending family storm.

Percy must have known what to expect. Bosie had kept him fully informed of their father's feud with Wilde. He knew about Queensberry's visit to Tite Street, about Bosie's letters, telegrams and postcards, and about Bosie's loaded revlver. He knew also just how vindictive both his father and his brother could be. But if he thought about these things, they did not worry him unduly. Percy arrived in England confident that he could smooth things over. He was an incurable optimist.

But he was reckoning without his father. Queensberry was then staying at the Grand Hotel in Carlisle. He had gone there after quarrelling bitterly with his agent (with whom he had been staying in Scotland) and was still brooding over this quarrel when Percy contacted him. The trouble, apparently had been caused by Queensberry giving offence to the agent's wife—'the holy christian Jane' Queensberry called her—who had refused to have him in the house any longer. 'All this,' he wrote to Percy's wife, 'has terribly upset me and I am homeless again and most uncomfortable and lonely.' Clearly he was in no mood for conciliatory gestures.

This did not deter Percy. According to his son, he went to Carlisle, met Queensberry, and promised to settle the quarrel with Bosie and Wilde. On returning to London, however, Percy changed his mind. Whether this was because he was won over by Bosie (whom he adored) or whether he developed a personal grievance against his father, is not certain. Unfortunately the only evidence for what happened after Percy's return to London is contained in letters written by Queensberry and these letters are, for the most part, rambling, muddled and undated. But it is fairly obvious that there was more involved than the quarrel between Queensberry and Wilde.

At this time, Percy's main concern was to establish his rights as his father's heir. Among other things he was anxious to have his allowance increased and for a settlement to be made on his wife in the event of his dying before his father. Queensberry adamantly refused to agree to either request. The more Percy argued, the more obstinate his father became. So abusive were Queensberry's letters that Percy was finally obliged to call in his lawyers. This only made things worse. 'I refuse,' Queensberry told his son, 'to be wheedled and coerced by this lawyer into carrying out this plan . . . they are trying to force me into making legal settlements on your wife during my life, a thing that has never before been done in the family. . . . Everything may go to the devil for you and your descendants.' Percy responded by refusing to receive any more letters from his father.

All the old attitudes, the resentments, the suspicions and prejudices, were revived. Queensberry raked up his objections to Percy's marriage and again began to attack Percy's wife. Percy sprang to his wife's defence and was supported by the rest of his family. Inevitably Queensberry became convinced that he was being conspired against. It was a conviction that influenced his later actions. He was determined to hit back at his family. 'There will be a scandal,' he warned Percy, 'and more disgrace to our family, but none to me. It is like you and your Montgomery lot to make my task more difficult.'

'Go and prove you're a man—' he sneered on another occasion, 'you having got the whole family to defy me in this way has made it ten times worse for you as far as I am concerned; you have made a quarrel between me and all of them which I will not forgive until they really apologise. It is about time I asserted myself and I intend to do so.'

Just how he intended to assert himself was soon to be made astonishingly clear.

[3]

Oscar Wilde's brilliant comedy *The Importance of Being Earnest* opened at the St James's Theatre on 14 February 1895. For Wilde it was a momentous event. The previous month he had scored an outstanding success with *An Ideal Husband*—which was still playing to packed houses in the Haymarket—and he had every reason to believe that his new play would be another triumph. 'My play,' he had boasted to Bosie earlier, 'is really very funny: I am quite delighted with it.' And despite wrangles with George Alexander, the actor-manager, who had demanded cuts and changes, his confidence had increased throughout rehearsals. Asked by a reporter if he thought *The Importance of Being Earnest* would be a success, he had airily replied: 'It already is: the only question is whether the first-night audience will be one too.'

But he left nothing to chance. The first-night audience was stage-managed with an attention to detail that Wilde had been denied during the rehearsals. He invited all his friends and decreed that lily-of-the-valley should be the flower of the evening. Women arrived at the theatre with sprays of lillies pinned to their puff-sleeved dresses and 'rows and rows' of elegant young men sported the flower in their buttonholes. The atmosphere in the scented foyer was, as a member of the audience remarked, one of 'gaiety, fashion and, apparently, ever-lasting popularity.' Wilde was everywhere. Dressed in a black velvet-collared coat, white waistcoat and white gloves, and wearing a green carnation, he was at his scintillating best: 'fertile, inventive, brilliant.' Few could have guessed that he was plagued by nerves, tortured with apprehension.

If anything dimmed the sparkle, it was the weather. That day—St Valentine's Day—had been a day of storm, the worst London had experienced for years, and a biting wind was blowing as the audience arrived. Snow lay thick in the streets; a jumble of hansom-cabs and private carriages, brought to a stand-still, blocked the approaches to the St James's. Latecomers had to push their way through the maze of vehicles and then battle with a crowd gathered at the theatre doors before reaching the brightly-lit foyer. The result was chaos. So much so, that the arrival of the Marquess of Queensberry, clutching a bunch of carrots and turnips and accompanied by one of his bruiser-like cronies, passed practically unnoticed. He lost no time, though, in making his presence felt.

Queensberry had not come to see the play. His only interest in *The Importance of Being Earnest* was its publicity value. He intended to turn Wilde's first night into a one-man show by repeating the act he had staged, some thirteen years earlier, at Tennyson's *Promise of May*. This time, however, he hoped to improve his performance by flinging his 'phallic' vegetable bouquet onto the stage when he rose to make his protest. Unfortunately his enthusiasm outran his enterprise. Always the exhibitionist, he could not resist boasting of his plan and word of it reached his family. They warned Wilde who immediately took action. On the day before the play was due to open, Wilde dashed off a note to the business manager of the St James's telling him to cancel Queensberry's booking and return his money. As an extra precaution he arranged for a police guard at all the theatre entrances.

Queensberry was not so easily put off. After being refused admission at the box office, he boldly marched to the gallery entrance where he was met by the police and again turned away. After that, according to Wilde, he 'prowled about for three hours, then left chattering like a monstrous ape.'

'He left a grotesque bouquet of vegetables for me!' Wilde wrote glee-fully to Bosie, who was on holiday in Algiers. 'This of course makes his conduct idiotic, robs it of dignity. He arrived with a prize-fighter!!'

Wilde was writing three days later. At first he had had no intention of telling Bosie about Queensberry's arrival at the theatre—'I had de-termined you should know nothing,' he said—but Percy had jumped the gun by wiring to his brother in Algiers and Wilde was left with no alternative but to laugh off the incident. The tone of his letter to Bosie is deceptively flippant. It gives the impression that he treated Queens-berry's antics as an ill-mannered joke—indeed this is what has always been assumed. Nothing could be further from the truth.

Wilde was both angry and alarmed by Queensberry's attempt to dis-rupt his first night. During the performance of the play he had spent most of his time in the wings; he was thought to be afraid that the 'screaming Scarlet Marquess' would try to enter the theatre disguised as a policeman. When the curtain came down to wild applause, Wilde did not take a call—which was not unusual—but he was clearly delighted with his success. He had climbed the stairs to the dressing rooms and joked with George Alexander. 'My dear Alec, it was charming, quite charming,' he laughed. 'And do you know, from time to time I was reminded of a play I once wrote myself called *The Importance of Being Earnest.*' It must have been after this that he was told that Queensberry had left his 'grotesque bouquet of vegetables' at the stage door. To the surprise of his friends, he did not join in the first night celebrations. He had other things on his mind.

His first thought was to sue Queensberry. Either that evening or the following day, he wrote to his solicitors telling them to commence legal proceedings. Once again he was thwarted. On 28 February, Messrs Humphreys, Son & Kershaw wrote to him to say that their efforts to obey his instructions had failed. 'Upon investigating the case,' they said, 'we have met with every obstruction from Mr George Alexander the Manager and his Staff at the Theatre who declined to give us any statements or to render any assistance to you in your desire to prosecute Lord Queensberry and without whose evidence and assistance we cannot advise you to venture upon a prosecution. You personally would of course be unable to give evidence of that which occurred behind your back as to which you have no personal knowledge beyond the information of others who apprised you of the insulting threats and conduct of his Lordship.'

Their letter must have infuriated Wilde. This was his second attempt to confront Queensberry and it was the second time he had been prevented from doing so by others. The solicitors, on the other hand, were not entirely discouraging. 'The only consolation we can offer you,' their letter concluded, 'is that such a persistent persecutor as Lord Queensberry will probably give you another opportunity sooner or later of seeking the protection of the Law in which event we shall be happy to render you every assistance in our power to bring him to Justice and thus secure you future Peace at his hands.'

The solicitors were wiser than they knew. The opportunity they forsaw of Wilde prosecuting Queensberry had come sooner rather than later. It had come, in fact, ten days earlier. Unbeknown to them it was to be acted upon shortly after they wrote their letter.

On 18 February—four days after the opening of *The Importance of Being Earnest*—Queensberry had written an angry letter to Percy's wife, Minnie. He was still smarting from a stormy meeting with Percy who had visited his hotel in Albemarle Street and accused him of creating a scandal at the St James's Theatre. Apparently Percy had refused to listen to his accusations against Bosie and, to prove himself right, Queensberry now told Minnie about the first attempt that had been made to blackmail Bosie at Oxford. 'If Percy does not choose to hear this,' he snarled, 'I shall feel bound to make use of it to clear myself from his wicked accusations. I have been most patient about all this and for two years sat still and did nothing, until everyone was saying "what is his father about, and why does he not interfere?" When I did so, I received nothing but insolence and defiance and impertinent telegrams . . . now I am to have my family taking sides on this question and taking sides with this wretched so-called son of mine. It is madness of Percy to allow quarrelling with me over it, for he knows nothing of what has been ignored.'

He was determined that Percy should know. Not only did he write to Minnie but, that same day, he took more decisive action.

Late that afternoon, Queensberry walked along the street from his hotel to Wilde's club, the Albemarle. On entering the club he went to the hall porter's desk, took out one of his visiting cards, and scrawled across it: 'For Oscar Wilde posing as somdomite.' 'Give that to Oscar Wilde,' he said to the porter.

The porter, Sidney Wright, looked at the card but was unable to understand what Queensberry had written. This is hardly surprising. In his fury, Queensberry had not only misspelt sodomite but had made the other key word, 'posing', indecipherable. (Later the porter was to say he mistook the word 'posing' for 'ponce.') However, after noting on the back of the card that it had been received at 4.30, the porter tactfully sealed it in an envelope and left it to await Wilde's next visit to the club.

Ironically, it was not until the 28 February—the very day the solicitors wrote saying they could not act against Queensberry—that Wilde called in at the Albemarle. Hardly had he walked through the door than the porter handed him the envelope containing Queensberry's card. Wilde took one look at the card and left the club. As he was then staying at an hotel in Piccadilly he went there and wrote to Bosie, now back from Algiers, and to his friend Robbie Ross.

'Bosie's father,' he told Ross, 'has left a card at my club with hideous words on it. I don't see anything now but a criminal prosecution. My whole life seems ruined by this man. The tower of ivory is assailed by the foul thing. On sand is my life spilt. I don't know what to do.'

But he knew full well what to do. He had to sue Queensberry. Ross called to see him that evening and Bosie arrived the following morning. There was no question, as is sometimes suggested, of their egging Wilde on. Wilde was not in need of advice; by that time he must have received the solicitor's letter. When, later that same day, the three of them went to consult Humphreys, the matter was settled. With the solicitors in full agreement, it was decided to commence proceedings against Queensberry.

If Wilde had any doubts at all, it was not about the wisdom of going to law but about the likely cost of the law suit. Here Bosie came to the rescue. His family, he said, would be 'only too delighted to pay all the necessary costs.' They regarded Queensberry as an 'incubus' and had 'often discussed the possibility of getting him put into a lunatic asylum.' He had no doubt they would be willing to pay any costs and expenses incurred by Wilde. This satisfied the solicitors and sent Wilde hurrying to the police court to apply for a warrant for Queensberry's arrest.

Detective-inspector Thomas Greet, of Scotland Yard's C. Division, arrested the Marquess of Queensberry at Carter's Hotel in Albemarle Street on Saturday morning, 2 March 1895. The arrival of the police with a warrant surprised Queensberry. 'In these cases,' he protested, 'I thought proceedings were generally taken by summons, but I suppose it is all right.' He then asked the date of the alleged libel. On being told it was 18 February, he seemed relieved. 'I have been wanting to find Mr Oscar Wilde for nine or ten days,' he smirked. 'This thing has been going on for about two years.'

[4]

Queensberry was formally charged at the Vine Street police station. He was then taken to appear before Mr Robert Milner Newton at the magistrate's court in Great Marlborough Street. By that time he had contacted Sir George Lewis, the clever, fashionable solicitor, who arrived at the court to act on his behalf. Wilde was represented by Charles Humphreys.

The brief proceedings were not without interest. Humphreys opened the case by outlining Wilde's grievances. His client, he said, was the victim of a long and 'most cruel persecution'. His firm had been made aware of this ten months earlier when Wilde had consulted them about the possibility of sueing Lord Queensberry for libel. The only reason they had not acted then was Wilde's concern for members of the Queensberry family. (For some reason Humphrey did not find it necessary to mention Wilde's more recent attempt to prosecute Queensberry. He did, though, hint at 'other libels.') Becoming more specific, Humphreys went on to explain how Queensberry had left his card to be read by the hall porter of the Albemarle Club: the writing on the card, he claimed, contained 'epithets of the foulest nature,' but one word was illegible. (Whether Humphreys and Wilde had themselves deciphered this word is not clear; if they had not, Wilde's haste in rushing into court was, to say the least, ill-advised.) Queensberry's meaning, however, was not left in doubt for long. Interrupting Humphreys, the Marquess offered to read the card himself. 'The word,' he hissed, 'was "posing".'

When Humphreys had finished speaking, Sir George Lewis asked for an adjournment before any evidence was taken. Humphreys objected and insisted on calling two witnesses. Sidney Wright, the hall porter, then vouched for having seen Queensberry's card and Inspector Greet gave evidence of Queensberry's arrest. Once again Lewis sprang to his feet to protest. Queensberry, he maintained, had acted under feelings of great indignation. 'I do not wish,' he went on, after being cautioned by the magistrate, 'this case to be adjourned without it being known that there is nothing against the honour of Lord Queensberry.' He then asked for Queensberry to be set 'at large on his entering into his own recognisances in £1,000.'

This resulted in another legal wrangle, Humphreys insisted on a surety. 'Lord Queensberry,' snapped Lewis, 'is not going to run away.' But the magistrate agreed with Humphreys and asked for a surety of an additional £500. Luckily for Queensberry, this was readily available. A Mr William Tyser 'merchant'—who he was or how he happened to be in court is not known—came forward and pledged himself as Queensberry's surety. The case was then adjourned for a week.

Queensberry must have been pleased with his solicitor. Lewis had shown the sort of fighting spirit he admired. His pleasure, though, was short lived. After leaving the court, Lewis returned his instructions to Queensberry and informed him that he could no longer act on his behalf. Why he did this is uncertain. The most feasible explanation is that, having known Wilde socially for some years, Sir George Lewis was reluctant to oppose him in what promised to be a sensational case. Whatever his reasons, his defection was a blow to Queensberry. On the brink of the most important fight in his career, the battling Marquess found himself deprived of legal support. He had to find another solicitor immediately.

He went to the firm of Day and Russell whose offices were in Norfolk Street. According to H. Montgomery Hyde, the authority on the legal aspects of the Wilde affair, these were the only solicitors' offices open that Saturday afternoon; Queensberry had no option but to apply to them. It was, as it happened, a stroke of luck. Charles Russell Jnr was at the office and agreed to accept the case. Quite by accident, Queensberry had stumbled upon a powerful ally. Not the least of Charles Russell's advantages was the fact that his father, Lord Russell of Killowen, was then the Lord Chief Justice of England.

The week that followed was one of frantic activity on both sides. Wilde's main concern was money. The help he had expected from the Queensberry family was not immediately available. Bosie's mother had promised to do what she could, but she was then in Italy; Percy had offered to pay half the costs, but he was in Devon; Bosie had only managed to rake up £360 in cash. Wilde needed much more. In desperation he appealed to Ernest Leverson—the husband of his devoted friend, Ada Leverson—and asked for a loan of £500 to see him through 'this tedious and dreadful trial.' Leverson sent the money by return and Wilde's confidence returned. He was now prepared to face the 'Scarlet Marquess.'

That he would get the better of Queensberry seemed a foregone conclusion. What had he to fear? How could Queensberry prove his accusations? Had he not repeatedly used, and even stressed, the word 'posing'? If he had any damaging evidence, why was Queensberry safeguarding himself in this way? A pose, even if proved, could mean anything or nothing. Indeed some might consider Queensberry was a *poseur* himself. What else, other than vague rumours, had he to go on? There were, of course, questionable passages in Wilde's novel *The Picture of Dorian Gray*, as well as in some of his other works. Whether Wilde knew it or not, Queensberry intended to quote these passages as evidence of Wilde's homosexual tendencies. But this would not have worried Wilde. There was nothing he enjoyed more than a literary debate. He had already defended *The Picture of Dorian Gray* in print and would have no qualms about doing so again in court. On the face of it, Wilde had every reason to feel confident.

Queensberry was indeed on very shaky ground. There was precious little substance in the case he presented to Charles Russell. He was relying on gossip, rumour, and his own interpretation of Wilde's writings. He had made no real effort to justify his accusations. There is evidence that he had been in touch with a private detective named Cook, who claimed to know a great deal about Wilde's activities, but this contact was purely incidental: it had resulted in nothing more than talk. Cook, Queensberry told Percy's wife, knew far more about Oscar Wilde than he did. This is not surprising. His own erratic enquiries had proved futile; the people he questioned had refused to provide him with answers. Even his literary researches were haphazard and, for the most part, unreliable. One of his proudest discoveries, for instance, had been a story called 'The Priest and the Acolyte' which he claimed Wilde had written for an Oxford undergraduate magazine. He described it as an 'odious work' which had been suppressed 'on account of its utter filth.' But Wilde had not written the story; he was to claim that he had protested to the editor about its inclusion in the magazine. 'It is strange indeed, then,' exclaimed Wilde's counsel, 'to find that publication put upon the particulars as justifying the charge against Mr Wilde.' Left to himself, Queensberry, for all his cunning, might well have walked blindly into his own booby-trap. He was saved from doing so by Charles Russell.

Russell's first move, after consulting his father, the Lord Chief Justice, was to brief the brilliant Irish barrister Edward Carson. Or rather, he took the papers to Carson and was turned down. Carson, who had been at Trinity College in Dublin with Wilde, was reluctant to act in a case involving a 'fellow alumnus and classmate.' According to one of Carson's biographers, Edward Marjoribanks, he was also doubtful about the validity of Queensberry's defence. 'There was nothing to go upon but hearsay,' says Marjoribanks, 'which would be as likely to ruin the young son whom the Marquess was nominally protecting as to have any other effect and the construction of certain books. . . . Carson could only fight if he could persuade himself of the moral justice of his cause.' (Similar doubts might, of course, have influenced Sir George Lewis.) Yet again Queensberry found himself rejected.

But his luck held. He decided, no doubt on Russell's advice, to hire a private detective. The man he chose was Inspector Littlechild. Once Littlechild began his investigations, things took a very different turn. Several stories were told about how Littlechild tracked down Wilde's homosexual associates. Most of these stories have to be treated with caution. One, for instance, has it that Littlechild stumbled upon a prostitute who accused Wilde and his friends of luring away her customers. So angry was she that she provided the detective with information which led him to Alfred Taylor (Wilde's friend who introduced 'gentlemen' to renters) and so exposed the goings-on at Taylor's rooms. There seems to be no real evidence for this story. It could have been inspired by the popular assumption that homosexuals are invariably traced through the criminal underworld. But it seems highly unlikely. Would any prostitute worth her money really have been incensed about losing her, presumably heterosexual, customers to homosexuals?

There is another, far more credible, explanation of Littlechild's detective work. Most of his information was supplied by a jaundiced actor. This was Charles Brookfield who was then appearing in a minor role in *An Ideal Husband*. He was known to be jealous of Wilde's success as a playwright. Brookfield apparently supplied Littlechild—without the help of prostitutes—with all the contacts he needed and put him on the trail of Alfred Taylor.

Once Taylor had been found, Wilde's chances of defeating Queensberry disappeared.

Littlechild's investigation took time. He had hardly got started when, on 9 March, Queensberry again appeared before Mr Newton at the Great Marlborough Street court. By that time, however, there had been an important development in Queensberry's favour. Either through Littlechild or some other contact, Charles Russell had obtained or been promised sufficient evidence of Wilde's homosexual activities to persuade Edward Carson to change his mind and accept the case. It is doubtful whether this evidence was substantial—Carson was not easily persuaded and he consulted a former Chancellor, Lord Halsbury, before finally agreeing—but it was incriminating enough to outrage Carson's moral sensibilities. 'The great thing,' Lord Halsbury had told him, 'is to arrive at justice, and it is you, I believe, who can best do it.' This was all Carson needed to overcome his earlier reservations. He agreed to appear as Queensberry's counsel at Great Marlborough Street.

When he was told he was to face Carson, Wilde was somewhat taken aback. 'No doubt,' he quipped, 'he will perform his task with the added bitterness of an old friend.'

Queensberry's second appearance in court was well publicised. A huge crowd gathered at Great Marlborough Street that morning. When the doors opened, at 11.30, there was a wild scramble for seats. Newspaper reporters were pushed aside, several 'prominent personages' were left standing and even the lawyers had difficulty in finding room for their clerks. By the time Queensberry turned up—muffled in a thick fur coat— the place was packed. Wilde was a little late. He arrived at quarter to twelve and, it was reported, was accompanied by 'a tall fair youth in a coat heavily collared and cuffed with fur.' Only later was it revealed that this youth was Lord Alfred Douglas, the son of the defendant. With Bosie and Wilde, also, was Percy who had returned from Devon for the hearing.

The sight of his two sons supporting Wilde in public infuriated Queensberry. He was only slightly mollified when the magistrate ordered them to leave. 'I hope you noticed,' he wrote to Percy's wife,

Minnie, 'that they were instantly ordered out of Court, which was some satisfaction to me. . . . I am doing all in my power to keep Alfred [Bosie] out of it. He goes and throws himself on our swords that are meant to hack the other fellow to pieces . . . you must all be mad.'

Again the proceedings were routine. Queensberry was allowed to sit on a chair outside the dock and Wilde was called to take the stand. He was examined by his solicitor, Charles Humphreys. His attitude was hardly that of the injured party. Asked whether he was by profession a dramatist and author, he could not resist flippancy. 'I believe,' he replied airily, 'I am well known in that capacity.' The magistrate was not amused. 'Only answer the questions, please,' he snapped. This was the first of many rebukes. Wilde's tendency to play to the gallery did him a great deal of harm.

The preliminaries over, Humphreys went on to question Wilde about his acquaintance with the Queensberry family. In doing so he referred to certain letters written by Queensberry containing libellous statements. The magistrate, however, objected to the introduction of these letters: they had no direct bearing on the issues before the court. 'At the trial,' he pointed out, 'you can say you have other libels against Mr Oscar Wilde and mention dates.'

Here Carson interrupted. He was anxious to have the letters produced and had little doubt that they would illustrate Queensberry's concern for his son. Somewhat to Humphrey's surprise, he announced that he had a copy of Queensberry's original attack on Wilde. (The wily Marquess had obviously safeguarded himself as far as his writing was concerned.) Humphreys, taken aback, submitted to the magistrate's ruling.

'It was never,' he explained, 'my intention to read the letters in public. I intended to produce them and ask you and the learned counsel to read them. In one particular letter the names of the exalted persons are used and I do not think it would be right that their names should be called in question in a matter of this description.' This was the first public mention of 'exalted persons' and, indirectly, of Rosebery.

Carson was prevented from cross-examining Wilde. He wanted to establish that Queensberry had acted solely as an aggrieved father but, again, the magistrate objected. Such a line of questioning, he ruled, would amount to quasi-justification and could not be allowed. Resignedly Carson resumed his seat.

The prosecution's case over, the magistrate turned to Queensberry. 'John Douglas,' he observed solemnly, 'having heard the evidence, now is the time to make an answer to the charge. . . . What have you to say? Queensberry, who had been sitting behind his counsel, rose to his feet. His reply was brief but direct.

'I have simply, your worship,' he declared, 'to say this. I wrote that card simply with the intention of bringing matters to a head, having been unable to meet Mr Wilde otherwise, and to save my son, and I abide by what I wrote.'

'Then,' said the magistrate, 'you will be committed for trial, and the same bail will be allowed you as before.'

Chapter Sixteen

The Queensberry Trial

Wilde still thought Queensberry was bluffing. He had no reason to think otherwise. So far everything had gone his way. He had sailed through the court hearing with great aplomb, even raised a smile or two, and his depositions had not been challenged. Knowing little of law, he was probably pleased with his performance. Queensberry, on the other hand, could hardly have been said to have shone. Press reports dismissed him as an unimpressive 'middle aged mutton-chopped man' and his lawyers had appeared to be clutching at straws. The stress Carson had placed on Queensberry's abusive letters had given the impression that these letters were vital to the defence case. If this were so, Wilde had little to fear. The letters were in the hands of his solicitors and, as he well knew, they contained nothing more than vague accusations based on hearsay. There had been not the slightest hint of more damaging evidence.

Whether Wilde's solicitors shared his confidence is another matter. Certainly Humphreys was taking no chances. Immediately after the court hearing he decided to brief Sir Edward Clarke, a well-known and highly experienced criminal lawyer, to act on Wilde's behalf. Evidently he considered it would require a man of Clarke's calibre to match up to Carson. Clarke had another advantage: he came to the case completely fresh. All he knew of Wilde was his reputation as a brilliant and successful playwright. So innocent was Clarke that when he was first introduced to Wilde he found it necessary to question him on the truth of the libel. Unblinkingly Wilde assured the lawyer that Queensberry's charges were completely without foundation.

That done, Wilde decided to take a holiday. Queensberry's trial was scheduled for the opening of the next Old Bailey sessions some three weeks later, and Wilde allowed Bosie to talk him into filling in the waiting period at Monte Carlo. It was, as he later realised, a very foolish decision. Not only was it a waste of the money he had borrowed to meet his costs, but a waste of precious time. He was to blame Bosie bitterly for this mistake. 'At a time when I should have been in London taking wise counsel . . .' he wrote in *De Profundis,* two years later, 'you insisted on my taking you to Monte Carlo, of all revolting places on God's earth, that all day, and all night as well, you might gamble as long as the Casino remained open. . . . You refused to discuss even for five minutes the position to which you and your father had brought me.' But he was writing from hindsight. At the time he could have needed little persuading. What, in any case, could he have told Sir Edward Clarke after denying the truth of Queensberry's charges?

A few days after Wilde and Bosie left England, the *Whitehall Review* reported that Queensberry was also in Monte Carlo. This was pure speculation. Journalists, remembering Queensberry's pursuit of Rosebery, were no doubt eager for a repeat performance; they were disappointed. Queensberry remained firmly in London. He had other ways of spending those critical three weeks.

Inspector Littlechild's investigation was in full swing. He was making rapid progress. One of his early successes was in tracking down a young soldier named Charles Parker who, before joining the army, had made a living of sorts (he was actually an unemployed valet) as a renter. A couple of years earlier, he and his brother William had been introduced to Wilde by the obliging Alfred Taylor. They had dined together at Kettner's and after dinner Wilde had whisked Charles Parker away to the Savoy Hotel where, as the young man later admitted, 'indecencies' had taken place. Wilde had paid Parker £2 and arranged to meet him at the Savoy a week later. The detective lost no time in persuading Parker to talk to Queensberry's solicitors.

Getting Parker to testify was not easy. In effect he was an accomplice and, as the solicitors were not acting for the Crown, he could not be promised immunity. Eventually, however, he was won over—helped, no doubt, by a judicious bribe—and his name was entered on Queensberry's plea of justification. Others followed. Littlechild and his assistants, helped by leads from the embittered actor, Charles Brookfield, collected the names of at least ten other young men who were alleged to be sexually involved with Wilde. Included among them was Alfred Wood, who had tried to blackmail Bosie; Maurice Schwabe, a nephew of the Solicitor-General's wife; Edward Shelley, a clerk at Wilde's publishers; and Herbert Tankard, a page at the Savoy Hotel.

That Queensberry took an active part in the investigation is unlikely. Stories of him scouring London with a team of ex-policemen are fanciful. He had neither the patience nor the perspicacity to play detective: his earlier attempts to obtain information against Wilde had failed dismally. For once, it seems, Queensberry was content to leave the footwork to the experts. His interest in this sport was in the kill, not the chase. Assessing the results kept him fully occupied.

And he had more on his mind than Wilde. Not the least of Queensberry's concerns at this time was his campaign against Percy. His second son's defection had hurt him deeply and, as always, his hurt had turned to spite. What spare time Queensberry had was spent in writing vitriolic letters to his daughter-in-law. This, as he repeatedly pointed out to Minnie, was his only means at hitting back at Percy.

As 'this good-for-nothing, white-livered son of mine, if he is so . . .' he exploded, after Percy had ignored his exposure of Bosie's activities at Oxford, 'refuses to receive or answer letters, the only way I could let him know was by writing to you. You must all be mad, and if you chose to make inquiries, you will find the whole town has been reeking with this hideous scandal of Oscar Wilde. . . . If I were to shoot this hideous monster in the street, I should be perfectly justified, for he has almost ruined my so-called son.'

Significantly Queensberry made no mention of Littlechild's investigation. That was something he was keeping to himself; he had no intention of putting Wilde on guard a second time. His letters to Minnie were a mixture of wild abuse and even wilder recrimination. It all became too much for poor Minnie. In desperation she instructed solicitors to inform Queensberry that she would not receive any more communications from him. This produced another explosion. 'Who the devil are you?' Queensberry screamed at the solicitors. 'I am not going to argue with you about this disgusting matter which is no earthly business of yours. . . . I can only suppose you are all raving lunatics, but I beg you will not worry or annoy me further with your impertinent interference.'

Cut off from both Percy and Minnie, Queensberry turned first on Bosie and then on Minnie's father. He became incoherent with rage; his writing was often indecipherable, his command of epithets nothing short of marvellous. Bosie was dismissed as a 'miserable misguided creature' who was 'insignificant, ridiculous and physically wretched' while Percy became 'your good-for-nothing, kicked-out, runaway, turned-up brother . . . a wretched creature . . . this squirming skunk.' He offered to fight Bosie with one arm tied behind his back and to give Percy 'the licking he deserves.' 'What you both require,' he stormed, 'is a damned good hiding . . . an unmerciful hiding to knock the conceit out of you.' Minnie's father was told he could take his daughter back and 'keep her and her pauper children, as I will disown them.'

Bosie found his father's letter waiting for him when he returned from Monte Carlo. There was a greater shock awaiting Wilde. By that time Queensberry's amended plea of justification had been completed and sent to Charles Humphreys. Its formal phraseology put Queensberry's invective to shame.

'John Sholto Douglas Marquess of Queensberry,' it declared, 'says that our Lady the Queen ought not further to prosecute the said Second Count of the said Indictment against him because he says that the said alleged libel according to the natural meaning of the words thereof is true in substance and fact.' There followed a list of persons with whom Oscar Fingal O'Flahertie Wills Wilde had committed 'sodomy and other acts of gross indecency and immorality' and the places and dates where and when these acts had been committed. The catalogue of offences ended with mention of works alleged to have been written by Wilde, including *The Picture of Dorian Gray* which, it was said, had been 'designed and intended' to describe 'the relations intimacies and passions of certain persons of sodomitical and unnatural habits tastes and practices.'

How Wilde reacted on being shown this frightening document can only be imagined. He must, to put it mildly, have been extremely worried. There was no escaping the thoroughness of Littlechild's investigation. Some of the incidents referred to were said to have occurred two or three years earlier; the places mentioned ranged from houses in Paris and Oxfordshire to the Savoy Hotel, the Albemarle Hotel and the Albion Hotel in Brighton. Yet, faced with all this, Wilde decided to brazen it out. The first shock over, he again insisted that there was no truth in the charges and that he was prepared to face Queensberry.

His friends thought him quite mad. Several of them—including Frank Harris and Bernard Shaw—urged him to leave the country. He refused to listen and was backed up in his obstinacy by Bosie. Two days before the Old Bailey trial the two of them, accompanied by Wilde's wife, attended a performance of *The Importance of Being Earnest*. During the interval Wilde went backstage to see George Alexander who also advised him to go abroad.

'Everyone,' sighed Wilde, 'wants me to go abroad. I have just been abroad, and now I am come home again. One can't keep going abroad, unless one is a missionary or, what comes to the same thing, a commercial traveller.'

His buoyant mood was not shared by his wife. Bosie was to remember Constance Wilde looking very agitated that evening and saying goodbye to him with tears in her eyes. It was the last time Bosie saw her.

Wilde's audacity was both typical and amazing. He placed his trust in himself and his stars. Earlier that week he had consulted a fortune teller and had come away full of confidence in her prediction that all would be well. The Sibyl, he wired to Ada Leverson, 'prophesied complete triumph.'

'Have no fear,' he told another friend, 'the working classes are with me—to a boy.'

[2]

Queensberry arrived early for the first day of his trial at the Old Bailey on 3 April 1895. He was neatly dressed in a navy blue overcoat and was wearing a light-blue hunting stock instead of a collar and tie. As he stood in front of the dock, waiting for the judge to arrive, he twiddled a small felt hat in his hands and gave the appearance of nervous uncertainty. He looked anything but aristocratic. 'He was short of stature,' noted an observer, 'with a round face, clean shaven except for a streak of red whisker. His lower lip drooped considerably.'

The small, rather dingy, court room was packed. A fashionably dressed crowd had queued from early that morning; when the doors opened, an hour before the trial, there had again been a wild scramble for seats. The gangways were jammed and as the men—there were no women— pushed against each other one of them raised a laugh by remarking on 'the importance of being early.' The joke was not inappropriate. For the most part, the mood of the crowd was that of a first night audience rather than of spectators at a solemn court hearing. They were not to be disappointed.

The leading actor arrived shortly after Queensberry. Wilde, wearing a frock coat and a flower in his buttonhole, entered the court accompanied by Bosie. Pushing his way to the front, he sat chatting to his lawyers. He appeared somewhat subdued. The jauntiness he had displayed in the police court was kept under tight control. Queensberry, standing a few yards away, scarcely glanced at him. His attention was concentrated on his solicitor, Charles Russell, who was locked in conversation with the redoubtable Inspector Littlechild. Whether, at that stage, Wilde realised who Littlechild was is not known. He was to find out later.

Percy was not in court. He and Bosie were represented by Mr Edward Besley Q. C. and Mr J. L. Monckton who held watching briefs for them. In Percy's case this was merely a safeguard. By an odd coincidence, Percy had met one of the young men named in his father's plea for justification, Ernest Scarfe, while travelling to Australia in 1893 and it was thought advisable for Percy to instruct counsel. Bosie, on the other hand, fully expected to be called as a witness. He was to claim that Sir Edward Clarke had given him a solemn promise that he would be allowed to testify against his father. His intention, he said, was to tell the court what an 'inhuman brute' Queensberry was and to explain how 'he had bullied and persecuted and outraged my mother for years . . . and for twenty years neglected and ill-treated his children and had forfeited all claim to a father's authority over them.'

Clarke denied having made such a promise. There was no reason for him to have done so. The issue before the court was Queensberry's alleged libel of Oscar Wilde by accusing him of posing as a sodomite. His character as a father was irrelevant; Bosie's testimony would not have been allowed by the judge. Indeed had Bosie appeared in the witness box at the outset of the case, as he wished, he might well have prejudiced the jury in Queensberry's favour. No jury, as Edward Marjoribanks pointed out, would have warmed to 'a young son attacking his father in a criminal trial before his father had said a word in his defence.' In any case Bosie, to his lasting chagrin, was not called.

The judge, Mr Justice Henn Collins, arrived ten minutes late and things got under way immediately. After the jury had been sworn in, Queensberry's name was called and he entered the dock. Speaking in a clear voice he pleaded not guilty and, glancing disdainfully at Wilde, declared that the words complained of were true and had been 'published' for the public benefit. Sir Edward Clarke, short and stout and looking, it is said, 'rather like an eighteenth-century parson', then rose to open the case for the prosecution.

Bosie, hoping for a scathing attack on his father, was scornful of Clarke's opening speech. The more experienced Edward Carson, though, had nothing but praise for his opponent's performance. 'I never,' he later told a friend in the House of Commons, 'heard anything to equal it in all my life.' There were no histrionics, no flights of rhetoric, no playing for effect. Only occasionally did Clarke allow himself a mild, but pointed quip. After outlining the nature of the alleged libel and touching on Wilde's relationship with the Queensberry family—including the attempt made by Alfred Wood to blackmail Bosie—he came to the written evidence. Skilfully he anticipated the defence's tactics by reading out Wilde's most compromising letter. This was the disastrous 'prose-poem'—'those red rose-leaf lips of yours . . . made no less for music of song than for the madness of kisses'—a copy of which was, by now, in Queensberry's hands.

'The words of that letter, gentlemen, may appear extravagant to those in the habit of writing commercial correspondence,' said Clarke, to loud laughter, 'or those ordinary letters which the necessities of life force upon one every day. But Mr Wilde is a poet, and the letter is considered by him a prose sonnet, and one of which he is in no way ashamed and is prepared to produce anywhere as the expression of true poetic feeling.'

It was a deft move. Wit and frankness helped to lower the jury's eyebrows and take the sting out of any later attack. He was also adroit in defending *The Picture of Dorian Gray* which, he pointed out, could 'be bought on any bookstall in London' and had been published five years ago. 'I shall be surprised,' he said, 'if my learned friend Mr Carson can pitch upon any passage in that book which does more than describe as novelists and dramatists may—nay, must—describe the passions and fashions of life.'

At the end of his speech, Clarke asked for the porter of the Albemarle Club to take the stand and repeat the evidence he had given before the magistrate. Carson did not cross-examine.

Then came the moment for which everyone had been waiting. Oscar Wilde was called. He presented a striking contrast to his dapper, tense-faced opponent in the dock. 'Ponderous and fleshy,' reads a contemporary description of him at this moment, 'his face a dusky red, and his hair brushed away from a middle parting in smooth waves, he folded his hands on the witness box, and replied in carefully modulated monosyllables.' Queensberry was seen to square his shoulders as Clarke began his examination.

Wilde was a model witness. He appeared (considering that he knew about the plea of justification) marvellously composed and answered Clarke's questions boldly. To the watchful Edward Carson his replies seemed, at times, a little too glib. Asked his age, for instance, he said unhesitatingly that he was thirty-nine. This caused Carson to look up sharply and make a hurried note. Queensberry was also scribbling away. He asked for pen and paper while Wilde was being questioned on his first meeting with Bosie and was soon writing furiously. His notes were later handed to Carson by an usher.

Oblivious of all this literary activity, Wilde continued with his evidence. Clarke led him through the routine business of establishing his position in society and his reputation as a literary figure and then questioned him about his relationship with the Queensberry family. There were several amusing passages. Wilde's version of his interview with Queensberry caused so much laughter that the judge threatened to clear the court. His account of Wood's attempt to blackmail him with the 'prose-poem' letter was hilarious.

'A very curious construction could be put on that letter,' one of Wood's associates had said. 'Art,' replied Wilde, 'is rarely intelligible to the criminal classes.' The blackmailer persisted. 'A man has offered me £60 for it,' he asserted. Wilde claimed to be flattered. 'If you take my advice,' he observed blandly, 'you will go to that man and sell it to him for £60. I myself have never received so large a sum for any prose work of that length, but I am glad to find that there is someone in England who considers a letter of mine worth £60.' Wilde admitted paying the man ten shillings for his trouble, but said he did so willingly. 'I am afraid,' he smiled as they parted, 'you are leading a wonderfully wicked life.'

This was Oscar at his best. By the time Clarke's examination ended, those who had come for a free performance of a Wilde comedy felt well rewarded. They fully expected that Bosie would be the next actor to appear, but they were disappointed. Clarke ended on a serious note.

'Is there any truth in any of these accusations?' he demanded.

'There is no truth in any one of them,' declared Wilde robustly.

The next act was opened by the long and lanky Edward Carson. Unfurling himself from his chair, he faced his ex-classmate and began his cross-examination. His first question was deadly. 'You stated,' he observed quietly, 'that your age was thirty-nine. I think you are forty. You were born on the 16th of October 1854?' He held up Wilde's birth certificate. For the first time the witness looked flustered: but he quickly recovered. 'I have no wish to pose as being young,' he purred. 'You have my certificate and that settles the matter.' Carson was not to be deflected. 'But being born in 1854,' he insisted, 'makes you more than forty?' 'Ah,' sighed Wilde, 'Very well.'

Carson had scored the first point. Trivial as it appeared, it was not without significance. Wilde, caught out in a silly lie, was now on the defensive. His discomfiture was apparent to the jury. There was more to come.

Carson went on to attack Wilde's writings. Coming to *The Picture of Dorian Gray* he suggested that it was open to the interpretation of being a 'perverted novel.' Here Wilde was on home ground; he gave back better than he got. 'That,' he replied disdainfully, 'could only be true to brutes and illiterates. The views of Philistines on art are incalculably stupid.' Unruffled Carson continued to hammer away at the book. He read out certain passages. 'But let us go over it phrase by phrase,' he urged, turning a page. ' "I quite admit that I adore you madly." What do you say to that? Have you ever adored a young man madly?' Wilde was not so easily caught. 'I have never,' he protested, 'given adoration to anybody except myself.' 'I suppose,' snapped Carson, when he could make himself heard above the laughter, 'you think that a very smart thing?' 'Not at all,' replied Wilde modestly.

And so it went on. As long as literature was being discussed, Wilde could more than hold his own. This was true even when it came to the extravagant letters he had written to Bosie. 'Is that an ordinary letter?' snorted Carson, after reading one of them. 'Everything I wrote is extraordinary,' retorted Wilde. 'I do not pose as being ordinary, great heavens! Ask me any questions you like about it.'

It was not until the names of the boys mentioned in the plea of justification were introduced that Wilde was again thrown off balance. Asked whether he had become fond of his publisher's 'office boy,' he became very heated. 'I really do not think,' he stormed, 'that is the proper form for the question to be addressed to me in. I deny that was the position of Mr Edward Shelley, to whom you are referring. I object to your description.' There was another uncomfortable moment when Carson produced a silver cigarette case, a silver-mounted walking-stick and a signed photograph which Wilde had given to another boy. Reluctantly he was also made to admit that he had supplied this boy with clothes and taken him to Brighton. His explanation that these gifts were 'a reward for his being a pleasant companion to myself and my children' was hardly convincing after Carson had pointed out that the boy was a newspaper seller. ('It is the first I have heard of his connection with literature,' quipped Wilde.)

Luckily it was late in the afternoon when Carson began questioning Wilde on his youthful companions and after he had dealt with the newsboy the court adjourned for the day. Wilde was given a much needed breathing space.

Queensberry had spent most of that afternoon lounging nonchalantly in the dock, gazing abstractedly round the court and appearing, at times, to be following the proceedings with only half an ear. His initial interest in Wilde's evidence seemed to subside once Carson began his cross-examination. What he thought of the day's proceedings is not known. He could not have drawn much comfort from the evening newspapers. Most reports of the case were inclined to favour the prosecutor. They were amused by Wilde, they described him as a 'lover of beauty' and admired the 'wonderful intellectual force and flow of perfect language with which he defended his position.' There were even some who saw him as a crusader in the cause of aestheticism, battling against the complacency of a philistine public.

These reports, however, had been rushed out before the court adjourned. Those reporters who waited until the end gained a somewhat different impression. They were aware of Wilde's touchiness when questioned about the boys with whom he had associated. So agitated did Wilde appear that a rumour spread that, after leaving court, he panicked and fled to Ostend. Late that night, the European correspondent of the *New York Herald* contacted Queensberry to find out if this were true. 'At one o'clock this morning,' he reported the following day, 'Lord Queensberry had heard nothing definite either in confirmation or denial of the rumour.'

But Wilde had not fled. If anything, he was pleased with his performance in court and encouraged by the early press reports. 'Everything,' he wired to Ada Leverson that evening, 'is very satisfactory.'

[3]

The court was packed again the next morning. Wilde arrived early, wearing a long black Chesterfield overcoat and carrying a silk high hat. His manner matched his sombre appearance: he was anything but jaunty. Queensberry followed shortly afterwards and took his stand 'with the same air of self-composure as marked his conduct the previous day.' The two men studiously ignored each other.

Wilde was called and, once he had entered the witness box, Carson resumed his cross-examination. He launched straight into Wilde's relationship with Alred Taylor. How friendly were they? (Wilde admitted he had known Taylor for two years.) Were not Taylor's rooms in Little College Street 'peculiar', heavily curtained, elaborately furnished and strongly perfumed? Did Wilde know that Taylor kept women's clothes in his rooms? Was he not notorious for introducing young men to older men? Had he ever arranged dinners for Wilde to meet young men?

Wilde denied knowledge of Taylor's habits, but admitted that Taylor had introduced him to 'about five' young men. 'Were these young men all about twenty?' asked Carson. 'Yes,' Wilde agreed, 'twenty or twenty-two. I like the society of young men.' Here Queensberry was seen to grin broadly. 'For a moment,' it was reported, 'he relaxed his fixed stare at the witness to gaze round the court, as though inviting attention to this answer.

Carson pressed on. What were the occupations of these young men? Was Charles Parker one of them? How old was he? ('Really,' exclaimed Wilde. 'I do not keep a census.') Was he intellectual? Where had they met? Did he know Parker's brother? Was not Parker a valet and his brother a groom? Did he call Parker 'Charlie' and Parker call him 'Oscar'? Had Wilde taken Parker to the Savoy Hotel?

Wilde was forced into some damaging admissions. His replies were often witty but there was no escaping the drive of Carson's questions. The lawyer was relentless. He was able to establish that Wilde had entertained the Parkers lavishly at Kettner's. That he had plied them with wine. That he had nothing in common with the young men. That he had taken a particular liking to Charles Parker and, despite a difference in age and interests, had treated him as an intimate friend. Wilde adamantly denied, however, that he had taken Parker to the Savoy Hotel. He had entertained other young men at the Savoy, he said, but not Parker.

What, Carson wanted to know, was Charlie Parker's attraction? Wilde's reply was disarmingly frank. 'I delight in the society of people much younger than myself,' he smiled. 'I like those who may be called idle and careless. I recognise no social distinctions of any kind; and to me youth, the mere fact of youth, is so wonderful that I would sooner talk to a young man for half-an-hour than be—well, cross-examined in court by an elderly Q.C.'

The 'elderly Q.C.' (Carson was Wilde's age) remained unmoved. Doggedly he continued with his questions about Wilde's boy friends. Having finished with Parker he turned to Fred Atkins, a bookmaker's tout whom Wilde had taken to Paris; and to Ernest Scarfe, a valet whom Wilde had met through Alfred Taylor; and to the slightly better educated Sidney Mavor, who was known to his friends as 'Jenny' and had spent a night as Wilde's guest at the Albemarle Hotel.

Wilde danced around Carson's thrusts, parried some, and occasionally scored a hit himself. A silver cigarette case was produced and Wilde was asked whether he recognised it as one he had given to Sidney Mavor. 'No really I could not,' he protested. 'I have given so many I could not recognise it.' His audience found this highly amusing. But that was the last laugh he got at Carson's expense. His next witticism proved fatal. It concerned a young boy named Walter Grainger, whom Bosie had once employed at Oxford and who had later worked for Wilde at Goring. Wilde admitted that he knew him and that he was sixteen when they first met.

'Did you ever kiss him?' asked Carson. 'Oh, dear no,' Wilde blurted out. 'He was a peculiarly plain boy. He was, unfortunately, ugly. I pitied him for it.' Carson pounced immediately. 'Was that the reason why you did not kiss him?' he demanded. Wilde recognised his mistake too late and made things worse by losing his temper. 'Oh! Mr Carson,' he snapped, 'you are pertinently insolent.' Carson was not put off by abuse. He now had Wilde on the run and was determined not to let up. 'Did you,' he thundered, 'say that in support of your statement that you never kissed him?' Wilde, by now, had become hopelessly confused. Embarrassed, angry, and near to tears, he could scarcely reply. He tried desperately to pull himself together. 'Why sir,' Carson persisted, 'did you mention that this boy was extremely ugly?' 'For this reason,' gasped Wilde. 'If I were asked why I did not kiss a door-mat, I should say because I do not like to kiss door-mats. I do not know why I mentioned that he was ugly, except that I was stung by the insolent question you put to me and the way you have insulted me throughout this hearing. . . .'

But it was no use. Wilde's speech was slurred, he was becoming increasingly incoherent. At last he had been made to realise that a court room was not a theatre; that there could be no throw-away lines, no playing to the gallery, no convenient exits. Carson had turned his comedy of manners into stark, real life tragedy. There was no mistaking the implication of Carson's sarcasm. He should never have joked about not kissing the boy. When questioned about other youths, he had flatly rejected any suggestion of 'improprieties' and, in so doing, had denied Carson an opening. Now he was dangerously exposed. One can only assume that, with Grainger, he felt himself to be on safer ground because he had not in fact kissed the boy. It was a foolish mistake.

Eventually, flushed with triumph, Carson let him off the hook. Wilde was forced to admit that 'at times one says things flippantly when one ought to speak more seriously.' 'Then you said it flippantly?' suggested Carson. 'Oh, yes,' Wilde sighed wearily, 'it was a flippant answer.'

The rest of the morning's hearing was an anti-climax. Carson concluded his cross-examination with a few innocuous questions and then sat down. Sir Edward Clarke was left with the thankless task of trying to restore confidence in his client.

Clarke began his re-examination by reading out the abusive letters Queensberry had written to his family. It was a shrewd, if belated, move. The letters were not designed to win sympathy for a solicitous father. Those addressed to Bosie, in which Queensberry questioned his son's legitimacy—'in this christian country . . . 'tis a wise father who knows his own child'—created a particularly bad impression. No one, however, was more affected by Clarke's reading than Queensberry himself. As the lawyer droned on, he stood snarling openly at Wilde; from time to time he shook his head violently and, at one stage, was seen to bite his lip as if trying to stifle his tears. The court's attention was evenly divided between the dock and the witness box.

Leaving the letters, Clarke went on to question Wilde about Alfred Taylor and some of the other young men. He did his best to counteract Carson's accusations by eliciting answers from Wilde that made these dubious acquaintances appear reasonably respectable. Taylor, for instance, was shown to be a former public schoolboy who played the piano 'very charmingly'; Edward Shelley not only worked for a publisher but had 'literary tastes' and admired Wilde's work. . . . It was a valiant effort on Clarke's part but the odds were against him.

Shortly after three that afternoon, Carson rose to make his opening speech for the defence. He was at his Irish best: persuasive, eloquent and fiery. It was his intention, he announced, to show that Lord Queensberry had been motivated by one desire—that of rescuing his son from the clutches of the prosecutor. He appealed to the jury, as fathers, for justice. Lord Queensberry, he said, had learned about the scandals associated with Wilde's name. He had been told about the incidents at the Savoy Hotel. He was aware that Wilde had befriended some of the most immoral characters in London.

'I refer above all others,' he rapped out, 'to the man Taylor, a most notorious character—as the police will tell the court—who occupied rooms which were nothing more than a shameful den.' He went on to elaborate on Taylor's debaucheries. He spoke of the 'orgies' at Taylor's rooms in which 'artists and valets' had taken part and of an occasion, the previous year, when the police had raided a house in Fitzroy Street and arrested eighteen homosexuals, Taylor and Charles Parker among them. 'Taylor,' he insisted, 'is really the pivot of the case . . . it was Taylor who introduced the young men to the prosecutor.'

Why then, he asked, had not Taylor been summoned as a witness? He was known to be in England, Wilde had remained friendly with him, why had he not appeared in court? 'Mr Oscar Wilde,' snorted Carson, 'has undertaken to prove enough to send Lord Queensberry to gaol and to brand him as a criminal, but it is remarkable that the only witness who could have supported Mr Wilde's asseverance of innocence has not been called.'

The court listened in silence. Carson spoke for nearly an hour. There was an occasional nod or whisper as he drove his points home, but it was not until he neared the end of his speech that comment rose above a whisper. For it was then that he sprang his greatest surprise.

The defence, he said, intended to call witnesses who would testify to Wilde's infamous practices. Various young men with whom Wilde was

alleged to have committed criminal offences would be put into the witness box. The first would be Alfred Wood, the boy who had tried to
blackmail Wilde and who was thought to be in America.

'But gentlemen,' barked Carson, after a dramatic pause, 'as a matter of
fact Wood is here and will be examined before you!'

There was a gasp of amazement. Carson had timed his announcement
well. He followed it up by reading out the 'prose-poem' letter. This time
the honeyed words fell on shocked ears.

'Before you condemn Lord Queensberry,' Carson concluded, 'I ask you
to read Mr Wilde's letter and say whether the gorge of any father ought
not to rise. I ask you to bear in mind that Lord Queensberry's son was so
dominated by Mr Wilde that he threatened to shoot his own father.
Gentlemen, Lord Queensberry did what he has done most deliberately,
and he is not afraid to abide by the issue he has raised in this court.'

It has been said that Wilde was stunned by Carson's announcement.
He is said not to have known that Wood and others would be called as
witnesses. This, however, is open to question. Wilde was no fool. He had
seen and recognised the names in the plea of justification. He knew those
names had not been sucked out of Queensberry's thumb. Could he really
have expected the case to end without those boys being called? It seems
highly unlikely. At the very least his lawyers should have warned him of
this possibility. If he was stunned it was because he realised how badly
the case was going against him; he was no longer sure of his ability to bluff
his way through. His fatal slip over the Grainger boy had thoroughly
unnerved him. The prospect of facing more detailed evidence, evidence
given by renters and chancers, was terrifying.

Certainly the case was going against him. Newspaper reports that
evening no longer made amusing reading. 'Things indeed,' commented
one journalist, 'have been fast reaching a point at which no man's name
has been safe, and it is therefore felt by everyone that Lord Queensberry
has rendered a positive service to the community. This at all events is the
opinion I have heard expressed on every hand today.' Again there were
rumours that Wide had fled the country.

The rumours became more persistent the following morning when
Wilde did not appear in court. His absence, however, was soon to be
explained. He had been advised to stay away by his counsel. After
listening to Carson, Sir Edward Clarke had decided it would be best for
Wilde to drop the case. He had met Wilde that morning and suggested
that he should, on Wilde's behalf, make a statement withdrawing from
the prosecution. No English jury, he argued, would be likely to convict a
father who appeared to be trying to save his son from an evil influence.
And if, as seemed possible, Queensberry was acquitted, then the judge
would undoubtedly order Wilde's arrest. His only hope was to withdraw
before Wood and the others were put on the stand. Wilde had no option

but to agree. He waited outside the court while Clarke went in to make his statement.

The trial was already in progress. Carson had resumed his opening speech and was detailing Wilde's relationship with the young newspaper seller when Clarke re-entered. He was stopped by Clarke plucking at his gown. The two lawyers held a whispered conversation and then Clarke addressed the court.

'I think it must have been present to your lordship's mind,' he announced, facing the judge, 'that those who represent Mr Wilde in this case have before them a very terrible anxiety. They cannot conceal from themselves that the judgement that might be formed on the literature involved in this case, and upon the conduct which has been admitted, might not improbably induce the jury to say that Lord Queensberry in using the word "posing" was using a word for which there was sufficient justification.' In the circumstances, he felt his client could not expect a favourable verdict. 'We should,' he pointed out, 'be going through, day after day, an investigation of matters of the most appalling character,' without reasonable hope of success. He was therefore prepared to accept a verdict of not guilty 'having reference to the word "posing".'

The judge was not happy with this. He objected to terms and limitations being set on the jury's verdict. 'The verdict,' he ruled, 'must be "Guilty" or "Not Guilty." ' The jury's deliberations took only a matter of minutes. Without leaving the jury box they found the plea of justification had been proved and declared Queensbery 'Not Guilty.'

The verdict was greeted with wild applause. Several of Queensberry's friends rushed to the dock to congratulate him and there was loud cheering as he reached over to grasp their hands. Outside the court he was met by a crowd of reporters. He told them he had sent a message to Wilde.

'If this country allows you to leave,' he was quoted as saying, 'all the better for the country. But if you take my son with you, I will follow you wherever you go and shoot you.'

Later Queensberry denied saying this. The message, he claimed, had been sent some days ago, not after the trial. He had not said he would shoot Wilde. What he had said was that if Wilde left the country and 'persuaded his misguided son to go with him, he would *feel quite justified* in shooting Wilde—did he feel inclined to do so, and were he worth the trouble.' It was a nice distinction. The battling Marquess had learned to measure his threats.

[4]

'The judge,' noted the approving *Daily Telegraph*, commenting on Queensberry's success, 'did not attempt to silence the irrepressible cheering in the court which greeted the acquital of this sorely-provoked and cruelly-injured father.'

This was the tone of most newspaper comment. Overnight the much-ridiculed and widely disliked Marquess had become a hero. His previous misdeeds and controversial activities—his agnosticism, his radical alliances, his dissolute life, his divorce, his neurotic behaviour and his violent, often public, outbursts of bigotry—were brushed aside and he was hailed as an upholder of Victorian propriety; a virtuous, self-sacrificing *pater familias*, a fighter for all that was good and decent, a noble public benefactor. Single-handed he had taken on the forces of evil and, with high-minded perseverance, exposed the corruption which threatened society. Beside him Oscar Wilde seemed the personification of wickedness.

'There is not a man or woman,' trumpeted the *National Observer*, 'in the English-speaking world possessed of the treasure of a wholesome mind who is not under a deep debt of gratitude to the Marquess of Queensberry for destroying the High Priest of the Decadents.'

Such pious acclaim might have embarrassed a more sensitive man. Not every rebel who had spent his life sneering at convention would have welcomed the role of moral guardian; not every agnostic whose letters denouncing Christianity had been read out in court would have allowed himself to be ranged so firmly on the side of the angels. But Queensberry was nothing if not an opportunist. He had not only accepted the homage but revelled in his new-found respectability.

The newspapers were not alone in their admiration. Hardly had Queensberry left court than he was deluged in congratulatory messages. 'You know,' he chuckled to an interviewer, 'I have not much to do with distinguished people, but I have had a very nice letter from Lord Claud Hamilton and a very kind telegram from Mr Charles Danby, the actor, with "Hearty Congratulations" etcetera. Various clubs have telegraphed also. Here is a message: "Every man in the City is with you. Kill the —" A couple of days later he was forced to apologise for not answering the 'hundreds of kind evidences of sympathy' that had poured in from all over the country. 'Their number,' said an announcement in the *Telegraph*, 'making it beyond his power to send separate replies or acknowledgements.'

Queensberry had every reason to be jubilant. He had done more than achieve acquittal and public acclaim; he had done what he had set out to do by completely turning the tables on his adversary. The inevitable result of the jury's verdict had been seen by an evening newspaper shortly after the trial ended. 'Lord Queensberry is triumphant,' it crowed, 'and Mr Oscar Wilde is "damned and done for." He may now change places with Lord Queensberry and go into the dock himself.' That prediction was soon to be realised.

Wilde had escaped the newspaper reporters at the Old Bailey. As soon as the trial ended, he and Bosie—together with Percy and Robbie Ross—had left the court and gone straight to the Holborn Viaduct Hotel. From there Wilde had scrawled a hurried note to the *Evening News*.

'It would have been impossible,' he wrote, 'for me to have proved my case without putting Lord Alfred Douglas in the witness box against his father. Lord Alfred Douglas was extremely anxious to go into the box, but I would not let him do so. Rather than put him into so painful a position I determined to retire from the case, and to bear on my own shoulders whatever ignominy and shame might result from my prosecuting Lord Queensberry.'

Sincere as Wilde was when he wrote this, it was a transparent evasion. There was no question of Bosie finding it painful to testify against his father. He, even more than Wilde, was lusting for revenge and would have delighted in denouncing Queensberry publicly. This was made clear by Percy, shortly after the note had been sent. When a reporter arrived at the Holborn Viaduct Hotel demanding a statement from Wilde, it was Percy who dealt with him. The interview he gave left no doubt as to his own and Bosie's feelings.

'He was,' Percy explained, 'together with his brother, Lord Alfred, under subpoena for the prosecution. He himself had been quite ready to go into the box, and his brother was most anxious to do so, and was exceedingly grieved that Mr Wilde had prevented him. It was to prevent that—and because he felt that "no man could bear to have every little act and indiscretion of his life, and every word and thought produced against him they perverted in the basest way and placed in their worst possible light" that Mr Wilde had resolved to retire from the prosecution.'

Percy claimed to be speaking on Wilde's behalf, but he was at pains to emphasise his personal disappointment at the way things had gone. 'You may say from me myself,' he told the reporter, 'that I and every member of our family, excepting my father, disbelieve absolutely and entirely the allegations of the defence. It is in my opinion, simply a part of the persecution which my father has carried on against us ever since I can remember. I think Mr Wilde and his counsel to blame for not showing, as they could have done, that was the fact.'

It was not the most judicious of statements. In one blow Percy had undermined Wilde's attempt to bow out of the case gracefully and had pointed to the fact that he was afraid of further disclosures. Worse still, he had unthinkingly dragged his entire family into the row. This, as he was quickly reminded, was exceeding his authority.

Until then Florrie and the Dowager Marchioness had maintained
silence. It is doubtful whether they fully appreciated the issues involved.
For Florrie it was no righteous, or at least humanitarian, cause that her
brother was defending; the Dowager Marchioness doubtless found it all
extremely distasteful. 'My sister and mother,' Queensberry had earlier
admitted, 'are utterly useless to me.' Percy's sweeping statements, however, put things on a different footing. With the family's loyalty being
questioned, both Florrie and her mother sprang to Queensberry's defence. Archie was called in and, after a hurried consultation, a short but
uncompromising statement was issued from Glen Stuart.

'My nephew, Lord Douglas of Hawick,' Archie announced to a press
agency, 'was certainly not authorised by my mother, my sister, or myself
to say, as was reported recently—"Every member of our family, except
my father, disbelieves, absolutely and entirely, the allegations of the
defence." We do most certainly believe them, and must repudiate any
sympathy with the statement of my nephew.'

This was the only reminder the public was given of Queensberry's
controversial relations. Usually so quick to offer their opinions, they were
on this occasion content to allow the nominal head of the family to battle
alone. He was, as they well knew, more than capable of handling a public
brawl without their interference.

Their trust was not misplaced. While Wilde brooded in his hotel,
Queensberry's solicitors had not been idle. At the conclusion of the trial,
Charles Russell had written to the Director of Public Prosecutions, the
Hon. Hamilton Cuffe, sending him copies of all the witnesses statements
and shorthand notes of the court proceedings in order, he said, 'that there
may be no miscarriage of justice.' It was then decided to apply for a
warrant for Wilde's arrest. The legal process was surprisingly slow. There
were several hours delay—deliberately contrived, it is thought, to give
Wilde time to leave the country—and it was not until after five o'clock that
evening that the warrant was eventually signed by Sir John Bridge, the
Bow Street magistrate. By then it was too late for Wilde to catch the boat
train, even had he wanted to.

He seems, in fact, to have given no serious thought to leaving.
Throughout the day friends had been urging him to make for Dover but
he had hardly listened to them. He appeared listless, preoccupied, almost
stupefied. Earlier that afternoon he had roused himself sufficiently to join
Bosie at the Cadogan Hotel but once there he again lapsed into a dazed
state and sat drinking glass after glass of hock and seltzer, as if waiting for
the inevitable to happen. Bosie found the tension unbearable. Eventually,
unable to stand it any longer, Bosie left for the House of Commons to
consult his cousin George Wyndham. He had not returned by six-thirty
that evening when two detectives arrived at the Cadogan with a warrant
for Wilde's arrest. They were shown to Wilde's room and found him

sitting in an armchair by the fireplace, smoking a cigarette. The floor was littered with copies of the evening papers. Solemnly they informed Wilde that he was charged with committing 'indecent acts'.

'Well,' sighed Wilde resignedly, 'if I must go, I will give you the least possible trouble.'

When Bosie arrived back at the Cadogan, he found a note waiting for him. 'I will be at Bow Street Police Station tonight—,' it read, 'no bail possible I am told. Will you ask Percy, and George Alexander, and Waller, at the Haymarket, to attend to give bail. Would you also wire Humphreys to appear at Bow Street for me . . . also, come to see me, Ever Yours, Oscar.'

Wilde had been half-drunk when he wrote the note. There was, as he had been warned, no chance of his being allowed bail. On the two occasions he appeared before the magistrate before being committed for trial—together with Alfred Taylor, who had courageously refused to give evidence against him and so had been charged himself—Sir John Bridge had dismissed all suggestions of bail. 'I think,' the magistrate declared ominously, 'there is no worse crime than that with which the prisoners are charged . . . and I shall therefore refuse bail.' Predictable as was this refusal, it smacked, as Bosie pointed out in a scathing letter to the *Star,* more of prejudice than of 'abstract justice.'

'Mr Wilde,' stormed the impassioned Bosie, 'as a matter of fact, is charged with a "misdemeanor" punishable by two years imprisonment with or without hard labour *as a maximum penalty;* therefore, the offence with which he is charged is, in the eye of the law, which Sir John Bridge is supposed to represent, comparatively trifling. I should very much like to know how, in view of this fact, Sir John Bridge can reconcile what he said with his conscience, and with his position as the absolutely impartial exponent of the law. . . .'

Bosie's outburst was doubly provoked. In attacking Sir John Bridge he was also attacking his father. His letter exploded in the midst of a battle that Queensberry was conducting in the correspondence columns of the *Star.* It had started with a brave attempt by Robert Buchanan, a fellow writer, to defend Wilde from those who were attacking him before he had been tried.

Most newspapers had been flooded with anti-Wilde letters at the conclusion of Queensberry's trial (an estimated quarter of a million extra evening papers had been sold that day) and Robert Buchanan was one of the very few to come to Wilde's defence. 'Let us,' he pleaded, in a letter published by the *Star* on 16 April, 'ask ourselves, moreover, who are casting these stones and whether they are "without sin amongst us" or those who are themselves notoriously corrupt.'

Queensberry, always sensitive to suggestions of corruption, took this as a direct attack on himself. He was quick to reply. 'Is Mr Buchanan without sin?' he fumed. 'I certainly don't claim to be so myself, though I was compelled to throw the first stone. Whether or not I am justly notoriously corrupt I am willing patiently to wait for the future to decide. Judge not that you be not judged—I, would add, until you were qualified to know all the actual facts of a man's life.'

Bosie's intervention was characteristic. Ostensibly he was criticising Sir John Bridge, but he could not resist a passing sneer at his father. 'There are a thousand other things that might be said,' he concluded, after accusing the magistrate of prejudice, 'but I am not the person to say them, nor is it my place to make any reply to the precious bit of cant and bad grammar which appears over Lord Queensberry's signature . . . and which I feel I may safely leave to the tender mercies of Mr Robert Buchanan.'

Queensberry was astute enough to ignore his son. To have answered Bosie would have ruined his image as a concerned and protective father. He had no such mercy on Mr Buchanan. The battle between them raged on. Others joined in and the issue became hopelessly confused. At one stage, Buchanan tried to call a truce by appealing to Queensberry as a fellow agnostic; his arguments, he insisted, was with 'these Christian publicists who were pronouncing upon Mr Wilde before he was even committed for trial.' But Queensberry refused to be appeased. He became even more annoyed when Buchanan claimed that he had heard 'from the Marquess of Queensberry's own lips that *he* would gladly, were it possible, set the public an example of sympathy and magnanimity.'

'I must,' retorted Queensberry, 'take exception to the word "sympathy" that has been placed in my mouth. I never used it. In my time I have helped to cut up and destroy sharks. I had no sympathy for them, but may have felt sorry and wished to put them out of pain as soon as possible. What I did say was that as Mr Wilde now seemed to be on his beam ends and utterly down, I did feel sorry for his awful position, and that, supposing he was convicted of those loathsome charges brought against him, that were I the authority that had to mete out to him his punishment, I would treat him with all possible consideration as a sexual pervert of an utterly diseased mind, and not as a sane criminal. If this is sympathy, Mr Wilde has it from me to that extent.'

Queensberry was always the sportsman. His letter was published the day before Wilde and Taylor were due to appear at the Old Bailey and, like so much that appeared in the press at that time, it was hardly designed to promote fair play. Bosie's earlier taunt that his friend was being tried 'by the newspapers before he has been tried by a jury' was no exaggeration. This, however, was to be Queensberry's last contribution to the debate. By the time his letter appeared in the *Star* his mind was on other things.

On that same day (25 April 1895) Queensberry had received some startling news from America. It concerned a pending trial, but had nothing to do with Oscar Wilde. A cable from San Francisco had informed him that his youngest son, Lord Sholto Douglas, had been arrested in Bakersfield, California, and was under close confinement in the county gaol on a charge of insanity.

Chapter Seventeen

Lord Sholto Goes West

Lord Sholto Douglas, the fourth son, is a shadowy figure in the Queensberry story. He is rarely mentioned in family letters and memoirs and when his nephew Francis, 11th Marquess of Queensberry, came to write the family history he had to consult Debrett to discover the most elementary facts about his uncle Sholto's life—and those 'facts' were not entirely accurate. All that is known of Sholto's early career is that, as a child, he so terrified his governess that the poor woman was forced to resign. He then attended Wixenford preparatory school with Bosie and later served briefly as a lieutenant in the 4th Battalion of the Northamptonshire Regiment.

Yet from what one can gather, and as later events bear out, Sholto was by no means a colourless character. He appears to have been a highly volatile, self-willed, extremely reckless and thoroughly troublesome young man. He was forever getting in scrapes. What evidence does exist of his youthful escapades indicates that he was a constant source of worry to his long-suffering mother. One of his many disappearances from home, for instance, proved so alarming that a private detective had to be employed to trace him. Precisely what caused him to disappear on this occasion is not known, but he was missing for ten days or more and the affair was considered sufficiently serious for his father to be consulted. (It was from the detective hired to trace Sholto that Queensberry first obtained hints of Wilde's homosexual associates.) In a family hardly remarkable for its white sheep, Sholto was probably the blackest.

Certainly he suffered the fate of a neer-do-well Victorian younger son. After his last and most controversial disappearance, it was decided that he should live abroad. That he was sent to America—rather than the more usual refuge of remittance men, the colonies—was due to the fact that his mother had recently acquired a fruit farm in California. It was thought that this would provide Sholto with the opportunity of making a career for himself as well as keeping him away from the flesh-pots of London. But that, as it turned out, was a forlorn hope.

Sholto was no more suited to manage a fruit farm that he had been to serve as an army officer. He was far too ill-disciplined, far too easily diverted and decidedly too irresponsible to knuckle down to hard work. What is worse, the place chosen for his exile was not chosen wisely. There was scant chance of California, in the 1890s, reforming the defiant and dissolute young Sholto.

Admittedly he was not exposed to the temptations of the larger Californian cities. Bakersfield, the nearest settlement to the 40-acre Queensberry farm, was a small, dusty, relatively remote town—over one hundred miles north of Los Angeles and nearly three hundred miles south of San Francisco—in the San Joaquin valley. But, for all its isolation, life in Bakersfield was far from tame. It was a brash, boisterous, hard-drinking, heavy-gambling place and, when Sholto arrived there in the middle of 1894, it was already recognised as the dumping ground for a weird collection of British expatriates. Like Sholto, these feckless young exiles were mostly remittance men with no knowledge of farming. They spent most of their days organising sporting events and most of their nights in the town's rowdy bars and gambling saloons. Wild, extravagant and totally unaccountable, they brought more than a whiff of decadence to the Californian wilderness. If the slums of Bakersfield, says a local historian, 'lacked anything that the young British bloods were used to they speedily arranged to supply the deficiency and give all vice a Western air and relish that the most artistic panderers to depravity in European capitals could not put to blush.' Sholto felt immediately at home.

He spent little time on the farm. Trading on his family's reputation, he was quickly acknowledged as a hard-riding sportsman and, when not in the saddle, was invariably to be found at the faro tables of the local saloons. One of Sholto's favourite haunts was Big Frank Carson's place on Twentieth Street. Here the attraction was not so much the gambling as the barmaid: a plump, pretty, black-haired and dark-eyed Irish girl known as Loretta Addis.

By all accounts, the eighteen-year-old Loretta Addis was an extremely accomplished young woman. Her real name was Maggie Mooney and she had only recently arrived in Bakersfield from San Francisco where she had made something of a name for herself as a singer and dancer. Besides serving drinks at Big Frank Carson's, Loretta and her decidedly less talented brother provided the nightly floor show. Their act was little more than amateur, some of Loretta's songs were slightly *risqué* but—pushed on by their formidably ambitious mother—they were considered one of Bakersfield's star attractions. Sholto, however, was captivated more by Loretta's charms than by her grossly exploited talent. 'The girl,' he declared, 'is too good for the business she is in. That brother of hers and her mother keep her in the business that they might live off her. Her money keeps the two of them.'

To rescue Loretta from her grasping family, Sholto took what proved to be a very unfortunate step. In the middle of April 1895, he announced that he intended to marry her. His friends were horrified. Misfits and outcasts as most of them were, they still prided themselves on being English gentlemen and the idea of little Maggie Mooney becoming Lady Sholto Douglas shocked them to the core. Having told Sholto this, they tried to frighten off Loretta. The Queensberrys, they warned her, were a very proud and ancient family and the Marquess, for all his eccentricities, would never sanction a marriage between his son and a barmaid. If she were so foolish as to accept Sholto's proposal, she was bound to be 'cast off and renounced' later on. This is what happened to upstart girls who tried to invade the aristocracy. Poor Loretta immediately took fright. Already suspicious of her good luck, she now began to have serious doubts. She told Sholto that she needed time to think things over. Loretta should have known Sholto better.

So, for that matter, should his friends. After all, he was a member of the Queensberry family and that in itself should have made them think twice before trying to pressure him into changing his mind. As it was, their heavy handed interference forced the issue. Sholto's reaction was predictable. Brushing aside all protests, he decided to make up Loretta's mind for her: on 23 April he marched to the county clerk's office and applied for a marriage licence.

Again he was reckoning without his friends. One of them, the one who claimed to be closest to him, M. G. Burwester, was convinced that Sholto had taken leave of his senses. He should, for his own good, be put under restraint. Burwester decided to act before it was too late. That same afternoon, he rounded up a magistrate and solemnly swore on affidavit that Lord Sholto Douglas 'was not sufficiently accountable for his actions' and should be declared insane. The magistrate had no option but to issue a warrant for Sholto's arrest.

Sholto was just about to go to bed when the deputy sheriff arrived at his hotel. He was flabbergasted on being shown the warrant. 'Insane!' he spluttered. 'Most extraordinary proceedings! Insane! One man can come up and swear you are insane! Most extraordinary country!'

Extraordinary or not, there was nothing he could do about it. Having scrambled into his clothes, Sholto was hauled off to gaol where he immediately sent for an attorney to represent him. He intended, he said, to demand an independent medical examination the following morning. He also made it clear that he would instruct his lawyers to 'set the law in motion for the prosecution of Mr Burwester.'

Coming hot on the heels of the Queensberry trial in London, Sholto's arrest created a nationwide sensation in America. 'The Douglas affair,' announced the local newspaper proudly the following morning, 'has brought the name of Bakersfield before the world. Last night the telegraph wires were kept hot with details of the Lord's escapade, papers from all parts of the country sending for full accounts. Even the staid old

Associate Press "got a move on" and ordered 500 words of special. Operator Merritt was kept busy until past midnight.'

The excitement continued throughout the following day. When Sholto's attorneys arrived at the gaol, early that morning, they were besieged by reporters. Smiling but tight-lipped, they refused to make a statement. They would have to see their client, they explained, before saying anything. Not all Sholto's friends were so reticent. Several of them turned up that morning and eventually one was trapped in a corridor and bombarded with questions. His replies were more colourful than accurate.

'Did he believe,' he was asked, 'that the Lord was really crazy?'

'No,' he laughed, 'but there is no doubt the entire family is "nutty". They are all peculiar.'

'Was Sholto Douglas really Lord Queensberry's son?'

'Yes, he is the son of the present Marquis. It was his grandfather [*sic*] who got up the famous prize ring rules. His father is a sporty bird. By the way, he has an aunt who was the cause of the death of the famous John Brown, the friend of the Queen. His aunt was assaulted or at any rate insulted by some fellow, and she applied to the Queen to have the matter investigated. The Queen sent Brown to look into the matter and while he was there he got wet, caught a cold and died. Another aunt married a baker who was taken as a child from a foundling asylum. So this is not the first attempt of the family to marry beneath its social station. . . .'

The questioning went on until the reporters were allowed to interview Sholto. They found him sitting cross-legged on his bed, reading the *Pall Mall Gazette*. Other newspapers, mostly American, were scattered about the floor. Sholto was enjoying his notoriety enormously. He gave a broad grin as the reporters trooped in. He was feeling very well, he told them, had slept soundly and expected to be medically examined the next day. What puzzled him was why he was there at all.

'Have you,' asked a reporter, 'retained the gentlemen who have just left here as counsel?'

'Yes. I have employed them to look after my case,' agreed Sholto, straightening up. 'But don't you know it is a remarkable proceeding to lock a man up on a charge of lunacy, on the charge of one man. In England they would have to had to take me before two physicians, who would certify my insanity before locking me up.'

He continued to grumble about the American law, even after it was pointed out to him that he could not have been examined unless he had been charged. When asked whether he had been visited that morning by Loretta's brother, he became more animated. 'He went on at a great rate to make a fool of himself,' he giggled. 'Didn't he tell you,' asked one of the newsmen, 'that he would kill you if you married the girl?' Sholto was highly indignant. 'No,' he snapped, 'but he said he would kill the girl.'

The journalists were left in no doubt that Lord Sholto Douglas was heartily sick of Loretta's family and was even having second thoughts about Loretta herself. 'I don't know,' he sulked, as the reporters left, 'that I care to marry the girl now.'

[2]

Whatever Sholto's thoughts on the matter, his friends were determined that the affair should end. Nor was it something they meant to leave to chance. With Sholto safely behind bars, they turned their attention to the thoroughly bemused Loretta. They were nothing if not persuasive. Her best plan, they told her, was to leave Bakersfield at once. Unless she did so her career would be ruined. The case had already attracted a consider-able amount of publicity and, as far as she was concerned, most of that publicity had been bad; she was being spoken of not as a talented singer but as a common barmaid with ideas above her station; however things worked out, whether she married Sholto or not, it would be difficult to live that sort of reputation down. Her only hope was to leave before Sholto was released.

Loretta needed little persuading. By that time, both she and her mother had abandoned all hopes of a romantic marriage. They were thinking solely in terms of future bookings. Bakersfield had, in any case, proved a dead end; neither of them were sorry to see the back of Big Frank Carson's sleazy saloon. With Sholto's friends offering to pay their fares, they were only too ready to pack their bags and return to San Francisco. Indeed they might have left there and then had it not been for two enterprising newspaper reporters.

The reporters were C. P. Fox and W. D. Young, the Bakersfield cor-respondents of two San Francisco newspapers—the *Chronicle* and the *Examiner*. They had rushed straight to Loretta's lodgings after interview-ing Sholto in his cell. They were very worried. Sholto's hint that he was thinking of calling off the marriage had come as a shock: it threatened to ruin the best story they had had for months. Bakersfield was not the most newsworthy of towns and, as its paupers far outnumbered its princes, stories of star-crossed lovers that had an international appeal did not crop up regularly; with their editors paying five dollars a column and willing to take whatever they could send, Mr Fox and Mr Young were not prepared to allow this romantic episode to fizzle out prematurely. Sholto's ardour would have to be rekindled and the only person who could do that was Loretta. Needless to say, they met with a very chilly reception from Miss Mooney.

Loretta refused to listen to them. She wanted nothing to do with the snooty British aristocracy. From what she had heard, she was convinced that the Marquess of Queensberry was a snob and a tyrant who would turn against her. Why should she expose herself to such ridicule? What, if she were spurned, would become of her career? They tried desperately to argue with her. She had, they said, been sadly misled. Sholto's friends were using her for their own ends. Queensberry was not the bigot they made him out to be. He was, claimed Fox, 'a true old sport, quick to recognise merit, not too fastidious in his associates and amusements and altogether unlikely to play the part of a prude or a pharisee.' If Loretta was presented to him as his daughter-in-law, he would be the first to recognise her charms. Barmaid or no barmaid, he would welcome her with open arms.

Loretta could not be moved. Her mind was made up. There was no future for her with Sholto, she insisted. She was very busy. She had a lot of packing to do. It was then, according to one account of this bizarre interview, that Young had a brilliant idea. Sentiment having failed, he appealed to Loretta's business sense. 'Let them renounce you if they dare,' he urged, 'and you go on the stage as Lady Sholto Douglas, daughter-in-law of the Marquess of Queensberry. With the talent you've got. . . .' There was no need for him to say any more. Loretta was immediately converted. She agreed to see Sholto that afternoon. Triumphantly Fox and Young accompanied her to the gaol.

How true this account is one does not know. In Bakersfield anything could happen and Fox and Young were shrewd enough to make the most of a good story. What is more certain is that Sholto and Loretta were reunited that afternoon; their reunion was broadcast to the world. Miss Mooney, stated the report which reached London, 'has visited Lord Sholto in gaol, and was very demonstrative in her manifestations of affection for the prisoner.' It went on to say that Sholto was still uncertain as to whether or not he would marry Loretta. The 'waitress', it observed, was said to be 'several months under age.'

Under age or not, Loretta proved more than a match for Sholto's friends. That same afternoon, the shamefaced Mr Burwester capitulated and 'formally withdrew all suggestions of insanity.' Sholto, still fulminating about the vagaries of Amerian law and the treachery of his friends, was promptly released. He went straight to his hotel from where, two days later, he told reporters that he had wired his father for permission to marry Loretta. 'Something has been said,' commented a correspondent of the *Daily Telegraph* 'about the young woman being under age, but this is not a serious obstacle to marriage in this country.'

Nor did Queensberry put any obstacles in the couple's way. Sholto could not have caught his father at a more fortunate moment. Flushed with his success against Wilde, still revelling in his role as a selfless and considerate parent, the Marquess was only too ready to display his magnanimity. He wired back immediately giving Sholto his permission and his blessing. Unfortunately his benevolent gesture was largely ignored by the British press.

Once the excitement of Sholto's release from prison had died down, he and Loretta went into hiding. They disappeared from Bakersfield overnight and were neither seen nor heard of for nearly a month. Their disappearance did not, of course, silence the press. Almost every day unconfirmed reports of their marriage appeared in gossip columns of the Californian newspapers. At one time or another they were said to have been married by an unknown Baptist minister, to have left for England for a London wedding, and—as was more widely believed—to have eloped to San Francisco and married in an Episcopal church.

The truth was not revealed until the last week in May. Then it was announced that the Roman Catholic Vicar General of San Francisco had 'issued a special dispensation . . . by virtue of which any priest under his jurisdiction might make Lord Sholto and Miss Mooney man and wife.' Loretta was taking no chances. Irish and Catholic, she wanted her marriage recognised by her own church: there were to be no theological quibbles over the matrimonial status of the new Lady Sholto Douglas. In fact Loretta made doubly sure of Sholto. The couple were married twice: first by a Justice of the Peace in San Jose and then—on 30 May—in the Catholic church at Oakland. Only then was the press informed.

'Loretta Mooney,' it was announced from San Francisco two days later, 'who also calls herself Addis in the variety theaters of California, is now Lady Sholto Douglas, daughter-in-law of the Marquis of Queensberry. She has a slender ring of gold which she demurely exhibits when she is asked if she is really the wife of Lord Sholto George Douglas. . . . She showed me her wedding ring, a plain gold band, lettered on the inside 'S to L May 30' and said she and Lord Sholto would keep house in this city.' But keeping house, as Loretta was quick to point out, was very different from becoming a housewife. Lady Sholto Douglas had more pleasing prospects. 'She will continue,' the report went on, 'to sing and dance and sell drinks in a resort which pays her $25 week.'

So much for Sholto's hopes of snatching Loretta from her money-grubbing family. He was no match for her mother. For it had been the indefatigable Mrs Mooney who had prevented the couple from returning to the Queensberry farm. She had touted her daughter's title and arranged for her to appear at a San Francisco theatre at what were considered very generous terms. Lady Sholto Douglas was to make the most of her aristocratic attractions, and that did not mean living as the wife of a remittance man. Unfortunately for Mrs Mooney, things did not work out quite as planned.

A few days later, Sholto and Loretta again disappeared. This time the hunt for them was led not so much by the press as by the outraged Mrs

Mooney. Distraught but determined, she dashed from town to town pleading for help in her search for her daughter. It gave the press a hilarious new slant on the marriage. 'Mrs Mooney, mother of the bride,' reported the San Jose *Daily Mercury*, 'and the man who has a contract from her to appear on the stage of an Ellis-street theater are suffering tortures of mind by her failure to return to San Francisco to regale open-mouthed spectators with her bad, but not wicked, song and inferior dancing.'

But Mrs Mooney need have had no worries on that score. The runaway couple had not absconded but were merely enjoying a few days' honeymoon in the country. They were eventually tracked down to a ranch near Los Gatos where they were reported to be 'taking matters easy.' Only the local newspaper pretended to be disappointed by the discovery. 'As Lord and Lady Douglas are honeymooning in this county,' it sighed in mock despair, 'it is pertinent to ask: What have we done to deserve it?' What indeed? Considering the publicity given to the affair, the question was somewhat superflous.

And that should have been that. Mrs Mooney, reunited with her daughter, was all smiles and forgiveness. She was not one to bear a grudge. Clutching the theatrical contract, she was fully prepared to overlook Loretta's little escapade and return to San Francisco in triumph. She was in for another shock.

Absurd, childish and ludicrous, as the entire episode had been, it ended with a twist that might have brought a blush to the most sentimental of Victorian novelists. Melodrama turned to pure pantomime. It can only be told as it was reported.

'LORD SHOLTO'S LUCK,' ran a headline in *Reynold's Newspaper* on 14 July 1895. 'A very substantial windfall, says a Daziel cablegram from Guelph Ontario, has just come to light, in which Lord and Lady Sholto Douglas, the newly-married couple, will share to a large extent. A tailor named William Mooney last week became the heir to a large estate in Ontario, and it was discovered that Lady Sholto, who as a variety actress on the Californian stage went under the name of Loretta Addis, is Mr Mooney's daughter. She has already been notified of the inheritance by her father, who intends making over to the couple half of it, amounting to half a million.'

Incredible as it appears, the story was true. At least it was true enough for Sholto and Loretta to kiss the thwarted Mrs Mooney goodbye and leave immediately for Canada. They settled in Ontario where Sholto became a farmer of sorts and where their two sons were born: Bruce Francis, in 1897, and Sholto Augustus in 1900.

It would be tempting to leave the Cinderella story there but the truth is that Sholto was badly cast as Prince Charming. Their marriage lasted for almost twenty years but it was not a success. In 1920, at the age of forty-eight, Sholto divorced Loretta. He was left to continue his comic-opera career alone.

[3]

Sholto's arrest in California distracted Queensberry, at least temporarily, from the Wilde case. As far as is known he was not once in court during the trial of Wilde and Alfred Taylor, which opened at the Old Bailey on 26 April 1895 and lasted for five days. Nor was Bosie there. Two days before the trial it was agreed between Wilde and Sir Edward Clarke—who had again offered to defend Wilde, this time without a fee—that it would be best if Bosie left the country. His presence in England, it was thought, could only prejudice Wilde's case. Reluctantly Bosie, who had faithfully visited Wilde in Holloway prison throughout his detention and who was still convinced that he should be called as a witness, accepted this decision and left for Calais. He and Wilde were not to meet again for over two years.

Queensberry's preoccupation, however, did not prevent him from continuing his feud against Percy. His eldest son's disloyalty, particularly his siding openly with Wilde after the first trial, undoubtedly incensed Queensberry more than Bosie's widely publicised hostility. Bosie, after all, could always be written off as a headstrong youngster who needed to be taught the error of his ways. Percy, on the other hand, was his heir—a future Marquess of Queensberry—and this made his actions appear all the more treacherous: he was defying his father in the name of his own family. Nor were things helped by the fact that Queensberry considered Percy's betrayal to be completely unprovoked. 'You began it,' he told Percy's wife. 'What possible business could it be of yours (you and Percy) interfering and taking sides? It was no business of any son of mine that I should insist that such an utterly disgraceful connection should be put a stop to between his brother and such a man.'

Queensberry was still having to use Minnie to hit back at his son. Percy refused even to acknowledge his letters. That Minnie had also called in lawyers in an attempt to put an end to the correspondence, Queensberry conveniently ignored. From the time his trial ended he directed a constant barrage of abuse at his unfortunate daughter-in-law. Things reached such a pitch that, three days before the Wilde trial opened, Percy applied to the Marlborough Street magistrate's court for a summons against his father on the grounds of 'threats contained in a letter written by Lord Queensberry.' The hearing was held in private and Percy's application was dismissed. This, for Queensberry, was the last straw. 'You may inform this so-called skunk of a son of mine (I never believed he was my son) . . .' he wrote to Percy's solicitors a few days later. 'That I will catch him some day and give him the warming he deserves, then we can raise the question whether a father has a right to thrash his son, particularly when he is old enough to protect himself.'

Although Queensberry did not attend the trial of Wilde and Alfred Taylor, there was no mistaking his influence on the case. The charges against Wilde were those revealed during his prosecution of Queensberry, the most damaging witnesses were the boys named in Queensberry's plea of justification—the Parker brothers, Alfred Wood, Edward Shelley, Sidney Mavor and Fred Atkins—and the third day of the hearing was devoted largely to the reading of evidence given at the Queensberry trial. Even the civilian clothes worn by Charles Parker during the trial (officially he was still in the army) were later admitted to have been provided by Queensberry's solicitors 'because the witness could not appear in the Queen's uniform.'

For Wilde the trial was a ghastly ordeal. He was indicted, as Hesketh Pearson has pointed out, 'under an Act that had only been passed ten years before, and which did not exist in any other civilised country' and was prosecuted by the Crown, represented by Charles Gill. From the moment he entered the dock beside Alfred Taylor, the physical effects of his detention in Holloway prison were obvious: he looked worn out, white faced and dishevelled.

He sat listening apathetically as the prosecution unfolded its case. He listened to Charles Gill describing Alfred Taylor's scented rooms in Little College Street and the young men who visited them 'giving their bodies, or selling them, to other men for the purpose of sodomy.' He listened as the procession of young renters described in graphic, sometimes lurid, detail his alleged attempts to seduce them—'He suggested two or three times that I would permit him to insert "it" in my mouth,' protested Charles Parker, 'but I never allowed that.' He heard Taylor's landlady tell of whisperings and laughter behind locked doors, of women's clothing kept in Taylor's wardrobe and to Charles Parker's landlady vouching for complaints about his furtive visits to her lodging house. The prosecution's case was formidable.

More encouraging were Sir Edward Clarke's cross-examinations. By skilful questioning Clarke managed to discredit some of the boys who gave evidence for the Crown, exposing their blackmailing activities and, in one case, nailing a blatant perjury. He also, on the fourth day, succeeded in having the charge of 'conspiracy' between Wilde and Taylor withdrawn. 'My Lord,' he said when the prosecuting counsel announced this withdrawl, 'if those counts had been withdrawn in the first instance, I should have made an application for the charges against the two prisoners to be heard separately.'

On that same day, Wilde was called to the witness box. He was far more subdued than when he had testified against Queensberry and only occasionally showed some of his old spirit. His most effective reply, a reply that drew applause and hisses from the public gallery, came when he was asked to explain a poem, written by Bosie, about the 'Love that dare not speak its name.'

'The "love that dare not speak its name" in this century,' Wilde declared, 'is such a great affection of an elder man for a younger man as there was between David and Jonathan, such as Plato made the very basis of his philosophy, and such as you find in the sonnets of Michelangelo and Shakespeare. It is that deep spiritual affection that is as pure as it is perfect. It dictates and pervades great works of art like those of Shakespeare and Michelangelo, and those two letters of mine, such as they are. It is in this century misunderstood, so much misunderstood that it may be described as "Love that dare not speak its name," and on account of it I am placed where I am now. It is beautiful, it is fine, it is the noblest form of affection. There is nothing unnatural about it. It is intellectual, and it repeatedly exists between an elder and a younger man, when the elder has intellect, and the younger man all the joy, hope, and glamour of life before him. That it should be so, the world does not understand. The world mocks at it and sometimes puts one in pillory for it.'

The following day Sir Edward Clarke made his closing speech. He was eloquent and persuasive. He tellingly contrasted Wilde 'a renowned and accomplished man of letters' with the 'harpies' and blackmailers who had testified against him. 'No jury,' he submitted towards the end of his speech, 'can find a man guilty on the evidence of these tainted witnesses. Nor did the jury find Wilde guilty. After retiring for over four hours, they returned without having reached agreement on a verdict. The judge dismissed them and announced there would be a retrial.

Five days later, after some legal quibbling, Wilde was released on bail. His bail was set at £5000, half of which he was required to guarantee himself while Percy and a sympathetic Church of England clergyman stood as sureties for the other half.

It was only after Wilde's release that Queensberry showed his hand again. He did so in a particularly vicious manner.

On leaving Bow Street Police Court, where his bail had been finalised, Wilde, accompanied by Percy, drove straight to the Midland Hotel, St Pancras. Two rooms had been booked for him at the hotel and that evening he invited Percy to stay to dinner. Just as they were about to sit down to their meal, however, the manager burst into the room and ordered Wilde to leave immediately. Queensberry, he said, was threatening trouble and he was not prepared to take any chances. Wilde had no option but to do what he was told. Saying goodbye to Percy, he set off in search of another hotel. He tried several before he found one—'in a distant part of London'—that would take him. Hardly had he settled into his room than the same performance was repeated. This time he was told that he had been followed by a gang of ruffians who were demanding he be thrown out. 'The men,' said the terrified landlord, 'say they will sack the house and raze the street if you stay here a moment longer.'

It was past midnight before Wilde shook off his pursuers. Harrassed, bewildered and nearing the point of exhaustion, he made his way to his mother's house in Chelsea. His faint knock was answered by his elder brother William Wilde. 'Give me shelter, Willie,' he gasped as he staggered in. 'Let me lie on the floor or I shall die in the streets.'

[4]

Wilde's stay at his mother's house was short. He was rescued by his old friend Ada Leverson who, arriving in a brougham, whisked him off to her house in Courtfield Gardens. 'He seemed so unhappy with his family at this time,' she explained, 'that we asked him to stay with us, feeling that he would be more at ease with friends than with relatives.' The nursery floor of the Leverson's house became Wilde's refuge until 20 May, the date fixed for his third trial.

Preparations for that trial were now going ahead. It was not long before news of how the trial was to be conducted leaked out. The prosecution, it was learned, had been entrusted to no less a person than Sir Frank Lockwood, the Solicitor-General. That such importance was attached to what, strictly speaking, was a relatively minor case caused considerable surprise in legal circles. No one was more astonished than Edward Carson who, having so brilliantly defended Queensberry, had subsequently washed his hands of the entire affair. The prosecution of Wilde, as far as he was concerned, was an extremely distasteful business. He told Sir Frank Lockwood as much when he heard the Solicitor-General had been assigned to the case.

'Cannot you let up on the fellow now?' he protested. 'He has suffered a great deal.'

'I would,' replied Lockwood, 'but we cannot: we dare not: it would at once be said, both in England and abroad, that owing to the names mentioned in Queensberry's letters we were forced to abandon it.'

Lockwood's anxiety is understandable. There were, by that time, serious political—as well as legal—issues at stake. The Solicitor-General and his superiors could not allow the Wilde case to peter out without making an effort to stifle the rumours that had started shortly before the Queensberry trial opened. These rumours implicated various members of the Liberal Government. Not the least involved were Sir Frank Lockwood himself and the then Prime Minister, Lord Rosebery.

The Solicitor-General's involvement was, in a way, incidental. It arose from the fact that his wife's nephew, Maurice Schwabe, had been named in the case. Schwabe was a friend of both Wilde and Taylor and was known to have introduced Taylor to one of the renters, Fred Atkins, who had appeared as a witness for the Crown. During the Queensberry trial, attempts had been made to hush-up Schwabe's association with Wilde. When for instance, Wilde had referred to Schwabe during his cross-examination by Carson, he had been told to write the young man's name on a piece of paper and hand it to the court usher. The usher had then passed the paper to Carson. However, at the second trial—that of Wilde and Taylor—Fred Atkins had inadvertently blurted out Schwabe's name. Atkins had told how, on a visit to Paris with Wilde, he had returned to their hotel late one night and found Wilde in bed with Schwabe. Surprisingly the press, for the most part, had ignored this slip; little or no mention of Schwabe's connection with the Solicitor-General had been made. Lockwood could not therefore have been unduly worried about his personal involvement.

With Lord Rosebery it was another matter. Here a number of embarrassing factors had arisen. There was, in the first place, Rosebery's known connection with Queensberry's eldest son. The Homburg incident, when the future Prime Minister had been wildly threatened by Queensberry, had not been forgotten. The sensation it had created had started rumours which, in the more fashionable London clubs and drawing rooms, were not confined to Drumlanrig's controversial peerage. This, in itself, was bad enough. What made things worse was the mention of Rosebery's name at the preliminary hearing by a grand jury of Wilde's original charge against Queensberry.

As the law then stood, such a hearing was an essential part of criminal procedure. A grand jury was expected to consider evidence presented by the prosecutor and then return a 'true-bill' before an accused person could be put on trial; if they found there was 'no true-bill' the prosecution automatically fell away. These preliminary hearings were held in private and the grand jury was usually selected from solid citizens with substantial property qualifications. In the Wilde vs Queensberry case, however, there was some confusion and a French journalist was summoned to serve on the jury by mistake. On arriving at the Old Bailey to excuse himself, the journalist learned that the Wilde case was due to come before the jury and this set his professional nose twitching. He decided to stay and, in staying, he heard mention of Rosebery's name. Whether, as was thought, the mention was merely that contained in one of Queensberry's letters is not certain but, whatever it was, it undoubtedly gave the journalist a good story. Hints that Rosebery was implicated in the Wilde case were soon appearing in the French press and the story was taken up by other Continental papers. Inevitably rumours drifted across the Channel and, although they were kept out of the British press, they were seized upon by the London gossips.

So conscious was Sir Edward Clarke of the Prime Minister's association with the case that, in his opening speech, he had made an embarrassing slip. Describing how Queensberry had tried to disrupt the opening night of *The Importance of Being Earnest*, Clarke had stumbled over the Marquess's name and called him 'Lord Rosebery.'

Carson had tackled the problem more robustly. He had drawn particular attention to the 'names of distinguished persons' mentioned in Queensberry's letters. 'It has been suggested,' he pointed out, 'that the names of those distinguished persons were in some way or other mixed up in Lord Queensberry's letters with the charges against Mr Wilde. The references were of a purely political character, arising out of the fact that the late Lord Drumlanrig, the eldest son of the Marquess, was made a member of the House of Lords, of which his father was not a member. Rightly or wrongly, Lord Queensberry felt aggrieved that an honour should have been conferred on his son which was not given to him. That was how the names of eminent politicians and statesmen came to be mentioned.'

It was a smooth, but not altogether convincing, explanation. There was more involved than a passing reference in Queensberry's letters. Otherwise why was so much fuss being made? Why was everyone so nervous? Only one of the letters submitted in court contained the names of 'distinguished persons.' This was the letter Queensberry had written to Alfred Montgomery. In it he had said that he considered Wilde to be a 'damned cur and coward of the Rosebery type' and later that he was convinced that the 'Rosebery-Gladstone-Royal insult' had been the work of his own wife. That was all. Given Queensberry's hot-headedness, given the insulting tone of most of his letters, was this so compromising? His quarrel with Rosebery was not exactly a secret. He had openly threatened to thrash Rosebery in Homburg and had prowled about his hotel with a dog whip. Why then should his renewed outburst in a private letter cause so much alarm? Was it so unusual that it required a pointed explanation from Carson? What reason was there for thinking that it was mixed up with 'the charges against Mr Wilde'? More important, did it warrant the Crown's relentless persecution of Wilde? Was Lockwood's claim that he 'dare not' drop the case justified?

There was, of course, the gossip. Members of the Government were not hermits; they must have been aware of what was being said both privately and publicly. Although the British press did not mention the Prime Minister by name, it was not entirely silent about the rumours concerning the Wilde case. There had been endless speculation about the impending arrest of 'highly-placed persons' and not a few hints at frantic back-stairs activity. As the time drew near for the second trial of Wilde and Taylor, this speculation was being reported throughout the English-speaking world.

'There is still,' reported the European edition of the *New York Herald*, on the day the trial opened, 'a continued prevalence of gossip concerning well-known people whom it is attempted by current rumour to connect with the case. It was stated yesterday that a conference of several hours duration took place between the police and Treasury officials relative to the advisability of issuing new warrants against persons whose names have been mentioned during the course of the Old Bailey trial and the Bow-Street proceedings.'

Who were these 'well-known' people whose names had been mentioned in court? Surely not little Maurice Schwabe. Hardly the worthy Mr Gladstone. That left only Lord Rosebery. The hints were vague enough to frighten even those whose names had not been mentioned. Throughout the Wilde case, it is said, the cross-Channel steamers were jam-packed with distinguished homosexuals who suddenly felt the need of a prolonged Continental holiday.

As it happened, Lord Rosebery was also out of the country. He had been advised to take a sea voyage by Queen Victoria who was concerned about his health. Early in March—two days after Queensberry's second appearance at Great Marlborough Street, the hearing at which 'exalted persons' were first mentioned—Rosebery had been struck down by a mysterious illness while attending the Queen at Windsor. He had suddenly become dizzy and the Queen had insisted that he sit down. His doctor was quite baffled by his collapse and his failure to recover. It was, he said, 'the most obstinate and puzzling case he had ever come across.' He put it down vaguely to 'long-continued derangement of the digestive organs' but admitted that Rosebery's appetite was 'pretty good.' The most obvious symptom was the Prime Minister's inability to sleep for more than three or four hours a night, which seems to indicate strain or a nervous disorder. Rosebery was prone to such attacks and had suffered a similar one three years earlier when he was being bombarded by abusive letters from Queensberry. On that occasion the doctor had recommended his ill-fated rest cure at Homburg. This time Rosebery took the Queen's advice. On 13 May, he accepted Lord Spencer's offer of a sea cruise in the Admiralty yacht *Enchantress*. He was sailing off the southern coast of England when the second trial of Wilde and Taylor opened.

Was he still being harrassed by Queensberry? The possibility cannot be ruled out. The vindictive Marquess was quite capable of threatening to make trouble if the Wilde case was dropped. Certainly Queensberry was active behind the scenes. Two days before Wilde was released on bail, he had paid a surprise visit to Holloway prison. 'The object of the visit of the Marquess to Holloway,' it was reported, 'has not transpired, but he had an interview with the chief prison officials. Oscar Wilde and Taylor apparently know nothing of the visit of his lordship, who did not remain at the prison long.'

How much the Queensberry family knew of all this is uncertain. It was not a subject they wanted to talk about. Whatever Rosebery's connection with the case might or might not have been, it was tied too closely to Drumlanrig for public discussion. They already had enough to do trying to clear Bosie. And Bosie was not helping them. He came very near, in fact, to a startling revelation. Writing to a French magazine a year later, he was unable to contain his anger at the way Wilde had been treated and he lashed out at those he considered responsible.

'I am confident,' he declared, 'that the Government did not wish to let the prosecution of Oscar Wilde take its regular course. . . . Why did the Crown take the very irregular course of having a second trial—why was the prosecution conducted with this extraordinary animosity; briefly why did the Crown manifest so eager a desire to obtain a verdict of guilty? The reason is very simple. The Government was intimidated; the second trial was the result of a political intrigue. I would wish to ask Mr Asquith, the then Home Secretary and an old friend of Oscar Wilde, if he was not threatened by Lord Rosebery that if a second trial was not instituted and a verdict of guilty obtained against Mr Wilde, the Liberal party would be removed from power. The fact is that the Liberal party then contained a large number of men whom I have referred to as the salt of the earth [homosexuals]. The maniacs of virtue threatened a series of legal actions which would have created an unprecedented scandal in Europe—a scandal in political circles. If Oscar Wilde was found guilty the matter would be hushed up. This was the cause of the second trial, and the verdict of guilty. It was a degrading *coup-d'état*—the sacrifice of a great poet to save a degraded band of politicians.'

Bosie could not be too specific. Suspicion may have fallen on a number of politicians, but it fell most heavily on Lord Rosebery. Amid all the hints and whispers it was Rosebery's relationship with Drumlanrig that inspired most of the gossip. The truth or otherwise of that gossip is beside the point: rumours were spread and those rumours were considered dangerous. Innocent or not, Lord Rosebery's involvement with the Queensberry family played an important part in sealing Oscar Wilde's fate.

Chapter Eighteen

The Tables Turned

On 20 May 1895 Oscar Wilde and Alfred Taylor again appeared at the Old Bailey to face charges under Section II of the Criminal Law Amendment Act of 1885. The clause in this Act which dealt with homosexual offences had been introduced by Henry Labouchere, the Radical MP, and in one of his letters to *The Star* Bosie accused Labouchere of being 'the inventor and supporter of the modern system of blackmail.' It was a taunt which the Wilde case did much to justify. The infamous Act later became known as the 'blackmailer's charter' and it was not until 1967 that the provisions penalising homosexual acts between adult males in private were finally removed. Neither Wilde nor Taylor could expect much leniency from this peculiarly British piece of legislation, backed as it was by hostile press comment and popular prejudice.

The presiding judge this time was the seventy-seven year old Sir Alfred Wills who, as a former president of the Alpine Club and an acquaintance of Queensberry's younger brother Francis, was no stranger to the Queensberry family's misfortunes. Nor, if newspaper gossip is to be believed, was he a stranger to Wilde. 'I am told,' observed a columnist of the London *Figaro*, 'that not only was Oscar Wilde a near neighbour of Mr Justice Wills in Tite Street—the former living at 16, and the latter at 42—but that the dramatist and the judge had for some time been on nodding terms.' The resolute and experienced Sir Frank Lockwood—he had earlier defended the notorious Charles Peace—appeared for the Crown; Wilde was again defended by Sir Edward Clarke and Taylor by Mr J. P. Grain.

The two defendants pleaded not guilty and, since the charge of conspiracy had been withdrawn, Sir Edward Clarke immediately applied for them to be tried separately. His application was granted but he was unsuccessful in his attempt to have Wilde's case heard first. Sir Alfred Wills refused to accept the argument that it would be unjust to Wilde, whose name appeared first on the indictment, to appear after the jury had heard evidence against Taylor. 'If there should be an acquittal [of Taylor]' reasoned the judge, 'so much the better for the other prisoner.' He upheld the prosecution's right to decide the order of the two trials. Lockwood, not surprisingly, opted to start with Taylor.

Taylor's trial lasted two days. On the morning of the second day, Queensberry made his first appearance in court since his own acquittal some six weeks earlier. Wearing a yellow rose in his buttonhole and twiddling his hat on the end of his walking stick, he looked extremely jaunty as he was shown to a special seat reserved for 'friends of the Corporation.' He was seen to grin broadly at Taylor's pathetic attempts to wriggle out of Sir Frank Lockwood's questioning.

About the outcome of the case there was never any serious doubt. The police had collected more positive evidence against Taylor than they had against Wilde. There were letters found in a hat-box in Taylor's room which left little doubt about his relationship with the young men who, as he freely admitted, had shared his bed; there was a young man with whom he was said to have gone through a form of mock 'marriage' and who wrote to him in intimate terms; and there was the ever-obliging Charles Parker who swore that Taylor had kept him in his rooms for a week, called him 'darling' and 'little wife', and promised to introduce him to rich clients. Lockwood was able to tie the hapless Taylor in knots and the jury had little hesitation in finding him guilty on two charges of indecent behaviour.

Queensberry left the court beaming. For him the verdict was a personal victory, a victory not so much over Wilde as over the 'Montgomery lot.' As always, he held his wife responsible for his misfortunes; it was to her side of the family that he traced his sons' weaknesses and the scandal associated with their names. Such an effete strain, he felt, could only have entered the Queensberry stock through his ladylike father-in-law.

Had he needed further proof of this, it had come in a letter he received from Bosie a few days earlier. Queensberry had immediately forwarded the letter to Minnie. 'I enclose letter,' he crowed, 'from the gilt soul whose rose-leaf lips are made for the madness of kissing. . . . Look out for your own children, there is such a thing as heredity, as is well-known, they throw back to the Montgomery grandpère.'

Unfortunately Bosie's letter has been lost. It was probably written to prove to his father that he was in France. This was something Queensberry refused to believe. He was convinced his son was hiding in London with Wilde and he had scoured London in an attempt to find them. Their most likely refuge had seemed to be Percy's house and it was there, a few days before Taylor's trial, that Queensberry had confronted his daughter-in-law. Minnie had been furious. She stoutly denied that she was harbouring Wilde and Bosie and told Queensberry he had no right to burst into her house. 'I have a right,' he stormed back at her in a letter the following day, 'and if I had not, it would be all the same—to force myself in anywhere to keep this wretched misguided boy apart from such a man. If I had not thought Wilde was there, as I believe he is or was, I should not have come. . . . I am unable to find out where Alfred is, as I am told

vaguely he is abroad by you all, in the meantime he was seen a few days
ago in London. . . . I think yours, you and Percy's, interference the most
impertinent interference I have ever heard of, and so do most people. You
talk of the way I treat you, but it is the way you have treated me.'

Queensberry was banging his head against a firmly closed door.
Having turned him out of her house, Minnie added to his fury by continuing to ignore his letters. This did not prevent him from writing. Two
days later he again accused her of hiding Wilde. 'I hope,' he spluttered,
'he is still enjoying the madness of kissing Boys and young men, but if
with you still, will hardly dare show his nose outside your gates.'
Queensberry was at a loss to know how to express his anger; he became
positively childish in his frustration. Seeing a picture of a grotesque
prehistoric iguanodon in the *Illustrated London News*, he tore out the page,
scrawled 'a possible ancestor of Oscar Wilde' across it, and sent it to
Minnie. 'I sent it to my son's wife,' he explained later, 'intending it more
as a good natured joke than anything else.' His son's wife was not
amused. Nor, for that matter, was her husband. They had both, by this
time, had more than enough of Queensberry's capers.

Queensberry, however, had several more good natured jokes on hand.
The Taylor verdict provided him with an excellent opportunity to play
one. On leaving the court that day he took a cab to St James Street and
then made straight for the nearest post office where he scribbled a hurried
telegram to Minnie.

'Must congratulate on verdict,' it read. 'Cannot on Percy's appearance.
Looked like a dug up corpse. Fear too much madness of kissing. Taylor
guilty. Wilde's turn tomorrow.'

Having fired off this banal squib, Queensberry marched up St James'
Street to Piccadilly. It was then that he spotted Percy. 'I was crossing over
to Albemarle Street,' he explained later, 'when by a coincidence that
seemed almost fateful, I saw my son some hundred yards away.' What
happened next was a matter of some confusion. Not one of the witnesses
to the incident tells the same story.

Queensberry himself claimed that it started with an unprovoked attack
by Percy. 'He came straight at me,' he said, 'almost at a run, and pushed
me up against a shop window, at the same time speaking at the top of his
voice. I struck him certainly but it was done in self defence.' Percy
heatedly denied this. His father, he claimed, was entirely responsible for
the attack. 'He must have seen me,' he insisted 'almost at the same
moment as I saw him and during the whole time he was crossing the
street he was making grimaces with the apparent idea of attracting my
attention. He reached the side of the street on which I was walking some
few paces in front of me. I walked up to him and said to him: 'Are you
going to cease writing these obscene and beastly letters to my wife . . .?
his only reply was to strike me violently under the left eye.' Frederick

Wisdom, a friend who was with Percy, more or less agreed. He swore that Percy had approached his father 'in a most respectful manner' and the 'Marquess replied by making a rude noise with his lips.'

However it started, there was no doubt about the fight which followed. Cheered on by a small crowd, father and son lashed out at each other. Percy's hat went flying, so did Queensberry's umbrella. It took two policemen to separate them, but they did not remain separated for long. When Queensberry tried to escape by crossing the street, Percy rushed after him and the fight began all over again. They were finally grabbed by the policemen and led away struggling and screaming abuse at each other.

Queensberry was still fuming when they reached the Vine Street Police Station. He told the constable who had arrested him that he was willing to fight his son 'anywhere in the country and wherever he liked' for £10,000. 'That is my son,' he yelled, 'who has bailed Oscar Wilde today. He has been following me about and struck me in Piccadilly.' Percy was slightly more restrained. When charged he merely replied that the fight was the result of his father 'writing letters of a most disgusting character to my wife.'

After signing to appear at Marlborough Street the following morning, they were both released.

[2]

'As to the reason for this attack by my son,' Queensberry told a reporter from the *New York Herald* that night, 'I can only imagine he was annoyed by the events of the day and felt foolishly exasperated against me. . . . Of course I regard this evening's affair as very painful from one point of view, but from another I am rather glad of it. There has been bad blood between my son and myself for some time and I think this encounter has probably let some of it out. At all events I feel more kindly disposed towards him than I have been for some years past, and I think very possibly he may think all the better of me.'

There was nothing, as far as Queensberry was concerned, that could not be settled by a good fight. His son, alas, thought otherwise. Returning home that evening, Percy was shown the telegram that Queensberry had sent to his wife. He considered it 'most disgusting and horrible' and sent for his solicitor immediately. The chances of a reconciliation between Queensberry and his son were more remote than ever.

For the reporter from the *New York Herald*, however, Queensberry's word was gospel. He was delighted with the interview and highly amused by the page from the *Illustrated London News* that Queensberry had sent to Minnie. 'There was a distinct touch of the humorous,' he wrote, 'about the dinosauron's [*sic*] attitude and the Marquess could not refrain from chuckling as he drew my attention to it.' Queensberry was still chuckling when the reporter left. The next morning the *Herald* boasted that it was the only newspaper to publish a full and accurate account of the Piccadilly *fracas*.

There was some truth in this. Most newspapers got the story hopelessly muddled. Several of them claimed it was Bosie, not Percy, who had attacked his father and then made things worse by giving Queensberry credit for flooring his son. Bosie, of course, was furious. Writing the following day to a Paris newspaper that carried the story, he demanded an apology. 'I have been in France for the past fifteen days,' he pointed out, 'and I regret that it was not I but my eldest brother, Lord Douglas of Hawick, who corrected the Marquis of Queensberry.' In a second letter, this time to *Le Temps,* Bosie was equally emphatic about his family's relationship with his father. 'Yet another somewhat serious error in your statement,' he complained, 'is to speak of my mother, the Marchioness of Queensberry, as the divorced wife of my father. Allow me to inform you, sir, that it is the Marquis who is the divorced husband of that lady, divorced on account of cruelty and adultery extending over a period of eight years.'

But if the public was misinformed, it was no less interested. The Marlborough Street Court was crowded when Queensberry and Percy appeared to answer charges of disorderly conduct. Not even the Wilde case, which opened at the Old Bailey that morning, could lure away Queensberry's faithful supporters.

It was the Wilde case, though, that was uppermost in Queensberry's mind. He made this quite clear the moment the magistrate, Mr Hannay, arrived in court. Springing to his feet, Queensberry said he wished to make an application. Hannay, taken by surprise, was nonplussed. 'Eh? What?' he spluttered. 'In my case,' Queensberry broke in before he could recover, 'and, I am sorry to say, my son, I appeal to you to take this case first, as I am extremely anxious to get down to hear another case.' Hardly waiting for Hannay to agree, he strode across the court and took his place in the dock. He was joined a few seconds later by Percy.

They were an ill-assorted couple. Queensberry, wearing a big old-fashioned white cravat, looked magnificently assured as he stood 'where the one gleam of sunshine that got into the court with the crowd lighted on his face and the big yellow rose in his buttonhole, making a fine splash of colour.' Beside him Percy, sporting a fancy waistcoat and an ugly black-eye, appeared highly embarrassed. It was noticed that they edged as far away from one another as 'the limits of their common habitation allowed.'

The proceedings were short. After a police constable had given evidence of his arrest, Queensberry announced that he would be defending himself. He cross-questioned the constable who readily admitted that Percy had been the aggressor. The constable who had arrested Percy agreed. 'Do you wish to put any more questions?' asked the magistrate. 'No-no-no,' replied Queensberry in what one journalist described as 'fine airy Old Bailey style.' Not until Percy's solicitor referred to the 'offensive letters' written to Minnie, did Queensberry become agitated. He insisted that there was nothing 'improper' about the letters and that they had only been written to protect his younger son. The magistrate was not interested. Having heard the witnesses—two shop assistants supported Queensberry—he was satisfied that a public disturbance had been created and that, as far as he was concerned, was that. A street brawl, he ruled, was a street brawl and how and why it started was immaterial. He held both the accused responsible and bound them over in their own bonds of £500 to keep the peace for six months.

Queensberry left the court immediately. He was followed to his cab by a wildly cheering crowd who then turned round to hiss and hoot at the departing Percy. Reports of this unseemly and, in view of the verdict, unwarranted display of partisanship brought another blast from across the Channel.

'Lord Queensberry,' Bosie observed sarcastically in a letter to *The Star,* 'seems to be rapidly taking the place of the great Duke of Wellington in the hearts of the British people. . . . Far be it from me to question the right of the great British public to choose as its heroes whom it wishes, but just as a matter of curiosity, I should like to know for which of his feats he was thus greeted. Was it for writing annoying letters to a young lady, or for giving his eldest son a black eye, or simply on account of his general character as shown by his conduct during the past dozen years? I wish somebody would tell me.'

[3]

The crowd who cheered Queensberry was not concerned with the rights and wrongs of his quarrel with his family. They saw him solely in terms of their own prejudices; they would have cheered him wherever and whenever he appeared in public. What did they care if he had tormented and betrayed his wife, hounded his sons and sent offensive letters to his daughter-in-law? Such behaviour was deplorable but at least it fell within the bounds of recognisable sexual conduct. Unlike the vices attributed to Wilde, it did not appear as a threat to the moral fabric of Victorian society; it was not considered depraved, unnatural and, by most people, unmentionable.

For the majority of Victorians, homosexuality was a taboo subject. That it existed could not be denied: homosexual offences were constantly being reported in the press—indeed in a widely publicised case Sir Frank Lockwood, before he became Solicitor-General, had himself defended a man accused of seducing a youth on the underground railway—but it was rarely discussed in conventional society. Even the most explicit Victorian pornography steered clear of homosexual acts. It was this suppression, this ignorance, this deep-rooted fear of the unspeakable, that provided Queensberry with his unlikely halo.

Compared with the enormity of the accusations levelled at Wilde, Queensberry's transgressions appeared trivial, almost commonplace. For once he found himself on the side of the angels. He was able to parade as the upholder of accepted values, to appeal to the very hypocrisy he claimed to despise. This was something Bosie never fully appreciated. He was convinced, and he remained convinced, that he could have won support for Wilde had he been allowed to expose his father's cruelty towards his family. Wilde was more perceptive. He recognised the strength of Queensberry's position, as well as the motives that had inspired it.

'What your father wanted, indeed,' he wrote to Bosie in *De Profundis*, 'was not the cessation of our friendship, but a public scandal. That is what he was striving for. His name had not been in the papers for years. He saw the opportunity of appearing before the British public in an entirely new character, that of the affectionate father. His sense of humour was roused. Had I severed my friendship with you it would have been a terrible disappointment for him, and the small notoriety of a second divorce suit, however revolting its details and origin, would have proved but little consolation to him. For what he was aiming at was popularity, and to pose as a champion of purity, as it is termed, is, in the present condition of the British public, the surest mode of becoming for the nonce a heroic figure. Of this public I have said in one of my plays that it is Caliban for one half of the year, it is Tartuffe for the other, and your father, in whom both characters may be said to have become incarnate, was in this way marked out as the proper representative of Puritanism in its most agressive and most characteristic form.'

Never was that puritanism more evident that during the Wilde trials. The crowds cheering Queensberry were no less vociferous than those denouncing Wilde. Long before he was brought to trial, Wilde, and everything associated with him, was mercilessly pilloried by an hysterical press and a self-righteous public. Hardly, for instance, had Queensberry been acquitted than Wilde's name was removed from the placards advertising his plays in the West End. His publisher, John Lane, not only wrote to *The Times* dissociating himself from the case (Edward Shelley, a clerk in his office, had been cited in Queensberry's plea of justification) but promptly stopped the sale of his books. Nor was such blatant prejudice confined to England. As early as 9 April—three days after Wilde was first charged at Bow Street—the *New York Herald* proudly announced that the committees of the public libraries in St Louis and Newark, New Jersey, had decided to 'withdraw from circulation and destroy all works bearing Oscar Wilde's name.' Press comment ranged from the vicious to the ridiculous. Any dirt that could be dug up and presented as evidence of encroaching 'corruption' was gleefully published. An item that appeared in the *Birmingham Post* was typical. Submitted by an anonymous correspondent and republished by the London Press, it read:

'I have heard on high authority that as a result of investigations which followed upon the Wilde trial, no fewer than sixteen boys have been expelled from one of the public schools. A peculiarly sad case is that of a lad of eleven who is among the sixteen subjects of discipline.'

How exaggerated, indeed how true, such stories were is neither here nor there. They were accepted without question. What they do illustrate—as does the cheering of Queensberry—is the widespread bias against Wilde after his arrest. When Sir Alfred Wills, in his wisdom, agreed to hear Taylor's case before Wilde's, he was quick to dismiss the suggestion that this would be to Wilde's detriment. Both he and the jury, he assured Wilde's counsel, would 'take care that the one trial should have no influence on the other.' He was expecting a great deal of the jury. Any guarantee of impartiality was questionable in the atmosphere, both inside and outside the court, that surrounded Wilde's second trial. Wilde was placed in the stocks long before he entered the dock.

His trial lasted four days—from the morning of 22 May until the evening of 25 May—and followed much the same course as the previous hearing. The same witnesses were called, the same stories were told, the same evidence was read, and the same accusations and denials were heard. Wilde again sat through it all looking haggard, drained of all spirit, partly numb. As he listened to the lawyers' arguments his stunned horror was tinged with bitter amusement. *'How splendid it would be,'* he mused during a diatribe from Sir Frank Lockwood, *'if I was saying all this about myself.'*

'I saw then at once,' he confessed later, 'that what is said of a man is nothing. The point is, who says it. A man's very highest moment is, I have no doubt at all, when he kneels in the dust, and beats his breast, and tells all the sins of his life.'

It was left to others to expose Wilde's sins. They did so in intimate, sometimes messy, detail. Among the few new witnesses were maids from the Savoy Hotel who told of the 'stained sheets' they had removed from Wilde's bed. Their evidence confirmed that of other hotel employees and provided the newspapers with the sort of headlines that are a feature of any sex-case when the secrets of the bedroom are coldly analysed in the court-room. Wilde's frailities were made to appear monstrous; he was judged not as a sinner but as a satyr.

Not only his own sins but those of others attributed to him. The most damaging evidence, he was to say, came from witnesses who had been coached by Queensberry and his solicitors 'not in reticences merely, but in assertions, in the absolute transference, deliberate, plotted and rehearsed, of the actions and doings of someone else on me.' That someone else was probably Bosie. There is no doubt that Bosie, as well as Wilde, entertained young men at the Savoy and that his activities at the hotel were deliberately hushed-up. The evidence of various renters about these occasions, as well as others, might well have been conveniently muddled on Queensberry's instructions. Certainly Bosie was the only person whom Queensberry would have tried to protect. He was also the person whom Wilde was most concerned to shield.

Wilde was to claim that, had he chosen, he could have torn the statements of Queensberry's witnesses to shreds. 'I could have walked out of Court with my tongue in my cheek, and my hands in my pockets, a free man,' he wrote in *De Profundis*. 'The strongest pressure was put on me to do so. . . . But I refused. I did not choose to do so. . . . Such a course of action would have been beneath me. Sins of the flesh are nothing. They are maladies for physicians to cure, if they should be cured. Sins of the soul alone are shameful. To have secured my acquittal by such means would have been life-long torture to me.'

But neither Wilde nor Queensberry was able to cover up for Bosie entirely. There were constant references to his friendship with Wilde, his letters, his poems and his quarrels with his father. So often was he mentioned that, during the judge's final address, the foreman of the jury interrupted to ask whether a warrant had ever been issued for his arrest. Sir Alfred Wills was plainly shocked by the suggestion. 'I should think not,' he snapped. 'We have not heard of it. . . . Lord Alfred Douglas, as you know, went to Paris at the request of the defendant, and there he has stayed, and I know absolutely nothing more about him. . . . It is a thing we cannot discuss.'

Queensberry was in court when this exchange took place. He seems to have attended the hearing for part of every day. On the third day, however, he had arrived late and, unable to find a seat, he had stood at the back of the court for sometime sucking the brim of his hat. Wilde was in the witness box at the time and became very agitated when he spotted Queensberry staring at him. He was seen to take frequent sips of water as he continued with his evidence. The sight of the wild-eyed Marquess was the ultimate horror of the trial. Wilde was always aware of him brooding, like a sour-faced inquisitor, in the background.

'I used to see your father,' he told Bosie, 'bustling in and out in the hopes of attracting public attention, as if anyone could fail to note or remember the stableman's gait and dress, the bowed legs, the twitching hands, the hanging lower lip, the bestial and half-witted grin. Even when he was not there, or was out of sight, I used to feel conscious of his presence, and the blank dreary walls of the great Court-room, the very air itself, seemed to me at times to be hung with multitudinous masks of that apelike face.'

The twitching hands and the bestial grin were very much in evidence when, after retiring for two and a half hours, the jury returned to give their verdict shortly before six in the evening of 25 May. They found Wilde and Taylor guilty on all but one of the eight charges against them. In passing sentence Sir Alfred Wills was merciless.

'Oscar Wilde and Alfred Taylor,' he pronounced, after overriding Sir Edward Clarke's request for a postponement of the sentence, 'the crime of which you have been convicted is so bad that one has to put stern restraint upon oneself to prevent oneself from describing, in language that I would rather not use, the sentiments which must arise to the breast of every man of honour who has heard the details of these two terrible trials. . . . It is no use for me to address you. People who can do these things must be dead to all sense of shame, and one cannot hope to produce any effect upon them. It is the worse case I have ever tried. That you, Taylor, kept a kind of male brothel it is impossible to doubt. And that you, Wilde, have been the centre of a circle of extensive corruption of the most hideous kind among young men, it is equally impossible to doubt. I shall, under the circumstances, be expected to pass the severest sentence that the law allows. In my judgement it is totally inadequate for such a case as this. The sentence of the Court is that each of you be imprisoned and kept to hard labour for two years.'

[4]

Queensberry's brief moment of glory was over. Now he had to count the cost. He did not emerge from the Wilde affair completely unscathed. Hardly had the prison gates clanged shut behind Wilde than murmurs of disapproval concerning Queensberry's role began to be heard. *Reynold's Newspaper*, for example, was highly critical of the sporting Marquess's unseemly delight at his opponent's downfall. 'Certainly,' it commented the day after Wilde was sentenced, 'we think it was indecent for the Marquis of Queensberry to remain in court a spectator of one of the most painful scenes that the historic Old Bailey has ever witnessed. We also thoroughly endorse the severe remarks of Mr Justice Wills as to the means by which Queensberry forced the whole matter to issue.' The following week a female correspondent to the same newspaper was even more outspoken in her condemnation. 'I cannot close this letter,' she fumed, after sympathising with Mr Wilde, 'without saying what I think of the creature who has flaunted about in and out of the Old Bailey with yellow roses in his buttonhole. . . . If I were a man I would meet him face to face, and give him his deserts with my own hands. My God, I would. He is the most outrageous little snob it is possible for one to conceive.'

But these isolated hisses were lost amid the thunderous applause for Wilde's conviction. Queensberry could afford to ignore them. Of more immediate concern was the financial loss he had sustained. The lawyers' costs, the expense of hiring detectives, of paying for evidence and of supporting witnesses throughout the case had, he estimated, set him back well over £2,000. As this money had been spent in what he considered to be a public service, he felt fully justified in petitioning the Treasury for partial repayment. Less than two days after the Wilde trial ended, Queensberry lodged his claim and let it be known that if he was not reimbursed he would ask an MP to bring the matter before Parliament.

Once again he came under attack from sections of the press. 'The Marquess of Queensberry,' sneered one newspaper, 'doubtless finds it agreeable to pose as a censor of morals, but he does not appear to derive the same satisfaction from paying for the privilege. He has a little lawyers' bill of some £2,000 to foot in connection with the recent proceedings, and he is endeavouring to induce the Treasury to take it off his hands. The Treasury has made him a sporting offer of £100, which seems to show they do not set very high value on his services in the cause of morality. As the Marquess was actuated quite as much by personal spite as by public spirit, it is not surprising that the Treasure should refuse to reimburse him. Revenge is sweet, but it is sometimes also expensive.' Not surprisingly, Queensberry refused to accept the Treasury's sporting offer.

Either he did not or could not get an MP to raise the matter in Parliament. Instead he seems to have contented himself with bragging about his great sacrifice in the London clubs. He was heard to say that, if the case had cost him £20,000, he would have considered the money well spent as 'he had extracted such enjoyment and delight and triumph out of it all.' His friends thought his attitude nothing short of noble. They were disgusted with the Treasury's refusal to compensate him and even considered organising a 'whip-round' on his behalf. 'Perhaps no other man in the kingdom,' claimed one of them, 'would have had the courage to act as Lord Queensberry acted. He was profusely thanked by the Press and by innumerable private correspondents of both sexes; but the fact remains that he had to bear the whole of the heavy expenses incidental to the getting up of his case against the wretched man who expiated his crime in a convict prison.'

There was nothing noble about Queensberry's continued persecution of the wretched man in the convict prison. Having failed to squeeze money from the Treasury, he decided to further embarrass Wilde. In June 1895 he instructed his solicitors to file a bankruptcy petition against Mr

Wilde, claiming £677 for his estimated costs in the action that Wilde had brought against him. A receiving order was issued and served on Wilde in Pentonville prison: it was Queensberry's final, humiliating thrust.

There was no way in which Wilde could avoid bankruptcy proceedings. He was penniless, without income, without possessions. His one vague hope that Percy would rescue him by paying Queensberry's costs was quickly dashed. Percy was caught up in his disastrous dealings on the Stock Exchange and in no position to help. In any case, costs or no costs, Percy had no intention of handing over money to his father. He was later to say that, rather than pay Queensberry, he had put aside £600 for Wilde's use when he came out of prison. (He might or might not have done this, but he certainly intended to assist Wilde. Unfortunately, when the time came, Percy—usually generous to a fault—was even further in debt and could not fulfill his promise. 'He is more to be pitied than blamed,' a friend told Wilde. 'He is completely without means for the present.')

As it was, the law, prodded by Queensberry, once again bore down on Wilde. At a meeting of his creditors, on 26 August 1895, it was Queensberry who proposed the motion declaring Wilde insolvent and placing his affairs in the hands of the Official Receiver. So began the long drawn-out and, for Wilde, traumatic bankruptcy proceedings—conducted for the most part in open court. This, claimed Wilde, was the 'complete and perfect victory' for Queensberry. 'Step by step with the Bankruptcy Receiver,' he recalled grimly, 'I had to go over every item in my life. It was horrible.' It turned him against the entire Queensberry family and led, indirectly, to his bitter attack on Bosie in *De Profundis*.

In that scathing document Wilde returned again and again to his bankruptcy 'Have you imagination enough to see,' he asked Bosie, 'what a fearful tragedy it was for me to have come across your family? What a tragedy it would have been for anyone at all, who had great position, a great name, anything important to lose? There is hardly one of the elders of your family—with the exception of Percy, who is really a good fellow—who did not in some way contribute to my ruin.' He saw himself, not as a victim of circumstances or prejudice, but of fate. 'Through your father,' he declared, 'you come of a race, marriage with whom is horrible, friendship fatal, and that lays violent hands either on its own life or on the lives of others.'

He was not alone in his misery. The malign Queensberry influence claimed another victim during the weeks that Wilde was on trial. Alfred Montgomery, that elegant, witty and seemingly insouciant old man, was completely crushed by the Wilde affair. He had never really recovered from the death of his beloved eldest grandson, Drumlanrig, and the new scandal, coming so soon afterwards and exposing his own relationship with Queensberry, proved more than he could bear. Shortly before Wilde appeared in the dock at the Old Bailey, Montgomery was taken seriously ill. The reports of his illness read more like obituaries. No mention was made of the impending trial, but the descriptions of him as a diner-out and a polished *raconteur* of an earlier, more gracious age, made comparisons with Wilde inevitable. 'He is one of the few of the old-fashioned wits who still remain,' observed a columnist of *The Graphic* pointedly, 'That thoughtful refined wit, just tinged with sarcasm, which was so greatly appreciated by the generation which preceded ours has few if any exponents now. The new humour relies more upon sound than upon sense, and owes much more to riskiness than to refinement.'

Alfred Montgomery lived just long enough to learn of Queensberry's triumph. He died at his London house on 5 April 1896, a broken and sadly disillusioned man. 'When I came to grief over the Wilde affair,' admitted Bosie in a rare moment of self reproach, 'I fear it was the finishing blow to him.'

His father-in-law's illness and death made no difference to Queensberry's vendetta against the 'Montgomery lot.' According to Bosie, he continued to persecute his wife with 'every fiendish ingenuity of cruelty and meaness that a man could devise.'

'Hardly a week passes without her receiving some letter from him containing some horrible insult,' wrote Bosie in a letter to the *Review of Reviews,* shortly after Wilde's imprisonment, 'he has been to beat on the door of her house when she was nearly dying upstairs, he has taken away from her every penny of money that as an honourable man he should have given her, and left her only that which he is forced to give her by Scotch law which is so hard on a woman who divorces her husband. In the meantime he flaunts about with prostitutes and kept women and spends on them the money which he should give to his children. . . . Not content with practising fornication and adultery, he has written pamphlets and given lectures advocating what he calls a "sort of polygamy" which is neither more nor less than free love. This is the man who has been made into a hero by the English people and *press*, who is cheered in the streets by the mob, and who has crowned his career by dishonouring and driving out of England his son.'

Perhaps it was just as well that this letter was not published. Not confined to denouncing Queensberry, it contained a long and spirited defence of homosexuality which, at that particular juncture, would not have won public sympathy. Like the rest of his impetuous family, Bosie never appreciated the value of dignified silence; he always considered attack the best form of defence. He had learned nothing from Wilde's experience. During the next few months he continued to indulge his passion for writing to the newspapers, in France as well as England, in the mistaken belief that he was furthering Wilde's cause.

It was Bosie's attempt to publish a lengthy apologia for his friend in the

Mercure de France that created a serious crisis. When Wilde learned about the proposed article, and that it would contain letters he had written to Bosie from Holloway prison, he was horrified. Those letters, he told Bosie, should have been 'sacred and secret beyond anything in the whole world!'; he shuddered at the thought of them appearing 'for the jaded *décadent* to wonder at, for the greedy *feuilletoniste* to chronicle, for the little lions of the *Quartier Latin* to gape at!' and refused to agree to their publication. Sickened by what he considered Bosie's betrayal, Wilde finally gave vent to his bile in *De Profundis*.

De Profundis is the long, breast-beating, self-pitying letter which Wilde wrote to Bosie during the last months of his imprisonment. Larded with grandiloquent phrases, pretentious allusions and distorted facts, it is Wilde's attempt to explain his friendship with Bosie and the effect of that friendship upon him as an artist. In it he repeatedly touches upon his fatal association with the Queensberry family and, in so doing, reveals his need to dignify what, in essence, was a degrading squabble.

'At the end,' he concludes, 'I was of course arrested and your father became the hero of the hour: more indeed than the hero of the hour: your family now ranks, strangely enough, with the Immortals: for with that grotesqueness of effect that is as it were a Gothic element in history, and makes Clio the least serious of all the Muses, your father will always live among the kind pure-minded parents of Sunday-school literature, your place is with the Infant Samuel, and in the lowest mire of Malebolge I sit between Giles de Retz and the Marquis de Sade.'

Wilde's sense of humour had for the moment deserted him. He was attempting to write out his despair, his humiliation, his frustration and his wounded vanity. He needed some means of release and sought it in hyperbole. Mercifully the letter was not delivered to Bosie, and Wilde, after leaving prison, showed little interest in what had become the manuscript. His bitterness, however, lived on and was not fully revealed until the complete text of *De Profundis* was published sixty-five years later. Significantly the parts which had been suppressed until then were those in which he most fiercely attacked the Queensberry family.

Wilde was released from Pentonville prison on 19 May 1897. He had served most of his sentence at Reading but officialdom demanded that he be discharged from the prison to which he had originally been committed. His friends were extremely worried about the publicity given to his release. Queensberry was again on the rampage. He had announced that he intended to wait for Wilde outside Pentonville and cause a disturbance. This threat was taken so seriously that Wilde had petitioned the Home Secretary for an early release and, when this request was refused, some of his friends had written to the prison authorities asking for him to be set free at least a day or two before the official date. They pointed out that Queensberry's thugs had previously hounded Wilde while he was on bail and there was reason to think that this would happen again. But the law stood firm and, as it happened, the alarm proved false. There was no sign of Queensberry when Wilde emerged from the prison gates to be met by his friends. He was whisked off in a brougham and that night caught the boat-train to France.

But even in France Wilde remained apprehensive. He confessed as much to Bosie. 'Of course at present it is impossible for us to meet . . .' he wrote to his 'dearest Boy' from Dieppe a month later, 'if your father—or rather Q, as I only know him and think of him—if Q came over and made a scene and scandal it would utterly destroy my possible future and alienate all my friends from me.' It was months before Wilde rid himself of that ape-like spectre with its bestial, half-witted grin, its stableman's gait and its twitching hands.

Chapter Nineteen

'The Douglas to the Dust'

Less than three years of life were left to Queensberry after Wilde's release from prison. They were lonely, purposeless, bitter years, the empty years of anti-climax, the years in which he was at last brought face to face with his own inadequacies.

Any hope of the pugnacious Marquess being accepted by respectable society in his quaint role as a moral crusader quickly faded. If anything, once the mindless cheering stopped, he was more heartily despised, more roundly condemned, more studiously avoided. There were those who were shocked by his treatment of his family. The contempt his sons expressed for him in court, his crude attacks on his wife and his daughter-in-law and his public brawl with Percy all helped to confirm what had earlier been rumoured. (In one of the few attempts to defend Wilde immediately after the trial, a French writer, Henri Bauër, described Queensberry as *'type de brute sportive malfaisante, mauvais mari, méchant père.'*) There were others, fired by press murmurings, who were disgusted at Queensberry's obvious delight at Wilde's downfall. And there were some who considered the Wilde scandal was not the sort of affair in which a 'gentleman' should have played a part, however public-spirited that part might appear. Ironically, Queensberry was made to suffer for his opponent's sins as well as his own.

And suffer he did. 'He really was ostracised and shunned, especially after the Wilde affair,' acknowledged Bosie. 'The victory he obtained over Oscar Wilde in the Law Courts was thus dearly bought, at a terrible price; for I doubt whether he ever knew a really happy hour after it happened . . . the satisfaction he got from his performance cannot have endured for much longer than a few weeks.' Even his more sympathetic friends found him remote and melancholy. 'He was almost universally misunderstood,' one of them protested. 'If ever an Englishman "took his pleasures sadly" that man was Lord Queensberry.'

Truth to tell, there were few pleasures left for Queensberry to take—sadly or otherwise. He had lost what interest he had in sport. He rarely attended a boxing match, his steeple-chasing days were over, he no longer hunted, and he appeared at the race-course simply as a spectator. Only when peddalling about the West End on his bicycle did he display a faint flicker of his old sporting spirit. And that flicker was becoming increasingly uncertain.

It certainly did not match up to the enthusiasm he had shown a few years earlier when the 'bicycling craze' had first swept fashionable London. Then he had helped to set the pace for the new sport. On one of his more memorable 'spins' Queensberry had greatly impressed his friends by puffing his way from the Star and Garter pub in Richmond to his rooms in James Street in forty minutes flat. Spurred on by this feat, he had teamed up with a local champion, known as 'Bath Road Smith,' and entered the various tandem events. The partnership had lasted until the doughty Mr Smith, while practising on his own, fell from his machine and almost broke his neck. Queensberry also took some nasty tumbles. One occurred between the hearings of the Wilde case and resulted in him being laid up for several days. After that he contented himself for the most part with tricycles. (Line drawings of him seated on his three-wheeler and wearing a deerstalker cap and knickerbockers featured prominently in American newspapers during Wilde's second trial.)

But it was all a far cry from his happy hunting days. He was now a sportsman in name only and well past his prime. His youthful ambitions, above all his hopes of winning the Grand National, had long since disappeared; with them had gone the remnants of his youthful philosophy. His faith in the immutable laws of nature, in the regenerative powers of a life force, in the need to strive for physical perfection had dismally failed to withstand the test of time. As his physical powers declined so, it seems, did his mental resources. He clung to his prejudices but rarely felt the need to defend them, let alone explain them. For one reason or another most of his old free-thinking friends had deserted him and only occasionally did he show interest in their activities. Once, on hearing that Annie Besant—Charles Bradlaugh's old friend and lieutenant—had been converted to Theosophy, he was sufficiently curious to write to her for advice. Her reply left him more mystified than ever. All the sorrows of his life, Mrs Besant assured him, 'were simply the result of "karma".' He did not, as far as is known, pursue the argument further.

Of greater concern were his financial worries. In the last years of his life, according to Bosie, Queensberry suffered from 'the strange delusion that he was almost entirely without money.' This—considering that when he died he left an estate valued at over £307,000 (a not inconsiderable sum for those days)—was extraordinary. On the other hand, his 'delusion' was not as strange as Bosie imagined. There can be no doubt that, over the years, Queensberry had squandered a small fortune. His own inheritance had been more than double that which he left and had included some valuable properties. These properties, mostly in Scotland, had gradually been sold off—first the Torthorwald and Tinwald estates and then, in 1896, the Cummertrees estate which included Kinmount—

until he was left with only Glen Stuart (rented to Florrie and Beau) and the small family burial ground. In July 1897, a year after the sale of Kinmount, the devastation was completed with the sale of the family pictures and heirlooms.

There is no telling what Queensberry did with his money. Extravagant he most certainly was not. His rooms in James Street were modest, he rarely entertained, he employed few servants, he allowed his wife only what he was forced to allow her and if, as Bosie claims, he spent the money on women he did not do so lavishly. He was considered every bit as mean as he was a bully. Even allowing for a certain recklessness as a young man—his stables, his mistresses and possibly his gambling—it is still difficult to fathom the continuing decline of his fortune. Admittedly his pig-headedness made him a bad business man. He neglected his estates, was suspicious of his managers, refused to take advice, and was forever quarrelling with his agents. This may have accounted for some of his losses—although the rentals from his Scottish properties remained fairly constant at between £12,000 and £13,000 a year—and one can only suppose foolish speculation accounted for the rest. There seems no other explanation, apart from what Bosie called 'melancholy madness', why such a notoriously tight-fisted man should be haunted by exaggerated fears of poverty. Whatever the reason, the result was unmistakable. As his fortune dwindled, Queensberry became more and more obsessed by the need to sell off his assets, to hoard and to economise. The last years of his life were plagued by these financial fears.

His sons refused to take his fears seriously. They saw the sale of Kinmount and the family estates as further proof of his vindictiveness. So cynical was Bosie that, shortly after the sale of the Scottish properties, he tried to have his allowance renewed. In 1898 he wrote to his cousin Algie Bourke asking him to intercede with Queensberry on his behalf and, if possible, to effect a reconciliation.

Bosie's *volte-face* was not as surprising as it first appears. Queensberry had already indicated that he was prepared to forgive his son. Shortly after the last Old Bailey trial, he had written to Bosie offering to supply him with money and an allowance if he would promise not to see Wilde again. With astonishing naivety he had suggested that Bosie should go to the South Sea Islands where he would find 'plenty of beautiful girls.' Bosie had dismissed this offer with contempt. At that time his only thought was to be reunited with Wilde (he knew nothing then of *De Profundis*) and he regarded his father's suggestion as obscene. Queensberry's idea of reformation, he snorted, was simply to substitute 'one vice for another.'

Now, three years later, Bosie viewed things in a different light. His longed-for reunion with Wilde had turned out a sad disappointment. After their first emotional meeting, Bosie and Wilde had been made to face reality. For a couple of months they had tried to live together in Naples but the experiment had failed. Pressure from their families and the inevitable problem of finance—neither of them was seriously prepared to work—had made any pretence of blissful companionship impossible. Finally Bosie's mother stepped in. She wrote to say that unless the 'scandalous Naples *ménage*' was broken up she would stop supplying her son with money. With that Bosie, fretful and bored, capitulated. He agreed to part from his friend and never to sleep under the same roof with him again, provided his mother paid Wilde £200 for his immediate living expenses. This payment, he argued, was part of the 'debt of honour' that the Queensberry family owed Wilde. On one point, however, Bosie was adamant: he refused to promise that he would not see Wilde again. This was his attitude when, on returning to England, he swallowed his pride and tried to drive the same bargain with his father.

Queensberry at first appeared amenable. When Algie Bourke showed him Bosie's letter he immediately agreed to a meeting; he seemed delighted at the prospect of welcoming back his prodigal son. They met in the smoking-room of Bailey's Hotel, where Queensberry was staying, and fell on each others necks. According to Bosie, it was a highly emotional occasion. Choking back his tears, Queensberry formally forgave his son several times and ended by calling him 'my poor darling boy.' There and then he promised to write to the man who managed his affairs authorising the renewal of the much-needed allowance. It all seemed too good to be true.

And of course it was. For all the tears and protestations of affection, the reunion smacked too much of opportunism on Bosie's part for it to be lasting. Within a matter of days Queensberry was having second thoughts. 'He whipped round on me again,' sighed the crestfallen Bosie, 'and wrote me an abusive letter in which he said that he did not intend to give me a penny until he knew exactly what my relations were with "that beast Wilde." ' It was hardly a novel situation. Nor is it surprising that Bosie retaliated by sending his father a 'suitable' reply, 'hurling back the celebrated and legendary "allowance" with stinging words.' Only poor Algie Bourke, caught in the cross-fire, could have been taken aback by this sudden switch from tears to tantrums.

Bosie never spoke to his father again. Some months later, though, he caught a glimpse of Queensberry in the street looking hollow-eyed and haggard. Bosie was in a cab at the time and did not stop but claims to have been overcome with compassion. On returning home he made enquiries about his father's health and was told by his brother-in-law, St George Fox-Pitt, that Queensberry was seriously ill. What was more alarming, Queensberry's illness seemed to be following an all-too-familiar pattern. He was suffering from delusions. He claimed to be 'persecuted by Oscar Wilders' who had driven him from various hotels and who woke him up at night by shouting obscene names at him. He was behaving, in fact, very much as his younger brother Jim had behaved shortly before he committed suicide.

Whether Bosie recognised the significance of these symptoms one does not know. He talks only about his shock at learning that his father held him responsible for his troubles. 'He was under the impression that I hated him,' says the suddenly surprised Bosie. The thought upset him dreadfully and he wrote a letter for his brother-in-law to give to Queensberry. In it he explained that he had been suffering from influenza when he last wrote and was scarcely responsible for what he said. He withdrew his 'stinging words' and assured his father of his love. Queensberry made no comment when he was shown the letter, but he appeared to calm down. 'I think he was pleased to see it,' Fox-Pitt later told Bosie.

[2]

St George Fox-Pitt was the only member of the family who was on speaking terms with Queensberry during the last months of his life. He was the husband of Queensberry's daughter, Edith, and in many ways a very remarkable man. Almost eighteen years older than his wife, Fox-Pitt was a most unlikely recruit to the hearty Queensberry clan. As a young man of twenty-two, he had startled the scientific world with his invention of a carbon filament lamp which many experts, including Thomas Edison, considered 'the decisive factor in the development of the commercial side of electric lighting.' Unfortunately the fortune which Fox-Pitt expected to make from this invention was lost when he was deprived of the patent rights in a lawsuit. Science was one of his early enthusiasms. Later his interests extended to every branch of philosophy, religion and politics. Fox-Pitt was one of the early members of the Society for Psychical Research, a vice-president of the Moral Education League, a candidate for the Liberal Party and the highly respected author of books on education and social problems. It was largely through his influence that Edith added an exotic touch to her family's religious ramifications by becoming a Buddhist.

Fox-Pitt's sympathy for Queensberry is an indication of his adaptability. It was a quality which his wife at times found difficult to appreciate. Very early on Edith had ranged herself firmly on the side of her mother and brothers in the family quarrel by roundly attacking her father for his opposition to Percy's marriage—'It has made trouble between I and Edie,' Queensberry had complained to Percy, 'that is hard to forgive'—and, although there had been an attempt at reconciliation, the rift had never properly healed. That is probably why, despite his approval of Fox-Pitt, Queensberry had shown no interest in his daughter's wedding. When the twenty-five year old Edith married her middle-aged husband at Holy Trinity Church, Sloane Street, in March 1899, she walked into the church, followed by nine bridesmaids, on the arm of her brother Percy.

It is impossible to say when Queensberry's 'delusions' started. He had always been prone to temperamental outbursts and his behaviour was, to say the least, often erratic; it is quite possible that the initial stages of this, his most serious mental derangement, passed unremarked. Unlike his brother Jim he had no one to keep a close watch on him. However, by the time Fox-Pitt reported to Bosie, probably in the latter half of 1899, there was no mistaking Queensberry's condition. His gaunt, wild-eyed looks, his rambling tales of persecution, his incoherent mutterings and his imaginary reversal of roles with Wilde could no longer be dismissed as mere eccentricity. He had, by that time, reached the slippery slopes of insanity.

Bosie was to claim that the last letter he wrote to his father 'put a stop to his delusions about persecution.' This seems most unlikely. He may have appeared to calm down—Jim had had intermittent periods of lucidity— but it needed more than a letter to soothe Queensberry's madness. Indeed it was never soothed: his ravings were halted in a more dramatic fashion. Towards the end of 1899, he suffered a stroke at the Raleigh Club in Regent Street which partly paralysed him. He was taken to rooms in Welbeck Street and lay there for several weeks, semi-conscious and scarcely able to recognise visitors.

One of the few visitors he did recognise was his wife. Having suffered so cruelly at the hands of her vindictive husband, Sybil was unable to ignore him on his death bed. She went to sit with him and, in one of his rare moments of sanity, they were reconciled. Emotional and unpredictable to the end, Queensberry begged his wife's forgiveness and told her that she was the only woman he had ever loved. His attitude towards his eldest son and heir was more characteristic. When Percy called at Welbeck Street, Queensberry simply sat up in bed and spat at him.

He died, aged fifty-five, on 31 January 1900. The cause of his death was announced as 'pneumonia'; no mention was made of his mental breakdown.

During the last days of his illness, Queensberry had been nursed by his brother Archie. Twelve years later Archie was to tell Bosie of his father's deathbed conversion to Catholicism. It was a salutary, but not very convincing story. According to Archie, that worthy Catholic priest, Queensberry in his dying hours had entirely renounced his agnostic views and professed his love for and faith in Jesus Christ to whom, he said, 'I have confessed all my sins.' Archie had then given him conditional absolution. Anything, of course, was possible with Queensberry and he was quite capable of touching wood at the last moment. But there is something suspect about Archie's story.

Why, for instance, did he wait twelve years before disclosing this extraordinary change of heart? And why, if it were true, did he deny his brother a Catholic burial? Indeed why did he allow the new convert to be buried in direct contravention of Catholic teaching? For, two days after his death, Queensberry was cremated at Woking and his ashes were taken to Kinmount. This, in a church which decreed that those who left instructions for their bodies to be cremated were as outcast as those who were excommunicated, seems strange indeed. But then Archie had also presided at the burial of his younger brother who, as a suicide, was subject to the same interdict. Perhaps the laws of the church did not apply to members of the Queensberry family. Or perhaps Archie's Catholicism, like his brother's agnosticism, was open to timely revision. However it happened, and whatever the truth, the legend that Queensberry died a Catholic lingered on.

There was no suggestion of a religious ceremony at his funeral. It was very much a private, family affair. Percy and Archie accompanied Queensberry's ashes to Scotland and his other two sons, Bosie and Sholto, as well as his daughter, Edith, his daughter-in-law, Minnie and his brother-in-law, Beau Dixie, were present when the Doulton ware casket was deposited in the family vault. His wife sent a wreath.

The only full account of the proceedings was that which appeared in the *Agnostic Journal*. 'I regarded him,' wrote the editor, W. Stewart Ross, who had known Queensberry for many years, 'with a great feeling akin to affection. He was a man whom those who only knew him partially were apt to quite misunderstand and grossly misrepresent. It may be that his procedure was not uniformly guided by prudence, and that he, on occasions, failed to exercise self-restraint; but a more sincere, single-minded, kind-hearted man did not live . . . it is not without a pang and a tear I have to give the Douglas to the dust.'

Other newspapers were not so kind. So scathing was *The Times* obituary that another of Queensberry's long-standing friends, Richard Edgcumbe, felt compelled to spring to his defence. 'A "curious figure" he may have been,' Edgcumbe protested. 'But he was undoubtedly a fearless, chivalrous English gentleman, who never told a lie in his life, who never did a shabby thing, who scorned hypocrisy, and who would willingly have suffered death if thereby he could have made his traducers better or happier.'

One wonders whether Oscar Wilde, then living in Paris, read this curious assessment of the man who had hounded him so mercilessly. He, like Queensberry's sons, would have found it difficult to swallow. 'Bosie is over here, with his brother,' he told a friend a few weeks later. 'They are in deep mourning and the highest spirits. The English are like that.' This was to be his last comment on Queensberry. Wilde survived his old enemy by a mere ten months. A more genuine death-bed convert to

Catholicism, Oscar Wilde died in a humble Paris hotel on 30 November 1900.

'If another century began and I were still alive,' he had told Bosie a few months earlier, 'I don't think the English could stand it.' For once, Queensberry might have agreed with him.

[3]

Neither Florrie nor her mother attended Queensberry's funeral. They were both too frail to risk the biting February winds. The redoubtable Florrie, who had inherited her twin brother's complaint and was crippled with arthritis, often had difficulty in walking these days and was forced to spend much of her time in a wheelchair. The Dowager Marchioness was similarly incapacitated. Now in her eighties, she tired easily and rarely ventured out of the house in the winter months. But, of all the family, it was probably Queensberry's sister and mother who were most deeply affected by his death. For all his faults, for all that others might think of him, the bigoted Marquess remained Florrie's hero and his mother's son.

It is doubtful whether Archie told the Dowager Marchioness of his brother's questionable conversion; or, at least, if he did so, it would not have been until after the funeral. Had she known earlier, the old lady would certainly have moved heaven and earth to have her son buried with the rites of the Catholic church. Her faith was as strong as ever. Her loyalty to the church had never wavered since her own conversion some forty years earlier: Ireland and Catholicism had dominated her life. She had defied her family, parted from her friends and shunned society for the sake of her religious convictions. Nothing would have consoled her more than the knowledge that her sceptical son had 'confessed his sins' on his death bed. True repentance was, as far as she was concerned, the only sure sign of salvation.

This—the need to return to the true faith—had become her *cri de coeur* for Ireland. She no longer trusted politicians. The older she grew the more convinced she became that a holy cause had been betrayed by unholy motives. In 1897 she had set out her views in a pamphlet entitled 'Let there be light' which she addressed to 'my brothers and sister of the Irish nation household.'

'As there is clearly but "one thing"—without the smallest possible doubt,' she pleaded, 'that is "needful" to save our country from its slavery and other ruin—nay death; above all it is to be commanded to be sought by Him who dare has the wisdom to know what is best; might I, as one of the least in our Father's house, be permitted to ask you why this "one thing needful" "the first to be sought" (according to His command) is overlooked by you all? This "one thing needful" it was which raised

Ireland under St Patrick's teaching to all her greatness and glory.
. . . This "one thing" has been set aside for centuries, to rest on men,
and still it is set aside seeking not the "one thing neefull' as commanded
but still for some "man."''

But, convinced as she was that Ireland had drifted from the paths of
faith, the Dowager Marchioness had never doubted the rightness of the
Irish cause. Her pen and her purse were always available to various
nationalist movements, however much she might distrust their leaders.
Not only did she honour her promise to support the dependants of the
'Manchester Martyrs' but she continued to finance Michael Larkin's
children long after they left school. She did so at no small cost to herself.
During the last years of her life she was almost entirely dependent on the
small annuity left to her by her father, but she never allowed her poverty
to interfere with what she considered a sacred trust.

Nor was her charity confined to Ireland. In Scotland she worked
tirelessly for local Catholic societies and was always at hand to help
Archie with his parish duties. Although there seems to be no truth in a
later rumour that she joined a religious order, her piety was such that the
tenants of the Kinmount estate always spoke of her as a 'Sister of Mercy.'

The Dowager Marchioness outlived Queensberry by four years, dying
at Glen Stuart on 14 February 1904. Her death passed almost unnoticed in
the English press. Those obituaries that were published tended to con-
centrate on her eccentricities—recalling her runaway marriage and describing her as the 'Gretna Green Marchioness' and 'a friend of the
Fenians'. Only in Ireland was she more fondly remembered.

'She was intensely religious,' noted the *Freeman's Journal*, 'and she felt
that everything done for Ireland was done for God. The memory of her
love for Ireland and her sacrifices in defence of Truth and Justice grateful
Irish hearts will not willingly let die. May the turf lay lightly on the grave
of a true friend of Ireland and a gentle and blameless lady.'

But it was in an Irish city with which she had no known connection that
she was best remembered. At that time a monument was being erected in
Cork to honour those who had died 'in the struggle for independence'
and the local branch of the Young Ireland Society wrote to Archie asking
permission to include his mother's name among the Fenians of 1867.
Archie was delighted. 'Her love for Ireland,' he wrote in reply, 'remained
to the end, and very, very often of late, especially as the end drew near,
the prayer, "God save Ireland", was on her lips . . . I shall feel highly
honoured in giving my assent to that proposal, asking, however, that the
inscription proposed shall first be submitted to me.'

Unfortunately, Archie's request appears to have been ignored. When
the monument at the junction of Grand Parade and South Mall in Cork
was unveiled two years later, it was revealed that Caroline, Marchioness
of Queensberry, had been mistakenly inscribed as 'Catherine, Mar-

chioness of Queensberry.' Not that this would have worried the daunt-less lady unduly. More to the point was the description of her as 'Friend of the Manchester Martyrs.' That is how she would have wished to be remembered.

Four years after his mother's death, Archie was transferred from St Columba's Church in Annan to a parish church in Girvan, Ayrshire. He was then in his mid-fifties and was to be the only member of his family to enjoy a tranquil old age. Unlike his more tempestuous brothers and sisters, Archie had never deliberately courted trouble and, though not the most orthodox of Catholic priests, his vocation appears to have brought him contentment.

Archie's later career was uneventful. For fourteen years he was happy enough pottering about his parish and when, in 1920, be became too old for parish duties he was appointed to the not over-exacting post of chaplain to a group of exiled French nuns at Cliffe, near Dover. Five years later he retired. At the age of seventy-five he went to live at St Anthony's Hospital in North Cheam, Surrey, where he died in February 1938.

Always the odd man out in his family, Archie remained—at his own request—aloof from them in death. The instructions he left for his burial were simple but explicit. 'I direct,' he wrote in a will drawn up seven years before his death, 'that I shall be laid out and placed in my coffin in my purple vestments as a Priest of the Roman Catholic Church and that I be buried in the nearest Catholic Cemetery and not in the family burial ground at Kinmount.'

His wishes were faithfully observed. The Reverend Lord Archibald Edward Douglas was buried in the Streatham Park cemetery and his meagre estate (valued at a little over £500) was placed at the disposal of the Catholic Bishop of Galloway.

[4]

There was nothing tranquil about Florrie's last years: she was too much of a fighter to settle for anything that smacked of resignation. Nothing, not even ill-health, could dampen her fiery spirit. Often immobilised by arthritis, huddled in a bath chair and sometimes scarcely able to hold a pen, Florrie never halted her campaigns on behalf of the oppressed, the neglected and the maltreated. Books, articles, pamphlets, tracts and letters to the press continued to pour out of Glen Stuart with amazing regularity. She wrote on animal cruelty, on vegetarianism, on religion, on dress reform, on Home Rule and, above all, on the rights of women. She republished the poems and plays she had written as a child, she recalled her own youth in thinly disguised autobiographical novels, she invented children's stories with fanciful titles—*Aniwee: or, the Warrior Queen, Little*

Cherie: or the Trainer's Daughter—and stern moral warnings. Every book she published, every article she wrote, was designed as propaganda for her various causes.

What she could not understand was the indifference with which so much of her pleading was received. So convinced was she of the rightness of her arguments that she found it astonishing that others did not think the same. This was particularly true of her crusade for women's rights. She was forever trying to prod her 'submissive sisters' into action.

'You must no longer acquiesce in your degradation by the false,' she railed in one of her attacks on Christianity. 'You must recognise that truth alone can save you. . . . You will give birth to sons who will oppress you by reason of their ignorance and acquired selfishness. The sons of free-born women would never act thus. Urgently needed is women's emancipation and her transformation from a bond slave to being born in freedom. Until this desirable object is effected, progress must be slow and the elevation of humanity be retarded.'

But she was preaching to deaf ears. Her views were too advanced, her voice too strident, for a conformist age. Not that this deterred her. The older she grew the more radical she became. Nowhere were her views on religion and politics more forcefully set out than in her last autobiographical novel, *Izra*. Her heroine, for instance, is obviously speaking for Florrie when she explains how the 'Brotherhood of Man' is to be achieved.

'By Co-operation alone,' she argues. 'Men and women must have equal chances and opportunities in life. From the day they are born equality must be theirs. The senseless social distinctions and barriers which call one man an aristocrat and another a plebian, giving to one privileges and witholding them from the other, awarding to one sex all power and keeping woman in helpless subjection, must be swept away, and *the one sound principle of Co-operation* prevail. To accomplish this we must destroy the dogmas of superstition, and uproot the false creed which they uphold, a creed which voices the savage and barbaric ideas of men in far-off ages gone. There should be no aristocracy but that of intellect and merit. Give all *human* beings fair play, and Nature will select her own aristocracy.'

Trite as it might now appear, this was considered fighting talk in Edwardian England. That Florrie's contemporaries regarded her as a red-hot revolutionary, a traitor to her class, is not surprising. Even her more progressive friends were inclined to speak of her as a crank when, on her rare visits to London, she embarrassed them by her outspokenness. Needless to say, she made few converts. Like so many ardent reformers, she was far too intense and didactic and her manner was too abrasive to win people over by personal persuasion.

There were, of course, exceptions. Among them was the beautiful Lady Warwick—Edward VII's 'Darling Daisy'—who claimed that it was Florrie who first interested her in socialism. But even Lady Warwick, much as she admired Florrie's 'eccentric and startling personality' had to admit that she could be frightening at times. 'She was a rough diamond', remembered the Countess, 'and as hard as nails, or even a little harder.'

Social prejudice was the least of Florrie's concerns. Unlike Queensberry she was never one to brood over trivialities; she made no pretence of her contempt for fashionable society. She was far happier in Scotland. Indeed she would have liked nothing better than to see Scotland shake off its ties with England and was genuinely ashamed of the fact that one of her ancestors—the second Duke of Queensberry—had helped forge the link between the two countries by securing the 1707 Act of Union, which was, she maintained, a betrayal of Scottish aspirations. Home Rule was as important for Scotland as it was for Ireland.

So, to her many causes and campaigns, Florrie added that of Scottish independence. When, in 1902, the Scottish Patriotic Association held a rally at Bannockburn to protest against the newly-crowned English King's assumption of the title Edward VII, she was quick to lend her support. Unable to attend the rally, she sent the organisers a spirited letter which was read out to the cheering crowd.

'When James VI of Scotland became King also of England, he was [Florrie wrote] styled James VI of Scotland, but James I both of England and of Great Britain. Why then, should Scotland be insulted now by being told that her King is Edward VII of Scotland? . . . Never give in on this point. To ignore it is to destroy historic truth and the glorious traditions of our native land, dear old Scotland.' She signed herself 'a Douglas to the backbone.'

Perhaps it was just as well that she omitted to mention that the presumptious Edward VII was an old friend of her husband's and godfather to one of her sons. Such associations belonged to her sporting past and, like her skill as her hunter, were best forgotten.

She no longer cared what her former friends thought of her. Her anti-bloodsports crusade was as vehement as ever. She revised her pamphlet *The Horrors of Sport*, wrote endless articles on the subject for British and American journals and was loud in her protests against vivisection. Experiments on animals, she insisted, were merely an excuse for humans to display their own brutality. Nor was her concern only for animals. In her gruff, no-nonsense way she was as active among the poor and sick of the Kinmount estate as was her mother. Not always the most gracious, and certainly not the richest, of Lady Bountifuls, Florrie was nevertheless able to hand out sound commonsense and practical advice. Among her more successful ventures was the scheme she originated for providing holiday camps at the seaside for poor children. Charity, she liked to boast, was not an exclusive Christian virtue. Her practical streak also led her to accept the honorary presidency of a ladies' football team.

'Football,' she stoutly maintained, 'was the ideal exercise for women.'

Florrie's enthusiasms were as unexpected as they were varied. One of the more surprising arose a year after her mother's death. It was sparked off by a curious telegram from Geneva which was published in the British press at the beginning of April 1905. It read:

'There is every probability that the body of Lord Francis Douglas will be delivered up by the slow moving glacier this summer. It is forty years since the terrible accident occurred by which Lord Francis Douglas lost his life during the first ascent of the Matterhorn. Despite prolonged search, no trace of the body of Lord Francis could ever be found. In the last 40 years, however, the Zmutt glacier has been descending regularly and rapidly, and, according to the natural laws, the portion of the glacier where the Alpinist fell should reach the valley this year. The body will be found in a perfect state of preservation, and easily recognisable.'

Florrie's first reaction to this startling information was one of dismay. It revived the spectre that had haunted her family for years and threatened, in a particularly gruesome way, to destroy what little consolation they had derived from Francis's disappearance. She had been a small child when the accident occurred but she vaguely remembered that, before leaving for Switzerland, her brother had forseen the possibility of his death and had given instructions that his remains should be recovered and buried on the spot. Determined that his wishes be obeyed, she dashed off an excited appeal to *The Times*. 'I shall take every step,' she declared, after quoting the telegram, 'to ascertain if my brother's body is yielded up by the glacier, and this is to ask the kind co-operation of anyone who may be in those parts who can greatly assist by keeping a sharp-look-out for the long lost body.' She did not question the prediction.

Once again Florrie found herself at the centre of a controversy. The story was taken up by other newspapers and soon she was being accused of morbid sensationalism. In the heated arguments that followed, the original telegram was ignored and it was even hinted that the story had been inspired by Florrie herself. Such a bizarre theory, it was thought, was typical of Lady Florence Dixie's over-heated imagination.

But the theory was not as bizarre as it appeared. Frozen bodies had been recovered from glaciers years after they had disappeared. This was pointed out by a former president of the Alpine Club, C. E. Mathews, who wrote to *The Times* a few days later. He quoted two known instances. One was that of three guides who had fallen to their death on Mont Blanc during an expedition in August 1820. Some forty years later, claimed Mathews, it had been correctly predicted that the bodies of these men would be brought down by a glacier and they were eventually found 'on dates varying from August 1861, to June 1863 and the head of one of the victims was actually identified after an entombment of 43 years.' The other case was that of Captain Arkright who had died on Mont Blanc in 1866 and whose body was recovered in 1897. Even Mr Mathews, however, doubted whether Francis's body would reappear. 'The opinion of competent mountaineers,' he concluded, 'is that the body was arrested in its fall and is still hidden in some fissure of those tremendous crags which form the north side of the Matterhorn.'

It was the mountaineers who convinced Florrie that another search would be futile. They wrote to her and explained that Francis had not fallen above the Zmutt glacier, as the telegram suggested, but above the 'Matterhorn glacier' which was shorter and steeper and had probably descended years earlier. 'Even if the body did reach the glacier and disappeared into a crevasse,' argued one of them, 'it is not likely that it should now be found.' Florrie could not but accept the verdict of experts. Among the many letters she received were some from climbers who were eager to organise a search party but Florrie turned their offers down. She was grateful, she said, but she considered the matter closed.

On one point, though, she refused to yield. She resented the taunts that she had instigated a hoax and adamantly denied that she was responsible for the newspaper reports. Francis's body was never found.

This was the last controversy in which Florrie was involved. She no longer had the strength or the inclination for public squabbling. The next few months saw a rapid deterioration in her health. Riddled with arthritis, unable to walk and sometimes unable even to stand, she was rarely seen out of doors. Occasionally, on a sunny day, she would be glimpsed in the grounds of Glen Stuart—sitting in her wheelchair, attended by Beau and a pack of yapping dogs—but, at the approach of strangers, she would be hurriedly trundled away. What little energy she had was spent in trying to complete her novel, *Izra*, which was then appearing in weekly instalments in the *Agnostic Journal*.

She was a regular contributor to this struggling little freethought weekly. Edited by Queensberry's old friend, William Stewart Ross—a former Presbyterian minister—it was the successor of the old *Secular Review* and catered for former member's of the British Secular Union who were unable to accept the politics of the more powerful National Secular Society. Its readers, a dwindling band, were mostly old-fashioned radicals who preferred their non-conformist religious views coated with a veneer of gentility. Florrie could have found no better audience. To these somewhat fastidious rebels her peculiar blend of reformist zeal, aristocratic patronage and sentimental socialism had an irresistible appeal. 'Though I did not know her in person,' sighed one of them after her death, 'I had, like all her readers, come to know and love her character. Was there ever a more beautiful one?'

He was not alone in his enthusiasm. *Izra*, a rambling semi-mystical, semi-autobiographical story of a roving 'free spirit,' was a tremendous success. It ran for several months in the *Agnostic Journal* and ended only with Florrie's death. Propped up in bed, flushed and breathless, she continued to churn out the weekly instalments of *Izra* until the end of October. Finally she was forced to give up. In the first week of November, the *Agnostic Journal* announced that 'owing to serious illness in the household of Lady Florence Dixie, *Izra* must, for the present, be discontinued.' It was never resumed.

Early in the morning of 7 November 1905, Florrie died. She was buried four days later at Kinmount. The funeral was a simple one, attended only by close members of the family, and conducted in accordance with her precise instructions. 'There was no ceremony,' it was reported, 'the religious tenets of the deceased proscribing this, and the consignment of the body to the "mother earth" was completed amid a respectful silence, to which the sobbing wet winds lent a note of acute poignancy.'

There was one notable absentee at the rain-soaked graveside. Beau, who had followed Florrie so faithfully to so many corners of the earth, was said to be too 'prostrated by illness' to follow her on her last bleak journey. His grief was monumental, his loss seemed irreparable. So great had been his dependence on his indomitable wife—a dependence that continued throughout her illness—that it was impossible to imagine a life for him without her. Yet, surprisingly, his recovery was as swift as it was unexpected. Within a matter of months he married a middle-aged widow from Jamaica with whom he lived contentedly until his death in 1924. As far as is known, he showed no further interest in Florrie's humanitarian concerns. The last years of his life were spent in Scarborough, Yorkshire, where his only recorded act of charity was an unsuccessful, though characteristic, attempt to 'provide free beer for the inmates of the workhouse at Christmas.'

But Beau had other claims to recognition; on his walks about the Falsgrave district of Scarborough, he was always on the look-out for unsuspecting strangers whom he could buttonhole and bore with stories of his far-flung adventures. His proudest boast, however, was probably the one that puzzled his new acquaintances most: for who, in the 1920s, cared that he had been the husband of Lady Florence Dixie?

'A notable career has been closed by the death of Lady Florence Dixie,' the *Morning Post* had remarked in its obituary notice. 'Her record whether as a sportswoman, explorer, politician, war correspondent, or authoress was one of untiring energy.' But this record meant nothing to a later generation. If Florrie's name roused any interest at all, it was not because of her accomplishments but because she had been born to a Douglas and, above all, because she was the sister of the notorious Marquess of Queensberry.

Chapter Twenty

The End of the Line

'Within eighteen months of my grandfather's death my father became a bankrupt,' Percy's son wrote ruefully in his book *The Sporting Queensberrys*. 'He could not even provide the two thousand pounds for his mother which he was obliged to do under the terms of my grandfather's will. . . . So the ushering in of the twentieth century found the Queensberry family without a penny.'

Financial prudence was never Percy's strong point. Half his inheritance was swallowed by the debts he had amassed before his father's death, the other half disappeared in madcap speculation. This, more or less, was to be the story of his life. Intelligent, hard-working, adventurous and quite the most endearing of Queensberry's sons, Percy was completely lacking in money sense.

He was plagued not so much by the 'fatal Douglas temperament' as by his own incurable optimism. Never able to admit defeat, Percy was plunged into one financial disaster after another. His resilience was remarkable. 'Failure meant less than nothing to him,' says his son. 'He believed he could make money—more than ever he could spend—and was convinced that at any moment the chance would come for him to make a bigger fortune than the inheritance that he had so swiftly squandered.'

It was not entirely a matter of wishful thinking, however. Vague as Percy's hopes sometimes appeared, they were backed by practical experience. In Australia he had gained a sound knowledge of gold mining and had seen how this knowledge could be put to good use. Admittedly he had lost more than he had made on the gold fields, but some of his more provident friends had cashed in on his pioneer work and some of them had him to thank for the great fortunes they had made in Australia. In theory, there was no reason why he should not strike it rich again. All that was needed was the right opportunity, a little luck and staying power. Unfortunately it was the last of these conditions that Percy, always eager for quick results, failed to appreciate.

The truth of this was clearly demonstrated when, having wasted his inheritance, he tried to recuperate by prospecting for gold in Canada. His search took him to the shores of Lake Huron where, although he found no gold, he was successful in uncovering huge nickel deposits. Yet the fortune he should have made from this discovery eluded him. The time was not right—there was no market for nickel—he lacked capital and, finally, an underground fire destroyed what little faith he had in the mine's potential. Had he been prepared to sit out the bad times he would undoubtedly have become a rich man. As it was, he returned despairingly to England. He was not to know that his mines, the 'Bruce Mines,' would one day become, according to Bosie, 'one of the largest sources of wealth' of the great tycoon Sir Alfred Mond.

Down one day, up the next, it was all much of a muchness to Percy. There were other ventures, other failures, more appearances in the bankruptcy court. He took them all in his stride, never for one moment doubting that he was destined to end up a millionaire. To his long-suffering family he seemed to personify the saying 'you can't keep a good man down'; they never knew what to expect of him. When he had money he lived in a grand, almost spectacular style—renting large country houses, shooting-boxes in Scotland and, on one occasion, leasing the island of Colonsay for the hunting season. He loved to play the grand seigneur, entertained lavishly, and was as open-hearted as he was open-handed. Many stories were told of his impulsive generosity, one of the more popular being of the bitterly cold night when, overcome by compassion, he was reputed to have handed out nearly £1,000 in bank notes to shivering derelicts on the Thames Embankment. 'Poor old Percy was recklessly generous, confiding and extravagant,' says Bosie, recalling this story. 'In certain moods he would almost literally "throw money out of the window". . . . He had an enormous number of friends of all classes all over the world.'

Percy's humanitarianism was not inspired solely by sentiment. There was a more reflective side to his generous nature, a side which, in 1908, led him to take a familiar Queensberry step by becoming a convert to Catholicism. His rejection of the established church in England was followed, three years later, by a rejection of the established order. In 1911 he announced that he was leaving for America where he intended to apply for American citizenship. Another familiar note was sounded in the statement he gave out before he left.

'We are played out here,' he declared with exceptional bitterness. 'The old order is passing away. I saw the storm clouds gathering for many years, and if the peers of England had given the slightest evidence of constructive statesmanship during that period, conceding to the growing spirit of democracy the reforms that have been wrested by force now, the House of Lords would have been strongly entrenched for generations to come. But the fools couldn't see anything, and wouldn't do anything. . . . I am a peer of Scotland and the only Marquess in the United Kingdom who is not a member of the House of Lords. Why? Because I am a Radical, and, although Scotland is overwhelmingly Liberal, its peers would never select me as a representative because of my known sympathy with progress and real reform. . . . So with the Lords against me because I am a Radical and the radical commoners opposed to me because I am a lord, I have been trimmed thoroughly as the Americans put it, and am seeking new fields in a new land to better my condition. . . . If I am successful over there I will send for my boys to join me as the day of the lord in England is over and I am going where not the title but the man counts.'

Percy's faith in American democracy was touching but transitory. It lasted no longer than his first attempt to find a job. Arriving penniless in Chicago he decided, *faute de mieux,* to apply for work at the *Daily Tribune.* With no qualifications as a journalist his chances were slim until it was discovered that he was the Marquess of Queensberry, son of the framer of the rules of boxing. Immediately the democratic doors flew open. The sports editor was sent for and Percy—who knew next to nothing about boxing—was offered the post of a sports writer at the equivalent of £30 a week. He worked on the *Tribune* for some weeks but, as far as is known, made no attempt to become an American citizen.

The American venture was, alas, another of his failures. After leaving Chicago he went to Canada and eventually returned to England. He was then in his mid-forties and still those elusive millions remained beyond his grasp. But he refused to give up. Cheerful as ever, he spent the next few years playing the Stock Exchange and planning further rainbow-chasing trips to north America. His family saw very little of him. Over the years he had developed into a hardened drinker and when he was in England much of his time was spent with drinking companions. Like his rakish ancestor, the incorrigible 'Old Q', Percy became known as a prankish gambler and delighted in pulling off outlandish bets. Once, for instance, having wagered that he would walk naked through the West End of London in broad daylight he fooled his friends by 'walking within the shelter of a four-wheeled cab the bottom of which had been removed.' He won his bet but it did nothing to improve the family fortunes.

In April 1917 his ill-starred wife, Minnie, died at a relatively early age. The following year Percy remarried. His second wife was Mrs Mary Louise Morgan, the widow of a prosperous Cardiff fish-merchant, who was well-known in hunting circles. To mark the marriage the new Marchioness presented her husband with a horse, Royal Bucks, which she bought for £3,000 from one of Bosie's racing friends. Both Percy and Bosie had high hopes of this horse: they had visions of reviving the old Queensberry colours and winning important racing events. But again success eluded Percy. Royal Bucks was indeed a winner—he won both the Lincoln Handicap and the City and Surburban that year—but his owner was prevented from sharing in his triumphs. Restless as ever, Percy had dashed off to America on one of his wildgoose chases and returned to find that the horse had run in his wife's name and that consequently the Queensberry colours had been altered. Such, it seems, was Percy's luck.

Not until the beginning of 1920 did things seem to brighten. The ray of light came unexpectedly from South Africa. In London Percy met a former journalist, William Bleloch, who—as agent for the Kalahari Diamond Company—was looking for someone to control prospecting operations in the nothern Transvaal. Percy leapt at the offer and set off for South Africa immediately.

At first all went well. Life in the Transvaal suited Percy. The crisp, sunny climate of the Transvaal, the free-and-easy atmosphere of the mining camps and the tantalising prospect of unearthing a fortune brought out the best in him. He was extremely popular with his colleagues. Any suspicions they had of his title were quickly dispelled by his down-to-earth manner, his breezy personality and his unmistakable talent. He was, one of them declared, 'a remarkable prospector.' Within two months the survey was completed and Percy was promptly offered the post of managing-director of another diamond company. His luck seemed at last to be on the turn.

Unhappily the turn came too late. Visiting Johannesburg towards the end of July, he complained of feeling ill. He told friends he had caught a chill. When the chill got no better he moved to a private house where he was nursed by two of his fellow guests, an American doctor and a dentist, but still he showed no signs of improvement. A local Indian doctor was consulted and then two more doctors were called in. One of these doctors, Dr Hans Sauer, diagnosed congestion of the lungs and recommended that Percy be moved to a nursing home. For some reason or other, Sauer's advice was not taken and when he called again Percy was 'beyond hope.'

Percy died early in the morning of 1 August, 1920, ten days after his arrival in Johannesburg. The doctors were baffled by the suddenness of his death. Inevitably there were rumours that all was not what it seemed. One of his friends reported to the authorities that he suspected Percy had died of 'phosporous poisoning.' He made 'certain allegations against some of the persons with whom [Percy] was closely connected while in South Africa.' Precisely why poisoning should have been suspected is not clear but the Criminal Investigation Department stepped in. Not until three weeks later, when an official inquest returned a verdict of 'death due to basal meningitis and abscess on the brain,' was permission given for the body to be shipped to England. Even so the rumours persisted.

Pecy was buried at Kensal Green cemetery in October 1920. At the Requiem Mass in Westminster Cathedral, which preceded his funeral, every available seat was taken. Literally hundreds of mourners, most of them complete strangers to his family, turned up for the service. Flower girls from Piccadilly, barmaids from Soho, taxi-drivers, waiters, down-and-outs and beggars all crowded into the pews to 'pay their last respects to a great-hearted gentleman who had handed out bank-notes as if they were coppers.' Never before had such a spontaneous demonstration of affection been accorded to a Marquess of Queensberry. In squandering the family fortune, Percy had redeemed the family name.

[2]

Lord Sholto Douglas, the eighth Marquess of Queensberry's youngest son, had all Percy's faults and none of his virtues. Selfish, extravagant, easily-influenced and totally irresponsible, he led a singularly pointless life. His only noteworthy achievement was his romantic marriage to Loretta Mooney but that, for all its initial promise, proved a sad disappointment. It brought Sholto neither the stability he needed nor the fortune he craved.

What happened to Loretta's much-reported inheritance is a mystery: certainly Sholto did not get his hands on it. A mere four years after their move to Canada, he was bemoaning the fact that he was entirely dependent on the £300 allowance he received from his father. Lack of money, he constantly complained, was the curse of his existence. On Queensberry's death, Sholto inherited £10,000 but this, needless to say, soon disappeared. By 1909 he was reduced to working as a commercial traveller for various American firms. A couple of years later he returned to England where, separated from Loretta, he lived on an allowance from a 'relative' —probably his mother—of £10 a week.

The outbreak of the First World War saw a further decline in Sholto's fortunes. In April 1915 his eldest son, Bruce, was killed in action shortly after his eighteenth birthday and all hopes of a reconciliation with Loretta ended. At the same time Sholto's meagre weekly allowance was stopped and, like Percy, he fell into the hands of professional money-lenders. Shortly before the war ended he made his first appearance in the bankruptcy courts where his debts were recorded as £279 and his assets nil. Somehow or other he managed to obtain his discharge in 1919 and the following year he finally divorced Loretta. The pattern of his life was, to all intents and purposes, set.

But Sholto, again like Percy, was nothing if not resilient. Free of his wife and his debts, he sought other means of survival. He did not have far to look. A few months after his divorce he met Mrs Georgina Barnard, the socially-ambitious daughter of a rich Dutch merchant, who promptly accepted his offer of marriage. What seemed to be an excellent match, turned out to be another of Sholto's mistakes. Ambitious as was the much married Mrs Barnard—she could count a son of the Sultan of Turkey among her three former husbands—she was nobody's fool. She lost no time in putting Sholto firmly in his place. At their showy wedding in the Covent Garden Register Office, on 23 April 1921, it was the bride—confidently overdressed in pink satin, black lace and furs—who footed the bill and hogged the limelight. There was to be no question of Sholto solving his problems at his wife's expense.

The cynical marriage of convenience was very much a one-sided affair. Georgina delighted in her title but she adamantly refused to finance her husband's chancy business ventures and would have nothing to do with his disreputable friends. As the new Lady Sholto Douglas, she spent huge sums on lavish entertainments at her Park Lane house—she had a *penchant* for English noblemen, foreign ambassadors and continental princesses—but not a penny did she fling in Sholto's direction. Having provided her husband with a good address, Georgina felt she had fulfilled her part of the bargain; except for the household expenses, Sholto was left to fend for himself.

This he spectacularly failed to do. A mere six months after the marriage Sholto was again declared bankrupt. At his second public examination, his lawyer admitted that Lord Sholto Douglas was without regular occupation and existed by transacting 'a little business in the City on commission terms.' His income was estimated at between £300 and £400 a year, his expenses at £700 a year and his liabilities at £4,500. (Among his creditors was a former landlady from whom he had arranged to buy a bracelet worth £500, agreeing 'to pay her three times its value.') Asked how he intended to meet his debts, Sholto replied lamely: 'An old friend of the family had promised to give me £12,000.' That friend was definitely not his wife.

There was no hope of the marriage lasting. Sholto's disgrace completely undermined Georgina's social pretensions. There were quarrels and reconciliations and they tottered on for a couple more years but it was a hopeless situation. Finally Georgina could stand it no longer and demanded a divorce. Sholto agreed to supply evidence of infidelity on condition that Georgina paid him £1,000 down and made him an allowance of £520 a year. Georgina reluctantly consented. In April 1924 a contract was drawn up by one of Sholto's shady associates—a former solicitor who had been gaoled for fraud and struck off the Roll—which, at the time, seemed to please everyone. Four days later Sholto popped an incriminating hotel bill into his wife's Park Lane letter box and the divorce proceedings went ahead. The suit was undefended and the decree was made absolute the following year.

Within a matter of months Sholto had married again. His third wife was a wealthy widow, Mrs Mendelssohn Pickles, with whom he lived for several years in Putney. All the same, he refused to let Georgina off the hook. Insisting that the dubious contract between them remained valid, he brushed aside Georgina's arguments that his new wife was rich enough to support him, and continued to demand payment of his £520 a year allowance. Lawyers' letters were sent, threats were made, writs were served—the battle lasted for years. Sholto's determination to squeeze money out of his former wife was equalled by no other action in his life. As late as October 1934, when he was in his sixties, he was still hauling the protesting Georgina into court. The failure of this, his last effort, left him without an allowance and without a cause. He died a poor, disgruntled old man eight years later.

[3]

'And the curious thing to me,' wrote Wilde in *De Profundis*, 'is that you should have tried to imitate your father in his chief characteristics. I cannot understand why he was to you an exemplar, where he should have been a warning. . . . I suppose that, by some strange law of the antipathy of similars, you loathed each other, not because in so many points you were different, but because in some you were so alike.'

Had Wilde lived longer he might have changed his tenses, but not his meaning. Of all Queensberry's sons, Bosie was most like his father. And the older he grew the more like his father he became. Bosie's looks and charm were inherited from the 'Montgomery lot', in temperament he was a true son of the 'mad bad line.' He had all his father's arrogance, conceit, vindictiveness and self-righteousness. Like Queensberry, Bosie was self-obsessed and neurotically sensitive to real or imagined slights; and he shared to the full Queensberry's capacity for hatred. These unfortunate traits—objectionable enough in a spoiled and pampered youth—were to turn him into a spiteful, querulous and, at times, perfectly insufferable middle-aged man.

Attempts have been made to excuse the fractiousness, the litigation, and the incessant quarrels that marred Bosie's later career. It is said that he was deeply wounded by the trauma of the Wilde affair and was made to suffer unfairly for the part he played in Wilde's downfall. The more enlightened blamed him for selfishly destroying Wilde's genius; fashionable 'Society' used him as a scapegoat for popular prejudice; Wilde's friends disowned him and the public at large continued to despise him. He returned to London after Wilde's death a sad and disillusioned young man.

There is some truth in all this. But it is not the entire story, not by a long chalk. It takes no account of Bosie's own faults; it glosses over his weaknesses—his vanity, his perversity, his emotional immaturity, his inability to withstand criticism—and totally ignores his turbulent family background. Wilde's earlier assessment is much nearer the mark. Bosie suffered but, like his father, much of his suffering was of his own making.

Perhaps his most disastrous flaw was his talent for self-deception. This talent was never more apparent than in the attitude he adopted towards sex. Shortly after Wilde's death Bosie convinced himself that he was a latent heterosexual, or at least bi-sexual with a sufficiently strong heterosexual bias to make a successful marriage. He began to look for a wife. At first he toyed with the idea of cashing in on his title—not an unusual thought in the Queensberry family—and marrying a rich American heiress. He seems, for some strange reason, to have been under the impression that a foreigner with a fortune could help him overcome any lingering sexual inhibitions. But his mercenary dream did not last long. It was shattered by a gushing letter from a young English girl who had read and admired his poetry. Flattered, Bosie replied and the two of them agreed to meet.

The girl was Olive Custance. She was the only daughter and heiress of Colonel Frederick Custance, a rich and distinguished soldier who had recently returned from fighting in South Africa. Like Bosie, Olive was a poet—her collection of poems, *Opals*, had been published the previous year—and the courtship which followed their first meeting was as soulful as it was, of necessity, secret.

Colonel Custance had hopes of his daughter making a brilliant match and, as those hopes did not include the notorious Lord Alfred Douglas, there could be no question of family approval. The threat of opposition added piquancy to the romance. Bosie and Olive needed no prompting in their roles of star-crossed lovers: there were clandestine meetings, wistful partings, furtive exchanges of letters and, inevitably, the trusted maid-servant. Throughout it all, it was Olive—as Bosie proudly admits—who set the pace. Her letters to her 'beautiful prince' were as flowery as they were intense. She was his 'little page' who longed for a glimpse from his 'clear brave eyes' and sighed at the thought of him being carried off by 'a beautiful rich princess.' They both acknowledged the hopelessness of their plight.

In October 1901, a year after they first met, Bosie actually went to America in search of a 'rich princess.' He visited New York and Boston and had a thoroughly pleasant time but, although several heiresses presented themselves, he found the idea of marrying for money less attractive in fact that in theory. Somewhat disconsolately he returned to Scotland to join Percy for the end of season shooting on the Isle of Colonsay. Hardly had he arrived than he received disturbing news. Olive wrote to tell him that she had become engaged to one of his former friends, George Montagu. There was, in the circumstances, only one thing a 'beautiful prince' could do and Bosie, like a true Douglas, did it. He rushed to London, met Olive, obtained a special licence, and, in all the flurry of an elopement, he and Olive were married at St George's, Hanover Square, on 4 March 1902.

Reading Bosie's account of his romantic courtship and marriage it is impossible not to be cynical. One only has his word for the main events and his word does not always ring true. When one considers his past, it is difficult to accept his picture of himself as a love-sick swain. He was, after all, thirty-one years of age and, until he met Olive, he had led an aggressive and, to all intents, exclusively homosexual life. Could his sexual orientation have changed so suddenly and so decisively? Could he have switched from what he admits was an indifference to girls to falling so blindly in love with a girl?

Admittedly the sexual spectrum is complex and is capable of endless, sometimes astonishing, variations. But Bosie's sexual somersault smacks too much of opportunism not to be questioned. The Wilde affair had soured his life; he needed desperately to live it down and to be accepted by a disapproving society. What better way than to marry? And what better marriage than one which appeared to be a genuine love match? Such expedient marriages are not unknown, even today, to insecure or socially ambitious homosexuals.

One's cynicism is increased by Bosie's explanation of his sexual ambivalence. He blames his homosexuality on his looks. Not only were men attracted to him, he says, but they pursued him and he was beguiled by their flattery. Girls, on the other hand, were more modest and so he remained unaware of their charms.

This, at best, is a half-truth. From what is known of Bosie's profligate homosexual activities he was more often the seducer than the seduced. With the notable exception of Wilde—where the attraction was more romantic than sexual—Bosie rarely capitulated to his more ardent male admirers. His taste was for renters, stable boys and valets who were not particularly interested in his looks. He sought them out and was known to chase after any likely lad who caught his fancy. 'Boys, brandy and betting,' Wilde wrote despairingly shortly before his death, 'monopolise his soul' Little more than two years after that was written Bosie married Olive. Was she really the first girl openly to admire him? Had he really been oblivious to the ways of the world until then? Why should any good-looking young man, particularly a Victorian, deliberately suppress his heterosexual instincts?

'Everyone should try to control his nature,' wrote Bosie in one of his rare attempts at self-analysis, 'but to try to distort it or force it is a great mistake, and leads to all sorts of miseries and misunderstandings, both for oneself and for others.' This was a truism which he failed to apply to himself. To his other foibles was added sexual repression—bad enough in itself, but disastrous in anyone so highly sexed. It helped to warp his already tortured personality.

Bosie could do nothing by halves. Having renounced his homo-sexuality—he was to denounce homosexuality as a terrible sin—he went on to forswear sex altogether. Some ten years after his marriage, and several years after the birth of his only son, Raymond, he became—perhaps not surprisingly—a Catholic and took a voluntary vow of chastity. He had intended, he said, to 'become a saint' but failing sainthood he settled for celibacy. 'I have been chaste,' he was to write in his *Autobiography*, published in 1929, 'for fourteen years roughly, and I am therefore able to look dispassionately at my own sex psychology.' Could any claim be more naïve?

His reluctance to face the truth about himself, combined with his newfound prejudice against homosexuality, marred all the accounts he wrote about the Wilde affair. Most of Bosie's autobiographical writing is centred on his association with Wilde and most of it is misleading. He was obsessed by his need to win sympathy for himself. He wished to be seen as a brave but misguided youth who, having seen the error of his ways, had emerged a nobler and decidedly wiser man. Had he indeed grown wiser he might have deserved the sympathy he sought; as it was, his lack of objectivity—his distortions, his evasions, his half-truths and, often, his down-right lies—makes it very difficult to feel sorry for Bosie.

His first attempt to justify himself, *Oscar Wilde and Myself*, was published in 1914 and is understandably bitter. It was written shortly after he had read the complete version of *De Profundis* and he was still smouldering under the fire of Wilde's attack. But, even allowing for pardonable resentment, his self-righteous tone makes sickening reading. The virulence with which he hit back at Wilde was worthy of his father. To be fair, he later admitted to being ashamed of the book (for which he blamed the influence of others) but this does not entirely excuse his spite. André Gide was to describe *Oscar Wilde and Myself* as 'Douglas's abominable book.'

'Hypocrisy,' Gide exploded in his journal, 'can go no further, nor falsehood be more impudent. . . . I should be aware he is lying, even if I had not been a direct witness to the acts of his life against which he protests and which he claims to whitewash. But this is not enough for him. He claims he was ignorant of Wilde's habits! and that he upheld him at first only because he thought him innocent! Whom will he convince?'

Bosie's later writing was more subtle. The digs at Wilde are not so obvious: they are softened by his professions of affection and occasional doses of worldly-wise 'candour', but the bias remains firmly in Bosie's favour. He omits far more than he admits; he is still the brave misguided youth, still more sinned against than sinning. What, for instance, is one to make of the assertion in his *Autobiography* that Wilde cheapened their friendship by his 'life of promiscuous nastiness.'? 'I was before the [Queensberry] trial,' he goes on, 'beginning to be a little tired of Oscar's "goings on" (even allowing for the fact that he of course concealed his "infidelities" as much as he could.)' One has only to turn to the period he is writing about to be aware of his hypocrisy.

He and Wilde were in Algiers immediately before the opening of *The Importance of Being Earnest*. There they met André Gide to whom Bosie confessed: 'I have a horror of women. I only like boys.' And the reason why Bosie did not return to London with Wilde for that fatal opening night was because he had made arrangements, as Gide puts it, 'to elope' with a young *caouadji* he wanted to take with him to Biskra.' Nor does one have to rely on Gide's word for this. A letter Bosie wrote to a friend in England at this time confirms that he went to the Biskra oasis with a 'marvellous' young arab. Were the truth known, it may well have been Wilde who was growing tired of Bosie's infidelities.

A respect for the truth does not shine among Bosie's much-proclaimed Christian virtues. His books do not bear close scrutiny. Was he really so relentlessly cold-shouldered for his association with Wilde? Or did he purposely exaggerate his isolation? Cold facts seem to indicate a familiar bias.

He claims, for example, that his friend George Montagu pointedly dropped him in October 1901 to avoid embarrassment in a political election campaign; but *Who's Who* shows that George Montagu fought and won that campaign a year earlier. He also claims that prejudice prevented him performing his patriotic duty. 'Directly after my father's death,' he writes in his *Autobiography* 'the South African war broke out. By the time war was declared I had already bought two or three horses, and they were being trained by George Woodhouse, at Chantilly. As soon as I heard the news I returned to London and offered myself as a trooper in "Paget's Horse." ' His noble gesture was spurned because of his association with Wilde. That, at least, is what he implies. The truth is a little different. His rush to volunteer seems less urgent when one discovers that the South African war broke out almost three months before Queensberry died; Bosie remained in England for at least another month and, by his own admission, he was in France long enough to buy two or three horses and arrange for them to be trained. It must have been April or May before he returned to England and by that time the war was on the turn and the demand for volunteers had lessened. One only has his word for his rejection.

Were these simply slips of memory? If they were, they were slips which enhanced his martyrdom. He wrote nothing to his own detriment and some of his more trivial embellishments are patently contrived. Take the stories he tells of his grandfather, Alfred Montgomery, in his book *Without Apology*. These mildly amusing anecdotes seem so harmless that one wonders why he should have lifted them from Sir Algernon West's *Recollections* and have shamelessly attributed them to himself. Perhaps he wished to be considered a *raconteur*. Whatever his reasons, they cannot be dismissed as slips of memory. Nor can many of his other distortions.

It would be tedious to labour the point. Tears shed for Bosie are quickly dried on the pages of any reliable reference book.

[4]

Of all the claims Bosie made for himself, perhaps the most valid was his claim to recognition as a poet. He was never the great poet he imagined himself to be but, within his self-imposed limits, he was a poet of distinction. Poetry for him was the supreme art; his struggle to perfect that art was the one thing that gave a sense of purpose to his otherwise feckless life.

Capricious and ill-disciplined in so many ways, Bosie brought a precision and elegance to his poetry that is sadly lacking in his prose writing. His almost fanatical respect for the rules of poetic form, a respect that was evident even during the rebellious phases of his personal life, both hindered his output and enhanced his style. 'He was happiest,' it was said when he died, 'within the most rigid limits that he could impose upon the most strict of forms—the Petrarchian sonnet. Thus he kept his poetry too small in volume for his powers, but as pure and firm as he could have desired.' Never was that curious combination of the traditionalist and the rebel, which so distinguished the Queensberry family, more apparent than it was in Bosie.

He published several collections of poetry—some of which were reprinted during his lifetime—as well as odd volumes of nonsense verse, satires and lampoons, but his bigoted conservatism alienated him from the mainstream of contemporary poetry. He openly despised Rupert Brook and the Georgians and dismissed T. S. Eliot and W. H. Auden as 'simply not poets at all.' His exclusion from *The Oxford Book of Modern Verse,* edited by W. B. Yeats, was one of the bitter disappointments of his life. He retaliated typically by sending an open telegram of protest to various national newspapers, accusing Yeats of adopting 'the attitude of the minor poet to the major one.' 'Had Thomas Moore been editing such a book,' he added pompously, 'he would have omitted Keats and Shelley.' Bosie was left to console himself with the thought that three of his sonnets had been included in *The Oxford Book of English Verse* and *The Oxford Book of Victorian Verse.* This, for the Bosie who had once basked in Oscar Wilde's limelight, was very much second best. He could never reconcile himself to his own limitations.

Bosie's desire for literary recognition was a source of unending frustration. What talent he had, outside his poetry, was ruined by his violent prejudices. Politically he liked to boast that he was 'a strong Conservative, of the "Diehard" variety'; what this meant was that he was the worst type of right-wing reactionary—authoritarian, elitist, xenophobic and anti-Semitic. His intolerance—political, religious and poetic—destroyed any hopes of success he had for the 'literary' magazines he edited. The *Academy*, in the early 1900s, *Plain English* and *Plain Speech* in the 1920s, all became outlets for his spite and brought him nothing but trouble. Time and again he was propelled into court to defend charges of libel and when he was not defending himself he was sueing others.

In middle-age, Lord Alfred Douglas became as notorious for his litigation as he had once been for his association with Oscar Wilde. He quarrelled with everyone. Some of these quarrels—like his long vendetta against Robbie Ross, Wilde's friend and literary executor—were complicated and probably unavoidable, but others he openly invited. Like his father he could never resist a fight; like his father he was always convinced of his own righteousness; and like his father he had neither the tact nor the grace to admit defeat.

The catalogue of his innumerable law suits makes depressing reading. For the most part they are best forgotten. He lost, both in reputation and financially, more than he ever gained from them. The results of three of the more important cases speak for themselves.

Whatever the rights and wrongs of his quarrel with Robbie Ross (there were undoubtedly faults on both sides) his harrassment of Ross—his public accusations of sodomy and corruption, his provoking of Ross into a libel action, his ferreting out of known homosexuals to support his plea of justification—was too reminiscent of the Queensberry case not to earn him the contempt of his former sympathisers. An earlier libel action brought by his father-in-law, after an unedifying tussle for the custody of his son (Bosie and Olive were then, 1913, temporarily separated) was too weakly defended not to end with a formal apology and withdrawal. The scurrilous pamphlet he published accusing Winston Churchill of conniving with 'rich Jews' to profit from reported disasters in the First World War and of assisting in the 'murder' of Lord Kitchener, was too preposterous not to earn him a six month prison sentence.

The cost of all this litigation was ruinous. Like his brothers, Bosie was no stranger to the money-lenders and the bankruptcy court. The 'odious question of finance', as he called it, dogged him all his life. Money trouble was behind the rumpus that led to his separation from his wife. Olive's father threatened to cut off her allowance unless she left Bosie—to whom he had never become properly reconciled—and by leaving Bosie, the penniless Oliver helped to weaken his case against her father. Four months later husband and wife met for a reconciliation but their marriage was never resumed. They remained good, loving friends but they did not live together. Bosie took refuge in chastity and, presumably, Olive's life was one of sexual frustration. Both their lives were saddened when, several years later, their son Raymond became psychologically disturbed and was confined to a mental home. The cause of the young man's illness is not known and, although he was released from confinement for a short period after his mother's death, he never fully recovered.

Throughout all his troubles, the one person Bosie could count on was his mother. Sybil, now the Dowager Marchioness of Queensberry, stood resolutely behind all her sons—she practically reared Sholto's eldest boy—but the hopelessly spoilt Bosie remained her favourite. She blindly supported him in all his quarrels, encouraged some of his wilder ventures and, at the age of seventy-seven, followed him into the Catholic Church. After he and Olive separated, Bosie and his mother lived together from time to time and drew, if anything, closer to each other. The love they shared was probably the greatest consolation either of them experienced. 'She gave me,' Bosie wrote when Sybil died in November 1935, 'the most wonderful and perfect love that ever mother gave to her son. . . . I don't know how I shall go on living without her.'

But he did go on living. He lived alone for the most part, in flats in Brighton and Hove. Surprisingly, this solitary life seemed to suit him. He was mellowed by old age, sweetened by new friendships. He could still be exasperating, edgy and snappish—particularly on the subject of his old enemies—and sometimes displayed a disconcerting conceit and high Tory intolerance, but he was no longer the snarling litigant or the insufferable moral crusader. Most people who met him during the latter part of his life were more impressed by his urbanity, his cultivated charm and delightful old world manners than by his occasional slips from grace.

With the exception of his sister Edith, who died in 1963, he outlived all his immediate family. But he never lacked for companions or near relatives. Olive followed him to Brighton and they met almost daily until her death in 1944. He kept in close touch with his nephews—Percy's sons, who helped to support him—and with his Wyndham cousins and seems to have been in contact with Florrie's sons to whom he occasionally sent copies of his books. Mostly, though, his friends were of a younger generation: writers attracted by his association with Wilde, students, admirers of his poetry, celebrity-hunters, professional gossips and homosexuals fascinated by the legend of the 'slim-gilt youth.' These were people with whom he could relax and reminisce; they listened to his stories, applauded his anecdotes, flattered him and winked at his prejudices and embroideries. They provided him with an outlet for his vanity and spared him the bitter isolation that had soured his father's last years.

Bosie died on 20 March 1945 and was buried next to his mother in the cemetery of the Franciscan Friary at Crawley in Sussex. Few of those who attended his funeral were old enough to remember clearly the notorious Old Bailey trials that had caused such a sensation fifty years earlier, but they were all aware of the role played by Bosie in the Wilde affair. Bosie had seen to that. He could never keep off the subject for long. His obsession with Wilde followed him to the grave.

Over the years his attitude towards that fatal friendship varied considerably. Love, hate, jealousy and admiration were too hopelessly entwined for him to come to any balanced judgement. In his later books, and to casual acquaintances, he would pose as Wilde's defender but occasionally, in private, he would attack his old friend with startling venom. Bosie, like the rest of his family, was never predictable in his emotions. His attitude towards his father was much the same. But there at least his religion helped him to resolve the central conflict.

'In spite of the hard things I may have been compelled to say about him,' he wrote of Queensberry in his *Autobiography*, 'I have got back much of my old love for him as I had it when I was a child. Needless to say I have never ceased to pray for him, and I look forward confidently to seeing him "hereafter in a better world than this," when all misunderstandings and obstacles to love and knowledge will be removed for ever.'

They would have found much in common, Bosie and his father. The differences that separated them in life would have faded into insignificance in their questionable heaven and they would have discovered themselves for what they were—the last true representatives of their 'mad bad line.'

Acknowledgements

The holders of the Queensberry title who feature in this book were known during their lifetimes as the 7th, 8th and 9th Marquesses of Queensberry. Later the numbering of the title was changed and, in some genealogies, they are now referred to as the 8th, 9th and 10th Marquesses of Queensberry. To avoid confusion I have retained the earlier numbering.

The change came about because James, son of the 2nd Duke of Queensberry (1672—1711) was reputedly 'an idiot from birth' and so was passed over in the entail of his father's estates and titles. Not until shortly after World War II, when the then 10th Marquess of Queensberry was ruled to be the 11th Marquess, was the discrepancy rectified. I am most grateful to Mr Patrick Montague-Smith, former editor of Debrett, for information concerning this renumbering of the Queensberry title.

In writing this book I have received help from a great many people. My chief debt is undoubtedly to Mr Theo Aronson whose unfailing interest, encouragement and expert advice have, as always, been of inestimable value. I must also express my warm thanks to Dr Bernard Aspinwall, of Glasgow University, Sister M. Eadmunda of St Joseph's Convent, Hendon, Sister Mary Claver of St Edward's Convent of Mercy, London, and the Rev. Dr Mark Dilworth of the Scottish Catholic Archives for assisting my exploration into the Catholic background of the Queensberry family. I am equally grateful to Mrs Suellen Zecchini and Mr John Bidwell of the William Andrews Clark Memorial Library, Los Angeles, for the trouble they took in unearthing unpublished material from the Wilde collection. Nor can I ignore the kind response of Ms. Marje Rump of the Kearn County Library, Bakersfield, California and the enthusiasm of Mr George Kobayashi of the California Room of the San Jose Public Library to my requests for information.

A special word of thanks must go to Mr J. Keith Killby, Mr Brian Masters, Mr John Anderson, Mr Patrick Strong and Mr David Burrell for their help and interest in various ways.

I have received assistance from several public institutions and would like, in particular, to thank: Mr John Preston, Regional Librarian, and the staff of the Ewart Library, Dumfries; Dr Frances J. Shaw, Senior Research Assistant, of the National Register of Archives (Scotland); Dr D. M.

Abbott, Research Assistant, of the Scottish Record Office; Mr Kieran Burke, Assistant Librarian, of the Cork City Library; R. D. Casey, Deputy City Librarian, of the Dublin Public Library; R. C. Howes, Assistant County Librarian, of the Buckinghamshire County Library; Mrs T. J. Himsworth, County Archivist, of the Surrey Record Office; Mr John A. Saunders, County Librarian, of the Surrey County Library; Mr A.W. Stevenson, Leicestershire Studies Librarian, of the County Library, Leicester; Mrs M. J. Guy, Divisional Librarian, of the Hampshire District Library Headquarters; Mr Alan Dearden of the North Yorkshire County Library; Ms Elain Farr of the Reference Division, British Library; the Librarian of the History Room, San Francisco Library, California; Miss L. Kennedy and staff of the Johannesburg Public Library, South Africa; and Mrs S. Bane and staff of the Frome Library, Somerset.

Two books have proved most helpful in my research. They are H. Montgomery Hyde's *The Trials of Oscar Wilde* and his excellent biography *Oscar Wilde*. I would like to record my indebtedness to Mr Hyde for his kind permission to quote from these books. I am likewise indebted to *The Irrepressible Victorian* by Leonard E. Naylor (Macdonald); *The Sporting Queensberrys* by the Marquess of Queensberry (Hutchinson, London, 1942); *Oscar Wilde and the Black Douglas* by the Marquess of Queensberry and Percy Colson (Hutchinson, London, 1949).

I must also thank Mr Edward Colman, literary executor of Lord Alfred Douglas, for permission to quote from *The Autobiography of Lord Alfred Douglas* (Martin Secker, 1931) and *Without Apology* by Lord Alfred Douglas (Martin Secker, 1920); Sir Rupert Hart-Davis and the Oxford University Press for permission to quote from *Selected Letters of Oscar Wilde* edited by Rupert Hart-Davis, 1979.

Bibliography

Andrews, Allen *The Splendid Pauper*, Harrap, London, 1968
Anonymous *Fifty Years in London Society*, E. Nash, London, 1920
Beerbohm, Max *Letters to Reggie Turner*, Hart-Davis, London, 1964
Brasol, Boris *Oscar Wilde: The Man, the Artist the Martyr*, Scribner, New York, 1938
Broad, Lewis *The Friendships and Follies of Oscar Wilde*, Hutchinson, London, 1954
Clayton, Sir William *Extracts from Sir William Clayton's Journals*, Privately printed, 1921
Crewe, Marquess of *Lord Rosebery*, (two vols) John Murray, London, 1931
Croft-Cooke, Rupert *Bosie*, W. H. Allen, London, 1963
— *The Unrecorded Life of Oscar Wilde*, W. H. Allen, London, 1972
De Crespigny, Sir Claud *Forty Years of a Sportsman's Life*, Mills & Boon, London, 1925
Deghy, Guy *Noble and Manly*, Hutchinson, London, 1956
Dixie, Lady Florence *Abel Avenged*, London, 1877
— *Across Patagonia*, R. Bentley, London, 1880
— *A Defence of Zululand and Its King*, Chatto & Windus, London, 1882
— *In the Land of Misfortune*, R. Bentley, London, 1882
— *Ireland and Her Shadows*, Sealy, Bryers & Walker, Dublin, 1882
— *Waifs and Strays*, Griffith, Farrer & Co, Edinburgh, 1884
— *Redeemed in Blood*, (3 vols) Henry & Co, London, 1889
— *Aniwee: or, the Warrior Queen*, Henry & Co, London, 1890
— *Gloriana: or, the revolution of 1900*, Henry & Co, London, 1890
— *The Young Castaways: or, the child hunters of Patagonia*, Shaw & Co, London, 1890
— *The Horrors of Sport*, Humanitarian League, London, 1891
— *Little Cherie: or, the Trainer's Daughter*, A. Treherne, London, 1901
— *Songs of a Child*, by 'Darling' (2 vols) Leadenhall Press, London, 1902–1903
— *Isola: or, the Disinherited*, Leadenhall Press, London, 1903
— *The Story of Ijain: or, the Evolution of a Mind*, Leadenhall Press, London, 1903
— *Izra: a child of solitude*, John Long, London, 1906
Douglas, Lord Alfred *Oscar Wilde and Myself*, John Long, London, 1914
— *The Autobiography of Lord Alfred Douglas*, Martin Secker, London, 1931
— *Without Apology*, Martin Secker, London, 1938
— *Oscar Wilde: A Summing Up*, Martin Secker, London, 1940
Douglas, Lady Gertrude *Brown as a Berry*, (as George Douglas) Tinsley Bros, London, 1874
— *Linked Lives*, Hurst & Blackett, London, 1876
(see also Stock, Lady Gertrude)
Douglas, Lord James *Royal Angus*, (2 vols) R. Bentley, London, 1882
— *Estcourt*, (2 vols) R. Bentley, London, 1883
— *Queen Mab*, (2 vols) R. Bentley, London, 1884
Drummond-Wolff, Sir Henry *Recollections 1832–1886*, (2 vols) Smith, Elder, London, 1899
Egremont, Lord *Wyndham and Children First*, Macmillan, London, 1969
Fane, Lady Augusta *Chit-Chat*, Thorton Butterworth, London, 1926
Freeman, William *The Life of Lord Alfred Douglas*, Herbert Joseph, London, 1948
Grolleau, Charles *The Trial of Oscar Wilde*, Privately printed, Paris 1906
Harris, Frank *Oscar Wilde*, Constable, London, 1938

Hart-Davis, Rupert (ed.) *The Letters of Oscar Wilde,* Hart-Davis, London, 1962
Hindley, Geoffrey *Roof of the World,* Aldus Books, London, 1971
Holyoake, George J. *Sixty Years of an Agitators Life,* (2 vols) T. Fisher Unwin, London, 1892
Hyde, H. Montgomery *The Trials of Oscar Wilde,* Dover Publications, New York, 1962
— *Oscar Wilde,* Eyre Methuen, London, 1976
Longford, Elizabeth *A Pilgrimage of Passion,* Weidenfeld & Nicolson, London, 1979
McCabe, Joseph *The Life and Letters of George Jacob Holyoake,* Watts, London, 1908
— *The Religion of Women,* Watts, London, 1905
Malmesberry, Earl of *Memoirs of an Ex-Minister,* (2 vols) Longmans, London, 1884
Manchester, Duke of *My Candid Recollections,* Grayson & Grayson, London, 1932
Marjoribanks, Edward *The Life of Lord Carson,* Gollancz, London, 1932
Mason, A. E. W. *Sir George Alexander and the St James Theatre,* Macmillan, London, 1935
Mason, Stuart *Oscar Wilde Three Times Tried,* Ferrestone Press, London, 1912
— *A Collection of Original Manuscripts . . . of Oscar Wilde,* Dulau & Co, London, (N.D.)
Menzies, Amy *Further Indiscretions of a Woman of No Importance,* Herbert Jenkins, London, 1918
Merle, Robert *Oscar Wilde,* Librairie Hachette, Paris, (N.D.)
Millard, C. (*see* Mason, Stuart)
Morgan, Wallace M. *History of Kern County,* Historic Record Co, Los Angeles, 1914
Morley, Sheridan *Oscar Wilde,* Weidenfeld & Nicolson, London, 1976
Naylor, Leonard E. *The Irrepressible Victorian,* MacDonald, London, 1965
Nethercott, Arthur H. *The First Five Lives of Annie Besant,* Hart-Davis, London, 1961
Nevill, Lady Dorothy *Reminiscences,* Edward Arnold, London, 1906
Nevill, Ralph *The World of Fashion 1837–1922,* Methuen, London, 1923
Newby, Eric *Great Ascents,* David & Charles, Newton Abbot, 1977
Newton, Stella M. *Health, Art and Reason,* John Murray, London, 1974
O'Brien, William & Ryan, Desmond *Devoys Post Bag* (2 vols) C. J. Fallon, Dublin, 1948–1953
Paget, Walpurga Lady *In My Tower,* (2 vols) Hutchinson, London, 1924
Pearson, Hesketh *The Life of Oscar Wilde,* Metheun, London, 1946
Pigott, Richard *Personal Recollections of an Irish National Journalist,* Hodge, Figgis & Co, Dublin, 1882
Portland, Duke of *Men, Women and Things,* Faber, London, 1937
Queensberry, 8th Marquess of *The Spirit of the Matterhorn,* Privately printed 1881
Queensberry, 10th Marquess of *The Sporting Queensberrys,* Hutchinson, London, 1942
— *Oscar Wilde and the Black Douglas,* (with Percy Colson) Hutchinson, London, 1949
Raymond, E. T. *Portraits of the Nineties,* T. Fisher Unwin, London, 1921
Redesdale, Lord *Memories,* Hutchinson, London 1915
Rhodes-James, Robert *Rosebery,* Weidenfeld & Nicolson, London, 1963
Ricketts, Charles *Oscar Wilde: Recollections,* Nonesuch Press, London, 1932
Ruitenbeek, Dr Hendrik *Homosexuality: a Changing Picture,* Souvenir Press, London, 1973
Russell, G. W. E. *Sketches and Snapshots,* Smith, Elder Co, London, 1910
Sherard, R. H. *The Life of Oscar Wilde,* T. Wernher Laurie, London, 1906.
Somerset, Duke of *Letters and Memoirs,* R. Bentley, London, 1893
Stephenson, John *A Royal Correspondence,* Macmillan, London, 1938
Stock, Lady Gertrude *Nature's Nursling,* (3 vols) Kegan Paul, Trench, London, 1889
Stone, J. M. *Eleanor Leslie,* Art and Book Company, London, 1898
Sullivan, T. D., A. M. & D. B. *Speeches from the Dock,* T. D. Sullivan, Dublin, 1887
Sutherland, Douglas *The Yellow Earl,* Cassell, London, 1965
Tennyson, Charles *Alfred Tennyson,* Macmillan, London 1949
Tisdale, E. E. P. *Queen Victoria's John Brown,* Stanley Paul, London, 1938
Trevor-Roper, Hugh *A Hidden Life,* Macmillan, London, 1976
Tribe, David *President Charles Bradlaugh, MP,* Elek Books, London, 1971
'Veritas' *Lady Florence Dixie Vindicated,* Sealy, Bryer and Walker, Dublin, 1883
Ward, Mrs E. M. *Memories of Ninety Years,* Hutchinson, London, 1924
Warwick, Frances, Countess of *Afterthoughts,* Cassell, London, 1931
— *Life's Ebb and Flow,* Hutchinson, London, 1929

West, Sir Algernon *Recollections 1832–1886*, (2 vols) Macmillan, London, 1899
— *Private Diaries*, John Murray, London, 1922
Whymper, Edward *The Ascent of the Matterhorn*, London, 1880
Winwar, Frances *Oscar Wilde and the Yellow Nineties*, Harper Bros, New York, 1940
Wyndham, Horace *Victorian Parade*, Muller, London, 1934
Wyndham, Violet *The Sphinx and Her Circle*, Andre Deutsch, London, 1963

Newspapers, Magazines and Periodicals
British: The Times, Daily Telegraph, Morning Post, Pall Mall Gazette, Evening News, Reynolds Newspaper, The Star, The Standard, The Echo, The Globe, London Figaro, St James Gazette, Daily News, Illustrated London News, The World, Graphic, The Queen, Whitehall Review, Vanity Fair, National Observer, Dumfries and Galloway Standard, Scottish Field, Moray and Nairn Express, Leicester Graphic, Scarborough Mercury, Eastbourne Gazette, Agnostic Journal, Secular Review, National Reformer, Weekly Register, The Tablet, Catholic Herald, Catholic Times, Court Journal, Court Circular, Gentleman's Magazine, Sporting Times, Sporting Chronicle, New Sporting Magazine, The Field.
Overseas: New York Herald, San Jose Daily Mercury, The Californian, Johannesburg Star, Natal Mercury, Natal Witness, Diamond Fields Advertiser, Cape Argus, South Africa, Irish Weekly Examiner, Freeman's Journal, Cork Constitution, Cork Examiner.

References

Unpublished Sources
The William Andrews Clark Memorial Library, University of California, Los Angeles, U.S.A.
Department of Western Manuscripts, Bodleian Library, Oxford.
Scottish Record Office, H.M. General Register House, Edinburgh.

Chapter One
p. 4   'The two gentlemen . . .' *The Times* 10/8/1858
        'weeping bitterly . . . something covered . . .' Dixie: *Story of Ijain*
        'It's papa . . .' Ibid
        'Sudden and sad . . .' *Dumfries Standard* 12/8/1858
p. 5   'One of the most universal . . .' *New Sporting Magazine* Sept. 1858
        'Of late years . . .' *The Field* 14/8/1858
        'It is surmised . . .' *Dumfries Standard* 18/8/1858
p. 6   'esteemed and deeply . . .' Ibid
        'In sporting circles . . .' Quoted: *The Complete Peerage*
p. 8   'the Bold and Gallant Drum' Dixie: *Songs of a Child*
        'A rare pugilist . . .' *Sporting Times* 13/6/1885
        'one of the hardest . . .' Ibid
p. 10   'Oh Archie . . .' *Dumfries & Galloway Standard* 17/2/1904
        'A fatal propensity . . .' *Sporting Times* 13/6/1885
p. 11   'moderate liberal' *Complete Peerage*
        'Nothing pleased him . . .' *Sporting Times* 13/6/1885
p. 12   'The betting was . . .' Ibid
        'bore undeniable tokens . . .' Ibid
        'He was far too wild . . .' *New Sporting Magazine* Sept. 1858
        'they never gave him . . .' Ibid
        'kindred pursuits . . .' *Dumfries Standard* 12/8/1858
        'Fox-hunting, steeple chasing . . .' *Sporting Times* 13/6/1885
p. 13   'uneventful and blameless . . .' Queensberry: *Oscar Wilde and the Black Douglas* p. 13
p. 14   'revived in his person . . .' *Gentleman's Magazine* 1858
        'Had prudence and patriotism . . .' *Dumfries Standard* 18/8/1858
        'swimming along beside . . .' *New Sporting Magazine* Sept. 1858
        'Lord Drumlanrig dropped in . . .' *Sporting Times* 13/6/1885
p. 15   'told its own . . . subsequently shown . . .' Ibid
p. 16   'I will kill myself . . .' Quoted: Croft-Cooke, *Bosie* p. 138

Chapter Two
p. 17   'fitted with a good deal . . .' *Scottish Field* June 1961
        'poor substitute . . .' Stock: *Nature's Nursling* p. 147
p. 18   'Glen Stuart, where . . .' Dixie: *Songs of a Child*
        'a gentle, kindly . . .' Dixie: *Story of Ijain*
        'We two are twins . . .' Dixie: *Songs of a Child*
p. 19   'Come kiss your boy . . .' Ibid

p. 20   'When I was a little . . .' McCabe: *Life & Letters of George Jacob Holyoake*
         'She absolutely and steadfastly . . .' Dixie: *Story of Ijain*
p. 21   'Police were after . . .' *Freeman's Journal* 18/2/1904
         'Lady Queensberry was allowed . . .' Stone: *Eleanor Leslie* p. 264
         'large old-fashioned . . .' Dixie: *Story of Ijain*
p. 22   'as they lay gasping . . .' Ibid
p. 23   'chopped and changed . . . single harness . . .' Ibid
         'That baptism . . .' Ibid
         'Papists as creations . . .' Ibid
         'a disinclination . . .' Ibid
p. 24   'until such times . . . further molestation' Ibid
p. 25   'Thinking over all . . .' Menzies: *Further Indiscretions* p. 209
p. 26   'They managed to make . . .' Dixie: *Story of Ijain*
         'a Hugenot . . . to see any child . . .' Ibid
p. 27   'fifteen policemen and sixty . . .' Stephenson: *A Royal Correspondence* p. 10
         'to take charge of . . .' Queensberry: *Oscar Wilde and the Black Douglas* p. 49
         'known a degree . . .' Douglas: *Oscar Wilde and Myself* p. 34
         'one of the best pedestrians . . .' De Crespigny: *Forty years of a Sportsman's Life* p. 79

Chapter Three
Unless otherwise stated the descriptions of the Matterhorn disaster, and events leading up
to it, are taken from Edward Whymper's *The Ascent of the Matterhorn*.
p. 34   'a kind of ladder . . .' *The Times* 22/7/1865
p. 38   'When we looked up . . .' Ibid
p. 39   'I have not been able . . .' Dixie: *Story of Ijain*
         'The brother of Lord Francis . . .' *Dumfries Standard* 16/8/1865
p. 40   'I was alone in my room . . .' Dixie: *Story of Ijain*
         'I can't tell you . . .' Ibid
         'He would probably . . .' *Dumfries Standard* 16/8/1865
p. 41   'Those thoughts . . . I thought and thought . . .' Dixie: *Story of Ijain*
         'A monument . . . For naught . . .' Queensberry: *The Spirit of the Matterhorn* p. 17
p. 42   'I shall come home . . .' Dixie: *Story of Ijain*
         'All at once . . .' *Dumfries Standard* 20/9/1865
         'when Lord Douglas . . .' *The Times* 21/7/1865
p. 43   'In regard to this . . .' Whymper: *The Ascent of the Matterhorn* p. 294
         'the most desperate . . .' Ibid p. 282
p. 44   'arrested on the rocks . . .' Ibid p. 295
         'that huge, majestic . . .' Dixie: *Songs of a Child*
p. 45   'the bosom of the . . .' *Dumfries Standard* 15/11/1865

Chapter Four
p. 46   'the Scottish Montgomeries . . .' Douglas: *Autobiography* p. 5
p. 47   'It would be interesting . . .' Douglas: *Without Apology* p. 234
         'I wonder how you . . .' Drummond-Wolff: *Rambling Recollections* Vol. 1, p. 76
         'His conversation . . .' Ibid
p. 48   'his bewitching attraction . . .' West: *Recollections* vol. 2, p. 140
         'confirmed bachelor . . .' Nevill: *Reminiscences* p. 144
p. 49   'Now at last . . .' Egremont: *Wyndham and Children First* p. 56
         'An actor cast . . .' Warwick: *Life's Ebb and Flow* p. 31
p. 50   'Having little or no . . .' Portland: *Men, Women and Things* p. 155
         'Do not forget . . .' Warwick: *Life's Ebb and Flow* p. 31
p. 51   'Her delicate features . . .' Stock: *Nature's Nursling*
         'He thought he loved . . .' Dixie: *Story of Ijain*
p. 52   'modern Babylon . . .' Ibid
p. 54   'Last night I wondered . . .' Ibid
         'Queensberry must have been . . .' Manchester: *My Candid Recollections* pp. 34–5

p. 57   'Lord Queensberry assured . . .' De Crespigny: *Forty years* p. 79
        'Who is there . . .' Menzies: *Further Indiscretions* pp. 205–6
p. 58   'the soundness of his . . .' *The Field* 3/2/1900

Chapter Five
p. 60   'For every Fenian . . .' Malmesbury: *Memoirs of an Ex-Minister* vol. 2, p. 375
        'unique reputation . . .' *The Echo* 20/3/1883
p. 61   'brothers and sisters . . .' *Dumfries Standard* 17/2/1904
        'We have daily Mass . . .' Sullivan: *Speeches from the Dock* pp. 282–3
        'Surely never was . . .' Ibid
p. 62   'The more audacious . . .' *The Echo* 20/3/1883
        'much opposed to . . .' Dixie: *Story of Ijain*
        'The twins were left . . .' Ibid
p. 63   'after hunting all day . . .' De Crespigny: *Forty years* p. 62
        'they had to cut . . .' Menzies: *Further Indiscretions* p. 205
p. 64   'He is very young . . .' Letter to Disraeli (31/8/68) Bodleian Library, Oxford.
        'You will know my . . .' Ibid
p. 66   'He was not altogether . . .' Menzies: *Further Indiscretions* p. 205
p. 67   Bulwer Lytton's sonnet. Dixie: *Songs of a Child*
p. 68   'I can handle a gun . . .' Dixie: *The Horrors of Sport* p. 1
        'to advise her sisters . . .' *Daily Telegraph* 8/11/1905
p. 70   'He did nothing . . .' Douglas: *Autobiography* p. 2
p. 71   'Well pulled . . . Down went . . .' Menzies: *Further Indiscretions* p. 204
        'His ambitions as . . .' Ibid
        'Those fits of insensate . . .' Queensberry: *The Sporting Queensberrys* p. 177
p. 72   'at home to anyone . . .' *The Times* 12/1/1887
        'My Lord . . .' Menzies: *Further Indiscretions* p. 203
        'Nothing came amiss . . .' Ibid
p. 73   'Montgomery lot . . .' Queensberry: *The Sporting Queensberrys* p. 166
        'the ideal grandfather . . .' Douglas: *Without Apology* p. 230

Chapter Six
p. 77   'standing erect and firm . . .' *Whitehall Review* 11/4/1883
        'Lady Florence Dixie and her . . .' Ibid 27/1/1877
p. 78   'too unorthodox' Dixie: *Songs of a Child*
        'English servants . . .' Dixie: *Across Patagonia* pp. 3–4.
p. 79–83   The Account of the Patagonian expedition is taken from Lady Florence Dixie's
        Across Patagonia.
p. 83   'I have done little . . .' Somerset: *Letters and Memoirs* p. 516
        'I shall never forget . . .' Warwick: *Afterthoughts* p. 73
        'Of course he wouldn't . . .' Douglas: *Without Apology* p. 245
p. 85   'Beau does not realise . . .' Naylor: *The Irrepressible Victorian* pp. 88–9
p. 86   'For some time past . . .' Ibid.

Chapter Seven
p. 88   'public discussion' Queensberry: *Spirit of the Matterhorn* p. 8
p. 90   'could never be made . . .' Holyoake: *Sixty Years of an Agitator's Life* vol. 2, p. 291
p. 91   'To myself . . .' Ibid
        'If a God . . .' Ibid p. 292
p. 92   'professor of polite . . .' Tribe: *President Charles Bradlaugh* p. 41
        'the ranks of that . . .' *Secular Review* 10/1/1880
p. 93   'The value of organisation . . .' *Moray and Nairn Express* 25/11/1882
        'Everything is fair . . .' *Daily News* 17/11/1882
        'over the seats of . . .' *Agnostic Journal* 18/11/1905
p. 94   'great misfortunes' Douglas: *Autobiography* p. 7

p. 95   'Belgravian loafers' Ibid p. 17
          'her sorrows and many . . .' Menzies: *Further Indiscretions* p. 204
p. 96   'on the fingers . . .' Douglas: *Autobiography* p. 92
          'I think it right . . .' Drummond-Wolff: *Rambling Recollections* vol 2, p. 255
p. 97   'an oath by an infidel . . .' Ibid p. 254
p. 98   'I have never at any time . . .' Queensberry: *Spirit of the Matterhorn* p. 5
p. 99   'To those who have . . .' Ibid p. 11
          'Who are the Lords? . . .' Tribe: *President Charles Bradlaugh* p. 68
p. 100   'allow me to tell you . . .' *National Reformer* 29/5/1881
          'who said he had lost . . .' *Tablet* 18/6/1881
          'invariably a size or so . . .' Menzies: *Further Indiscretions* p. 208

Chapter Eight
Unless otherwise stated the quotes in this chapter are taken from Lady Florence Dixie's *In the Land of Misfortune*
p. 105   'an ignorant and bloodthirsty . . .' Dixie: *A Defence of Zululand*
p. 113   'Undaunted by the effects . . .' *Natal Mercury*
          'When this appears . . .' *Nineteenth Century* August 1882
p. 115   'Sir Always and Lady Sometimes Tipsy' Fane: *Chit Chat* p. 69

Chapter Nine
p. 116   'to caricature and misrepresent . . .' *The Globe* 21/11/1882
          'Godless gloom . . .' *Nineteenth Century* November 1881
p. 117   'The moment that the play . . .' *Morning Post* 13/11/1882
          'These are the sentiments . . .' *Daily Telegraph* 15/11/1882
p. 118   'Apparently under the . . .' *Reynolds Newspaper* 19/11/1882
          'I was forcibly . . .' *Daily Telegraph* 15/11/1882
p. 119   'She must be gone . . .' Wyndham: *Victorian Parade* p. 70
          'much confused . . . professing orthodox . . .' *The Globe* 20/11/1882
          'the mouth of . . .' Ibid 21/11/1882
p. 120   'Marriage ought to be . . .' *Daily News* 17/11/1882
          'He had himself been . . .' *Moray and Nairn Express* 25/11/1882
p. 123   'the Woman's Rights mania . . . mate for everyone' Douglas: *Brown as a Berry* pp.
              104–105
          'matters have been on . . .' *Dumfries & Galloway Standard* 22/11/1882
          'that admirably kept . . .' *The World* 29/11/1882
p. 124   'His Lordship was greatly . . .' *Dumfries & Galloway Standard* 22/11/1882
          'sister of a well-known . . .' Ibid
          'It is needless to say . . .' Quoted: Ibid
          'outdone by that . . .' *The World* 29/11/1882
p. 125   'the mutations of opinion . . .' *Whitehall Review* 30/11/1882
          'The marriage was an experiment . . .' Quoted: Wyndham: *Victorian Parade* p. 74
          'The society organs . . .' Ibid
          'best-looking boy . . .' Beases Dictionary A-D.
          'turned from carrying out . . .' Quoted: *Dumfries & Galloway Standard* 25/11/1882

Chapter Ten
p. 128   'It was raised . . .' *The Times* 14/3/1882
p. 128   'intend to take any . . .' Ibid 19/3/1882
          'The window to the right . . .' *Illustrated London News* 24/3/1882
p. 130   'Sir Beaumont something . . .' Wyndham: *Victorian Parade* p. 86
          The knife came . . .' *The Times* 19/3/1882
          'Two men have . . .' Ibid 21/3/1883
p. 131   'Eton boys' Wyndham: *Victorian Parade* p. 79
          'The particulars are . . .' *The Times* 19/3/1883

'very large feet' *Reynolds Newspaper* 27/3/1883
'light loose clothes . . .' *The Times* 21/3/1883
p. 132   'I have never said . . .' Ibid
'What a thing . . .' Tisdale: *Queen Victoria's John Brown* p. 221
p. 133   'She was certainly very . . .' Ward: *Memories of Ninety Years* pp. 188–89
'I am not a person . . .' *The Times* 21/3/1883
p. 134   'The Queensberry family . . .' *The Echo* 20/3/1883
'The family is a . . .' *Reynolds Newspaper* 25/3/1883
'for a purpose . . .' Ibid
'inflict personal chastisement . . .' *Whitehall Review* 28/3/1883
pp. 134–35   The Commons debate. *Reynolds Newspaper* 25/3/1883

Chapter Eleven
p. 137   'his whole character . . .' Douglas: *Without Apology* p. 247
p. 138   The Queensberry divorce. *The Times* 24/1/1887
p. 139   'It is a pity . . .' *The World* 2/2/1887
p. 140   'With a rapid . . .' Douglas: *Royal Angus* vol. 2, p. 296
'He will be a very . . .' *St James Gazette* 20/11/1882
p. 142   'an exceedingly exciteable man' *The Globe* 6/5/1891
'I wish your uncle . . .' Douglas: *Without Apology* p. 240
p. 143   'he might one day . . .' *The Times* 7/5/1891
'thought it a good joke' *Reynolds Newspaper* 26/4/1891
p. 144   'Facts lies' *The Globe* 5/4/1891
p. 145   'as he had shown . . .' *The Times* 7/4/1891
'evidently cut his throat . . .' *The Globe* 6/4/1891
'that state' Douglas: *Without Apology* p. 243
'My God how I loved . . .' Ibid p. 244
p. 146   'expression of pious . . . Loved with . . .' *Agnostic Review* 25/11/1905

Chapter Twelve
p. 147   'I have quite given . . .' Andrews: *The Splendid Pauper* p. 144
'He had a disconcerting . . .' Douglas: *Without Apology* p. 238
'He was incapable . . .' Ibid p. 237
p. 148   'My father was a . . .' Douglas: *Autobiography* p. 93
p. 150   'His prejudices once formed . . .' Ibid p. 17
pp. 150–3   Bosie at Winchester and Oxford. Ibid
p. 152   'nothing in the least . . .' Croft-Cooke: *Bosie* p. 41
p. 153   'fatal Douglas temperament' Hart-Davis: *Letters of Oscar Wilde* p. 433
'lot of good lines' Douglas: *Without Apology* p. 14
p. 154   'Oscar took a violent . . .' Ibid p. 122
p. 155   'a very pathetic letter . . .' Hart-Davis: *Letters of Oscar Wilde* p. 281
p. 156   'was indiscreet to a . . .' Croft-Cooke: *Bosie* p. 47
Crabbet Club incident Longford: *A Pilgrimage of Passion* p. 289
p. 157   'not unkind or offensive' Douglas: *Autobiography* p. 98
'charming fellow . . .' Ibid p. 99
p. 158   'pleasant state . . .' Ibid
'the Douglas fighting . . .' Ibid p. 285
'to shed a single tear' Hart-Davis: *Letters of Oscar Wilde* p. 439
'a highly nervous boy . . .' Queensberry: *Oscar Wilde and the Black Douglas* p. 51
'an excellent amiable . . . He imparted to . . .' Paget: *In My Tower* pp. 5–6
p. 159   'Grandpapa was absolutely . . .' Douglas: *Without Apology* p. 230
'He wrote to Gladstone . . .' Douglas: *Autobiography* p. 94
p. 160   'Lord Queensberry was far . . .' West: *Private Diaries* p. 163
'to be pursued by . . .' Rhodes-James: *Rosebery* p. 287
'The Marquess of Queensberry . . .' Ibid
p. 161   'My brother Percy . . .' Douglas: *Autobiography* p. 95

p. 162 'Just what happened . . .' Queensberry: *The Sporting Queensberrys* p. 162
'One admiral said . . .' Queensberry: *Oscar Wilde and the Black Douglas* p. 64
'paid work . . .' *Star* (Johannesburg) 2/8/1920
p. 163 'I could not have . . .' Queensberry: *The Sporting Queensberrys* p. 162
p. 164 'Why indeed if you . . .' Ibid
'cascade of vitriolic . . .' Ibid pp. 129–30
'stuck-up, pauper . . .' Queensberry: *Oscar Wilde and the Black Douglas* p. 61
p. 165 'All my life . . .' *Star* (Johannesburg) 2/8/1920

Chapter Thirteen
p. 169 'Lady Florence Dixie . . .' *Natal Mercury* May 1883
'a true representative . . .' *Vanity Fair* 5/1/1884
'is Home Rule . . .' Dixie: *Izra* pp. 613–14
p. 170 'tramp the turnips . . .' Dixie: *Horrors of Sport* pp. 4–5
'The memory of those . . .' Ibid
p. 171 Killing of the stag. Ibid pp. 9–12
'Much of the barbarous. . .' Ibid p. 7
p. 172 'For breakfast she had . . .' *Daily Telegraph* 8/11/1905
p. 173 'Woman submits . . .' McCabe: *Religion of Women* p. 5
p. 174 'thanked her for . . .' Wyndham: *Victorian Parade* p. 106
'a style of dress . . .' Newton: *Health, Art and Reason* p. 117
'Stick to your stays . . .' Ibid
'Though she did not . . .' *Daily Telegraph* 8/11/1905
p. 175 'No sir – a comfortable . . .' *Agnostic Journal* 25/11/1905
p. 176 'considerable space would . . .' Anon: *Fifty Years in London Society* p. 212
'Who is this Lobengula . . .' *Pall Mall Gazette* 2/11/1893
p. 177 'conveyance like a gipsy . . .' *The Tablet* 19/2/1938
'in which his ancestors . . .' *The Times* 16/2/1938
p. 178 'Embodying, as it does . . .' *Dumfries and Galloway Standard* 29/11/1893

Chapter Fourteen
p. 180 'The Marquess of Queensberry married . . .' *Eastbourne Gazette* 11/11/1893
'She is tall . . .' Ibid
p. 181 'a sort of plurality . . .' London *Figaro* 14/3/1895
'the lecture was expected . . .' Ibid
'on the following day . . .' Hyde: *The Trials of Oscar Wilde* p. 344
'a young lady . . .' *Eastbourne Gazette* 15/11/1893
'full age' Marriage Certificate: No 3417D 1893
p. 182 'the hearing resulted . . .' *The Times* 25/11/1894
'quite astonishing . . .' Hart-Davis: *Letters of Oscar Wilde* p. 376
pp. 182–3 Account of Lord Drumlanrig's death. *The Times* 25/10/1894
p. 183 'The young man who . . .' *The World* 24/10/1894
p. 184 'a dark horse . . .' Crewe: *Lord Rosebery* p. 631
'an incalculable man . . .' Russell: *Sketches and Snapshots* p. 350
'to marry a great heiress . . .' Raymond: *Portraits of the Nineties* p. 22
p. 185 'considering some of the things . . .' Trevor-Roper: *A Hidden Life* p. 262
'No two men . . .' Douglas: *Oscar Wilde and Myself* pp. 72–3
'left London to avoid . . .' Queensberry: *Oscar Wilde and the Black Douglas* p. 57
p. 186 'Drumlanrig is going . . .' Trevor-Roper: *A Hidden Life* p. 262
p. 187 'substituting himself for Drumlanrig . . .' Ibid p. 263
'taken his own life . . .' Hyde: *Oscar Wilde* p. 219
'Your intimacy with . . .' Mason: *Oscar Wilde Three Times Tried* pp. 91–92
'What a funny . . .' Mason: *Oscar Wilde Three Times Tried* p. 92
p. 188 'You impertinent . . .' Ibid
'He might have guessed . . .' Douglas: *Without Apology* p. 235
'She saw of course . . .' Hart-Davis: *Letters of Oscar Wilde* p. 433

p. 189 'violent and invincible' Douglas: *Oscar Wilde and Myself* pp. 72–3
'The only thing . . .' Redesdale: *Memories* p. 543
p. 190 'infamous conduct . . .' Queensberry: *Oscar Wilde and the Black Douglas* p. 63
'not exactly a professional . . .' Croft-Cooke: *Bosie* p. 63
'My Own Boy . . .' Mason: Oscar *Wilde Three Times Tried* p. 27
p. 191 'When you left . . .' Hart-Davis: *Letters of Oscar Wilde* p. 431
'Bosie you must not make . . .' Ibid p. 336
In intellectual calibre . . . *The World* 26/4/1893
p. 192 'Am I to understand . . .' Mason: *Oscar Wilde Three Times Tried* pp. 91–2
'an irrevocable parting . . .' Hart-Davis: *Letters of Oscar Wilde* p. 430
'Bosie seems to me . . .' Ibid p. 346
p. 193 'I have in my blood . . .' Quoted: Croft-Cooke: *Bosie* pp. 94–5
'I assured her . . .' Hart-Davis: *Letters of Oscar Wilde* p. 434
p. 194 'a threat of suicide . . .' Ibid p. 435
'You had yourself . . .' Ibid
p. 195 'I saw at once . . .' Ibid p. 445

Chapter Fifteen
p. 197 Interview between Wilde and Queensberry. Mason: *Oscar Wilde Three Times Tried*
pp. 37–9
p. 198 'stinking scandal' Ibid p. 93
'exalted personages . . . most foully' *Daily Telegraph* 5/4/1895
Correspondence with solicitors. Mason: *Oscar Wilde Three Times Tried* pp. 104–105
p. 199 'plausible George Wyndham' Hart-Davis: *Letters of Oscar Wilde* p. 497
'gradually drop . . .' Ibid
'Why should I come . . .' Mason: *Oscar Wilde Three Times Tried* pp. 93–4
p. 200 'Your father . . .' Hart-Davis: *Letters of Oscar Wilde* p. 360
'If I shoot you . . .' *Daily Telegraph* 5/4/1895
'I have heard . . .' Mason: *Oscar Wilde Three Times Tried* pp. 105–106
'If my father . . .' Douglas: *Autobiography* p. 101
p. 201 'I have received your . . .' Mason: *Oscar Wilde Three Times Tried* p. 95
p. 202 'made a fortune by . . .' *Star* (Johannesburg) 2/8/1920
'I was not intending . . .' Queensberry: *The Sporting Queensberrys* p. 152
'If I go anywhere . . .' Ibid p. 151
'the holy christian . . .' Ibid p. 155
'All this has terribly . . .' Ibid p. 151
p. 203 'I refuse to be . . .' Ibid pp. 160–1
'There will be a scandal . . .' Ibid p. 166
'Go and prove . . .' Ibid p. 163
p. 204 'My play is really . . .' Hart-Davis: *Letters of Oscar Wilde* p. 362
'It is already . . .' Morely: *Oscar Wilde* p. 102
'rows and rows . . . gaiety, fashion . . .' Wyndham: *The Sphinx and Her Circle* p. 109
p. 205 'prowled about . . . He left . . .' Hart-Davis: *Letters of Oscar Wilde* p. 383
'My dear Alec . . .' Hyde: *Oscar Wilde* p. 251
'Upon investigating the case . . .' William Andrews Clark Memorial Library: Ref.
H927L/W6721
p. 206 'If Percy does not choose . . .' Queensberry: *Oscar Wilde and the Black Douglas* p. 55
p. 207 'Bosie's father has left . . .' Mason: *Collection of Original Mss* p. 18
'only too delighted . . .' Hart-Davis: *Letters of Oscar Wilde* p. 442
'In these cases . . .' Mason: *Oscar Wilde Three Times Tried* p. 3
pp. 208–13 Magistrate's Court hearing. Hyde: *Trials of Oscar Wilde* pp. 80–1; *The Times*
4/3/1895
p. 209 'this tedious and dreadful . . .' Hart-Davis: *Letters of Oscar Wilde* p. 385
p. 210 'odious work' Queensberry: *Oscar Wilde and the Black Douglas* p. 58
'fellow alumnus . . . There was nothing . . .' Marjoribanks: *Life of Lord Carson* pp.
198–9

p. 211   'The great thing . . .' Ibid
         'No doubt . . .' Morley: *Oscar Wilde* p. 108
         'I hope you noticed . . .' Queensberry: *Oscar Wilde and the Black Douglas* p. 59
         Second hearing at Magistrate's Court. Hyde: *Trials of Oscar Wilde* pp. 83–6; Mason:
             Oscar Wilde Three Times Tried pp. 4–14; *Daily Telegraph, Pall Mall Gazette* 9/3/1895;
             Reynolds Newspaper 10/3/1895

Chapter Sixteen
p. 214   'At a time . . .' Hart-Davis: *Letters of Oscar Wilde* p. 430
p. 216   'this good-for-nothing . . .' Queensberry: *Oscar Wilde and the Black Douglas* p. 58
         'Who the devil . . .' Ibid pp. 61–2
         'miserable misguided creature . . .' Ibid pp. 59–60
         Queensberry's plea of justification. Hyde: *Trials of Oscar Wilde* pp. 323–7
p. 217   'Everyone wants me . . .' Hyde: *Oscar Wilde* p. 265
         'prophesied a complete triumph . . .' Hart-Davis: *Letters of Oscar Wilde* p. 385
         'Have no fear . . .' Morley: *Trials of Oscar Wilde* p. 110
pp. 217–27   Unless otherwise stated the account of the Queensberry trial is taken from:
             Hyde: *The Trials of Oscar Wilde* and Mason: *Oscar Wilde Three Times Tried*.
p. 218   'the importance of being early' Marjoribanks: *Life of Carson* p. 204
         'inhuman brute . . . he had bullied' Douglas: *Autobiography* p. 91
p. 219   'rather like an eighteenth . . .' Marjoribanks: *Life of Carson* p. 205
         'I never heard . . .' Ibid
         'Ponderous and fleshy . . .' *Reynolds Newspaper* 7/4/1895
p. 220   'a very curious construction . . .' Marjoribanks: *Life of Carson* p. 210
p. 222   'lover of beauty . . . wonderful intellectual . . .' Ibid p. 216
         'At one o'clock this morning . . .' *New York Herald* (International) 6/4/1895
         'Everything is very . . .' Hart-Davis: *Letters of Oscar Wilde* p. 385
         'with the same air . . .' *Reynolds Newspaper* 7/4/1895
p. 226   'Things indeed have . . .' *New York Herald* (International) 6/4/1895
p. 227   'If this country allows . . .' Mason: *Oscar Wilde Three Times Tried* pp. 134–5
p. 228   'The judge did not attempt . . .' *Daily Telegraph* 9/4/1895
         'There is not a man . . .' *National Observer* 6/4/1895
         'You know I have . . .' *Reynolds Newspaper* 7/4/1895
         'hundreds of kind evidences . . .' *Daily Telegraph* 9/4/1895
p. 229   'Lord Queensberry is triumphant . . .' *The Echo* 5/4/1895
         'It would have been impossible . . .' *Evening News* 5/4/1895
         'He was, together . . .' *Reynolds Newspaper* 7/4/1895
p. 230   'My sister and mother . . .' Queensberry: *The Sporting Queensberrys* p. 152
         'My nephew, Lord Douglas . . .' *Reynolds Newspaper* 7/4/1895
p. 231   'Well, if I must go . . .' Hyde: *Oscar Wilde* p. 290
         'I will be at Bow Street . . .' Hart-Davis: *Letters of Oscar Wilde* p. 386
pp. 231–2   Queensberry–Buchanan controversy. *The Star* 15–25 April 1895

Chapter Seventeen
p. 235   'lacked anything that the . . .' Morgan: *History of Kern County* p. 114
         'The girl is too good . . .' *The Californian* 25/4/1895
p. 236   'cast off and renounced' Morgan: *History of Kern County* p. 114
         'was not sufficiently . . .' *Pall Mall Gazette* 25/4/1895
         'Insane! Most extraordinary . . .' *The Californian* 23/4/1895
         'set the law in motion . . .' *Pall Mall Gazette* 25/4/1895
         'The Douglas affair . . .' *The Californian* 24/4/1895
pp. 237–8   Interview at Bakersfield gaol. Ibid
p. 239   'a true old sport . . .' Morgan: *History of Kern County* p. 115
         'Let them renounce you . . .' Ibid
         'has visited Lord Sholto . . .' *Pall Mall Gazette* 25/4/1895
         'formally withdrew . . .' *The Star* 26/4/1895

p. 240 'issued a special dispensation . . .' *New York Herald* (International) 1/6/1895
'Loretta Mooney who also . . .' Ibid
p. 241 'Mrs Mooney, mother of the . . .' *Daily Mercury* (San Jose) 7/6/1895
'As Lord and Lady Douglas . . .' Ibid
'LORD SHOLTO'S LUCK . . .' *Reynold's Newspaper* 14/7/1895
p. 242 'You began it . . .' Queensberry: *Oscar Wilde and the Black Douglas* p. 65
'threats contained in a . . .' *Reynolds Newspaper* 28/4/1895
'You may inform . . .' Queensberry: *Oscar Wilde and the Black Douglas* p. 63
p. 243 'because the witness could . . .' Mason: *Oscar Wilde Three Times Tried* p. 433
'under an Act . . .' Pearson: *Life of Oscar Wilde* p. 302
'giving their bodies . . .' Hyde: *Trials of Oscar Wilde* p. 169
'He suggested two or three . . .' Ibid p. 172
'My Lord, if these counts . . .' Ibid p. 195
p. 244 'The love that dare not . . .' Ibid p. 201
p. 245 'The men say . . .' Brasol: *Oscar Wilde* p. 278
'Give me shelter . . .' Pearson: *Life of Oscar Wilde* p. 305
'He seemed so . . .' Wyndham: *The Sphinx and Her Circle* p. 115
'Cannot you let up . . .' Marjoribanks: *Life of Carson* p. 230
p. 247 'It has been suggested . . .' Mason: *Oscar Wilde Three Times Tried* p. 108
p. 248 'There is still a continued . . .' *New York Herald* (International) 20/5/1895
'the most obstinate . . .' Crewe: *Lord Rosebery* vol. 2, p. 501
'the object of the visit . . .' *Reynolds Newspaper* 5/5/1895
p. 249 'I am confident . . .' Hyde: *Trials of Oscar Wilde* p. 346

Chapter Eighteen
p. 250 'The inventor and supporter . . .' *The Star* 23/4/1895
'I am told . . .' London *Figaro* 30/5/1895
p. 251 Taylor's trial. Hyde: *Trials of Oscar Wilde* pp 227–31
'I enclose letter . . .' Queensberry: *Oscar Wilde and the Black Douglas* p. 66
'I have a right . . .' Ibid p. 65
p. 252 'I hope he is still . . .' Ibid p. 66
'a possible ancestor . . . I sent it . . .' *New York Herald* (International) 22/5/1895
'must congratulate . . .' Mason: *Oscar Wilde Three Times Tried* p. 373
pp. 252–3 Piccadilly incident Queensberry: *Oscar Wilde and the Black Douglas* pp. 67–8;
Mason: *Oscar Wilde Three Times Tried* pp 373–7; *Pall Mall Gazette* 22/5/1895
p. 254 'I have been in France . . .' Quoted: *New York Herald* (International) 24/5/1895
'Yet another somewhat . . .' Ibid
pp. 254–5 Queensberry/Percy court hearing. *Pall Mall Gazette* 22/5/1895
p. 255 'Lord Queensberry seems to be . . .' *The Star* 25/5/1895
p. 256 'What your father . . .' Hart-Davis: *Letters of Oscar Wilde* p. 497
p. 257 'withdraw from circulation . . .' *New York Herald* (International) 10/4/1895
'I have heard . . .' *Reynolds Newspaper* 9/6/1895
'How splendid it would . . .' Hart-Davis: *Letters of Oscar Wilde* p. 502
p. 258 'not in reticences merely . . .' Ibid p. 452
'I could have walked . . .' Ibid
'I should think not . . . Hyde: *Trials of Oscar Wilde* p. 265
'I used to see your father . . .' Hart-Davis: *Letters of Oscar Wilde* p. 492
p. 259 'Oscar Wilde and Alfred Taylor . . .' Hyde: *Trials of Oscar Wilde* p. 272
'Certainly we think . . .' *Reynolds Newspaper* 26/5/1895
'I cannot close . . .' Ibid 2/6/1895
p. 260 'The Marquess of Queensberry . . .' London *Figaro* 30/5/1895
'he had extracted such . . .' Hart-Davis: *Letters of Oscar Wilde* p. 451
'Perhaps no other man . . .' Anon: *Fifty Years in London Society* pp. 153–4
p. 261 'He is more to be pitied . . .' Hart-Davis: *Letters of Oscar Wilde* p. 551
'Have you imagination . . .' Ibid p. 495
'Through your father . . .' Ibid p. 440

p. 262   'He is one of the few . . .' *The Graphic* 13/4/1895
       'When I came to grief . . .' Douglas: *Without Apology* p. 230
       'Hardly a week passes . . .' Hyde: *Trials of Oscar Wilde* pp 343–4
p. 263   'sacred and secret . . .' Hart-Davis: *Letters of Oscar Wilde* p. 455
       'At the end I was . . .' Ibid p. 431
p. 264   'Of course at present . . .' Ibid

Chapter Nineteen
p. 265   *'type de brute* . . .' Hart-Davis: *Letters of Oscar Wilde* p. 455
       'He really was ostracised . . .' Douglas: *Without Apology* p. 248
       'He was almost . . .' *The Times* 7/2/1900
p. 266   'were simply the result . . .' Nethercot: *First Five Lives of Annie Besant* p. 389
       'the strange delusion . . .' Douglas: *Without Apology* p. 241
p. 267   'plenty of beautiful girls . . .' Douglas: *Autobiography* p. 121
p. 268   'my poor darling boy . . .' Ibid p. 123
       'He whipped round . . .' Ibid
       'hurling back . . .' Ibid p. 124
       'persecuted by Oscar Wilders' Ibid
p. 269   'He was under the impression . . .' Ibid
       'I think he was pleased . . .' Ibid p. 125
       'the decisive factor . . .' *The Times* 9/4/1932
       'It has made trouble . . .' Queensberry: *The Sporting Queensberrys* p. 152
p. 270   'put a stop to his delusions . . .' *Autobiography* p. 125
p. 271   'I regarded him . . .' *Agnostic Journal* 10/2/1900
       'A "curious figure" . . .' *The Times*
       'Bosie is over here . . .' Hart-Davis: *Letters of Oscar Wilde* p. 816
p. 272   'If another century . . .' Morley: *Oscar Wilde* p. 149
       'As there is clearly . . .' *Dumfries & Galloway Standard* 17/2/1904
p. 273   'She was intensely religious . . .' *Freeman's Journal* 18/2/1904
       'Her love for Ireland . . .' *Cork Examiner* 26/2/1904
p. 274   'I direct that I shall . . .' Scottish Record Office: Record of invts. 1938 vol 993, p. 407
p. 275   'You must no longer . . .' McCabe: *The Religion of Women* p. 7
       'By Co-operation alone . . .' Dixie: *Izra* pp. 613–614
p. 276   'eccentric and startling . . .' Warwick: *Afterthoughts* p. 73
       'When James VI of Scotland . . .' *Dumfries and Galloway Standard* 8/11/1905
p. 277   'Football was the ideal . . .' *Star* (Johannesburg) 3/8/1920
       'There is every probability . . .' *The Times* 18/4/1905
       'I shall take . . .' *The Times* 18/4/1905
       'on dates varying . . .' Ibid 20/4/1905
p. 278   'In the opinion . . .' Ibid
       'Even if the body . . .' Ibid 24/4/1905
       'Though I did not . . .' *Agnostic Journal* 18/11/1905
p. 279   'owing to serious illness . . .' Ibid 4/11/1905
       'There was no ceremony . . .' Ibid 25/11/1905
       'provide free beer . . .' *The Times* 22/8/1924
       'a notable career . . .' *Morning Post* 8/11/1905

Chapter Twenty
p. 280   'Within eighteen months . . .' Queensberry: *The Sporting Queensberrys* p. 190
       'Failure meant less . . .' Ibid p. 133
p. 281   'One of the largest . . .' Douglas: *Autobiography* p. 186
       'Poor old Percy . . .' Ibid
       'We are played out . . .' *Star* (Johannesburg) 2/8/1920
p. 282   'walking within the shelter . . .' Nevill: *The World of Fashion* p. 132
p. 283   'remarkable prospector . . .' *Star* (Johannesburg) 2/8/1920
       'phosphoros poison' *South Africa* 28/8/1920

'certain allegations . . .' Ibid 7/8/1920
'death due . . .' Ibid 28/8/1920
p. 284 'pay their last respects . . .' Queensberry: *The Sporting Queensberrys* p. 128
p. 285 Sholto's bankruptcy. *The Times* 29/10/1921 & 1/12/1921
p. 286 'And the curious thing . . .' Hart-Davis: *Letters of Oscar Wilde* p. 493
p. 288 'Boys, brandy and betting . . .' Ibid p. 831
'Everyone should try . . .' Douglas: *Autobiography* p. 213
p. 289 'become a saint' Ibid p. 247
'Douglas's abominable book . . . Hypocrisy . . .' Quoted; Croft-Cooke: *Bosie* p. 250
'Life of promiscuous . . .' Douglas: *Autobiography* pp. 121–2
p. 290 'I have a horror . . .' Croft-Cooke: *Bosie* p. 110
'to elope with . . .' Quoted: Ibid p. 111
'marvellous' young Arab. Quoted: Ibid p. 112
'Directly after my father's . . .' Douglas: *Autobiograpy* p. 168
p. 291 'He was happiest . . .' *The Times* obituary
'Had Thomas Moore . . .' Quoted: Croft-Cooke: *Bosie*
'a strong Conservative . . .' Douglas: *Autobiography* p. 220
p. 292 'odious question of finance' Ibid p. 81
p. 293 'She gave me the most . . .' Quoted: Croft-Cooke: *Bosie* p. 338
p. 294 'In spite of the hard . . .' Douglas: *Autobiography* p. 125

Index